TRUST IN THE LAND

TRUST IN THE LAND

New Directions in Tribal Conservation

Beth Rose Middleton

Foreword by Clifford Trafzer

FIRST PEOPLES
New Directions in Indigenous Studies

The University of Arizona Press   Tucson

The University of Arizona Press
© 2011 The Arizona Board of Regents
All rights reserved

www.uapress.arizona.edu

Library of Congress Cataloging-in-Publication Data
Middleton, Beth Rose, 1979–
Trust in the land : new directions in tribal conservation / Beth
Rose Middleton ; foreword by Clifford Trafzer.
p. cm. — (First peoples : new directions in indigenous studies)
Includes bibliographical references and index.
ISBN 978-0-8165-2928-5 (pbk. : alk. paper)
1. Indians of North America—Land tenure—Case studies.
2. Land trusts—United States—Case studies. 3. Conservation
easements—United States—Case studies. 4. Natural areas—
United States—Case studies. 5. Nature conservation—United
States—Case studies. I. Title.
E98.L3M53   2011
333.2–dc22   2010028738

Publication of this book was made possible, in part, with a grant
from the Andrew W. Mellon Foundation.

All proceeds from this book will go to the InterTribal Sinkyone
Wilderness Council and the Native American Land Conservancy.

Contents

Illustrations

Foreword

When I was a small boy, I was afraid of the dark. One evening, my mother was baking some bread, and she ran out of flour for the second or third bake. She asked me to walk across the country road and go to our neighbor's house to borrow some flour, but I told her I could not go alone. I explained that I was afraid to go outside alone, so she quietly removed her apron, took me by the hand, and led me outside. Our house faced east, and by the light of the moon, I remember the stands of tall oak, maple, and elm that lined the woods behind our neighbor's house. The moonlight silhouetted the trees and that sight is deeply embedded in my mind. Once outside, we walked halfway to my neighbor's house. My mother said nothing at first. She simply stood quietly behind me and held my upper arms with her hands.

"What do you see?" she asked.

Still facing east, I told her I could see our neighbor's house and the big trees lining the woods.

"What else do you see?"

I told her I saw the moon and stars. The Milky Way showed bright in the night sky, and she had already taught me how to find the Big Dipper. Remaining behind me, she turned me to the south and asked, "What do you see?" I told her I saw some houses and trees, the moonlight and stars.

She turned me to the west and asked, "What do you see, now?"

I told her I saw our house and behind it the cemetery running along Chamber's Road. I told her I saw the trees.

Finally, she turned me to the north and asked, "What do you see?"

I told her I saw Big Hill, lights down the road, the Bailey House, Robin's Tree, and the Big Dipper.

"That's right," she said. "Do you see anything bad, anything that might hurt you?"

I told her I saw nothing bad, nothing that would hurt me. She told me that thousands of former relatives surrounded me, the spirit people that lived all around us and protected us. She told me I was standing in the middle of the earth where our people once lived. She said that our Wyandot relatives and their former neighbors in the woodlands still love this land and had never left it. The spirit of the land, trees, streams, gardens, sunlight, and night still live.

The lands of the Americas are Indian lands, and contemporary American Indian people continue to have a relationship with the land, whether they are living on or off reservations and tribal lands.

My mother taught me that wherever I travel in America, I would be on Indian lands, where the spirits still live. She taught me to respect the first nations wherever I travel or live. My mother's words and her lesson have stuck with me for more than sixty years, guiding me in my work with the Native American Land Conservancy. These lessons were most constructive because of our own relationship with the environment, which is part of our past and certainly our future. We have to preserve that which the Creator provided us at the beginning of time. The Creator instructed us to care for and protect Indian land from desecration.

According to many tribes, creation took place over time and never ended. Creation continues, but when holy forces first put the earth into motion and life began in so many forms, divine beings made the land, water, plants, animals, fire. Spiritual characters also named the lands for tribal people, marking the boundaries and teaching humans of their special relationship to the land through songs and stories. Tribal people remember many of these lessons today, singing and remembering their sacred landscapes. The earth is a storied landscape.

Chemehuevi and Southern Paiute people of California, Arizona, and Nevada still sing Salt Songs. Matthew Leivas, Vivienne Jake, Larry Eddy, Bettie Cornelius, Robert Chavez, and others still sing Salt Songs. The song sequences last all night, telling of two women who traveled together from a cave on the Bill Williams River in Arizona to the Colorado River, inland to the Hualapai Indians, and northwest toward present-day Las Vegas, Nevada. At midnight, singers tell of the parting of the two sisters, as one travels north, taking her songs to the people there. The other sister travels south, into the Mojave Desert, past the Old Woman Mountains, over the Little San Bernardino Mountains, and east to the Colorado River where the songs end in the cave where the adventure had begun. The Salt Song Trail marks a sacred landscape of the people, a storied landscape significant to many Paiute-speaking people. Most of the lands mentioned in the Salt Songs do not belong to Native people, but they remain Indian lands in the hearts and minds of the people. The lands mentioned in the Salt Songs are generally off the reservations and threatened by development—a common scenario in Indian Country today.

But just as Paiutes still love the lands described in the Salt Songs, the Indian people of the Pacific Northwest revere the Columbia and Snake rivers, the great volcanic mountains that cast their shadows over the land, and the Pacific Ocean of the West.

The ancestors of contemporary people eloquently mentioned their love of the earth during the treaty councils with representatives of the United States in 1854 and 1855. During the Walla Walla Council, Chief Owhi of the Yakama explained: "God gave us day and night, the night to rest in, and the day to see, and that as long as the earth shall last, he gave us the morning with our breath; and so he takes care of us on this earth and here we have met under his care. Is the earth before the day or the day before the earth? God was before the earth, the heavens were clear and good and all things in the heavens were good. God looked one way then the other and names our lands for us to take care of."[1]

Like all Indians, the Creator charged the Plateau people with the responsibility of caring for and protecting the earth. As Owhi said, the spirit had named the lands that the people were to care for and protect. Throughout Indian Country today, people take seriously their stewardship of the earth. People engage in the active preservation of their environment because it is a holy task, spoken about by past and present elders. During the Walla Walla Council of 1855, Cayuse Chief Young Chief explained the relationship of humans to the earth in his recorded testimony:

> I wonder if this ground has anything to say: I wonder if the ground is listening to what is said. I wonder if the ground would come to life and what is on it; though I hear what this earth says, the earth says, God has placed me here. The Earth says that God tells me to take care of the Indians on this earth; the Earth says to the Indians that stop on the Earth feed them right. God named the roots that he should feed the Indians on: The water speaks the same way: God says feed the Indians upon the earth: the grass says the same thing: feed the horses and cattle. The Earth and water and grass says God has given our names and we are told those names; neither the Indians or the Whites have a right to change those names: The Earth says, God has placed me here to produce all that grows upon me, the trees, fruits, etc. The same way the Earth says, it was from her man was made. God on placing them on the earth desired them to take good care of the earth and do each other no harm.[2]

When the United States established reservations on Indian lands, the Plateau Indians lost millions of acres, and the tribes were able to preserve for themselves only a small portion of their former homelands. Still, the Plateau Indians have a relationship with the lands the Creator had designated for them. Although other people, newcomers, may say they own the land, American Indian people have a special relationship with these lands, the quiet places of the Plateau Country. Perhaps the people will create a land trust or conservancy to protect their former homelands. But whether they do or not, they continue to have a sacred relationship with a vast landscape, filled with plants and animals that Coyote had placed on earth at the beginning of time. The power remains in the land and still influences the lives of many.

On my last visit to Quebec, I had a lengthy conversation with Dr. Eleonore Sioui, an extraordinary spiritual leader and medicine woman among Wyandot people. She was a Keeper of the Council Fire and Spiritual Mother of many. She was my elder teacher. As we walked on the great ledge overlooking the St. Lawrence River, Sioui shared many things with me, including the power of place, plants, and animals. When I pressed her on the use of plants for healing, she stopped and said, "It's not just the plants, you see. It is the power that flows into the plants that does the healing."

As we anticipate the greater use of Indian land conservancies, easements, and trusts, we must remember Sioui's words. It is not just the land. The spirit of the land is the power that continues to influence people in their relationships with each other and the natural environment. The authors of this useful and colorful book have given us a gift of words, experiences, and spirit that will help contemporary people navigate the world of preservation. This work, infused with spirit, will forever change mankind and the earth upon which we live.

Clifford E. Trafzer, Professor of American Indian History
Rupert Costo Chair in American Indian Affairs
University of California, Riverside

Preface

The Heart K Ranch

In May 2009, I joined a Sierra Institute[1] tour of the Heart K Ranch in Genesee Valley in California, entitled "Maidu Way of Life" and led by Farrell Cunningham (Mountain Maidu), his father Marvin Cunningham (Mountain Maidu), and members of the Feather River Land Trust Board and staff. The forty-odd participants followed Farrell and Marvin through the apple orchards, planted in the 1860s by homesteader Harvey Ingalls. As we examined the stands of willow that had been tended by Maidu families for generations and observed the erosion on the banks of Indian Creek, I reflected on the many times I had visited this property with members of the Cunningham family. They had invited me here to tend and harvest traditional plants, to pick apples in the old orchard, to check on the old farmhouse, to show my family the area, to learn how to make cordage from milkweed, to camp out when the deer were rutting, and to attend their family reunions and other family events. The place holds many memories for me, even as a relative newcomer. My friends in the Davis/Cunningham family have been interacting with this land for generations, as far back as memories and oral histories extend.

The ranch consists of a scenic expanse of pastureland that slopes nearly imperceptibly down to Indian Creek. Rising up from the valley floor are forested uplands topped by high, rocky, and often snowy peaks. Several structures stand on the 883-acre property, including three homes, located between one-quarter and one-half mile from one another, two large barns, and a granary. Before it became known as the "Heart K," 480 acres of the ranch belonged to the Davis family.[2] John Davis, a Welsh immigrant, married a local Mountain Maidu woman, Mary Yatkin, from the nearby Maidu town of Coppertown. He acquired the ranch in sections through a combination of two purchases and one homesteading claim. Before the establishment of Coppertown, many Maidu villages were located in the Valley, which is known as *yatometo koyo*, or valley surrounded by mountains. The valley's Maidu residents have been stewarding its resources for many, many years, following a seasonal cycle that includes harvesting bulbs in the higher country in the summer and harvesting acorns in the valley in the fall.[3]

Davis and his wife had several children, and one, Charles Davis, built a ranch house on the land in late 1800s or early 1900s.[4] The home still stands, and Marvin Cunningham grew up there, helping in the fields and catching the bus to school in Greenville. Charles Davis willed the ranch to his daughter, Marvin's mother Evelyn, and when she passed away, the ranch went to her husband Jack Cunningham and their six sons, including Marvin. In 1960, the ranch was transferred from the family to Kathleen Garr, although not all of the heirs seemed to be aware of or had consented to the land transfer.[5] Garr sold the parcel to a Mr. Reininghaus in 1998, and, in the early 2000s, Reininghaus began to talk of subdividing it and building houses on it to sell. In 2002, hoping to save the $3 million property from development, the Feather River Land Trust (FRLT) began exploring possibilities for purchasing it.

Local resident Paul Hardy and several other community members had established the land trust just two years earlier, in 2000, and it was entirely run by volunteers. Although FRLT did not have the funds to purchase the land outright, it had already established a productive partnership with The Nature Conservancy (TNC), which had both the money and an interest in the property. However, TNC was largely concerned with the property's biodiversity values, whereas FRLT recognized both biodiversity values and the community and cultural values associated with the land. These differences did not seem large at first, but when TNC staff changed, the differences became more striking.

Acquiring the Heart K

At the time of the land transaction, pressure was high as the two conservation organizations worked to save the parcel from development. Reininghaus subdivided the 1,267-acre property into eleven parcels and quickly began selling them, dropping the total available acreage to 883 acres in seven parcels. Working with FRLT, TNC made an unsuccessful offer on the property in 2002, and FRLT made another in 2003. Finally, at the end of 2004, TNC made an offer and purchased the property directly from Reininghaus, using its internal revolving loan fund that is set aside for quick acquisitions of threatened properties.

FRLT had partnered with TNC on fundraising and negotiations for the property, and the idea was that, once TNC acquired the land, the title would go to FRLT. However, when TNC's California state director and Northern Sierra project director both left the organization, the new staff decided to place conservation easements on the property and sell it to "conservation buyers" (buyers willing to live with the restrictive easements), in order to replenish TNC's revolving fund. According to Hardy, TNC was considering selling the 883-acre ranch to as many as three different buyers. "The plan was good for biodiversity conservation and scenery, but . . . it would have been seen locally as an unsuccessful outcome, in which out-of-area buyers purchase the property . . . are only on the property for part of the year, and usually mandate no trespassing and very little community engagement [with] the property."[6] In response, FRLT decided to take out a loan and buy the property directly from TNC. TNC was amenable to the plan, stopped showing potential buyers the land, and gave FRLT the time it needed to raise the money. In 2006, FRLT secured a $2.5 million, three-year loan from the Packard Foundation. "Part of the reason we chose to do it was to keep relationships to the place alive. . . . That is why we took the risk," Hardy explained.[7]

The Heart K came to illustrate a substantial discrepancy between TNC's and FRLT's conservation strategies. TNC protects many acres of land by engaging in conservation-buyer sales, which put money back into its revolving loan fund for emergency acquisitions.[8] Although Hardy sees the value of the conservation outcomes of this approach, he also sees the ways in which it can disenfranchise local stakeholders. FRLT came to articulate its own, multifaceted public-benefit focus, by charting a "middle ground" between these different models. The land trust considers the scale of the development threat, yet it also consistently affirms its identity as a "locally based conservation organization" that takes community interests into account. Although FRLT still emphasizes biodiversity conservation, weighting it slightly more than educational, cultural, and scenic property values, it typically selects properties that meet all of these criteria. The Heart K, for example, is in a valley bottom, has cultural importance, has recently been a working ranch, includes a riparian corridor, is extremely scenic, and holds great importance for the local community. Because of its passion for protecting the Heart K, the FRLT was faced with a loan principle amount of $2.5 million, due in December 2009. At that point, the organization had raised only about $1.6 million, and the Packard Foundation granted FRLT an eighteen-month extension to raise the remainder. The FRLT will continue to pursue federal, state, tribal, and private sources. One potential funding opportunity may involve selling a riparian conservation easement to the California Department of Fish and Game on the stream corridor that traverses the property. The revenue from the easement sale would go toward paying down the loan principle. If the FRLT is not able to raise the required amount, it will have to sell one or two of the seven remaining parcels in the 883-acre Heart K Ranch. Hardy sees this as a "last resort."

Accountability and Involvement

As a nonprofit land trust with a legal mandate to protect land for conservation and public benefit, the FRLT is accountable to a diverse constituency of members and communities who hold a variety of goals for the organization. The FRLT must balance multiple values on the Heart K and its other properties, including Maidu cultural values.[9] On the Heart K, in particular, the land trust has been challenged to build a relationship with the Davis/ Cunningham family that simultaneously respects the family's deep and abiding relationship with the land and honors the land trust's mandate to preserve lands for broader public benefits. For example, the FRLT stopped the "fragmentation of habitat and loss of public access"[10] that were likely to accompany subdivision and construction, but it has not offered Marvin the opportunity to rent or purchase the home his grandfather built, adjacent to the family cemetery. According to land trust staff, this is partially because the home itself has been declared uninhabitable until the septic system is replaced, and basic repairs must be completed on the structure to make it legally rentable.[11] Leaving aside these legal and financial issues, Hardy indicated a willingness to discuss this further with Marvin.[12]

In 2003, Hardy asked me, a young African American/multiracial researcher working in the local Maidu community, if I knew of any other examples and models of land trusts successfully collaborating with tribes, Native nonprofits, and Native families. It was that question, and my being concerned about the separation of the ranch from the Davis/Cunningham family, that led to the development of this book. At the time, I was a graduate student in the Department of Environmental Science, Policy, and Management, Division of Society and the Environment, at the University of California, Berkeley. I was working with the Cunningham family and other Maidu families, community members, and organizations, supporting their efforts to reacquire lands and to gain increased opportunities to protect and steward Mountain Maidu resources and cultural sites. I had been listening to and discussing concerns about the Heart K Ranch with Farrell and Trina Cunningham, in particular.

When I first met with Hardy in 2002, the FRLT mirrored the demographics of many other fledgling, local land trusts around the United States. It was small, largely Anglo, with a part-time staff of two,[13] and a grand vision for preserving habitat, scenery, working ranches, and conservation values in the 2.4-million-acre Feather River watershed, the headwaters for the California State Water Project. The board of directors consisted of local businesspeople, back-to-the-landers, conservationists, botanists, and those employed in forestry and other natural-resource-sector jobs. With some success, the land trust has consistently attempted to have at least one representative from the Mountain Maidu community serve on the board. The first representative was Warren Gorbet, from 2000 to 2002, and Trina Cunningham, Marvin's eldest daughter and a descendant of the Davis family that owned the Heart K Ranch, served from 2001 to 2010.[14] Trina and her older brothers spent part of their childhood in the house built by their great-grandfather Charles Davis, when Marvin rented it from Garr in the 1970s.

Trina explained her decision to join the FRLT board at a 2009 workshop I had organized on Cultural Conservation Easements at the Public Interest Environmental Law Conference:

> I was asked to be on the board of the Feather River Land Trust, and the reason that I accepted that position was because, as an un-federally recognized tribal person in my own homeland, we didn't have access to the resources that we need to perpetuate our culture, the way that we need to, and our language, to be able to practice our ceremonies, to be able to gather the plants that we need. And so I thought at that time that being on the board of the Feather River Land Trust could help assist in that goal, because, even though they didn't have anything cultural in there whatsoever, it was still protecting our land that we wanted to have protected so, to me, it doesn't matter who does it, as long as it's getting done. And so, at the same time it was pretty frustrating because, you know, there is nothing cultural going on [in the land trust], and yeah, it's great, you know, I agree, the black-tailed mule deer need to be protected, and the cottonwood stands need to be protected, but, you know, where's the human factor within that?[15]

Trina has played an important role on the land trust board, in terms of helping the organization to recognize the cultural importance of the lands they are protecting within the Maidu homeland.[16] However, as a board member, she cannot directly advocate for her father to live on the land because that would constitute a conflict of interest. According to Hardy, although the land trust realizes that the Davis/Cunningham family has a longstanding tie to the ranch, they are concerned about privileging the concerns of one Maidu family over those of other Maidu or members of the public regarding the ranch.[17] Trina also explained that the land trust does not want to get into the business of being a landlord by renting out structures on their properties. Further, the land trust does not want to incur the costs associated with subdividing a property in order to sell a structure.[18]

As Hardy's 2003 question to me about other examples of land trusts that successfully collaborate with Native peoples indicated, the land trust was also unsure of which actors in the Native community—the nearest recognized tribe, Maidu nonprofits, or specific families—would be most appropriate partners for FRLT. California agencies and external organizations have expressed similar confusion about whom to work with in Maidu country and often focus on working solely with the recognized tribe. The distinction between recognized and unrecognized tribes is rooted in California Indian genocide and land appropriation. When treaties negotiated with California Indians in 1854 were "lost" in the Senate for fifty years and never ratified,[19] the Mountain Maidu, like many other tribes throughout the state, were left landless and without federal recognition as a tribe. Federal recognition establishes a government-to-government relationship between tribes and the federal government, formally recognizes tribal sovereignty, and provides federal funding for tribal health care and education (among other services). In addition, federal recognition establishes a trust relationship, whereby the federal government holds certain resources in trust for the tribe and manages these in the tribe's best interest. Today, the nearest recognized tribal governments to the Genesee Valley are six rancherias in Plumas, Lassen, and Butte counties.[20] Most rancherias began as lands set aside for California Indians who had been displaced from their homes as a result of the influx of non-Native miners, farmers, homesteaders, entrepreneurs, and other settlers.[21] The Cunningham/Davis family still owned the ranch at the time the local rancherias were established. Consequently, they are not members of the nearest recognized tribe, the Greenville Rancheria, whom most outside entities consult when planning a land action in the area.[22]

Prior to European contact, California Indian families had particular areas that they stewarded, and the boundaries between areas of use were well respected.[23] When European settlers homesteaded particular areas and married into Maidu families, some Maidu family resource-procurement areas became part of these homesteaded ranches. In cases such as these, questions about the land's management may need to be directed to the Maidu-white family linked to that particular site rather than to the nearest recognized tribe. For California Indian tribes that are not federally recognized, the nearest rancheria tribal government may actually be located at a considerable distance from specific local properties. Given this context, the FRLT has sought to work with the Cunningham family, particularly Marvin, Trina, and Farrell, as well as working through Trina and former board member Jeanene Hafen[24] to communicate with other Maidu and Native constituents, such as the Maidu Summit Consortium.

The FRLT board allows traditional cultural uses of the property, including willow coppicing, acorn harvesting, and ceremonials. However, no formal agreements have been signed with the Cunningham family or any Maidu government or group. Once the FRLT has paid off the loan and secured title to the property, Paul Hardy foresees more agreements, comanagement efforts, and overall hands-on management of the land. Work on the land thus far has included willow planting in Indian Creek, repairing the main barn, hazardous fuel reduction around the main house, irrigation repair and installation of a solar-powered water system, and removal of trees that pose hazards.[25] Some community members—Maidu and non-Maidu alike—have expressed a desire to see more intensive management, Maidu involvement, and daily Maidu stewardship on the property.[26] But the FRLT Board is focused on securing ownership of the property before initiating additional agreements or management actions. As Hardy explained, "We partly haven't done as much as we would like to because of the situation of trying to raise $3 million [$2.5 million loan, $.5 million endowment for long-term management]. The Heart K lends itself to so many important stewardship, restoration, and education projects, but to some degree, it's first things first. You have to accomplish the holding action of owning the property before you can delve too deeply into actions on the property."[27] In 2010, the FRLT is also working on twenty other acquisitions in addition to paying off the Heart K, a testimony to the organization's growth in staff members and operating budget since it first worked with TNC to make an offer on the Heart K in 2002.

However, despite the expanding scope of FRLT's work, the Heart K remains unique among its properties because of the ranch's degree of cultural importance and community involvement. These aspects of the property and Trina Cunningham's active role on the FRLT board have also helped to change the personality of the entire organization. According to Hardy, FRLT has become a more "people/community/service oriented" body, which "bodes well for [its support of] cultural conservation."[28] Hardy attributes this change to board members like Cunningham. In contrast to the current board, the founding board of the FRLT focused more on environmental science and evaluated parcels largely on ecological criteria. Now, Hardy explains, "we are becoming more aware. Generally, the work of a land trust has to be broader. It's part of a maturity process within the organization and more of a sincere desire to serve the communities we work in."[29]

The FRLT is now working on developing easement language that addresses cultural access to and protection of cultural resources on properties it holds easements on or owns. As part of this effort, the FRLT is also initiating a program area called People on the Land. The FRLT has two existing program areas, Land Protection (the acquisition of publicly important properties and conservation easements) and Land Stewardship (the restoration, management, and monitoring of these properties and easements).[30] People and the Land will focus on protecting and restoring people's relationship to place. The program will include cultural conservation, as well as acquainting children with the land and partnering with multigenerational agricultural families.

Conclusion

In 2003, after Hardy asked me what I thought of the situation on the ranch, and I had heard the concerns of the Cunningham/Davis family and other Maidu people in the area, I began researching existing collaborations and statutory developments in Native-private conservation. This work was also applicable to another project I was involved with in Maidu country—the Maidu Stewardship Project. When I first began collaborating with the Maidu Cultural and Development Group in 2001 on the Stewardship Project, they were finishing the environmental analysis required by the National Environmental Policy Act to begin work on a 1,600-acre parcel of U.S. Forest Service land outside of Greenville, California. The project is still underway, but it has hit several roadblocks. Some Maidu ascribe these to the federal government's bureaucratic resistance to adaptive management and innovative contracting.[31] As the project stalled, community members started to ask if it might be easier to collaborate with private landowners or to raise the funds to buy their own parcel of land. This raised the question of whether private lands offered more opportunities than public lands for both innovation and security of land tenure. Working on private lands might require use of private conservation tools, such as easements and land trusts, which are relatively new applications in Indian country.

Drawing on both of these experiences, in which there was a need for more information on how tribes can use private conservation tools, this book looks at examples of partnership for management and stewardship of

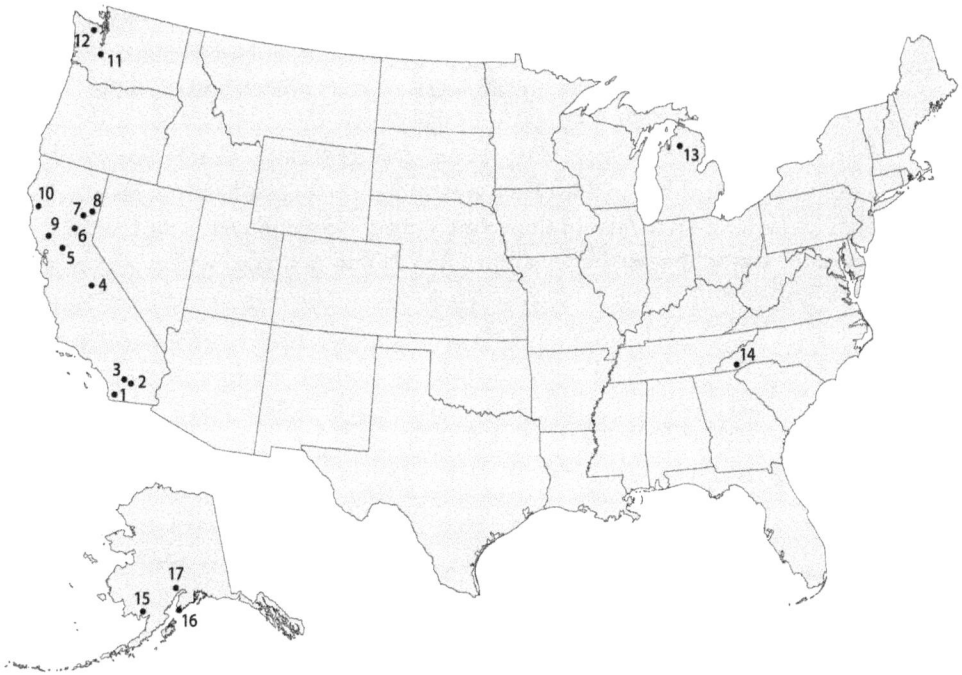

1. Kumeyaay-Diegueño Land Conservancy
2. Native American Land Conservancy
3. Morongo Band of Mission Indians
4. Coarsegold Resource Conservation District
5. Cache Creek Conservancy /
   Tending and Gathering Garden
6. Tsi-Akim Maidu / Nevada County Land Trust
7. Maidu Summit / Feather River Land Trust
8. Susanville Indian Rancheria
9. Yocha Dehe Wintun Nation
10. InterTribal Sinkyone Wilderness
11. Nisqually Indian Tribe / Nisqually Land Trust

12. Jamestown S'Klallam / North Olympic Land Trust
13. Little Traverse Bay Bands of Odawa Indians /
    Little Traverse Conservancy
14. Eastern Band of Cherokee /
    Land Trust for the Little Tennessee
15. Nushagak–Mulchatna Wood–Tikchik Land Trust
16. Kachemak Heritage Land Trust
17. Tyonek Native Corporation /
    Chuitna Conservation Easement

Data Sources: US Census (Boundaries),
Middleton Research (Project Locations)
Projections: US Albers, Alaska Albers (GCS NAD 1983)
Map by Joshua Perlman

FIGURE P.1. Map of case-study sites. (Prepared by Joshua Perlman) privately owned lands. It examines how tribes and land trusts might best work together, how tribes might form their own land trusts and conservancies, and how they also might employ conservation easements and land trusts as tools for cultural and natural resource preservation. In this book, I have worked to answer Hardy's question in a way that would simultaneously expand Native families' and organizations'—and recognized and unrecognized tribes'—possibilities for regaining access to culturally vital lands and other resources while also providing resources and reasons for land trusts to improve their relationships with Native partners. The book offers a series of examples focused on the use of these emerging conservation tools for environmental justice and legal innovation and in support of tribal sovereignty.

Acknowledgments

I am extremely grateful for the assistance and partnership of Reina Rogers (NRCS-Tribal Liaison), without whom this project would not have been completed. I also owe a debt of gratitude to Hawk Rosales (InterTribal Sinkyone Wilderness Council) and Kurt Russo (Native American Land Conservancy), each of whom went over multiple drafts and answered many questions. Innumerable thanks are also due to each interviewee who took the time to share his or her opinions, provide additional resources (often from afar), and review and comment on text. I am grateful specifically to Curtis Berkey, Chuck Sams III, and Tim Troll for correspondence on taxation and other legal questions; my Ph.D. advisor Dr. Louise Fortmann (UC Berkeley) for her support of the project; David Case for reviewing sidebar text and sharing his expertise on Alaska Native land claims settlement laws; my doctoral mentor Dr. Jeff Romm at UC Berkeley and my postdoctoral mentors at UC Davis, Dr. Ben Orlove and Dr. Stephen Crum, for advice and encouragement; to Dr. M. Kat Anderson, for comments on early drafts; 7th Generation and Chris "Mo" Hollis for recording the Cultural Conservation Easements workshop and collaborating on the video project; colleague Josh Perlman for cartography; Mary Ann King, who initiated this project with me in 2004; my aunt and uncle Diane and Joe Ide for consulting on the title; and my parents, Lyrissa and Herb Middleton. I am also grateful to three anonymous reviewers, who offered excellent suggestions; to copy editor Patricia Rosas; and to Patti Hartmann, Senior Acquisitions Editor, and Nancy Arora, Production Editor, both with the University of Arizona Press, for supporting the project; and to all people whose deepest faith is in their connection to the land.

TRUST IN THE LAND

Introduction

Bottom line is, our land is our life. Whatever mechanism you use in present terms, in the present law, is fine, but the bottom line is we've never broken the covenant that we have with Creator, across Indian Country. That is first and foremost the law that most Native peoples refer back to, it is also a law that we have been able to put into the conservation and cultural easements.

—Charles Sams III, Executive Director, Indian Country Conservancy[1]

Land trusts did not originate in Native America, but the traditions of working to buy back confiscated lands and to retain rights to lands not in tribal ownership are well known in Indian Country. Tribes have long been working to buy back or petition for the restitution of culturally important lands taken from their communities during the European settlement of the United States.[2] Tribes have also consistently worked to assert rights to resources that are not in tribal ownership, including traditional hunting, fishing, and gathering sites.[3] Given the growth of private conservation throughout the United States to protect biologically and recreationally important lands, this book explores how private conservation tools—despite their neoliberal, neocolonial roots—can actually be used for Native goals, thereby expanding the reach and relevance of the conservation movement itself. The book examines the tools themselves and then explores where, and under what conditions, we can productively use them in Indian Country to meet Native land priorities.

The fourteen case studies illustrate the ways in which tribes have applied private conservation methods to protect culturally important resources, acquire alienated lands, mitigate tribal development projects, and ensure the health and sustainability of traditional resources. The text is organized along two axes. First, cases are grouped into three different institutional mechanisms. Looking at the institutional character of the partnership and the partners, and the conservation tool used, allows an exploration of how differences are resolved and similarities enhanced in the development of collaborative conservation agreements. Second, looking at land-tenure arrangements (easement holder or landowner) provides important insights into the possible power dynamics of a partnership, in which a landowner may or may not have more leverage to choose a partner and to direct the outcomes.

The two cases in Section One, "Native American Land Conservation Organizations," focus on Native land trusts and conservancies. Although both of these Native conservancies own land, the chapters emphasize not only their land ownership but also their partnerships, organizational form, history, goals, governance, and projects. The two cases are united by being Native land trusts, yet they differ enough from one another to illustrate the variations that can occur under one institutional arrangement.

The nine cases in Section Two, "Collaborations between Tribes and Land Trusts," explore collaborations between Native entities, including recognized tribes, petitioning tribes, and Native nonprofits, and land conservancies or trusts. The cases in this section represent a range of land-tenure arrangements, in which the tribe, the conservancy, or a non-Native private holder own the land. Tribes' use of Senate Bill 18 (SB-18, California) is included in this section because SB-18 specifically names tribes as easement holders, and SB-18 consultation involves tribes using statutes and partnerships with surrounding jurisdictions to negotiate for conservation and resource protection on private lands. Collaborations between tribes and non-Native land trusts to protect parcels not in tribal ownership are similar to SB-18 negotiations to protect off-reservation lands. The nine case studies in this section are grouped into eight chapters (the Alaska chapter contains two). These cases are placed in dialogue with one another in the book's Conclusion to glean lessons learned that may be applied across Indian country and throughout the land trust movement.

The third section, "Tribes and NRCS Conservation Tools" contains a single chapter that is narrowly focused on the ways in which tribes can work with the conservation tools and programs of one federal agency, the Natural Resources Conservation Service (NRCS). The NRCS focuses on private-land conservation and is the only federal agency that is directly instrumental in and supportive of tribes creating tribal resource conservation districts. The Susanville Indian Rancheria mini-case study in this chapter shows how tribes can tailor an NRCS tool to tribal needs. This section has an institutional focus on arrangements involving tribes and the NRCS.

Theoretical Frame

Environmental justice is analytically important to private conservation, yet it remains under-discussed and under-utilized in the conservation field. As Mary Christina Wood and Zachary Welcker note, "by integrating humans back into conserved landscapes, the tribal trust movement will draw attention to the role of land in the pursuit of social justice and human rights. This dimension has been much ignored by the conservation movement."[4] An environmental justice analysis is essential for expanding conservation tools that have heretofore been used for relatively narrow conservation purposes. The cultural foundations of the notions of conservation and public benefit must be interrogated. Tribes lost most of their lands to the expansion of the American state, which included the expansion of American conservation. America was and is home to a great diversity of individual Native nations, each with a practical and spiritual relationship to a homeland. Europeans attempted to sever this relationship by confiscating Native lands and suppressing Native practices. "Losing their lands has had a profound impact on Native people. Many tribal leaders believe it is the most significant factor in the economic, cultural, health, social, and spiritual challenges facing Native Americans today."[5] Rather than undertaking conservation atop this foundation of injustice, we must examine conservation practices for their relevancy to the first peoples of this land. Are conservation tools, which are aimed at conserving Native homelands (although they may not be recognized as such), legally, politically, culturally, and socially available for tribes and Native organizations to use to meet their goals, in their own places?

Environmental justice examines the distribution of environmental benefits and harms and the rights of all people, particularly people of color and low-income people, to participate in environmental planning and decision making. Perhaps conservation tools and private conservation practices do not include a mandate to discriminate against poor people and people of color, but if they do so in practice, the tools themselves must be changed to confer benefits on all members of the population. This book also argues that Native Americans have a particular right to be involved in conservation planning and decision making as the first peoples of this land.

When private conservation tools are examined and altered to create more just and evenly distributed outcomes, new legal arrangements often emerge. We must expect that these new arrangements will issue from an arena that brings together conservation statutes and precedent, public-lands law, and traditional, tribal, and federal Indian law. The cases included in this book offer some examples of innovative legal arrangements; raise questions as to why certain institutional arrangements (such as tribes holding conservation easements) are not emerging; and push legal analysts, conservation practitioners, and tribal leaders to think creatively about possible arrangements that would bring existing laws together in ways that support tribes' diverse goals and motivations for land conservation.

Environmental justice and legal innovation are taken together to explore the hypothesis that tribal engagement in private conservation, as exemplified by a range of institutional arrangements, achieves environmental justice and lights the way toward new legal mechanisms. The text travels from California north to Washington and Alaska, and east to Michigan, and southeast to North Carolina. The book does not contain a comprehensive review of all tribe–land trust collaborations and Native land trusts, but those discussed here provide a sample of existing institutional arrangements and practices.

The book invites tribes, land trusts, and agencies considering conservation partnerships to think carefully about points and locations of common interest; possible structures of agreement (such as memorandums of understanding, lease agreements, short-term easements, perpetual easements); and possible institutional formations (including Native land trusts, collaborations with non-Native land trusts, and collaborations with federal conservation agencies). As practitioners continue to develop agreements, this book also invites readers to encourage lawmakers; legal counsel; the Internal Revenue Service; federal, state, and local agencies; and umbrella conservation organizations, such as the Land Trust Alliance (LTA), to examine how conservation easements and land trusts might be rethought from the premise that they could be used by tribes and Native organizations to meet tribal goals for land restitution and cultural and natural resource protection: "By fostering greater tribal involvement, LTA will stimulate private conservation even more and help introduce a much needed Native perspective into the broader environmental movement."[6]

Incorporating Native interests into LTA goals may require land trusts to become knowledgeable about federal Indian policy (historic and contemporary) and individual tribal traditional goals, as well as understanding how these interface with contemporary enabling statutes for conservation easements and land trusts. Ultimately, the goals for a tribal agenda using private conservation tools will come from Native organizations and from tribal members, such as the leaders who organized a workshop on Native land trusts at the 2009 LTA Rally.[7] Non-Native land trusts, agencies, and private conservationists will be working toward environmental justice and undoing historical wrongs if they give priority to establishing relationships with local tribal governments, Native organizations, and Native families, and to accompanying them in this work, rather than opposing it by further enclosing Native homelands.

Lines of Inquiry

The case studies and analysis explore two principal questions. The first asks: what are the challenges for using private conservation tools on tribal lands? As the cases show, the challenges range from legal ones, in that the tools were not created to serve Native contexts and must be adapted to that, to cultural and social considerations, in that private conservation tools have been used in ways that have disenfranchised or, at the very least, simply did not include Native Americans. Given the role that conservation has played in divesting Native homelands, tribes may approach private conservation organizations or mainstream conservation practitioners with mistrust. However, some legal tools and conservation approaches that have been used against Native claims to Native homelands may now be reused by tribes to reclaim lands and to reassert relationships with place and the right to manage resources.

The second line of inquiry gleans lessons and guidelines from successful projects. A "lessons learned" section in the conclusion looks at cases thematically to extract both applied and theoretical lessons. Some key applied lessons that will be discussed throughout the text and in the conclusion include:

- establishing clear spheres of influence for the different partners;
- developing formal agreements;
- respecting one another's differences, but finding key points of similarity and common ground;
- clearly defining the purpose of the collaboration;
- developing, as needed, unique legal arrangements to fit the contexts of cross-cultural partnerships that involve a range of land-tenure situations and legal statuses.

The Work Ahead

The conservation tools discussed in this text provide a new format for partnerships so that tribes can achieve either ownership with some conservation restrictions or, at least, an interest in alienated lands and a place at the table in determining their future. This book takes as a starting point the notion that conservation easements and land trusts are also conservation tools for

Native Americans and Native lands. The work now is to determine precisely how the characteristics of application, incentive structure, and enabling statutes need to be amended to embrace and support further Native application of these tools.

In this era of increasing disinvestment in federal institutions, growth in privatization, and ongoing climate change,[8] the role of private-land conservation in preserving natural and cultural resources will only expand. However, as the next chapter will explain, these "private" land conservation tools are hardly private, because public statutes, funding, and incentives enable them. Land trusts preserve private lands in order to achieve public benefits, but they often do so without much input from the public, which can create a confusing institutional condition. In terms of land trust partnerships, formation, and acquisitions, the relative lack of bureaucracy compared to public land acquisition and management may create increased opportunities for tribal land acquisition, stewardship, and protection. To assert their role in the stewardship of culturally important, privately conserved lands, tribes may choose to form their own land trusts or to partner with existing non-tribal land trusts.

Easements and land trusts can fit within a portfolio of admirable work "in which Indians and their representatives have used the judicial and legislative processes to reclaim land, natural resources, and political power."[9] Conservation easements and land trusts are enabled by state and federal statutes that by and large do not recognize the possible links between easement law, on the one hand, and tribal sovereignty, traditional land rights, treaty rights, and federal Indian law, on the other. The information in this book may offer suggestions to lawmakers, judges, and attorneys, as well as to tribal leaders and conservationists working on tribal lands, regarding how to interpret and amend these statutes in order to recognize their applicability to tribal land conservation, acquisition, stewardship, and consolidation. As Vine Deloria Jr. argued, "Policy objectives should be oriented toward restitution of Indian communities with rights they enjoyed for centuries before the coming of the white man."[10]

2

Context of Private Conservation

The use and applicability of private conservation tools, such as conservation easements and land trusts or conservancies, has expanded exponentially over the last two decades. According to the 2005 land trust census taken by the Land Trust Alliance (LTA), there were 1,667 land trusts in the United States, up 32 percent from 2000.[1] The 2005 census calculated the total acreage conserved by local, state, and national land trusts at 37 million acres, or "an area 16 and one-half times the size of Yellowstone National Park." As of 2009, the number of land trusts surpassed 1,700.[2] The overall rate of proliferation of land trusts in the last two decades has been similarly astonishing. In Mary Ann King and Sally Fairfax's analysis of the LTA census, for example,

> the number of land trusts ha[d] increased 26 percent between 1998 and 2003 alone. The number of [conservation easements] . . . also increased dramatically in the same period. Total acreage conserved by local and regional land trusts doubled, from 4.7 million to 8.4 million, and [conservation easements] account for most of that increase: local and regional land trusts hold 17,847 [easements], up from 7,392 in 1998, and the total acreage protected by [those easements] has increased 266 percent since 1998.[3]

This analysis only includes local and regional land trusts, and not the rate of protection by international land trusts, such as The Nature Conservancy, and national land trusts, such as The Conservation Fund and the Trust for Public Land. Still, private conservation through direct purchase of land by trusts or the use of conservation easements is growing at a much faster rate than parks, preserves, wilderness areas, and other methods of public conservation.

But what do land trusts do? What communities do they serve? Within a context of neocolonial conservation policy, do they act to increase equity and justice? Or do they simply protect lands for privileged, middle- and upper-class nature lovers? Since the incentives for conservation that land trusts provide may have greater appeal for individuals with financial or property-based assets, can they really enable rural people to continue to work farms, forests, and ranches that have ceased, in a globalized economy, to support themselves?[4] And which rural people may benefit? Rural workers? Or rural landowners? Or both? Finally, will land trusts really continue "in perpetuity"? The questions surrounding the purpose of utilizing land trusts and conservation easements are many, and this book focuses specifically on how land trusts and conservation easements can support, rather than encroach upon, Native lands.

Although land trusts have recently proliferated, the concept of pur-chasing land and setting it aside for conservation is not new in the United States. Citizen groups working together to preserve local resources have been around since well before the term "land trust" came about.[5] Sally K. Fairfax and her coauthors describe such early private conservation orga-nizations as the Bunker Hill Monument Association, formed in 1823 to raise funds to memorialize the American Revolution, and the Mt. Vernon Ladies Association, which bought George Washington's estate in 1861.[6] Most scholars of land trusts also point to the Boston-based "Trustees of [Public] Reservations," founded in 1891, as one of the oldest private land trusts in the United States.[7] Although the Trustees promulgated a notion of purchasing historic and scenic land and holding it for public benefit, we have to imagine that the meaning of the deserving "public" was very different at that time, and it did not include most Native Americans or African Americans. This raises the question of what "public" is being served by contemporary private conservation. In many cases the "public good" does not include formal participation of ancestral owners of the land (tribal members), and it does not provide mechanisms for ensuring the protection and stewardship of culturally important places.

To return to the history of private-land conservation, as Fairfax and her coauthors remind us, "Private actors have played a vital role in acquisi-tion and conservation efforts for more than 180 years."[8] The early Anglo private acquisitions, with some federal funding and support, took place in a climate of "strong property rights and weak federal authority."[9] Similarly, during the Reagan and Bush Sr. administrations, when those conditions also existed, the number of land trusts increased. However, land trusts continued to increase in the Clinton, and now, the Obama administrations, so Republican leadership is not the only factor. This raises the question of what type of climate is needed for tribes to take full advantage of private conservation tools, that is, to apply tribal sovereignty and these tools to assert partial nonpossessory claims or full ownership rights over off-reservation properties.

Law and policy must be friendly specifically to tribal and cultural conservation, by creating statutes (such as SB-18) that affirm the rights of recognized and unrecognized tribes to hold easements. Additionally, the Internal Revenue Code (IRC) should state specifically that landowners can receive a tax deduction for donating or selling a conservation easement to a tribe. Although the LTA works hard to maintain the tax incentives for conservation,[10] it has yet to call for incentives to increase tribal conservation. At the 2009 LTA Rally, a group of indigenous people and their allies drafted a summary of standards and practices for how land trusts should engage with tribes and Native communities.[11]

Like contemporary land trusts, the early forms of private conservation existed in a gray area between public and private conservation. As King and Fairfax note, "Conservation easements were in 1980, and remain today, a combination of public and private leadership, management, and funding."[12] Historically and contemporaneously, land trusts are private groups that draw on both public and private funding to conserve lands with importance to both public and private constituencies. Legal scholar Nancy McLaughlin, who has published extensively on conservation easements and land trusts, notes that, "Virtually all land trusts function as publicly supported charitable organizations."[13] Land trusts are public in that they are subject to the laws and regulations that make them qualified holders of property for a public conservation purpose,[14] yet they are private because they are not federal nor state entities.[15]

Despite such pluralistic legal and fiscal origins, land trusts are governed by private boards, which make land-use decisions with private landowners and funders that may affect thousands of acres. Parties that may not have a voice in these decisions include tribes and other Native entities (nonprofits, families, and so forth) with ties to those lands. King and Fairfax have argued that because land trusts function in a public manner but are seen as private entities, they should be subject to greater public oversight.[16] This oversight would make land trusts more accountable to stakeholders, ensure broader public participation in land-use decisions, and provide more assurance that land trusts were performing their easement-enforcement duties. Further, an external monitor could keep track of the land trust's use of public funds and measure its achievement of goals and broad public outcomes.[17] Another recommendation should be added to this list: a monitor could determine how a land trust is working to increase justice by collaborating with the first peoples in its area of interest.

Conservation Easements

A conservation easement is an agreement between a landowner and another party restricting or prohibiting development of a parcel for a defined length of time. In 1959, William Whyte was one of the first people to use the term "conservation easement," in an attempt to convey the multiple conservation benefits it could provide the public.[18] The federal enabling statute for conservation easements, the Uniform Conservation Easement Act (UCEA) defines conservation easements as

> a nonpossessory interest of a holder in real property imposing limitations or affirmative obligations the purposes of which include retaining or protecting natural, scenic, or open-space values of real property, assuring its availability for agricultural, forest, recreational, or open-space use, protecting natural resources, maintaining or enhancing air or water quality, or preserving the historical, architectural, archaeological, or cultural aspects of real property.[19]

As Federico Cheever aptly describes, conservation easements create "property rights in conservation."[20] As such, they make "conservation/development" one stick in the bundle of sticks that constitute a property right. Property values are divided into components using the "bundle of sticks" metaphor, in which property ownership consists of a bundle of sticks, or distinct rights. All of the sticks together compose the ownership of a piece of land. One of the individual sticks is the right to develop the land. The landowner (individual, tribe, corporation, and so forth) can sell or donate the right to develop by placing a conservation easement on the property. The conservation easement is held and enforced by an entity that is legally approved to do that. Although the landowner has sold or donated the development rights by creating a conservation easement, that person retains the rest of the sticks (property rights) in the bundle.

Conservation easements can be used to protect ecological, cultural, economic, scenic, historical, or related values. Although a conservation easement restricts the development values of a property, it may also enhance these other values. Conservation easements can help tribes to gain access to and stewardship of culturally important species; protect off-reservation treaty fishing and hunting rights; memorialize and cleanse sites where massacres occurred; reacquire alienated tribal lands; find a secure land base for ceremonies; and mitigate on- and off-reservation development projects that impact tribes and resources.

A Legal Anomaly

Conservation easements are a radical legal tool in the United States because they stray from English common law, which underlies much American law. Under common law, easements are servitudes, or private interests in property that do not constitute full ownership. They are usually affirmative, in that they typically allow use of another's property—for example, to run a power line or an access road across the land. They are also appurtenant, in that they are created to serve a neighboring parcel. Common law servitudes are generally not negative, in that they do not prohibit certain actions. They are also not in gross, that is, providing benefits to groups that do not own either parcel.

Conservation easements, in contrast, are simultaneously negative, affirmative, and in gross, and they are typically referred to as negative servitudes in gross. They are "in gross" because benefits accrue to the "public," rather than to a specific, neighboring landowner.[21] Conservation easements offer both negative rights ("such as the right to restrict development or regulate farming practices") and positive rights ("such as the right to plant vegetation or construct trails").[22] One similarity between common-law easements and easements in gross is that the easement continues in force even when the ownership of the land changes. Conservation easements are different, however, because the easement is tied to both the property and to a specific easement holder that is facilitating public benefit by monitoring and enforcing the easement, even when land changes hands.[23]

Conservation easements are also odd because they are both public and private. Although property theorists have long argued that our concept of private property is inherently pluralistic,[24] conservation easements particularly magnify this intersection of the public and the private. In "Public Good and Private Magic," Cheever explains that although they are persistently considered "private," easements are a form of public conservation on at least three levels.[25] Easements could not exist without public interventions, which indicate federal, state, and local governments' acknowledgment of the importance of private conservation. A state government's adoption of the Uniform Conservation Easement Act or similar legislation allows conservation easements to be used in that state and identifies which entities can hold easements. The Internal Revenue Code's substantial tax savings for private landowners with lands encumbered by conservation easements give some landowners an incentive to donate an easement to a designated holder. State, federal, and local governments support land trusts and other legal easement holders by giving potential holders a financial incentive to purchase easements. Ultimately, the public sphere enables the concept, the practice, and the application of valuing easements.

Applying Easements

Conservation easements are legally enforceable encumbrances on title that stay on the deed through subsequent land sales. If the easement is "in perpetuity" or permanent, when a landowner sells the property, the conservation easement will apply to all subsequent owners. They will be prohibited from developing the property and will coordinate the monitoring of its protection with the easement holder. A landowner and the party buying or holding the easement can negotiate shorter-term easements, as Susanville Indian Rancheria has done (see chapter 16). However, short-term easements are not eligible for the federal tax incentives for conservation-easement donations, and some states may have minimum terms for conservation easements. California, for example, requires all conservation easements to remain in force for at least ten years.[26]

Some ecologists and landowners prefer conservation easements because they enable "site-specific" conservation that involves planning that is uniquely tailored to a particular site.[27] However, research has shown that the location of easements and other protective covenants does not necessarily match the areas where there is the most need for conservation.[28] This is partially because individual landowner choice and the interests of the funders influence the shape of conservation easements and land trust acquisitions. There is always a possibility that a landowner in a high-priority habitat or cultural resource area may choose not to collaborate with a land trust, tribe, or other entity seeking a stake in the property's ownership. This is a weakness in the ability of conservation easements and other private conservation tools to protect areas that are most in need.

Usually with legal assistance, the landowner and the future easement holder negotiate to allow or disallow particular land uses. Easements can be very specific, allowing certain types of low-impact development, such as temporary structures, hiking trails, or restoration of historic buildings, or they can require no development at all. Conservation easements generally allow or mandate one or more of the following: recreation, education, habitat protection and enhancement, restoration, traditional Native cultural activities, preservation of historic and archaeological sites, grazing, forestry, farming, and ongoing traditional uses. Many land trusts focus on habitat value, which is due to their scientific roots. The Nature Conservancy, for example, was created by a group of biologists concerned about environmental destruction.[29]

In the conservation movement, the term "traditional use" has often referred to farming and ranching activities. This may be due to an American romanticism associated with working the land, which land trusts capitalized on during the Reagan era, when conservation dollars were few but funds for farm subsidies remained substantial.[30] Easements have helped farmers and ranchers maintain their land-based livelihoods as the financial viability of their occupations has decreased. A farmer or rancher can sell development rights in the form of a conservation easement, receive a cash return or a tax deduction, and simultaneously ensure that the property will not be developed and taken out of its customary use.

This book focuses on a different type of "traditional use": Native stewardship of natural resources for cultural and subsistence values. Fourteen case studies in five states look at how tribes are working with easements and land trusts for traditional, ongoing indigenous resource use and enhancement.

Appraising Easements

As a first step in creating an easement, a qualified appraiser[31] calculates the fair-market value of the land with and without development restrictions (the latter taking into account the full "bundle of sticks," that is, property rights). The landowner is typically paid the difference between these two values in exchange for giving up the development rights to the property. The agreement to cede those rights is set forth in the conservation easement, which also names an approved entity to monitor and enforce it. Baseline evaluation of the conservation values of the property is preferably done before the easement is transferred. This step documents the condition of the land and its features, so that the holder can monitor and enforce the land's conservation.[32] The easement holder can be a state or federal agency or a nonprofit land trust or conservancy. Depending on the regulations of the state where the transaction takes place, a federally recognized or unrecognized tribe or Native nonprofit organization may also be able to hold an easement. For example, SB-18 modified the list of entities that could hold conservation easements in California so that it included federally recognized and unrecognized tribes.[33]

The landowner can either donate, sell, or engage in a bargain sale, in which part of the value of the easement is donated and the remainder is sold.[34] The holder can either pay the landowner outright or raise state, federal, or private-foundation funding to pay for the easement. In addition to the actual cost of the easement acquisition, the holder must raise adequate funds to cover the long-term monitoring and enforcement. Many of the land trusts profiled in this text conduct monitoring at least annually to ensure that the baseline conditions are being upheld. Funding for monitoring can come from investments of landowner stewardship donations or endowments; state, federal, or private conservation grants; or land trust campaigns and fundraisers.

The landowner donating a conservation easement can receive a federal tax deduction and possibly a state tax deduction. Some states offer tax incentives to landowners, particularly productive rural landowners, such as farmers and ranchers, who place permanent conservation easements on their properties.[35] Under the federal tax incentive, qualifying family farmers, ranchers, and other moderate-income landowners who donate conservation easements can deduct up to 100 percent of their income, annually, for up to fifteen years or until they reach the full value of the gift, whichever comes first. The LTA continues to lobby for the renewal of these tax incentives, which expired on December 31, 2009.[36] Other tax benefits may include lower estate taxes for heirs of properties with conservation easements; lower gift taxes for landowners gifting portions of a protected property; and finally, lowered property taxes based on the reduced value of the land after development rights are ceded.[37]

To be eligible for the federal income tax incentive, the IRC requires that the easement must be a "qualified conservation contribution," that is, a real gift of a "qualified real property interest" to a "qualified organization" that has conservation as its mission. The gift must be made in perpetuity and explicitly designated for "conservation purposes."[38] These purposes include preservation for outdoor recreation or education, habitat protection, preservation of open space for public benefit, and preservation of a "historically important land area or a certified historic structure."[39] Although landowners who donate shorter-term easements will not get the tax break, they can work with certain federal programs, such as the U.S. Department of Agriculture's Natural Resources Conservation Service Wetlands Reserve Program, to obtain project-based funding. The Wetlands Reserve Program specifically offers landowners funds to complete restoration projects in exchange for permanent or short-term easements of up to thirty years. This will be discussed further in Section Three, chapter 16.

Doubts and Concerns

The majority of the easements discussed in this document are "perpetual" easements, intended to protect lands from development forever. The question of how to ensure perpetuity of restriction, both practically and legally, has been the subject of much debate in the literature on conservation easements. Although some authors argue against the wisdom of imposing a "dead hand" on future property owners,[40] others question the enforceability of easements over time, noting that there are ways to get around them or even annul them.[41]

Concerns center on the durability of a private, usually small nonprofit land trust that is committing to overseeing a parcel of land forever. Cheever, Fairfax, McLaughlin, and others have played the legal devil's advocate to the land trust movement, by calling on land trust proponents to consider possible weaknesses in structure, enforceability, and life expectations of these trusts and, by extension, of the conservation easements they hold.[42] *Trust in the Land* asks whether these same weaknesses exist when tribes use conservation easements or land trusts. Tribes' distinct legal status and different applications of conservation tools may ameliorate those concerns.

Land trusts can be challenged in court regarding their legitimacy as conservation nonprofits. Past cases have revealed problems with land trusts that have cooperated for mutual benefit with for-profit entities, such as developers of neighboring lands, who donate either easements or funds to buy easements on properties adjacent to land trusts. The developers benefit with increased property values (by ensuring that their buyers will have scenic viewsheds in perpetuity), but the land trust may be compromised by working for a private rather than a public good.[43] Similarly, landowners and easement holders may be accused of engaging in the conservation deal as a form of collusion simply to benefit the landowner rather than for any public benefit.

Easements themselves can also potentially be annulled by landowners who no longer want the restriction on their property. There may be quite valid reasons for this, for example, if the property is no longer meeting or perhaps even harming the conservation purposes for which it was developed. Easements may be nullified under the doctrine of *cy pres*, which applies to charitable gifts. If the purpose of the gift is no longer being achieved, then a court may develop a new plan for the gift in order for it to better serve its original purpose.[44] McLaughlin argues that *cy pres* may be an apt tool to address problematic easements in the future, because it addresses a situation very similar to that of conservation easements, in which there is a need to balance the donor's wishes to control the use of the gift far into the future, and "society's interest in ensuring that assets perpetually devoted to charitable purposes continue to provide benefits to the public."[45]

Other scholars have responded to the problem of perpetuity by proposing an adaptive structure for easements. Greene, for example, advocates "dynamic" conservation easements, "whose terms provide land use restrictions that may change over time."[46] These dynamic easements would rely on adaptive management principles, in which monitoring would provide information that would be fed back into management. Duncan Greene also reminds readers that rather than being concerned about easements "locking up" land that may be needed for future uses, we should be attentive to the fact that development also "locks up" land, with lasting consequences for species survival and habitat viability.[47] Easement language should be carefully developed so that once it is recorded, there is little or no need for amendments, which can be costly, time-consuming, and possibly place the easement in jeopardy if a violation of conservation purposes is suspected.[48]

Landowners can also simply blatantly disregard the terms of an easement, knowing that most land trusts are understaffed and may not do complete monitoring. For example, in states with a short statute of limitations, once it notices the damage, the land trust may no longer legitimately be able to bring a suit or other enforcement actions against the landowner.[49] There is also the concern that landowners and land trusts may ignore an easement's public aspects and work privately to modify it to better fit either party's needs.[50]

The reasonable-duration and the relative-hardship doctrines also threaten the perpetuity of easements. The first allows the court to place a reasonable duration on an action that has no endpoint. If an action becomes unnecessary, the court can respond by saying that the requirement for it should reasonably sunset at a certain point. Under the second doctrine, the court can recognize whether a mandated action is causing undue hardship relative to the amount of benefit it is supposed to produce. If the hardship outweighs the benefit, the covenant—in this case, the easement—can be nullified.[51]

Conservation easements may also be vulnerable to the government's power of eminent domain, by which the government can condemn land needed for a public purpose, pay the landowner, and assume ownership and the right to modify the parcel. Eminent domain has been used to widen highways, for example. If the government applied eminent domain to a parcel protected by an easement, would the easement remain in force? The answer depends at least partly on the character of the easement holder. For instance, an easement held by a federal agency cannot be annulled by a state or county declaration of eminent domain. Some states also have statutes protecting lands with easements from state or county eminent-domain declarations.[52]

It is also possible that perpetual conservation easements could be cancelled by applying the doctrine of changed conditions to argue that the purpose of the easement is no longer being served.[53] This could be a valid argument if, for example, the climate changes so much that a certain protected species is no longer living on a site with an easement intended to protect it. Conservationists, however, are concerned about misuses of this doctrine by landowners who want to remove easements. Wood and O'Brien note that tribes provide a better defense against the concerns over misuse of the "changed-conditions" argument, simply because tribes have been working with the land longer and have adapted to many changing conditions over time: "The intergenerational perspective of tribal people, their capacity to adapt to changing environmental and societal conditions, and their ancient knowledge of ceded lands make tribes and Native land trusts better situated than other land trusts to design, draft, and defend conservation easements in a way that protects against the changed-circumstances argument."[54]

Although the concerns listed above may make it appear that easements are ineffective, the reality is quite the contrary. The point of listing these concerns is that tribes and their partner land trusts and lawyers should review these challenges and explicitly and creatively take steps to prevent them from affecting their agreements.[55] One strategy to address these threats is to include a third party in the transaction, particularly a governmental entity, which could be a tribe, that commits to taking responsibility for the easement if the land trust closes.[56] Having a backup holder on an easement can increase trust in the transaction.[57]

Cultural Conservation Easements

Conservation easements can both restrict and affirm rights on a property. By restricting development and mandating conservation, easements often include requirements for restoration and light management to preserve a property. In contrast, cultural conservation easements place greater emphasis on the stewardship and use of a property in order to perpetuate cultural practices and enhance culturally important plant and animal species. These easements affirm certain land uses, such as tending and harvesting culturally important plants. These practices often cannot occur if the property is developed. Therefore, cultural conservation easements may include the elements and mandates of a conservation easement, such as restricted use and access. Despite overlap between the two types of easements, the term "cultural" draws attention to a specific purpose of the easement. As they grow in popularity, cultural conservation easements may serve to push conservation easements to become more attentive to cultural land uses and cultural preservation.

One of the most devastating impacts of colonization was the destruction of resources that tribal members tended for generations. Tribes were violently driven from their lands for reclamation projects and industrial development. This displacement and genocide form a backdrop for contemporary American Indian environmental struggles.[58] Cultural conservation easements can affirm Native entities' stake in the ownership and stewardship of ancestral lands that are no longer tribally held. Native Americans were and are well aware of the multiple benefits inhering in a diverse and nuanced system of Native land stewardship. Today, Native Americans and their allies continue to apply this stewardship, in a context of reduced land access, increased land-use regulations, and a decline in endemic species. As the publisher of *News from Native California* Malcolm Margolin explained:

> Early European visitors to California did not find polluted waterholes, diminished game, or impoverished vegetation. Far from it. California was a land of "inexpressible fertility." . . . It was no accident that such a dense population could sustain this abundance. It came about through conscious and highly evolved policies of what we now call conservation. . . . By regular burning the land, by pruning and coppicing certain shrubs, by carefully timing the digging of bulbs, and by other, often sophisticated practices, Native people consciously managed the land so as to preserve its wealth and increase its productivity. It is important to realize that California's bountiful harvests existed not despite a significant human presence but because of it.[59]

Cultural conservation easements can set aside lands in perpetuity for traditional stewardship, as well as for many other culturally important uses. Hawk Rosales, Executive Director of the InterTribal Sinkyone Wilderness Council, argued for the importance of cultural conservation easements during a 2009 presentation at the Public Interest Environmental Law Conference:

> Notwithstanding Native people's loss of control over most of their aboriginal land base, America still is and always will be Indian land. All of it. Native people retain crucial spiritual and cultural connections to vast areas of ancestral lands that are currently outside the reservation boundaries, not in the stewardship or the ownership of tribes or tribal members. . . . The challenge is that tribal members often cannot freely access portions of their ancestral lands that are culturally important and vital to their traditional lifeways. But tribal governments and organizations can hold title to deeds of cultural conservation easements, and these easements would enable tribal members access to and use of private properties in perpetuity.[60]

Native land stewardship ethics generally have a multigenerational orienta-tion.[61] For example, as the Trust for Public Lands' Tribal and Native Lands Program Executive Director Chuck Sams III (Cayuse, Cocopah, Yankton, Assiniboine) explained:

> Land conservation and the idea of the stewardship of that land begins thousands of years ago here on Turtle Island—tens of thousands of years ago. . . . [The covenant that we have with the land] is the oldest law in North America . . . As I've traveled across the United States, I've seen tribe after tribe recognize that that is the law that they were given. The divine law, that Creator sewed up that covenant, that . . . the human would be the protector of the land, of the water, of the sky, and of the creatures that live on it."[62]

The role of protector carries great responsibility that is not temporally limited. Conservation easements or "the conservation trust"[63] preserve land in perpetuity and may therefore be a good fit for achieving Native conserva-tion goals. According to Dune Lankard, founder of the Native Conservancy Land Trust in Alaska, "[I] started the Native Conservancy Land Trust to protect not only endangered plants and animals but endangered peoples and their culture, and rather than lock the land up in state and federal parks and kick everybody out, lock people in to be the stewards and protectors of land in perpetuity."[64]

By using conservation tools, tribes and other Native entities can enshrine their ties to the land and resources in a legal document that will enable them to access and care for a particular site in perpetuity. In the preface, I described one impetus I had for writing this book: the Maidu Stewardship Project, in which Maidu traditional practitioners are work-ing to implement traditional ecological knowledge on a portion of public land. The Maidu Summit Consortium negotiated a ten-year contract, but its vision for the land needs at least a one-hundred-year contract. Utilizing a conservation easement in perpetuity would enable a contractual period that is more in line with Native goals for the land.

Cultural conservation easements can be mutually beneficial for non-Native landowners and land trusts. First, there is a possibly significant tax incentive if the parties and the easement meet the requirements of the Inter-nal Revenue Code,[65] and if the landowner has the resources to benefit from the deduction.[66] Second, as Rosales argues, in terms of enhanced steward-ship, "the landowner and the land benefit tremendously by welcoming back the land's first people."[67] Cultural conservation easements can be specifically tailored to promote and foster the revitalization of traditional Native use of the land, while simultaneously protecting open space and conservation values and allowing for nondisruptive recreational and educational use. Rosales offered a list of possible uses that cultural conservation easements could enhance and protect: "Traditional harvest of culturally important plants and animals, ceremonial uses, protection and stewardship of cultural sites, access to conduct restoration of the property's cultural and ecological values, cultural recreational activities, cultural educational programs, access for youth and elders gatherings, and monitoring of timber harvesting to protect cultural resources."[68] Chapter 4 will discuss the ways in which the InterTribal Sinkyone Wilderness Council has cooperatively developed easements to meet these needs, as well as any additional, compatible needs of the land trust/conservancy and conservation agency.

Cultural conservation easements offer an emerging direction in conservation-easement policy that grows out of Native self-determination, environmental justice, and a desire on the part of some conservationists to right past wrongs. The United States has a history of alienating tribal lands from tribes and then making it difficult for tribes to adequately protect their sacred sites, whether on public or private land.[69] Cultural conservation easements are simultaneously a conservation- and a justice-oriented strategy that serves to enable direct Native protection of important sites, as well as access to and use of these sites for ongoing cultural and community stability. As Farrell Cunningham (Maidu) states in the Maidu Summit Land Management Proposal submitted to the Stewardship Council:[70]

> These lands, once owned by the Maidu, eventually came under the ownership of the United States of America. . . . However, throughout time and regardless of deed ownership, these lands have continued to be important to the Maidu. . . . Maidu ownership of these lands will allow Maidu to become an integral part of Maidu cultural perpetuation as well as a place where an empowered Maidu community can add to overall land-management practice and methodology while also accessing essential natural resources."[71]

Full restitution of ownership of culturally important lands remains the essential goal, and cultural conservation easements can also be used when the Native entity is the property owner. For example, the Little Traverse Bay Bands of Odawa own the Taimi Lynne Hoag Natural Area, but they worked to design conservation agreements with a non-Native land trust that will protect the property's cultural and conservation values in perpetuity.

Cultural conservation easements are also good tools in situations where the tribe or Native nonprofit is not the landowner. Historically, culturally important areas where the landowner or agency retained private owner-ship could be vulnerable to trespass or vandalism, or tribal members would be barred from coming onto the property for cultural purposes, including tending plants that had long been family resources. As Rosales described, "Unfortunately for private property situations, tribal members have to sneak onto these lands sometimes, and risk getting caught and cited for trespass-ing. . . . What a cultural conservation easement can do, it can formalize a legal arrangement, a binding arrangement, between a tribal entity and the landowner [so that] those sorts of obstacles can be overcome."[72] In Maidu country, for example, the Cunningham family hosts an annual Bear Dance in Taylorsville, but they do not own nor have permanent access to a dance ground. Instead, they host the dance on county property, with the explicit support of the board of supervisors. However, an ongoing problem has been the site manager scheduling other, unrelated events on the same date as the Bear Dance. The lack of title to land suitable for this dance or an ease-ment in perpetuity so that it could be held at a particular location threatens the continuation of this traditional event. Although the preferred option is tribal ownership of a parcel of land, a cultural conservation easement is also an enforceable legal tool that would enable Maidu individuals access to and use of land suitable for the dance. Chapter 9 will discuss cultural con-servation easements, with attention to the collaboration between the Little Traverse Conservancy and the Little Traverse Bay Bands of Odawa Indians.

Cultural conservation easements are permitted under the Uniform Conservation Easement Act (UCEA), which recognizes that easements may be used to preserve the "historical, . . . archaeological, or *cultural* [emphasis mine] aspects of real property."[73] However, the use of these easements to protect cultural resources and enable stewardship activities has not been widespread. Although the act allows for cultural protection under conserva-tion easements, it has been primarily used for environmental protection. As such, parties developing cultural conservation easements under the act must be careful to ensure that these easements also fall within the existing bound-aries of state law.[74] States must either adopt the federal UCEA or assert their own statutes enabling conservation easements as "negative easements in gross" and list legally acceptable holders. Some states, such as California,[75] are quite clear that tribes *can* hold easements, whereas others, such as New Mexico,[76] are equally clear that they *cannot*. Still other states rely on the UCEA, which defines a "qualified holder" as a conservation nonprofit or government entity. Tribes are government entities, but most applications of conservation easements have involved holders that are federal, state, or county government entities. Whether the statute meant for tribes to be included in the group of "government entities" authorized to hold easements may be challenged.

If states do not explicitly list protection of cultural resources in their enabling statute for conservation easements, then protection of cultural resources, or of natural resources for cultural purposes, will not qualify as an acceptable use. At least one state (New Mexico) has created a Cultural Properties Preservation Easement Act (CPPEA), which is separate legislation to address cultural protection. This statute is congruent with the UCEA, including the requirement that cultural properties be defined, in general, as those eligible for listing on the National Register of Historic Places. The CPPEA and the UCEA make cultural conservation easements legally enforceable and subject to IRS tax deductions for the landowner.[77]

Tribes are treated as states for purposes of charitable gift deductions and federal income-tax deductions under Section 7871 of the Internal Revenue Code. States are organizations qualified to receive conservation easement donations under the IRC's Section 170(h)(3). It follows that a landowner could get a tax deduction from donating an easement to a federally recognized tribe or a Native nonprofit organization.[78] In the list of conservation purposes that qualify a parcel for a tax deduction, Native land uses and sacred sites could fall under "habitat protection," "preservation of open space," or "preservation of a historically important land area or a certified historic structure."[79] "Certified," in this case, means being eligible for listing in the National Register of Historic Places. The criteria for qualifying to be in the National Register are general, raising the concern that the eligibility of a cultural site to be protected under a cultural conservation easement, and the associated tax benefit to a landowner, could be questioned.[80] Prudent landowners should ensure that their culturally important properties have confirmation of eligibility for listing or are already listed on the National Register before they receive a tax benefit for donating those properties through an easement.[81] Sites may be eligible for listing even if they are not structures. The National Register categorizes undisturbed sites imbued with cultural values as Traditional Cultural Properties (TCPs).[82]

Another concern is that the IRC notes that deductions for donations to states (remember that tribes are treated as states for the purposes of charitable donations) and other governmental entities must be for "exclusively public purposes."[83] Wood and O'Brien note that there is legal precedent for the protection of archaeological and cultural or historic sites as a matter of public interest.[84] They also persuasively argue that tribal conservation activities are readily construed as publicly beneficial, both intuitively and with legal precedent.[85] For example, actions to preserve fish habitat, as discussed in the

Nisqually, Jamestown S'Klallam, and Alaska cases in this volume, serve the tribe as well as the broader public. As tribes and Native land trusts continue using private conservation tools to acquire and restore lands in a growing context of climate change, the public will continue to see numerous benefits from tribally led ecological and cultural restoration.

In the meantime, Lawrence R. Kueter and Christopher S. Jensen suggest that, when drafting a cultural conservation easement, authors should foreground the environmental values of a property, as that is the type of protection that conservation-easement statutes are really intended to address: "To the extent that conservation easements protecting cultural resource values also protect environmental values, the certainty of their tax deductibility may be strengthened by the long-recognized validity of environmental conservation purposes."[86] Wood and O'Brien offer a similar recommendation, noting that Native land trusts should focus on conservation purposes mentioned in the Internal Revenue Code 170(h)(4)(A): "For example, instead of 'To conserve medicinal plant life so as to ensure adequate supply for the tribe,' a conservation easement might propose 'To conserve native vegetation from adverse land use and invasive species.' Likewise, 'To ensure open-space features of Protected Property sufficiently to accommodate tribal ceremonies' might be riskier than 'To ensure open-space features for low-impact cultural and recreational purposes.'"[87] Tribal goals for the land should still be included, but placing them within a context that uses the language of broader environmental concerns may make easements immune to possible challenges. As cultural conservation easements become more common, federal and state enabling legislation and the IRC should be adapted to specifically address tribal and cultural applications.

Valuing Resources: Cultural Differences

In all of these institutional situations, advocating for the protection and conservation of resources often comes down to a contested process of determining the economic value of the conservation easement.[88] "Developing conserved areas into marketable products involves understanding the specific nature of the site and the benefits to be derived from it, and finding mechanisms by which those benefits might be transferred to willing purchasers."[89] The valuation of conservation easements has been based on the "highest and best use" of the land, which is usually defined as development.[90] Setting aside the land for permanent conservation reduces the value of the land and, in turn, its taxation rate. If the development potential of the property is appraised at a high value, the conservation easement will be expensive—resulting in a substantial payment to or tax deduction for the landowner. Because land conservation is seen as a "public value," governmental agencies and nonprofit organizations can raise public and private funds to buy conservation easements.

In some cases, appraising traditional land and resources is challenging. For example, salmon has both an economic and a spiritual value for tribes. Sams described his understanding of the Umatilla and Cayuse peoples' role as keepers of the salmon: "At the time of the creation of human beings, salmon gave humans its voice, which became the Chinook language, and its body, for the nourishment of human beings. In return, salmon asked that humans be its keeper, protecting salmon and its relations all over the earth."[91] Even when tribes assert the economic value of a particular resource, they may be met with competing assertions of economic value from commercial users. The court may choose to weigh these as equal claims to a resource, without taking into account the tribes' longstanding, possibly unquantifiable, relationship to the resource.[92] In order to begin a process of buying and selling conservation interests, we must clearly define the resources, their value, and how to acquire them.

Tribal, Federal, and State Jurisdiction

Using conservation easements on lands owned by tribes raises multiple jurisdictional questions. First, as government entities, tribes cannot be sued unless they consent. If the tribe holding a conservation easement does not agree to waive its immunity from suit, it may be difficult to enforce the easement's terms. The tribes and land trusts profiled in the case studies have dealt with sovereign immunity in different ways, ranging from tribes waiving it in order to negotiate easements that are enforceable in a local or state jurisdiction (Jamestown S'Klallam Tribe) to tribes negotiating additional legal agreements that function like conservation easements on trust lands (Little Traverse Bay Bands of Odawa Indians).

Tribal land may be under either state or federal jurisdiction. If the land is in private fee simple tribal ownership, it will be subject to state law. If the land is held in trust for the tribe by the Bureau of Indian Affairs (BIA), it is federally owned for the benefit of the tribe. The BIA has certain requirements for lands it takes into trust for tribes. For example, the BIA particularly scrutinizes lands that have encumbrances or restrictive covenants, such as conservation easements, on the title. At its own discretion and on a case-by-case basis, the BIA may or may not request the removal of these encumbrances before accepting the land into trust.[93] If the federal government is the easement holder, as in the case of Susanville Indian Rancheria and the Wetlands Reserve Program, the easement remains legally enforceable even if the land goes from private fee into federal trust status. However, if the easement holder is not a federal entity, it is unclear if the easement will be enforceable once the land is in trust. This raises several questions in tribe–land trust collaborations, including: Is a conservation easement held by a private land trust enforceable on both tribal fee and trust properties? Will having a conservation easement on property owned in fee by the tribe or by an individual Indian landowner make it more difficult to have that land placed into trust? The cases offer several responses to these questions.

Some legal scholars and tribal leaders alike have compared having a conservation easement on land to having the BIA hold land in trust for a tribe.[94] In the case of the BIA holding land in trust, it is reserved for the tribe in perpetuity and free from taxes.[95] In the case of a land trust holding an easement on land owned by a Native entity, taxes are greatly reduced because the land value drops, and the land is protected from certain uses in perpetuity. The choice then becomes a question of which partner is better for the Native entity—the BIA or a local or regional Native land trust or conservancy? For example, if the Native owner wants to initiate a certain management action or plan on the land, a conservancy may be less bureau-cratic because the two parties can review the proposal and make a decision, avoiding the possibly lengthy approval process if the partner is a federal agency. However, given the debate about the permanence of land trusts and easements, the BIA may be a more stable partner.[96] On the other hand, because some have described the BIA as working to "get out of the Indian business,"[97] a land trust may be preferable.

As private conservation pacts become more common between tribes and land trusts, the BIA may release specific guidelines addressing a con-servation easement as a distinct covenant that is enforceable or not under certain conditions. Currently, a range of cooperative scenarios are taking place across Indian country—ranging from tribal land encumbered with a conservation easement going into trust with assumed easement enforce-ability to extensive efforts to establish additional layers of conservation protection for trust lands.

Land Trusts

What Is a Land Trust?

Land trusts are nonprofit organizations that raise funds to purchase conserva-tion easements or accept and oversee donated easements on properties within their area of focus. The Land Trust Alliance (LTA) defines a land trust as: "a nonprofit organization that, as all or part of its mission, actively works to conserve land by undertaking or assisting in land or conservation easement acquisition, or by its stewardship of such land or easements."[98] The LTA is an umbrella organization that offers training, professional accreditation, and other resources to its member land trusts and conservancies that hold conservation easements. Individual land trusts prioritize certain values, such as preserving or restoring lands for habitat for certain species, protecting historical or archaeological sites, maintaining rural working landscapes, or protecting cultural uses and resources. Land trusts also focus on particular areas, which may extend over a specific region, an individual watershed, or a certain land-use type. The Native American Land Conservancy, for example, focuses on conserving healing landscapes that are sacred to Native American people.

Land trusts operate in four principal ways: they buy or acquire donated conservation easements; they buy entire parcels to conserve them; they buy parcels, retain the conservation easement, and sell the rest of the parcel to a private owner; and they act as middlemen, by buying parcels and then selling them to other conservation managers. The Trust for Public Land (TPL), for example, is well known for its role as an expert in land transactions. TPL works to bring all parties to the table and to develop terms that work for all concerned. Once the land trust holds either a parcel or an easement, it has committed to monitoring and enforcing the terms of the easement.

Although state and federal governments also contribute significantly to funding land trusts' transactions, land trusts also receive funds from private donors, private foundations, and direct donations of conservation easements, entire properties, and funds for stewardship and monitoring. Landowners who either donate or sell their properties or easements to land trusts and conservancies have a say in how these lands are managed, including what type of public access is allowed on them. This differs substantially from federal or state conservation, where no single member of the public can control conservation planning and management on a piece of property.

Land trusts have not focused on preserving Native American land uses and stewardship as "traditional" uses. However, the case studies in this book highlight land trusts that are actively collaborating with tribes to achieve tribal land conservation goals. The cases also include Native land conservancies that are acquiring properties and easements for specific Native conservation and cultural purposes. Overall, the cases focus on emerging practices in conservation that recognize Native tribes, communities, and individuals as key partners and leaders in land stewardship and that understand that

Native land uses are ongoing and key to the health of communities, Native nations, and natural resources.

A Leading Example: Trust for Public Land's Tribal and Native Lands Program

The only national non-Native land trust that has created a program specifically to focus on tribal-land stewardship and preservation goals is the Trust for Public Land (TPL). Although this book contains examples of collaborations with The Nature Conservancy and The Conservation Fund, these large land trusts do not have specific nationwide programs targeting Native conservation. Indeed, Sarah Greensfelder, former executive director of the California Indian Basketweavers Association, commented on the challenge of communicating with conservation organizations focused primarily on habitat rather than on cultural needs: "I have . . . found that it is very useful to introduce the concepts and techniques of traditional Indian plant gathering practices to people in The [Nature] Conservancy.[99] In general, there is a great gap between the American environmental movement's idea of untouched 'wilderness' and the Native American perspective in which humans are a part of the natural world. The latter includes taking an active role to ensure the health and growth of plants."[100] TPL's view is similar to Greensfelder's articulation of Native stewardship, as the organization is known for its focus on "conserving land for people,"[101] making it a good fit for Native land conservation goals. As former TPL senior vice president Bowen Blair noted, "TPL protects land for communities, not from communities."[102] Moreover, TPL is quite aware of the history of taking lands from Native Americans and how that history has created a current situation in which many culturally important places are no longer owned by tribes.

In 1996, TPL acquired a 10,000-acre parcel within the ancestral homeland of the Nez Percé and transferred it to the tribe. The land is said to be quite near where Chief Joseph was born and where his father is buried.[103] This purchase and reconveyance was an important return home:

> Chief Joseph and his band lived peacefully in these river valleys and mountains until 1877, when they—with their horses and whatever possessions they could hurriedly gather—were forced by the U.S. Army across the freezing spring torrents of the Snake River, leaving behind Oregon and their Wallowa homeland. . . . The Trust for Public Land spent years negotiating and funding the acquisition of this property so that the Nez Percé could return to the Wallowas for the first time since 1877.[104]

Following this initial, successful acquisition, TPL created the Tribal and Native Lands Program in 1999, which focuses on collaborating with tribes and tribal governments to protect and return Native homelands to Native people:

> TPL's Tribal and Native Lands Program was created to expand partnerships with tribes to assist them in reversing a history of dispossession. Tribes are proven leaders as natural resource stewards and restoring traditional lands to tribal ownership—or under public ownership where tribal values are afforded legal protection—assists native communities in meeting their land conservation, natural resource restoration, and cultural heritage objectives. Clearly, TPL's mission and the needs of land-based tribal communities are closely aligned.[105]

The Tribal and Native Lands Program has three main areas of focus, which it pursues with Native partners throughout the United States, including Hawaii and Alaska: conservation of natural resources, traditional economic revitalization, and preservation of culturally significant sites.[106] This work strengthens tribal culture and communities, addresses intergenerational trauma by returning and protecting lands, and contributes to conserving lands and heritage in a way that benefits all Americans.

The Tribal and Native Lands Program has a sixteen-member advisory council composed of Native leaders, Native scholars, and Native and non-Native legal and conservation professionals. According to Sams, prior to European contact, tribes controlled and maintained 2 billion acres of land.[107] Today, Sams estimates that tribes control 45 million acres of trust land, 11 million acres of allotted land, and in Alaska, another 44 million acres, all split among more than 370 tribal ethnicities and 565 federally recognized tribal governments (including tribes, pueblos, and rancherias). Since its inception a decade ago, the Tribal and Native Lands Program has worked to complete sixty-five projects with seventy-two tribes across the United States. Using conservation covenants, the program has moved 134,000 acres back into tribal and community hands. With tribal support, they have also transferred an additional 70,000 acres to federal and state agencies that committed to protect Native constituents' usual and accustomed rights to these parcels.[108]

Sams underscores the importance of establishing trust and understanding, rather than adversarial relationships, with non-Native landowners: "building the trust [with the landowner], educating them . . . on the tens of thousands of years of history that are on those pieces of property, is the key element in building that partnership so that we can coexist and steward this land the way it's supposed to be."[109] Sams is also clear that he does not give the tribes he collaborates with typical boilerplate language for their easements. Rather, he encourages them to draw as much as possible on their traditional laws, as codified in oral histories and creation stories that outline the foundation of their people's relationship with the land. This is directly in line with both Stephen Cornell and Joseph Kalt's and Robert Williams's suggestions for successful tribal governance, built upon the unique traditional cultural values of the tribe.[110] As Sams explains: "When I go out there, I work with the different tribes and ask them what are their laws? What were the laws that they were given since time began? How can we incorporate that into the language? Because that will codify those [laws] from here into eternity."[111] Through the development of cultural conservation easements, conservation easements, memorandums of understanding or agreement, and tribal land conservancies, tribes can articulate their own laws and regulations with conservation statutes.[112] The tribal laws exemplify adaptability and contemporary relevance. TPL also provides technical assistance, helping tribes with real estate transactions and fundraising. In sum, TPL's Tribal and Native Lands Program supports tribal sovereignty, self-determination, land stewardship, and cultural perpetuation.

As of 2010, TPL's Tribal and Native Lands Program had grown so much that it spawned a separate entity, managed and overseen by Native people, called Indian Country Conservancy (ICC). According to Sams, who serves as the president and CEO of ICC, TPL and ICC will continue to work closely together. With a combination of Native leaders and former-TPL real estate and conservation experts, the ICC brings together unique experience, skills, and scope: "Until today, no organization existed with the primary mission to restore conservation lands to Native people and the real estate capability to attain this mission nationally."[113] The ICC has four goals: acquiring conservation lands and placing them in Native hands, increasing conservation funding sources for tribes, training tribal staff on conservation fundraising and acquisitions, and helping tribes build GIS capabilities to guide and inform land planning and acquisition.

Tribes and Land Trusts

The case studies in Section Two describe several situations in which partnerships with land trusts, often using conservation easements, have been useful to tribes. Tribes can collaborate with land trusts, public agencies, and other entities to acquire interests in parcels no longer tribally held by, for example, purchasing conservation easements or buying entire properties and placing conservation easements on them. Tribes can also work with land trusts to protect watersheds by removing specific properties from development. The Nisqually, Jamestown S'Klallam, and Alaska cases provide examples of this use of conservation easements.

Tribes also collaborate with land trusts to use easements as mitigation for development, whether it is development the tribe itself is undertaking on tribal lands or development that is happening on culturally significant sites not on tribal lands. In the Yocha Dehe case, the tribe transferred a conservation easement to a land trust on property it set aside as mitigation for a tribal development. In Southern California, tribes including the Torres Martinez Desert Cahuilla Tribe and the Morongo Band of Mission Indians protected cultural resources by negotiating open-space easements within housing developments off of tribal lands. In the latter case, tribes used a state statute to negotiate mitigation because the development required a general-plan amendment, triggering consultation under SB-18.

Tribes have also partnered with land trusts to employ easements to maintain traditional cultural and ceremonial uses on off-reservation lands. In the case of the Little Traverse Bay Bands of Odawa Indians, the tribe and the local land trust are pioneering a cultural conservation easement structure that will enable specific cultural activities to take place on non-tribal properties. The Little Traverse Bay Bands also created a unique supplemental conservation agreement, which functions like a conservation easement, except that it specifically addresses conservation encumbrances on lands held in trust for the tribe.

Negotiating conservation easements on tribal fee or trust lands may also help tribes to raise the necessary funds to purchase cultural properties that they no longer possess. For example, collaborating with the Land Trust for the Little Tennessee and placing easements on the Cowee Mound property enabled the Eastern Band of Cherokee to access additional grant funding to purchase the historic Cowee Mound. In the case of the Susanville Indian Rancheria in northeastern California, the tribe drew on USDA's Natural Resources Conservation Service Wetlands Reserve Program funds to assist with the restoration of a rural parcel in exchange for a conservation easement. In addition to expanding the rancheria's landholdings, this property provides opportunities for ongoing training and employment for a rancheria work crew.

Working with land trusts can also be a way for federally unrecognized tribes, which do not have a government-to-government relationship with the federal government, to gain a stake in culturally important lands. The Tsi-Akim Maidu have partnered with the Nevada County Land Trust (NCLT) to create a living cultural center on NCLT property that contains cultural resources. As the Cache Creek Conservancy case shows, indigenous people from different tribes can also negotiate land uses with a land trust or conservancy. In this case, a graduate student worked with the Cache Creek Conservancy and a group of weavers, which had limited access to reliable, clean basket weaving materials, to build a partnership that resulted in a living resource for weavers on the conservancy's property. Named the Tending and Gathering Garden and located in the Jan T. Lowrey Cache Creek Nature Preserve, the site has received nationwide attention.

The cases of the Sinkyone InterTribal Wilderness Council and the Native American Land Conservancy, respectively, demonstrate that tribes are forming successful intertribal land trusts, conservancies, or nonprofits. These organizations can receive donated easements themselves or raise the funds to purchase easements or properties. Native land trusts and conservancies exist all around the United States, and more are developing. As part of its mission, the Native American Land Conservancy works to assist nascent Native land trusts. The newly developed Indian Country Conservancy also supports the formation of Native land trusts and may serve as an intermediary and consultant in collaborations between Native entities (tribes, land trusts, nonprofits) and land trusts (Native or non-Native). Federal and state agencies have also supported Native land conservancies and collaborations between Native groups and conservation organizations—as shown in cases of the Native American Land Conservancy, the Nisqually Tribe, and Eastern Band of Cherokee Indians.

Mutual Benefit

As funding for conservation declines, non-Native land trusts and conservationists know that collaborating with tribes may allow them to access additional funding sources. Land trusts collaborating with tribes may also benefit from increasing support from philanthropic private individuals and foundations that support social justice as well as conservation. In addition, if land trusts want to increase their membership base to encompass businesses, they can expand their scope of work to include tribal interests, because tribes often have business entities and are respected in the business world. Indeed, the majority of the cases allude to the tribes' economic use of protected resources, such as ongoing harvesting of salmon following watershed restoration to increase the salmon population. As Wood and Welcker explain: "[The tribe's] economic use of fisheries sets them apart from environmental groups that are often accused of having little or no economic stake in an outcome of an environmental justice conflict. Economic interests cannot easily dismiss the tribal voice, for traditional economies are more longstanding than virtually any Western economic enterprise."[114] Conservation easements have brought environmentalists together with farmers and ranchers to ensure protected, mutually beneficial working landscapes. Land trusts and tribes may similarly support working landscapes, as well as cultural preservation, social justice, and tribal sovereignty.

There are also legal reasons for quasi-public entities like land trusts to support the protection of tribes' traditional homelands. All tribes have traditional rights to their homelands and to the resources contained therein. Some tribes have these rights codified in treaties, treaty substitutes, and executive orders. Treaties were negotiated between 1778 and 1868, and they provided a limited means for tribes to affirm their rights to certain areas of resource stewardship and habitation.[115] These treaties are agreements between sovereigns,[116] often recognizing tribal members' inherent, preexisting rights to access "usual and accustomed"[117] areas to fish, hunt, and steward resources. The American government broke many of the treaties it made with tribes. As Deloria famously wrote: "America has yet to keep one Indian treaty or agreement despite the fact that the U.S. government signed over four hundred such treaties and agreements with Indian tribes."[118]

Treaties were also misrepresented as enabling the federal government to generously "grant" lands and other resources to the tribe. In reality, however, treaties actually ceded *tribally owned* lands to the new U.S. government.[119] Although the courts have not generally been willing to confirm tribal rights,[120] tribes have been able to use their treaty-guaranteed rights in court to hold the federal government responsible for ensuring that the resources are maintained in a healthy enough condition so that the tribes can continue to harvest them. Tribes have had to continually remind federal agencies to exercise this responsibility by regulating resource use by other non-tribal parties (including private entities, such as farmers and fishing interests) in order to protect tribes' treaty-guaranteed rights.[121] As Andrew Gulliford explains: "Today's native descendants expect their treaty rights on ceded lands to be protected. They view hunting, fishing, and the gathering of roots, berries, sweetgrass, and sage not as sport and recreation but as vital seasonal activities that are essential for cultural continuity and the maintenance of family, clan, and tribal ties."[122] Treaties represent only a small portion of Native rights to lands that are not in tribal ownership or held in trust for tribes. Although conservation tools can and are being used to protect treaty-guaranteed rights, they can also be used to protect traditional rights that are not in treaties, treaty substitutes, or executive orders.

Conclusion

From a theoretical point of view, the long-term orientation of conservation-easement statute and practice mirrors a long-term, indigenous approach to land management, in which resources are left alone, protected, or tended judiciously so that they will be available for generations to come:[123]

> Many Indian people still insist that there are places that really should be left as they are, because of the graves of ancestors, because of the stories (including religious beliefs) that are tied to certain places, because of the plants and animals that need certain places for their survival. From an Indian perspective, a person who owns the land at such a place cannot hold an absolute right to take anything from the land that can be converted into financial gain; rather, the rights of such a landowner must be tempered by responsibilities to care for such places.[124]

Conservation easements and land trusts offer a relatively unique opportunity to codify this orientation for the careful stewardship of land into the future.

Environmental Justice and Tribal Conservation

The book's cases are examined through the lens of conservation easements and land trusts for both procedural and distributive environmental justice. A comprehensive look at environmental activism over the last two centuries shows that environmental justice is actually an old concept.[1] Although the idea of "environment" has been construed (via membership in conservation organizations, for example) as a narrowly white, middle-class conception of place, environmental activism has actually long been on the agenda of women, poor people, and people of color, and it has been explicitly linked to justice.[2] The State of California is particularly illustrative for exploring the theme of environmental justice. California is home to an enormous diversity of tribes, tribal homelands, and Native languages,[3] as well as one of the most egregious histories of genocide of Native peoples and disregard for Native land rights. Although the majority of the case studies in this book are from California, each of the other states included here—North Carolina, Alaska, and Washington—as well as the remaining U.S. states all have their own painful histories of injustice.

Given this context, conservation easements and land trusts are one of many valuable legal and political tools that tribes can use to achieve much-needed land restitution. Depending on state statutes, these tools can be used to reacquire lands wherever they were confiscated or compromised. Reservations all over the United States were fragmented by allotments, many of which were sold to non-Natives, drastically reduced in size by Congressional action, and eroded by land claims settlements. Conservation easements and land trusts provide innovative frameworks for organizing alliances, marshaling resources from conservation and tribal sources, and working to provide tax incentives for landowners to return some of these lands. The tools are imperfect, of course, and this book will explore their deficiencies as well as their opportunities. It takes, however, as its starting point that tribes can use these tools for land restitution.

Procedural Justice

Using conservation easements and land trusts to achieve Native goals employs two key aspects of environmental justice:[4] procedural justice and distributive justice.[5] Procedural justice focuses on ensuring that all communities, particularly those that often "lose" in environmental planning, are able to participate in processes. Procedural justice is further divided into two concerns: "procedural fairness and the effective ability of groups to participate."[6] Processes may follow an equitable series of steps, but if people cannot attend the meetings because child care or transportation are unavailable or they cannot participate because there is no interpreter, then the process is procedurally unjust. Looking at conservation easements and land trusts through an environmental justice, and, specifically, a procedural justice, lens means that private transactions that lock up lands in perpetuity should never proceed without the participation of tribes and Native families with ties to the land. Non-Native land trusts, conservation funders, and conservation agencies must recognize federally recognized and unrecognized tribes as essential partners in conservation decision making.

Since conservation easements and land trusts involve private transactions, they are not typically subject to public environmental processes requiring public comment. Applying standards of procedural justice to easements and land trust actions would require that tribes, as cultural and political sovereigns with ties to the land, would have the right to meaningfully participate in these transactions. Given the history of California Indian policy, including the nonratification of treaties that resulted, ultimately, in numerous federally unrecognized tribes, it may be difficult to discern which tribal entity to collaborate with regarding land-use decisions. This is no excuse, however, for not working to involve Native stakeholders with ties to the land (including tribes, Native nonprofits, and Native individuals and families) in the conservation planning process. The history of land dispossession, Native individual and family ties to the land, and tribal jurisdiction must be considered and addressed in each place and situation.

The application of procedural environmental justice is particularly important in the context of land conservation. Although the concept of "public good" is often linked to the preservation of resources, this preservation has a deeply colonial past and present: "Environmentalism has not always been so innocent of colonial involvement . . . in the imperial era, these two geopolitical agendas . . . were almost inextricably intertwined. Precisely because environmentalism still makes sense to us today, . . . it is imperative to recognize that its specifically colonial realization was irretrievably tainted with social and human injustice."[7] Indeed, there is a long negative history of indigenous people being pushed out of reserves, wilderness areas, and other conservation designations.[8] Scholars of British colonialism linked the establishment of reserves to capitalist expansion. Certain areas were set aside for recreation, at the expense of others targeted for intensive production. This "partitioning" of the land was mirrored in social and class divisions determining who could live where and enjoy which lands:[9] "If there is a lesson to be learned from a[n] . . . imperial era, it is that environmental rhetoric needs to be carefully analyzed for its impacts on social and political justice, where it can be said that all that is green does not glitter."[10] Research has also shown that indigenous people beneficially managed ecosystems.[11] Although parks and wilderness areas were created in part to halt industrial land uses, they also expelled indigenous people, thereby changing ecosystems and relationships that had developed over millennia. As a result, some of the ecosystems set aside for preservation, such as grassland habitats, are disappearing.[12]

Conservation: A Policy of Attempted Exclusion

Exclusion of tribes was the rule in the late-nineteenth- and early-twentieth-century formation of public lands,[13] and tribes are acting now to ensure that private conservation does not follow the same path. Conservation legislation had its heyday over one hundred years ago, with the passage of the Forest Reserve Act (1891), the establishment of the U.S. Forest Service (1905), the National Park Service (1916),[14] and predecessors to the U.S. Fish and Wildlife Service, including the Bureau of Biological Survey (1906) and the Bureau of Fisheries (1871). The Bureau of Land Management was established a little later, in a 1946 merger of the General Land Office and the Grazing Service. The creation of the Forest Reserve Act, and the establishment of the Forest Service and the National Park Service, in particular, had devastating effects on tribes. As Karl Jacoby explains:

> The [conservation] movement's arrival shut off vast portions of tribal hunting and foraging areas while also inhibiting Native Americans' use of fire to shape the landscape around them. Even more strikingly,

conservation interlocked on multiple levels with other, ongoing efforts—treaties, the establishment of reservations, allotment—to displace Indians' claims on the natural world in order to open up such areas to non-Indians. In this sense, conservation was for Native Americans inextricably bound up with conquest—with a larger conflict over land and resources that predated conservation's rise.[15]

Suddenly, lands that had been stewarded for centuries were declared forest reserves, then national forests and national parks. They were off-limits, except for certain permitted uses, and Native land management practices were criminalized.

The creation of conservation areas seemed to have at least three purposes: conserving resources from being overharvested and destroyed by settlers; setting aside resources for industrial production (timber harvest, among other things);[16] and removing Indian people from lands that could be used for industrial management, permitted uses, or recreation. Often, Indian people were not even allowed to engage in permitted use of these lands. This has had ongoing consequences for indigenous culture, identity, and survival:

> Much of an individual's identity—as male, as female, as a member of the Havasupai tribe—was linked to how they interacted with the landscape around them. And so, from the perspective of the Havasupai and other groups like them, conservation represented an assault not only on the material underpinnings of their existence, but also on many of the less tangible, but no less real, spiritual and moral understandings that gave their lives meaning.[17]

Similarly, the Timbisha Shoshone of Death Valley were blatantly disregarded during the planning process to establish Death Valley National Monument.[18] They were initially relocated out of the park, and although they continued their traditional "use of and relationship with the land," Park Service regulations criminalized their time-honored stewardship. Elders resisted requesting permits from the park to be allowed to perform generations-old land management actions. As Robert J. Paton reports: "The bitter irony is that indigenous people throughout the world have sophisticated knowledge of the intricacies of nature but are all too often the first victims of programs that propose to protect the land."[19]

Another, more recent clash with a park occurred in the far northwestern corner of California, when Yurok traditionalist Merk Oliver was investigated for allegedly killing two Roosevelt Elk in the Redwood National Park in 1999. The park had been established in 1978, placing a new layer of bureaucracy over ongoing indigenous stewardship practices. As Marina Drummer described Oliver's 2001 hearing at the Federal 9th Circuit Court in San Francisco: "Oliver spoke with great emotion about the difficulty of living in two worlds. In his world, the Yurok constitution gives tribal members the right to hunt, fish, and gather on their aboriginal grounds. When Redwood National Park was created on aboriginal grounds, that right was taken away."[20]

Our contemporary public lands are also composed of remnants of individually held Indian allotments, granted following the Dawes (Allotment) Act of 1887. These allotments were often cancelled and reabsorbed into the General Land Office, which served as the "'breadbasket' of lands" for other agencies.[21] Lands that were not allotted to tribes, and many lands that were allotted and then cancelled, went to the General Land Office.[22] This completely disregarded tribal land claims. Moreover, this so-called public domain land was taken from tribes, even though the United States had no specific use planned for it.

These histories clarify the reality that tribes are much more than stakeholders in decision-making processes for what are now public lands—they are former landowners who were often not justly compensated. Moreover, they continue to have a relationship with alienated lands—stewarding particular plants and visiting particular spiritual sites, for example. Thus, they deserve, at the very least, a prominent and permanent place at the table in land-use decisions. As Eric Freedman writes in his description of a conflict in Minnesota between Superior National Forest administrators and indigenous fishers with an 1854 treaty right[23] to fish in the Boundary Waters Canoe Wilderness Area:

> Wilderness designations and the regulations that enforce them can conflict with preexisting property rights and claims, including those of Native Americans who have treaty-based and traditional tribal rights. The ensuing conflicts may pit Native Americans against environmentalists and recreational users, while placing public lands managers in the middle as they attempt to enforce the laws and satisfy the often competing demands of multiple constituencies.[24]

The federal government has invested more or less heavily in conservation and the creation of increased public lands during specific historical periods. Following the Depression, for example, the government allocated funds to conservation agencies to buy lands as a form of economic stimulus.[25] The Bureau of Biological Survey was the first agency to invest heavily in conservation easements, buying the rights to protect land and build wild-life habitat, and leaving the fee title with the landowner.[26] There was never any similar investment in tribes so that they could buy back alienated lands. Instead, the development of conservation statutes, agencies, and regulations is intertwined with the confiscation of Native lands and associated assimilation policies.[27] The proliferation of conservation agencies post–World War II was echoed only by the proliferation of environmental statutes in the 1970s, including the National Environmental Policy Act (1970), the Clean Air Act (1970), the Clean Water Act (1972), and others. Policies protecting tribal resources came slightly later, with the American Indian Religious Freedom Act (1978), the Archaeological Resources Protection Act (1979), and the Native American Graves Protection and Repatriation Act (1990).[28]

Tribes have consistently developed creative applications for the (largely procedural) environmental statutes and relatively underfunded and unenforced statutes designed to protect cultural resources and elevate Native concerns. This may be a form of what Tsosie terms "cultural sovereignty," or a broader notion of sovereignty that addresses resources and populations not directly under tribal governmental jurisdiction. Cultural sovereignty "implicates the philosophical core of Native people's belief systems and requires them to create their own appraisal of what 'sovereignty' means and what rights, duties, and responsibilities are entailed in their relationships to each other, to the federal or state governments, and to ancestors and future generations. The exercise of cultural sovereignty evokes a process of repatriation of land, traditional knowledge, and cultural identity."[29] Tribes have also established formal relationships with the resource management agencies charged with overseeing portions of their homelands. Tribes have pushed these agencies to increase their understanding of tribal values and to apply environmental statutes in ways that increase protection of cultural resources.[30] Relationships with the agencies have often been fraught with tension, but they have also resulted in productive comanagement agreements,[31] memorandums of understanding for access and protection,[32] and, as some of the cases will show, unique coordination of land protection using private conservation tools.

Generally, tribes are better able to protect culturally important sites on public lands. If a proposed agency action on public land threatens cultural sites, the Section 106 consultation process of the National Historic Preservation Act takes effect, and the tribe can come to the table.[33] If the land is private and threatened by a private action, tribal involvement and protection of cultural sites is more difficult: "My experience relating to instances involving damage to tribal sacred places on private lands reinforces my opinion that many people in the dominant American society have very little understanding of or respect for tribal religious beliefs or practices."[34] This gulf of understanding is apparent in the struggle to protect traditional sacred sites that do not contain structures or features, but "are important in maintaining the continuing cultural identity of the community."[35] Nontribal conservation organizations and public-resource agencies can purchase entire parcels, or the rights to manage them, from public or private landowners without an understanding of their cultural significance for local tribes, and they can then displace or exclude tribal access.[36] As private land trusts become major players in land planning and use,[37] this new era of enclosure may become of increasing concern to tribes.[38] The LTA could help address this by requiring its member land trusts to adopt a commitment to work with local Native entities on conservation planning, acquisition, stewardship, and monitoring.

Easements and land trusts may also offer expanded opportunities for tribes. For example, tribes can take the lead in partnering with existing conservation organizations to set a regional conservation agenda and to assert a role in the management and oversight of private conservation purchases. Indeed, private conservation organizations have realized that they must partner with diverse private and public stakeholders in order to protect threatened regions, rather than focusing only on specific parcels that landowners are willing to sell: "It seems logical that a more holistic approach to environmental protection, looking at habitat rather than species preservation and regional rather than local land protection, demands the cooperation of private organizations with public agencies and local communities."[39] The case studies of Nisqually and Jamestown S'Klallam tribes, for example, show how numerous partners are collaborating with these two tribal governments to protect local watersheds.

With clear recognition of the colonial history of conservation, and as tribes emerge as political, cultural, and economic leaders, land conservation interests and tribes may be able to collaborate and develop shared goals. However, certain principles must be respected, including that tribes are not to be lumped in with interest groups, such as rock climbers[40] and hard-rock miners.[41] Conservationists must be attentive to a history in which tribal rights were disregarded, and tribes were violently dispossessed of their lands. Further, tribes are sovereigns that predate the creation of the United States, and they have historical, cultural relationships with lands, which extend back to before Europeans came to North America: "Native peoples' interests as 'stakeholders' must be differentiated from their rights as separate nations that have a trust relationship with the U.S. government. . . . Indian nations, as sovereigns, have a unique range of interests and rights, both cultural and political, which should be given independent weight in the policy battles over public lands."[42] Recognizing Native sovereignty, knowledge, history, and relationship with the land can be the foundation for collaboration between a Native and a non-Native landowning or nonprofit entity.

Distributive Justice

The second aspect of environmental justice, distributive justice, is intertwined with the very notion of purchasing lands or rights to lands, in order to set them aside from development. These conserved lands are all Native lands, and the majority of Native communities have members that retain deep ties to the lands and extensive knowledge about their cultural and natural components. We must guard against a definition of justice that calls for a "redistribution of the power and loot deriving from the occupation of Native North America, even as the occupation continues."[43] Conservation easements and land trusts represent an important private conservation tool to "redistribute" these lands to tribal entities.

Within the contemporary environmental justice movement, distributive justice is understood as equally distributing the benefits and harms of environmental planning. This responds to the situation of poor communities and communities of color that are disproportionately affected by environmental pollution, as a result of the siting of polluting facilities (such as incinerators, toxic dumps, refineries, and so forth) or polluting activities (such as nuclear testing and pesticide application, among others) in or near these communities. Distributive justice can go beyond "egalitarian (equality-based) standards" that would provide the same level of harms and benefits to each place, to "equity-based standards,"[44] which take into account that some groups have historically suffered more harm and are more vulnerable. Equity-based standards then act to reduce the harms in these communities more than in the communities that have suffered less or are less vulnerable.

The conservation planning, of which easements and land trusts are a part, often differentially confers benefits, such as increased environmental amenities, protection of valued sites, increased land value because of proximity to conserved areas, and tax deductions. In order to carry out their conservation purposes, land trusts are often dependent on wealthy donors who may have undue influence on organizational choices of which lands to conserve and whether or not to make them publicly available.[45] The goal, then, is to even out the benefits, so that tribes benefit as much from the use of these conservation tools as, for example, wealthy landowners who can donate easements in order to get tax breaks. Within this framework, conserved land should incorporate not just values as defined by land trusts ("traditional" ranching and farming, recreation opportunities, scenery, and biodiversity, for example) but also the Native cultural and spiritual values related to the resource. These values long predate not just the arrival of Europeans,[46] but even more, the Euro-American hybrid structure of a land trust or conservation easement.

Conclusion

"Buying nature began as the noticeably clubby concern of elites. . . . They have met their own needs and impressed their vision on the landscape in the process. But they have also left a legacy—of land, institutions, and civic participation. . . . We have a more-than-adequate foundation for adding equity and accountability to the architecture and evaluation of conservation mosaics."[47]

The cases and analysis that follow demonstrate that tribes are bringing these tools to bear to meet their own cultural and community needs. Tribes are continuing to assert their sovereignty and undivided claim to their homelands. Conservation easements and land trusts are just another tool tribes can use for land acquisition, protection, and stewardship. Now, let us take a look at a sample of diverse situations and partnerships in which tribes, Native organizations, and their allies are applying these tools.

Native American Land Conservation Organizations

This section focuses on the development and sustainability of specifically Native American land trusts and conservancies. In these cases, tribes and individual Native Americans have adapted the land trust model to a Native framework. The two cases in this section are not representative of all Native land trusts and are merely meant to provide a source of information and inspiration about possible paths a Native-led conservation organization might follow. The InterTribal Sinkyone Wilderness Council (henceforth, the Council), for example, has created a nonprofit land conservancy governed by representatives of ten member tribes. The Native American Land Conservancy (NALC) is also a nonprofit land trust, but one with Native and non-Native board members cooperating to preserve healing landscapes that are sacred to Native Americans. The NALC has a predominantly Native-American board, but the members do not formally represent their tribes. Although they have different strategies, both the Council and the NALC have successfully raised funds to acquire and steward culturally important lands.

This section will begin with a case study of the Council. It includes background information and a detailed account of how its members organized to maintain and sustain title to the InterTribal Sinkyone Wilderness. A case study of the NALC follows, which will also include information on emerging Native land trusts—like the Kumeyaay Diegueño Land Conservancy—that the NALC is helping to support.

The section will conclude with a special chapter written by Dr. Kurt Russo, Executive Director of the NALC. This chapter was requested by NALC board members, who wanted to see a guide developed from their experiences to help other Native organizations embarking on a Native land conservation effort. Although Dr. Russo's chapter contains step-by-step information that will be helpful for developing organizations, each case study in this book also contains general advice on how to develop Native land conservation initiatives. Interviewees in each community were asked to reflect on how they would advise others to form, sustain, operate, and succeed in a cooperative Native land conservation effort. The goals of individual organizations, reflections from partners across the continent, and Dr. Russo's recommendations can all be taken together to assist in the spread of Native land conservation.

4

InterTribal Sinkyone Wilderness Council (California)

In 1986, seven California Indian tribes formed the first intertribal Native American land-conservation organization in the United States to protect the Sinkyone rain forest and its numerous cultural and ecological values.[1] The organization's member tribes retain deep historic, cultural, and ancestral ties to the Sinkyone tribal territory located between the Pacific Ocean and the vicinity of the South Fork and main stem of the Eel River in Northern Mendocino and Southern Humboldt Counties.

The Sinkyone, an Athabascan-speaking people, were massacred and subjected to forced removals from their homelands by white settlers and the government in the mid-1800s.[2] Sinkyone survivors became members of neighboring tribes that had received federal recognition and reservation lands. The InterTribal Sinkyone Wilderness Council (hereafter, the Council) now has ten federally recognized member tribes and holds fee title to the 3,845-acre InterTribal Sinkyone Wilderness—the first such wilderness area of its kind, yet only a small portion of the vast area of land once inhabited by the Sinkyone.

The ten member tribes and their appointed Council representatives are: Cahto Tribe of Laytonville Rancheria (Richard J. Smith), Coyote Valley Band of Pomo Indians (currently vacant), Hopland Band of Pomo Indians (Shawn Pady), Pinoleville Pomo Nation (David Edmunds), Potter Valley Tribe (Salvador Rosales), Redwood Valley Band of Pomo Indians (Elizabeth Hansen), Robinson Rancheria Band of Pomo Indians (Stoney Timmons), Round Valley Indian Tribes (Mona Oandasan), Scotts Valley Band of Pomo Indians (Crista Ray), and Sherwood Valley Band of Pomo Indians (Daniel

Rockey, Sr.). Martha Knight, a member of the Pinoleville Pomo Nation, serves as board secretary. Priscilla Hunter, a founder and the Chairperson of the Council, is a member of the Coyote Valley Band of Pomo Indians.

The Sally Bell Grove

In early September 1983, the California Department of Forestry and Fire Protection (CDF) approved a 75-acre Timber Harvest Plan (THP) filed by landowner Georgia-Pacific Corporation for an area of its Sinkyone property that environmental activists dubbed the "Sally Bell Grove" after a Sinkyone Indian survivor who had witnessed the brutal massacre of her family by white vigilantes in the late 1850s or early 1860s.[3] Sally Bell recounted the massacre to ethnographer Gladys Nomland in 1928:

> My grandfather and all of my family—my mother, my father, and we— were around the house and not hurting anyone. Soon, about ten o'clock in the morning, some white men came. They killed my grandfather and my mother and my father. I saw them do it. I was a big girl at the time. Then they killed my baby sister and cut her heart out and threw it in the brush where I ran and hid. My little sister was a baby, just crawling around. I didn't know what to do. I was so scared that I guess I just hid there a long time with my little sister's heart in my hands.[4]

Bell goes on to describe living in the woods with a few other survivors, eating what they could find and making do without clothes or blankets in the cold spring weather. She was eventually rescued by her brother and taken to a white family, where she stayed until she grew older. Needless to say, the activists' choice in dubbing the land the "Sally Bell Grove"[5] power-fully linked the horrific depredations the Indian community had suffered to contemporary injustices.

Litigation

In late September 1983, a group of plaintiffs including the International Indian Treaty Council, the Environmental Protection Information Center (EPIC), Fred "Coyote" Downey, Robert Sutherland, and Richard Gienger challenged the approval of Georgia-Pacific's Timber Harvest Plan (THP) in a landmark case known as *EPIC v. Johnson*.[6] Sharon Duggan represented the plaintiffs, and the defendants were the CDF, the State Board of Forestry, and Georgia-Pacific. The lawsuit described the grove and surrounding area as having been "once inhabited by members of the Sinkyone nation."[7]

In July 1985, the California Court of Appeals, District Five, found Georgia-Pacific to be out of compliance with the California Environmental Quality Act (CEQA). The ruling noted that Georgia-Pacific and CDF had failed to: (a) adequately consult with Native Americans, (b) protect Native American cultural resources, (c) provide adequate public notice regarding the THP, and (d) consider cumulative impacts. The decision led the State Board of Forestry to revamp the THP approval process statewide.

Planning for the Future of the Land

Shortly after the *EPIC v. Johnson* decision, four conservation groups began discussing how they could pool their resources to acquire and conserve a large block of Georgia-Pacific's Sinkyone property that included the Sally Bell Grove. The groups were the California State Parks, Save-the-Redwoods League, California Coastal Conservancy, and the Trust for Public Land. Georgia-Pacific voluntarily agreed to sell 7,100 acres of its coastal Sinkyone holdings to the Trust for Public Land (TPL). In December 1986, TPL deposited a certain amount to place a hold on the property and agreed to pay the full price within a designated period. TPL raised funds and completed the purchase with additional funding from the Save-the-Redwoods League, a California-based conservation organization (hereafter, the League), and the California Coastal Conservancy (hereafter, the Coastal Conservancy), a state agency focused on protecting California coastal resources and improving public access.[8] Nearly half of the land—3,255 coastal acres—was soon added to the south end of the Sinkyone State Park, established in 1975.[9] The fate of the remaining 3,845-acre Sinkyone Upland Remainder Parcel (hereafter, Upland Parcel) remained in question.

Within the context of extreme conflict over the use or preservation of California coastal redwoods, the Mendocino County Board of Supervisors asked the Coastal Conservancy to mediate the disposition of the Upland Parcel. The conservancy did not fiscally support TPL's purchase until the supervisors were agreeable to TPL's acquisition of the land. Although the supervisors at that time did not directly support TPL's acquisition, they supported the Coastal Conservancy by providing funding for TPL's purchase because it gave them (as representatives of the County of Mendocino and constituents of the state conservancy) some stake in what happened to the land.[10] Just after TPL optioned the property, and before TPL received any funding from the conservancy, the supervisors stated their support for TPL's purchase. As Neal Fishman, current Coastal Conservancy deputy executive officer and a longtime employee who was closely involved in these negotiations, explained: "Our putting money into the deal, after the fact, with the proviso that we would control its eventual disposition after developing a management plan, gave the Board [of Supervisors] political leverage on the eventual use of the land, though not an actual legal right. We made a commitment to an eventual disposal of the land consistent with the wishes of the board."[11] At that time, the board wanted "multiple use" of the land, including logging.

The InterTribal Sinkyone Wilderness Council formed in response to the anticipated divestiture of the Upland Parcel. The tribes creating the Council were concerned that if they did not intervene, the land would be transferred to another industrial timber entity. This was a valid concern because half of the land had gone into permanent conservation to expand the Sinkyone Wilderness State Park, and the general expectation of the state and the county—as well as the timber industry—was that the other half would be put into multiple use. According to Council Chairperson Hunter, "The Indian tribes in this area wanted to prevent future industrial logging on this Sinkyone land. The tribes saw that to achieve this, they would need to form a nonprofit to acquire and protect this land by designating it as the nation's first intertribal wilderness area."[12]

Hunter circulated a letter of intent among the local tribes, expressing the tribes' desire to form an intertribal consortium to protect the Sinkyone land from future logging. Tribal chairpersons signed the letter, and soon thereafter, the tribes passed resolutions supporting the formation of the Council and acquisition of Sinkyone land for an intertribal wilderness area. Ricardo Tapia, the Council's first director, assisted Hunter and others in drafting its articles of incorporation and bylaws.[13] As Hunter remembered, "There was the clear perception in the Indian community of the cultural significance of, and the threat to, this land. This informed the urgency to unite and form a tribally based Indian organization that would serve as the official platform for gaining support and negotiating with the state of California and TPL to acquire this land."[14]

In December 1986—less than two weeks before Georgia-Pacific agreed to sell the land to TPL—the Council officially formed as a nonprofit and began positioning itself to obtain the land. According to Hawk Rosales, who has worked with the Council since 1990 and is now its executive director, "We were so intent on making this happen, and we were able to show important connections between the Sinkyone land, the Sinkyone ancestors, and the Sinkyone descendants of today. That struck a chord in everyone's heart."[15] Ultimately, the Council was able to garner local, state, national, and international support, and the opposing commercial interests vying for the land were unable to compete.

The Council's proactive approach included developing restoration and stewardship projects, which the TPL and the Coastal Conservancy supported. These projects helped foster a new, innovative Sinkyone conservation partnership and built the awareness and capacity that enabled the reestablishment of Indian stewardship on the land. Collaborative work in Sinkyone between the Council and leaders in TPL (such as Ted Harrison and Martin Rosen) laid the groundwork for TPL's national Tribal and Native Lands Program. As described in chapter 2, it is the only such program in a national conservation organization, and it has been active nationally in numerous projects involving Native land and communities.

New Alliances

The effort to stop logging in the area that is now the Sinkyone State Park and the InterTribal Sinkyone Wilderness represented the first time locally that the Indian community had allied with the environmental activist community. Tribal representatives and environmentalists were politically active in Sinkyone as early as 1983, when they began the work to prevent the clear-cutting of the Sally Bell Grove. During this time, people began discussing ways of getting the Sinkyone land back into Native hands. At the time, environmentalists and timber industry representatives were sharply at odds regarding resource management. It was understood that TPL would hold title to the Sinkyone Upland Parcel only temporarily, until the Coastal Conservancy helped to find a local nonprofit organization to permanently hold and manage the land.[16] Meanwhile, the Council and the conservancy built a relationship by representatives attending one another's meetings and collaborating on projects. The Council publicly asserted its interest in and qualifications to manage the Upland Parcel. Council representatives also went to public meetings about the property and networked with local and regional environmental organizations and environmental justice supporters.

In 1993, TPL approached a new forest conservation organization, the Pacific Forest Trust (PFT), about becoming involved in the land transaction. After a series of conversations between TPL, the Coastal Conservancy, the Council, and the PFT, the conservancy asked the PFT to develop a conservation easement for the property. According to the PFT President Laurie Wayburn, the easement would acknowledge and respect Native American ownership, allow for restoration, leave the potential for some economic activity, and conserve the "full range of public trust values, from water and wildlife to opportunities for recreation."[17]

In order to develop the easement, the PFT worked closely with Rosales, Hunter, and other members of the Council's board, and Sharon Duggan. After developing the draft terms of a conservation easement, the PFT held public outreach sessions to get feedback from stakeholders in Mendocino and southern Humboldt counties. Then, the PFT drafted a resolution for the Mendocino County Board of Supervisors to consider. The resolution supported conveying the land to the Council and the placement of protective conservation easements on the property. It also recognized the Council's ongoing educational and restoration activities on the parcel.

In December 1994—eleven years after the initial lawsuit—the supervisors unanimously passed this resolution supporting the Council in its bid for the land. Both Fishman and Wayburn observed that the decade-long time lapse changed the climate and the players surrounding the Sinkyone Upland Parcel.[18] During that period, the composition of the Board of Supervisors and their constituencies changed to one that would accept a tribal wilderness, and the Council had worked successfully to garner diverse local and regional support. Other interested groups, such as the Mendocino Forest Conservation Trust, which had expressed a desire to see the land become a working forest, also had time to develop a proposal, raise funds and support, and present proposals to the supervisors and the Coastal Conservancy. However, according to Fishman, they "could not match [the Council's] progress" in gaining funding and support.[19]

Building Support for an InterTribal Wilderness

The Trees Foundation, a conservation resource center based in rural Garberville, California, was instrumental in building local and regional support for the tribal acquisition of Sinkyone land.[20] The Trees Foundation organized the Friends of the Sinkyone—a grassroots network of largely local northwestern California residents who supported and helped to raise funds for the Council. Another group that built momentum for the success of the Sinkyone acquisition was the Bay Area Friends of Sinkyone (BAFOS), which formed in 1992–1993 and was based on the campus of University of California, Berkeley. The BAFOS raised thousands of dollars for the Council, organized bike-a-thons from campus to the Sinkyone, and developed classes geared toward research in and support of the Sinkyone. The Council also collaborated with individuals and groups in 1994 to create a forty-five-minute documentary film—*The Run to Save Sinkyone,* which went to the famed Sundance Film Festival in 1995 and then traveled to ten other film festivals. This greatly helped to build awareness about the Sinkyone lands.[21]

Members of the Indian and non-Indian communities volunteered their time to build support for transferring land to the Council. According to Hunter,

> We worked hard to secure this support. We had already done several successful projects on the land, which created employment, and a lot of pride for local Indian communities. We had to fight for this land because there was a competing timber industry group that had formed a land trust, and they were trying to convince the conservancy that they should be the buyer. There was animosity and resistance toward the idea of returning this land to the Indian people, but we persevered and were able to win this fight to save the land.[22]

At a 1995 public meeting held in Fort Bragg, the Coastal Conservancy approved a deal to sell the land to the Council, provided that the Council could raise $1.4 million to purchase the property within three years.[23] During the meeting, Council members were pleased to hear overwhelming public sentiment that the land be given to them, and they were prepared to raise the required purchase price, which would allow the conservancy and TPL to recoup their costs. The Council had already raised over $100,000 when a board member from the Lannan Foundation read about the situation in an April 1995 *Los Angeles Times* article.[24] The Lannan Foundation invited Council members to a meeting to discuss the Council's plans to raise funds to buy the land. Lannan board members were so impressed by the Council's vision, as articulated by Rosales and Hunter, that they stepped outside of their regular grant-making guidelines and made a grant of $1.3 million to the Council for purchase of the Sinkyone land.[25] The Lannan Foundation has also provided support for other Council projects.

Easement Structure

On July 11, 1996, just before selling the land to the Council, TPL sold a primary conservation easement to the Pacific Forest Trust. The Coastal Conservancy was intimately involved in this multilayered transaction—at the same meeting that the conservancy approved TPL's sale of the land to the Council, they also granted the PFT $2 million to buy the easement. Because of the terms of the agreement between the conservancy and TPL, in which state funds for conservation were put toward TPL's purchase of the land, a conservation easement had to be in place before TPL could sell the land. The easement also ensured the protection of the land for cultural uses. As Wayburn explained, "It's the same for anyone looking at creating something that can be used seven generations into the future. The legal tools to do this are limited, and conservation easements are the best for this purpose. The tribes hadn't used a conservation easement before, but it turned out to be a very elegant tool to accomplish their cultural goals as well as natural resource protection."[26] The easement also provided public benefits through land, water, and forest conservation, and it reduced the price of the property to $1.4 million.[27] In August 1997, the Council took title to the property.

There are currently two conservation easements on the property. The PFT drafted the primary one in 1993, and it took three years to negotiate. Five teams of attorneys (one each representing the Council, TPL, the PFT, the Coastal Conservancy, and the Lannan Foundation) reviewed and commented on the easement. Its terms were designed to hold in perpetuity and to accommodate the Council as owner. "We were very, very careful to have language that respected the tribes' desire for confidentiality regarding their cultural heritage," Wayburn said.[28] The easement includes agreed-upon language establishing clear restrictions—for example, on occupancy, use of horses, timber harvest, and development—in order to minimize impacts on parcel resources. The Council and the PFT discuss these restrictions annually to ensure that they are being respected. However, the easement does not detail the tribes' traditional use of resources.

It is believed that when the property was transferred in 1997, the Council became the first tribal entity in the United States to have entered into a conservation easement with a private land trust:[29] "This was the very first conservation easement with a group of federally recognized tribes in the United States. It was not only new for Pacific Forest Trust, but it was new, period."[30] The PFT recognized the precedent-setting nature of this agreement and entered into it carefully. Conversations between the PFT and the Council addressed numerous issues. Wayburn, for example, raised some questions about holding an easement on land owned by an organization not accustomed to using that type of instrument: "Would it be seen as cultural imperialism? Was it a sign of lack of trust? Or was it a sign of equality? Would this be enforced in tribal court or U.S. court? We wanted to be extremely respectful of those issues, the history of those issues, and the emotional and identity impact of those issues."[31]

The Council and the PFT also explored whether the PFT was the right group to hold the easement. Although the PFT has extensive experience in forestry, restoration, and protecting conservation values, they had not previously worked with a Native American landholder. In order to test the waters, the PFT and the Council built a five-year decision period into their agreement, at the end of which time they could reassess to see if both parties were still comfortable working together or if the easement should be transferred to another conservation organization. After five years, the Council formally requested that the PFT continue to hold the easement.

Not only did the PFT and the Council have to be comfortable with the terms of the easement and with working together, the Coastal Conservancy also had to be confident that both parties involved in the easement would comply with its terms. According to Fishman, the conservancy felt comfortable working with the Council to negotiate and establish these easements precisely because of the Council's nonprofit status.[32] For the PFT, this was less of an issue, as the key concern about working with tribal governments on easements is actually the status of the land.[33] Because the land is in fee status and not held in trust by the federal government, state and federal laws enforce the easement. Although the Council is composed of sovereign tribal governments, as an entity, it functions as a nonprofit organization.

The PFT monitors the easement annually, walking the property with Council staff, and the trust is also involved throughout the year if the Council is doing restoration or other projects on the land. Because of the communication channels established between the PFT and the Council, which are codified in the easement, the Council notifies the PFT when and where they are doing restoration work that involves heavy equipment, so that the PFT knows what resources may be affected and can review the work plan. The PFT and Sanctuary Forest have also been key partners with the Council in addressing issues of trespass.[34] The organizations have worked together to help ensure that others respect the protected resources on the property: "Those resources are not only owned by the Council but protected by the PFT. That has been a productive and positive relationship."[35]

Sharon Duggan represented the InterTribal Sinkyone Wilderness Council in the easement negotiations: "It is rare that one has the opportunity to see things come full circle. Many times one lawyer litigates, and another does the transactional work, so it was unique for me to have the ability to act as litigator and then to be engaged in a public policy transactional role for the purposes of seeing the property protected and returned to what I would consider to be rightful ownership."[36] Both the InterTribal Sinkyone land-ownership structure and conservation easements can be seen as unique and innovative arrangements. Unlike most tribal lands, the InterTribal Sinkyone Wilderness is not held in trust by the federal government on behalf of Indian tribes. Rather, the nonprofit InterTribal Sinkyone Wilderness Council—on behalf of its member tribes—holds fee title to the land, making the easement enforceable under state law: "The Council has a tradition and a history and a vision about what needs to happen to that property, [which] is, in some respects, parallel to what you would see in typical conservation easement, and in other respects, not."[37] Typically, the easement holder has authority to monitor and enforce compliance with the easement, and this had to be balanced with the tribal sovereignty of the Council's members: "It was important that the Council had the autonomy that it needed, within the context of protecting the resource."[38]

As an environmental litigator, Duggan was also struck by the depth of relationship between the Native people and the resources. Although most conservation easements include individuals and groups asserting some relationship to the resources they want to protect, in the Sinkyone case, the relationship had a different tone: "[The Council has] a profound relationship to the land and resources, as well as to the culture of the place and the people, embodied by generations and thousands of years. Because of the past treatment of the Indian people, in some ways that deep relationship was broken. Now there is cultural restoration and healing."[39] Years of collaboration were required to create easements that balanced respecting this cultural relationship and Native autonomy while ensuring environmental protection.

The Coastal Conservancy's collaborative process with multiple stakeholders (including timber industry representatives, local tribes, local government, state agencies, local citizens, and environmental groups) resulted in a requirement that the future landowner of the Upland Parcel would have to have the ability to commercially harvest timber on the property to "offset" the strictly conservation-oriented management of the neighboring State Park property. The intent of the PFT-held easement is "to foster the restoration of a mature native redwood forest type or Douglas fir forest type, depending on the natural occurrence of these types on the property."[40] As such, the PFT easement allows—but does not compel—the Council to conduct sustainable commercial timber management that fulfills that intent. However, the easement itself is so restrictive that it would be difficult to find enough sites within the appropriate zones to make commercial harvesting cost-effective.

Despite these restrictions, in 1997, the Council executed a secondary easement with the land conservation trust Sanctuary Forest. It prohibits future commercial harvesting, thereby ensuring that industrial timber management would never compromise the fundamental cultural conservation goals. Members of Sanctuary Forest had worked alongside Native people to protect Sinkyone lands from further clear-cutting in the mid-1980s.[41] The Sanctuary Forest easement underscores the sentiment stated in the PFT's easement about cutting only for restoration. The Sanctuary Forest easement explicitly allows the Council to cut trees only as part of its "restoration activities necessary to preserve and enhance the forest habitat and ecology" and "for non-commercial local California Indian traditional purposes."[42] Both the Pacific Forest Trust and Sanctuary Forest conduct annual monitoring on the property to evaluate compliance with their easements' terms and conditions.

According to Sanctuary Forest's former Executive Director Eric Goldsmith, the secondary easement represents the Council's vision for the property: "[The Council] wanted to make any forestry that would occur there congruent with the cultural values of the Sinkyone people. This was one of the first easements to incorporate Native American cultural values as a significant part of easement terms."[43] It remains distinct from other easements that Sanctuary Forest holds because of its emphasis on cultural values, the sense of a "higher principle" of returning sovereignty over the land to a consortium representing descendants of the original inhabitants, and the cultural sensitivity required to monitor easement compliance. For example, Sanctuary Forest monitors where and how many trees were cut for cultural purposes, but it does not ask what those purposes were and why those particular trees were chosen. As Goldsmith notes, "As a tree-hugger, I might not like to see a tree cut, but I have no need nor place to ask why, unless it was sold, or a case could be made that such action undermines the underlying conservation values articulated in the easement."[44] Sanctuary Forest sees itself as a partner with the Council to steward the property, and they do the annual monitoring together, including taking photographs from established photo-monitoring points and conducting specific studies of long-term trends.

Two additional restrictions apply to the property. These are actually "irrevocable offers to dedicate," which will become easements held by a third party only if the landowner fails to comply with their terms. The effect of these offers to dedicate (OTDs) is to require the landowner (rather than the holder of the OTD) to implement the conservation agreements. If the landowner fails to do so, then the legal holder can intervene and enforce the agreements' terms. These offers, which provide for limited public access and the protection of cultural resources, are made in favor of the Coastal Conservancy (which would hold the easements if the landowner failed to meet the requirements specified in the OTDs). Offers to dedicate are conservancy policy on all lands that draw on public money to fund acquisition or preservation.[45] In case the nonprofit property owner ceases to exist, the OTD allows the state to step back in and, in this case, enforce the terms of the OTD by ensuring limited public access. However, since the Council was formed largely to address the conservation and land management concerns included in the easement, it makes sense for it to oversee and fulfill the terms of these OTDs: "The Council's purpose has always been and will always be to protect this land's cultural resources. The Council, as landowner, is able to provide this cultural protection better than anyone else."[46] The Council also wanted to develop and manage public access in a way that simultaneously safeguards Sinkyone's conservation values and expands opportunities for people to enjoy the land. According to Hunter, the Coastal Conservancy understood these needs and worked productively with the Council to develop and execute OTDs that address both organizations' interests and concerns.[47]

InterTribal Sinkyone Wilderness Council: A Cultural and Environmental Vision

The focus of the Council's work is cultural land conservation within the historic boundaries of Sinkyone tribal territory (fig. 4.1). It achieves this goal through the acquisition, conservation, and stewardship of land; the revitalization of Native cultural land uses; and the preservation and restoration of important cultural-ecological resources within Sinkyone lands.

Luwana Quitiquit, a former Council board member, who represented Robinson Rancheria from the Council's inception until 2009, is particularly interested in the stewardship of native plants on the InterTribal Sinkyone Wilderness land. As a traditional basketweaver, Quitiquit struggles to find Native basketry plants that are in good condition and accessible to Native weavers. She described going to gather weaving materials on federal and private lands, only to find sedges and other native plants "in disarray," and "inappropriate for use." The best way to ensure healthy native plants, she explained, is to have your own land, which would make it possible to manage, encourage, and care for the plants that are vital for traditional basketry.[48]

Weavers like Quitiquit are working to establish Native gardens, and the InterTribal Sinkyone land represents a huge area that can be managed to ensure the abundance and well-being of native plants that are needed for continuing age-old basket-weaving traditions: "I have an interest in what's going on in our environment. I'm watching the native plants. I'm very interested in having the [Sinkyone land] for our Native people. . . . It's really remarkable that we can do this for our people, to be able to have a sanctuary for ourselves. My interest is very deep."[49] At past annual cultural gatherings at Sinkyone, Quitiquit has coordinated educational workshops for youth on the land—teaching them to identify at least twenty plants per day. Once the children are confident in their knowledge, Quitiquit takes

FIGURE 4.1. Dancer at Sinkyone Cultural Gathering, August 2008. (Photo courtesy of and copyright by Hawk Rosales)

them on a walk with the elders and the two groups identify and discuss the plants as they walk along together.

Quitiquit envisions the Council becoming a resource and providing workshops to other Native groups interested in forming Native land organizations focused on regaining Native lands for cultural conservation: "There is not enough of what we are doing going on in other places, so we are like an example to other communities. I think other people would be doing what we're doing if they knew. It wasn't something that just happened overnight, but I think other communities could move faster based on what we have done."[50]

InterTribal Sinkyone Wilderness Council: Governance Structure

Federally recognized tribes with ancestral and cultural ties to the aboriginal Sinkyone tribal territory have become members of the Council through certified tribal resolutions. These resolutions from individual tribal councils indicate the tribes' commitment to support and contribute to the Council. Member tribes then identify a tribal representative to serve on the Council's board of directors. The Council admits only federally recognized local tribes to the organization: "The Council was formed by and for these federally recognized tribes—sovereign Indian communities that have recognizable tribal governments with the ability, authority, and responsibility to govern their own people, and to legitimately represent them."[51] The Council incorporated as a nonprofit in order to acquire and protect the Sinkyone Upland Parcel, and to raise awareness and support for its conservation work throughout the Sinkyone region. Priscilla Hunter has served as chairperson since the Council began, and several board members have been with the Council for over fifteen years. According to Hunter, board members' long-term leadership "gives the Council a great measure of stability." The Council is consciously intertribal in nature, with equal representation accorded to each member tribe. Chairperson Hunter reported that she had "never seen any serious conflicts within the board. The Council is really focused on developing and implementing very positive initiatives that benefit the land and our communities."[52]

The board makes decisions by a combination of voting and consensus, and board members volunteer their time and expertise in a variety of ways. Council treasurer and Redwood Valley Little River Band of Pomo Indians representative Elizabeth Hansen has been active with the Council for fifteen years: "It's a lot of work, and it takes a lot of your time, but that's part of being on the board. I've seen the Council grow as the project grows. [I am] looking at how our people benefit from this, from the land, from involving the youth. It's the first intertribal Indian wilderness area in the nation; we can say, 'yes, this is ours.'"[53] Board members also gain valuable insights and tools from their participation on the Council, which they can then take back to their individual tribes. "The Council has shown us about networking, building alliances, and managing resources in a way that is consistent with cultural values," said David Edmunds, the recently appointed representative to the Council from the Pinoleville Pomo Nation.[54] Pinoleville is working to establish gardens of traditional plants, undertake restoration projects on degraded sites, and develop protocols and agreements for accessing traditional resources on privately owned lands.

Plans for the Land

The Council's plan for limited public access provides protection for the land's cultural-ecological resources and cultural privacy, and it promotes the Council's original intent to revitalize traditional tribal uses and stewardship.

After the environmental review phase is complete, the Council will seek funding to complete the construction of a maximum of three public-access trails and camping areas, located near the trailheads. These trails will tie into existing ones that traverse the longest stretch of permanently protected coastal wilderness in the lower forty-eight states. Sanctuary Forest, which holds the secondary easement on the Council land, owns property and easements nearby, so the two entities are examining ways in which they may be able to create connections between their parcels through hiking trails. "We are neighbors in land ownership, and we share stewardship goals for the larger landscape," Goldsmith added.[55]

Since 1992, the Council and the California State Parks have collaborated on numerous restoration and stewardship projects in the Sinkyone Wilderness State Park, including salmonid restoration and a major overhaul of the Hotel Gulch Trail. In May 2009, Rosales—on behalf of the Council—received the 2008 State Parks Dewitt Award for Partnership from California State Parks Director Ruth Coleman.[56] According to Rosales, State Parks has been an excellent partner on the Council's trails project because of the agency's nationally renowned trail design-and-construction program, which is headquartered at the North Coast Redwoods District Office in Eureka.[57] Tribal members will be involved in construction, as they are in all of the Council's on-the-ground work. "We have created a significant block of employment for this geographic area," Rosales said.[58] Thus far, the Council's numerous cultural conservation projects have employed approximately eighty tribal members and twenty-five non-tribal members in seasonal positions. Funds for these projects come from state agency grants and contracts, as well as from donations and private foundation grants. To date, the Coastal Conservancy has provided the majority of funding support for the Council's InterTribal Trails Project.

The Council conducts cultural resource monitoring, education, land restoration, and other aspects of cultural conservation work on public and private lands throughout Sinkyone territory.[59] It assisted California State Parks with the decommissioning of more than 50 miles of abandoned logging roads and stream crossings in the Sinkyone State Park, which led to its official designation as a State Wilderness Area in November 2006. According to Rosales, in upcoming years the Council plans to eventually decommission most of the abandoned logging roads, landings, and stream crossings located within the InterTribal Wilderness.[60] This effort will entail a multiyear planning and implementation program, beginning with wildlife and cultural resource assessments. The Council also plans to eradicate exotic plant species on the InterTribal land, thus promoting the return of native plants and a more balanced ecosystem. The Council is engaged in ongoing ethno-historical research on the language, culture, land-use patterns, trade practices, relations with neighboring tribes, and the territorial boundaries of the original Sinkyone peoples.

According to Council research, the Sinkyone people comprised approximately twelve tribelets with common cultural practices.[61] Since 1993, the Council has been engaged in salmonid habitat improvement in Wolf Creek, the largest stream on the InterTribal property. The Council will continue its native fisheries restoration work in Wolf Creek and hopes to eventually expand its restoration work to other Sinkyone streams. The Council also has plans for seasonal cultural camps featuring bark and pole frame structures built using local traditional materials and construction methods. These camps are identified as a "permitted use" in the Pacific Forest Trust and Sanctuary Forest conservation easements. The Council also plans to develop a program to encourage tribal members to harvest, utilize, and care for the land's traditional cultural-use plants. Ultimately, the Council's desire is to expand its cultural conservation program to include other locations within the Sinkyone territory considered as candidates for protection and cultural stewardship due to threats posed by development or industrial extraction.

Advice for Native Conservation Groups

The InterTribal Sinkyone Wilderness Council has been successful over the past two decades in maintaining cohesion within the organization, accomplishing conservation work throughout Sinkyone territory, and attracting monetary support to acquire and manage cultural properties. The Council believes that there is a growing need for Native-led land conservation efforts in Indian country. In the Council's experience, the most successful Native conservation organizations are those that establish and maintain sound fiscal management practices, develop and expand effective infrastructure, and collaborate via long-term partnerships with other organizations and agencies.

Atta Stevenson, a former Council board member who represented the Cahto Tribe of Laytonville Rancheria, drew on her personal experiences as a Tribal Person and an activist when she joined the Council. Stevenson had been involved for years in the Cahto Tribe's efforts to ensure access to seaweed, kelp, abalone, mussels, fish, and other living marine life that they have respectfully harvested for thousands of years. Stevenson emphasized that the practice of harvesting transcends simple access to encompass a holistic understanding of the tides and the fluctuations in ocean temperature and other conditions. She recalls a time when federal and state agencies disregarded the importance of Native land stewardship: "Our tribe would migrate to the coast and gather all of our sustenance for the rest of the year and bring it home. [The agencies] did not acknowledge it as a meaningful way of life."[62] Stevenson believes this can still be a problem.

Although there are ongoing struggles to educate outsiders, when tribes throughout the region began working together in efforts including the formation of the Council, they achieved broader recognition for their traditional lifeways and rights: "Wherever they went, they talked about conservation, how tribes wanted to preserve pristine waters, natural habitat, forestry range, and to provide cultural awareness."[63] Lessons continue to be learned from these collective Native efforts to protect and ensure access to the land. Stevenson reflected on the importance of face-to-face conversations within tribal communities before beginning to work with outside parties. She also cautioned against writing down plans too soon and not including elders and culture-keepers in plan development: "Before you take action and put words to paper, you should sit down through some really heartfelt sessions with your elders. When you do leadership meetings, you should go out of your way to invite traditional practitioners and elder practitioners, who are not always the same people."[64]

Although Stevenson also acknowledged the importance of collaborating with outside specialists, such as scientists with expertise in species preservation, she felt that any interaction with scientists in particular had to be preceded by in-depth training to raise cultural awareness. This is partially due to the power of science to determine conservation objectives, which thereby excludes other perspectives on how to manage the land: "When those people come in, you need to . . . sit down and walk them through your history and the obstacles you are trying to overcome. [Then,] when their knowledge is needed, they will be able to form [plans] with a more compassionate directive."[65] The Council has worked with numerous parties to acquire and steward the Sinkyone parcel, including federal and state agencies, public and private funders, conservancies and land trusts, and lawyers: "Partnerships, with people above or around you, are important. You need to sit down with them and say, 'this is what we intend to do with this land for one hundred years,' and maybe we can help you by . . . doing traditional burns that prepare the land and protect it from fire [for example]."[66]

Stevenson also suggested that Native groups examine the health of all elements of the resource they intend to preserve and utilize, including the air. Because of its location and characteristics, the Sinkyone parcel, she felt, is an ideal place for land preservation. "It's adjacent to a State Park, the land is undeveloped, and it contains old-growth trees," she explained. Stevenson encouraged tribes to be open to partnerships—with other tribes and with outside groups that share Native conservation values.[67]

Overview of the Council's Strategy

According to Rosales, those seeking to establish initiatives like the Council and the InterTribal Wilderness should have clear ideas about the cultural priorities they want to address, how they will revitalize and sustain a Native land stewardship ethic, and how their efforts will serve the needs of their tribal communities:

> The ultimate success of such cultural conservation efforts requires that they originate from within the tribal communities themselves and are accompanied by investments of long-term involvement and strong, committed tribal leadership. The movement itself must emanate from within the tribal communities that, since time immemorial, have maintained traditional beliefs and cultural values, including important relationships with their aboriginal lands.[68]

Of course, the Council has been working on this process of articulating traditional values with contemporary organizational and management structures for more than twenty years. Hansen offered some words of encouragement to groups just starting out, based on her own long participation with the Council: "Keep with it, keep with your goals. You will have your ups and downs, but just stay with it. That's what we did here. We had moments of saying, 'Where are we going? What are we doing?' but you have to focus on the positive [and] on what you want to do."[69]

Advice for Non-Native Land Trusts Working with Native Groups

From the point of view of non-Native land trusts collaborating with the Council, Wayburn of the PFT and Goldsmith, formerly of Sanctuary Forest, offered some recommendations for non-Native land trusts beginning cooperative work with Native entities. First, Goldsmith recommended that land trusts "do their homework," and understand the status and structure of the Native entity with which they will be collaborating. This includes understanding the more subtle "lay of the land" in the tribal community before wading in with the idea of "helping."[70] Goldsmith also encouraged

groups to be very clear about their roles in collaborating with Native entities. In this vein, Wayburn encouraged acknowledging any issues and talking about them from the start. The PFT and the Council exemplified this
in their dialogues about whether a conservation easement held by the PFT
was going to be the right thing for the Council.[71]

According to Goldsmith, the role of a non-Native land trust may not
be "to understand the resource and what it means to the Native people," but
to "have the rapport and sensitivity to know what is and is not appropriate
in terms of what you need to know to fulfill your responsibility to protect
that resource."[72] Non-Native land trusts also need to become aware of the
protocols surrounding archaeological sites, traditional cultural properties,
and other cultural resources. To this end, Goldsmith advised land trusts
to consult with professional archaeologists, and Rosales and others underscored the importance of talking with the Native people themselves about
archaeological sites and their management and protection.[73]

Both Wayburn and Goldsmith recommended investing time in building
good cross-cultural communication. Goldsmith emphasized that good communication allows both parties to feel comfortable telling each other when
they may have asked something inappropriate.[74] And Wayburn underscored
the importance of communication in making the agreement viable over
time:

> You do the best that you can with documents, and you try to be as clear
> as you can, so that the intent will be clear—not just in ten to twenty
> years, but in fifty to one hundred years—and then you rely on the
> kinds of relationships you have built with your partners to carry that
> through. The Council has been such a great partner, so committed and
> dedicated to it. . . . What makes [documents] effective is the quality of
> communication and the relationship.[75]

Goldsmith added that land conservancies need to be aware of the time
required to establish the trust and communication to be able to come to
a shared set of values and practices for an easement. Any cross-cultural
partnership requires in-depth discussion of, and ultimate consensus on, a
set of values that will underlie the easement agreement. This can be challenging when, as Goldsmith noted, the preservation ethic that underlies
the land conservation movement may be strikingly different from a Native
conservation ethic in which stewardship is an active part of conserving and
maintaining a relationship with the resources in question: "The conservation ethic is more geared towards the idea of preventing bad management
and that nature left on its own would be the ultimate ideal. This is very

different from many Native cultures that view management of the land as integral to sustaining its full natural value."[76]

Ultimately, the Council's partnerships and easements with the PFT and Sanctuary Forest, as well as the OTDs with the Coastal Conservancy, exemplify conservation arrangements that finely balance the needs of the landowner, the land trust, the state, and the public. These partnerships are sustained by communication, trust, and a common commitment to fulfill the jointly developed terms of these unique conservation agreements.

Native American Land Conservancy (California/ National)

The sacred lands that the Native American Land Conservancy (NALC) focuses on are vital to cultural identity, historical continuity, and contemporary healing from intergenerational trauma due to the historic and contemporary impacts of colonialism. According to Winona LaDuke, "By the 1930s, Native territories had been reduced to about 4 percent of our original land base. More than 75 percent of our sacred sites have been removed from our care and jurisdiction."[1] In California alone, more than 333,346 Native Americans[2] (from tribes originally located throughout the United States) are limited to 463,000 acres of individual and collective trust land.[3] This land base is just 5 percent of what the nearly 300,000 Native Californians "were promised in the treaties of 1852 and a mere fraction of California's aboriginal territory."[4] The NALC specifically works to preserve "healing landscapes," or places that are restorative, reawakening, and recentering for human beings. The need for this healing can be understood on individual, community, national, and even international levels. As Kurt Russo explains in *In the Land of Three Peaks*, "in the case of Native America, whole cultures . . . must come to terms with the pain of unresolved, intergenerational grief."[5]

The NALC works with tribes and other organizations to achieve land preservation and protection through direct acquisition or the use of conservation easements. As of 2008, it had raised more than $1.5 million, ensured the protection of 10,000 acres of lands sacred to Native American people,

and organized three national conferences and many smaller meetings dedicated to educating the public on the threats to sacred lands and strategies
to protect them.[6]

Beginnings

The NALC grew out of a series of meetings of an intertribal cultural committee in the Coachella Valley, located in Southern California's Riverside
County. The committee included tribal people from Imperial, Riverside,
and San Bernardino counties, and it focused primarily on preserving the
endangered Chemehuevi and Cahuilla languages. Two of the leaders of the
committee were Theresa Mike (Lummi) and her husband Dean Mike, tribal
chairman of the Twenty-Nine Palms Band of Mission Indians. Throughout
the growth of the NALC, this band has provided critical encouragement
and financial support for the NALC's vision and operations. As Dean Mike
explained at the 2009 NALC conference, "Desertlands/Sacred Lands," held
in Palm Desert, California, the NALC operates to protect and preserve lands
important to Native Americans, and the NALC believes that these lands are
"not just 'that place' and 'this place,' but the connections between them."[7]

The importance of the regional efforts of the intertribal cultural committee provided what NALC Executive Director Dr. Kurt Russo calls "a
growing point" for several associations and activities, including the NALC.
The NALC was created when the Mikes brought their colleagues and friends
together in response to landowner Tom Askew's efforts to transfer a parcel
of land in the Old Woman Mountains to a Native organization. Tribes in
the region had long been active to protect the Old Woman Mountains from
a proposed radioactive dump in nearby Ward Valley.[8] The Colorado River,
Ward Valley, Chemehuevi Valley, the Turtle Mountains, Spirit Mountain,
and the Old Woman Mountains encircle an area considered sacred by the
lower Colorado River Indian tribes.[9]

Acquiring the Old Woman Mountains

The Old Woman Mountains are a range of peaks rising as high as 5,000
feet, located in the eastern Mojave Desert, 220 miles east of the City of
Los Angeles. They are within the Nuwuvi, or Southern Paiute and Chemehuevi, homelands.[10] The sacred Salt Songs, discussed below, sing of this
landscape.[11] In 1923, Tom Askew's grandfather purchased a small parcel, and
eventually, he acquired eleven sections (7,500 acres) of this range. Tom first
visited the property in 1955, at the age of nine, and he lived on the land

as an adult. When his grandfather passed away, Tom inherited 40 percent of the property, with the remainder willed to other family members and to charities, including a local Presbyterian church, a rehabilitation hospital, and the Boys and Girls Scouts, in undivided interests. Tom had spent the most time on the property of any of the heirs, and he became impassioned with the goal of returning it to the local Native people: "I wanted to turn it back to the tribes because it was theirs, and I felt they needed it."[12] One day, Tom went into Spotlight 29 Casino and found Dean Mike. Tom remembers giving him a picture of the painted rock on the site and saying, "Here is a picture of your property, this belonged to your ancestors, so, if you're interested, give me a call."[13]

Theresa Mike discussed the offer with UC Riverside History Professor Dr. Clifford Trafzer (Wyandot), who was already working with Twenty-Nine Palms Band on historical preservation projects, and Russo, who has worked for Theresa's tribe in Washington State since the 1980s. Russo, Trafzer, Mike, and others began brainstorming about how to form an organization that could take title to the land. As Russo recalled, "This is one of those things that really started on a napkin, with a couple of folks sitting around thinking, 'What is the best way to do this?' No one had ever looked into land conservancies—it emerged out of a small group of people with creative minds, [who were] willing to look in new places for new solutions to old problems."[14] In 1998, Mike, Trafzer, and Russo worked with the Twenty-Nine Palms Band to officially form the NALC as a 501(c)(3) nonprofit organization to "protect the endangered plants, animals, and Native homelands." The NALC is an innovative, multi-tribal, multiregional, nonprofit land conservancy formed in 1997 to "protect and preserve sacred landscapes important to Native American people."[15] As of mid-2010, the NALC was working intensively with thirty-two tribal communities from San Diego to the Colorado River, north to Las Vegas and east to the Kaibab Plateau, in addition to developing and maintaining relationships with groups farther afield.[16]

According to Trafzer, the process of getting 501(c)(3) status took longer than usual because the IRS questioned the group's intentions: "The IRS kept thinking that if there is a tribe involved, there must be casinos. On two occasions, we had to explain to them that you have to have federal trust land for a casino, and we had no plans for that. That's not what we are trying to do."[17] Ultimately, the IRS granted the NALC nonprofit 501(c)(3) status, and "we began our process of learning, mostly learning by doing," Trafzer said. The NALC also sought the help of existing land conservancies, including The Nature Conservancy and a successful local wildlands conservancy, and conservation groups, such as the Audubon Society and the Sierra Club, but none showed interest or offered assistance. At the time, the NALC was not aware of the Trust for Public Lands' Tribal and Native Lands Program, which has been instrumental in forming Native land trusts and Native conservation initiatives. The NALC's difficult experience strengthened its commitment to help other Native land trusts and tribes doing conservation projects. "It is very important," Trafzer said. "Indians need to help other Indians—and anyone else who is trying to do preservation."[18]

Even after they formed the NALC to serve as a new instrument for obtaining and setting aside Native lands, purchasing the Old Woman Mountains parcel was complex because of the five owners with undivided interests. Although the Scouts were willing to donate the property if the others would agree to donate as well, the church in particular wanted to receive some payment for the land. The land was appraised at $200 per acre, and the NALC offered all of the owners $100 per acre on the 2,500-acre parcel, which is remote land with virtually no mineral value but invaluable cultural resources. Each of the heirs accepted the $100 per acre in cash and donated $100 per acre in tax write-offs to the NALC.[19] After eight years of developing agreements and obtaining funding to buy the land, the NALC successfully acquired the Old Woman Mountains parcel in 2002.

Trafzer recognized board member and NALC cofounder Theresa Mike's commitment to the process of negotiating with the church and other parties, even when reaching an agreement seemed nearly impossible. Russo also cited her guidance as foundational to the successful growth of the organization: "As a member of the board of directors, [Theresa's] leadership has been critical for the emergence of the NALC as one of the preeminent intertribal, grassroots, nonprofit organizations dedicated to the acquisition and preservation of Native American sacred lands."[20] It was Theresa who invited Askew to attend the ongoing Cultural Committee meetings, which resulted in the eventual successful acquisition of the land by the NALC and the growth of the NALC as an organization.

Vision

The NALC carefully selects healing landscapes, like the Old Woman Mountains, and then introduces people to them in a specific series of orientations (physical, visual and spatial, emotional, psychological, and temporal) that engage different human senses. These orientations are combined with an introduction to Native stewardship and land ethics, including learning to recognize the visible and invisible (story, song, energetic) elements of a landscape.[21] According to NALC board member Mike Madrigal, the places

NALC works to preserve "have a very deep history," and they are sources of power and strength that Native families have returned to in order to keep their traditions alive.[22]

Askew also came to the NALC with a vision for the Old Woman Mountains parcel, based on his own experience of the land. "This area has a [Native American] history going back over three thousand years. . . . I wanted to bring it back. I'm not Indian but felt it was really important."[23] Askew wanted to see the property become a "symbol of healing" to the Chemehuevi and Mojave peoples and to make it "a functioning asset" for everyone involved.[24] These sentiments fit with NALC's vision and mission to steward healing landscapes, perpetuate ancestral knowledge, and provide educational and cultural experiences in the Old Woman Mountains Preserve.

Governance

Like any California nonprofit organization, the NALC has a Board of Directors with four officers—a president, vice president, treasurer, and secretary. The NALC board began with five Native and non-Native people who were close friends, trusted one another, and "took an interest in leaving a legacy for future generations."[25] The board has grown to more than twelve members, the majority being Native people. There are nine tribes (Cahuilla, Chemehuevi, Kumeyaay, Yakama, Ojibwe, Modoc, Lummi, Wyandot, and Seneca) represented on the board, but members are not appointed by their respective tribal councils. "This is not a political organization at all," Russo explained.[26] However, all of the board members are actively engaged and influential in their home communities.

Not being a political organization sometimes places the NALC in a contested middle ground, in which its members may find themselves actually competing with tribes for specific grants or taking stances on land management that may differ from those taken by neighboring tribal councils. As an intertribal, multicultural conservancy focused on protecting culturally important Native lands, the NALC is also an organization that is not easily categorized by funders and governmental entities. Strategies for addressing these challenges evolve as the NALC continues its work, in which it has been largely successful and well supported by both tribes and non Native entities. When the NALC competes with tribes for federal grants, the organization is clear that it is applying for a specific and distinct category of funding—learning landscapes, for example, rather than the water-quality-monitoring funds a neighboring tribe may be seeking. The NALC is also strategic about which board members it sends as representatives to regional meetings about development, for example. Board members wear multiple hats, as university professors, traditionalists, and business leaders, in addition to their commitment to the principles of cultural conservation. Those with the best combination of roles for specific meetings are sent to represent the NALC.

The diversity of the board means it includes participants who are known in civic, cultural, and business circles and who intimately know the desert landscape. With the participation of both "people of means and people without running water," according to Russo, the NALC Board demonstrates that people from very different backgrounds can work together successfully for a common purpose.[27] Board members join for different reasons but become committed to the organization's vision and offer their skills and resources to serve the NALC. Cross-cultural communication occurs at every board meeting. For example, Russo described a presentation by board member Matthew Leivas Sr., a leader of the Salt Song Project, who explained the images on a rock in the Old Woman Mountains:

> He took them on a journey, a lucid dream—he is gifted at that. Some of the non-Native people [who] were fortunate enough to be there get a glimpse into the power of oratory that most non-Natives only read about or get a glimpse of peripherally. They get excited about a tradition that is trying to be preserved through these places—they really get it, they develop a passion. The Native and non-Native [board] members trust each other to share what they know. These are cultural encounters.[28]

It is part of the NALC's strategy to include non-Native Board members, so that it becomes an organization that bridges Native and non-Native understandings of place and can therefore make a case for why all people should care about sacred-site preservation.

The NALC board does not work entirely by either consensus or hierarchical decision making; instead, they rely on a hybrid structure that incorporates elements of both. The board has navigated conflicts successfully since its founding eleven years ago, with one fundamental issue revolving around a sense of comfort with risk taking. "Some of our board members were very cautious—risk averse—and others felt 'no risk, no reward,'" Russo explained. In one instance, the NALC had $140,000 in the bank and the board was contemplating dedicating $100,000 of it to acquiring a parcel that needed protection. If the deal went well, the NALC would get its money back; if not, the money would be gone. In the end, the NALC took the risk and eventually got its money back—with interest. Discussing whether or not to take this risk "resulted in some disputes," according to Russo. "People didn't get mad and storm out, but it was up for debate."[29] All board members agree on the importance of the NALC and its goals, but they have differing opinions about how much risk to take to reach those goals. Russo noted that there are two spheres in which decision making occurs: board meetings and board relations, or informal communications between board members. Issues are generally aired out at meetings, and then worked out privately in board relations.[30]

Fundraising

The diversity of the board leads to eclectic fundraising strategies that also serve to educate and energize participants. "We are a Native Conservancy that has golf tournaments and fashion shows to raise money," Russo remarked.[31] Although people do not necessarily come to these events with a passion for Native rock art and desert tortoises, they may leave with an understanding of their importance. Each fundraiser features presentations on the culturally important desert landscapes that the NALC is working to raise funds to protect. The December 2009 golf tournament netted the NALC $40,000, and the 2010 fashion show brought in an additional $45,000. These funds will be used for land acquisition through the NALC's Land Endowment Fund and to provide scholarships for Native American college students through its Theresa A. Mike Scholarship Fund.[32]

The NALC works on a task-force basis, addressing particular lands, groups, fundraising strategies, and other efforts as a group. The NALC is nontraditional, in that it has no full-time staff or office. With little overhead, the funds the organization raises to fulfill its mission go primarily to projects: "We don't spend our money on the organization. . . . We want to spend our money on the purpose of the organization."[33] This non-bureaucratic approach focuses on getting the greatest benefit from the least resources. The board has met at the facilities made available by its members, such as meeting rooms in the casino complex of the Twenty-Nine Palms Band of Mission Indians. However, as the organization expands and takes on more projects, it may need a modest office, and board members are exploring how to balance this with continuing the NALC's project-based focus: "We've been going now for ten years, and we are talking about finding a permanent home—a presence and a place of our own that we can invite people to and perhaps do some interpretation."[34] Russo has been successful in acquiring grants to support the NALC's land conservation work, and the organization is working to raise money to host a conference on Sacred Landscapes in Santa Fe, New Mexico.[35]

Conferences

The NALC organizes large conferences focused on sacred-lands preservation, bringing together tribal, government, and community stakeholders. The conferences are prime opportunities to brainstorm about projects and strategies; direct attention to specific lands and constituencies; and build networks for collaborations, fundraising, and organizational development. When the NALC was in the process of negotiating the purchase of the Old Woman Mountains parcel, they organized a high-profile conference highlighting all of the people—including landowners—who were helping the NALC to obtain this land. Russo felt that the conference was "one of several factors" that persuaded the church (one of the last of the five landowners to agree to sell the parcel to the NALC).[36]

The 2006 Sacred Lands Conference was held in San Diego, as a means to help grow the Kumeyaay-Diegueño Land Conservancy (KDLC). Among other parties, the NALC invited the National Park Service (NPS). At the Conference, the NPS and the Kumeyaay-Diegueño Conservancy were able to meet, and when the NALC and the Kumeyaay-Diegueño Conservancy later applied for a grant from the NPS, it was funded.[37] The first KDLC executive director, Louis Guassac, reflected that the conference was helpful in that it presented the funding sources that might be available to the conservancy once it was operational.[38]

The 2008 conference, entitled "Lifeways and Landforms: Stewarding Sacred Lands," was held in Boulder, Colorado, to bring attention to the efforts of the Valmont Butte Heritage Alliance. Russo described all of the NALC's conferences as issuing from this question: "What can we do and how do we do it in an ingenious way that leads to the ultimate growth of the effort?"[39] This effort is the NALC's broader vision to see "indigenous land conservancies from the Pacific Ocean to the Colorado River."[40]

Project Strategies

The NALC is a Native nonprofit with a history of successfully owning and managing land. It can leverage that identity to assist other groups with land acquisition. The NALC helps those groups to raise funds, or it temporarily holds land until the group attains the nonprofit status and funds needed to assume ownership. The NALC maintains a $100,000 land endowment, and "in the event that an organization is moving along and it wants to get a traditional cultural property, it is possible that we might use some or all of that money to help with that."[41] The NALC may loan the organization the money to purchase land, but, more often, the NALC offers to hold the land for an organization and help the organization grow its capacity. According to Russo, "We can't buy it for you, but we can work with you to get the money."[42]

Organizations like the Kumeyaay-Diegueño Land Conservancy, the Valmont Butte Heritage Alliance, and the Maidu Summit may form partnerships with the NALC, drawing on the latter's expertise and reputation to do successful fundraising, land acquisition, and stewardship planning. The strategies to accomplish land acquisitions vary by location and situation. For example, the NALC now holds title to a 37-acre historic site near San Diego, while the KDLC awaits the granting of its nonprofit status, at which time the land will be transferred from the NALC to the KDLC.[43] Russo encourages Native groups to trust the NALC as a partner. "There is no hidden agenda here," he explained.[44] The NALC is guided by a desire to leave a natural and cultural legacy for future generations.

The NALC board also tries to build partnerships across cultures and lifestyles with individuals and groups that are not part of the organization. For example, the board is working to build communication with the Off-Highway Vehicle (OHV) community that utilizes the area in and around the landscapes the NALC is trying to protect. Engaging this community in the NALC's projects, goals, and efforts will help the NALC to protect sites that are too distant to be monitored on a daily basis. The NALC's 2009 conference included the participation of the Off-Road Business Association, as well as environmental, civic, military, and various Native stakeholders.

Project Management

Old Woman Mountains Preserve

After an extended period of planning and negotiation with partners, including the National Fish and Wildlife Foundation, the philanthropic community, the Bureau of Land Management, and several Southern California tribes, the NALC purchased the 2,500-acre parcel in the Old Woman Mountains. The Old Woman Mountains are known for *bajadas*, or "shallow slopes that lie at the base of rocky hills, where materials accumulate from the weathering of the rocks."[45] These materials create a base of soil that hosts diverse desert plants. Springs also help support an array of wildlife, including bighorn sheep, mule deer, coyotes, and desert tortoises.[46] The land's faunal and floral diversity, as well as its archaeological sites and cultural importance, caught the attention of funders and supporters who helped the NALC to acquire the parcel. In January 2004, the U.S. Fish and Wildlife Service (USFWS) announced a $217,000 grant to the Twenty-Nine Palms Band to support the NALC's purchase. According to USFWS Tribal Liaison Scott Aiken, as quoted in a local paper, "For the tribes, it is more than just experiencing nature. It is just a natural, living church there."[47]

In cooperation with the San Bernardino County Museum and the Sweeney-Granite Mountain Research Station, and with funding from the U.S. Fish and Wildlife Service, the NALC completed the first comprehensive inventory of the plants and animals in the preserve—including developing an extensive ethnobotanical manual. Based on this inventory, the NALC developed an Adaptive Management Plan, which includes a comprehensive assessment of "what should be there, what is there, and how to monitor for the protection and enhancement of native plants and animals," said Russo.[48]

The NALC is also providing educational programs, including fellowships from the Theresa A. Mike Scholarship Fund, and the NALC has published a book, *In the Land of Three Peaks: The Old Woman Mountains Preserve*, on the unique aspects of the Old Woman Mountains preserve and the organization's actions to protect it. This is the flagship project of the NALC, in terms of acquisition and protective management and efforts to provide healing and learning landscapes. To protect and monitor the site, the NALC has hired Askew, the landowner who initially proposed the sale of his parcel to a Native organization.[49]

Askew has lived in the desert for most of his life and intimately knows the Old Woman Mountains. NALC pays him to protect the site three days per week. When people illegally ride off-road vehicles or target shoot, Askew does everything he can to change their way of seeing the desert. "He has a passion for protecting rock art," Russo explained.[50] Askew knows the cultural resources on the site are irreplaceable, and he is also aware of how quickly they can be destroyed: "We have to have someone available to educate people who don't understand how to be good stewards of the land . . . for eighty years my family has been a steward and watch guard of the property. . . . [The land] has a rich history that is unbelievable."[51] The NALC recently received a letter from some archaeologists who met Askew when they went to the site to look at the petroglyphs. According to Russo, the archaeologists "didn't know of any other preserve in the country that could actually protect these places" the way Askew and the NALC are protecting the Old Woman Mountains site.[52]

Cahuilla Historic "Fish Traps" Site

The NALC worked with the Trust for Public Land, Anza Borrego State Park, and the Torres Martinez Tribe to raise $4 million to purchase a 4,000-acre

Cahuilla historic site on the Salton Sea in Southern California. Preserving this site fits within a larger land ethic, as articulated by Katherine Saubel (Cahuilla): "I remember we were told as youngsters that you never destroy plants around you, or trees around you, or rocks around you. They are alive, that is where you get your energy, from all these things around you. So, you don't destroy all these things. That's what we were told."[53] This particular site consists of former shoreline land to ancient Lake Cahuilla, including rock arrangements that archaeologists have identified as fish traps. At one time, Lake Cahuilla was larger than the Salton Sea, 100 miles in length and 40 miles wide.

According to William Madrigal, Jr., an NALC site monitor who is training to be an archaeologist and who works to protect the traps, when the Colorado River delta would periodically fill with silt, water was diverted inland, raising the level of Lake Cahuilla until it became a giant sea that stretched from the present-day cities of Indio and La Quinta in the Coachella Valley into Mexico. According to both oral histories and archaeological evidence, this has happened three times since 900 AD. The sea would take twelve to twenty years to fill and sixty years to evaporate. Lake Cahuilla was last full in 1600 AD, and the fish traps, fire pits, and trails are reminders of this and earlier times. As Benjamin Spillman reported in a local paper, "They're evidence of an ancient lake where the earliest residents of the Colorado Desert hauled in catches that would have included razorback suckers and bonytail chub. . . . Visiting the fish traps—pointed rock arrangements where tribal people may have herded fish—it is easy to envision the shoreline. Shells dot the ground and many rocks still sport a layer of tufa, a hardened lime deposit that forms along freshwater shorelines."[54]

The NALC initially contacted the Trust for Public Land about preserving the site, and TPL granted funds to an archaeological conservancy to purchase 360 acres. In 2005, the conservancy had an option to purchase the remaining 4,000 acres, which it then planned to transfer to the Anza Borrego Desert State Park.[55] The NALC helped to raise the money to assist the archaeological conservancy and TPL to buy and transfer the site. A Memorandum of Understanding (MOU) between the State Park, the NALC, and the Torres Martinez Desert Cahuilla Tribe accompanied the land transfer and detailed how to ensure protection of cultural resources. If the state, as the landowner, does not abide by the MOU, the NALC is empowered to ensure that the conditions of the MOU are enforced.

The NALC received a $50,000 grant to initiate a stewardship effort to begin site monitoring, and all but $2,000 of these funds went directly to the Torres-Martinez Desert Cahuilla Indians to implement the project.

The MOU delegates monitoring and protective management to the tribe, under the general oversight of the NALC, which serves as fiscal agent for the grant.[56] The most pressing concern is the threat of incursion by OHVs, which can cause long-term damage to the landscape and destroy the fragile archaeological resources. As of October 2009, partners were working on a general plan outlining the archaeological and cultural resources and how to preserve them.[57]

Horse Canyon

Horse Canyon, located in the Santa Rosa Mountains east of San Diego, California, includes a Cahuilla village site. The 1,600-acre area was slated for a housing development, but the NALC raised $100,000 and worked with the California State Parks and the Anza Borrego Foundation to purchase the land and transfer it to the State Parks. A MOU between the Cahuilla people and the State Parks accompanied the land transfer and detailed how to manage cultural resources on site. "We midwife these processes," said Russo. "We step in with money and leverage it to protect sacred lands."[58] On April 9, 2005, the NALC, the Anza Borrego Foundation and Institute, and Cahuilla community members held a lecture, dedication ceremony, and reception to celebrate their joint acquisition of Horse Canyon.[59] The Cahuilla people, the State Parks, and the NALC worked together to develop a plan for how the cultural resources will be managed.

NALC Partnerships

Salt Song Project

The NALC is working with the Cultural Conservancy and Chemehuevi and Paiute traditionalists on the Salt Song Project, a unique collaboration to help preserve the Salt Songs and their landscape. The NALC's specific role is to help provide protective management of the Salt Song Trail, which includes sites associated with these traditional songs that tell the story of the landscape from the perspective of the region's indigenous peoples.

According to a 1998 interview with Chemehuevi elder Gertrude Leivas, the Salt Songs issue from a cave on the Bill Williams River, where two sisters camped and learned the songs. The sisters then travelled down the Bill Williams to the Colorado River, up to the Point Mojave area, over to Mineral Peak and then Hualapi Valley, then across the Colorado River and down to Las Vegas, where they parted ways. One sister went to the Northern Paiutes, and the other went south, near the Old Woman Mountains, then to Twenty-Nine Palms, and on south to the area of present-day Blythe.[60] In

FIGURE 5.1. Southern Paiute elders work on the Salt Song Trail map. The map is available through The Cultural Conservancy Web site at www.nativeland.org. (Photo courtesy of Philip M. Klasky)

his introduction to the Salt Song recordings, Chemehuevi leader Matthew Leivas explains: "The Salt Songs tell about the different sacred sites on the thousand-mile journey . . . visiting all the sacred sites. . . . It explains the whole history of our people and the connections we have with the elements."[61] NALC board member and California Native American Heritage Commission legal counsel Anthony Madrigal (Cahuilla) refers to these connections with the elements as "cultural sovereignty," or the sovereignty that issues from culture and tradition, rooted in relationship to land and all beings. "This sovereignty has successfully guided tribes and Native people in their independent existence since their beginnings,"[62] he writes, and this sovereignty is reflected in the continuing relationship tribal members have to the Salt Songs and the lands along the Salt Song trail (fig. 5.1).

As Gertrude Leivas' account noted, the Salt Songs include parts of the Old Woman Mountains. The NALC's approach to conserving these mountains includes preserving the active cultural practice of the songs: "The NALC is leading the way toward a nexus of cultural preservation and environmental protection and the recognition of the intimacy of human relations with the landscape in a way that is designed to promote biological and cultural diversity."[63] At a recent NALC educational event for Native youth in the Old Woman Mountains, the young people were given the opportunity to hear and participate in some of the traditional Salt Songs and Bird Songs. As Russo described:

> [We do] ethnohistory learning during the day, [and] at night [we are] by the fireside, and the singers are singing songs from that rock, for three hours, incredible songs, and every one of those youth were singing the songs. One youth turned to me said, "I don't understand what I'm singing, I don't know these songs," and Matt Leivas explained to him, "These songs find you." We will be doing four such educational events with youth next year. They are not just good for the youth and the elders, but [they are] good for the rock too.[64]

Protecting the Old Woman Mountains and other sites described in the Salt Songs, and educating Native youth and others about their importance, are central to preserving the unique understandings of the Chemehuevi, Mojave, Paiute, and other tribes in the region.

The Cultural Conservancy began recording the Salt Songs in 2001, at the request of Chemehuevi traditionalists led by Matthew Leivas and Vivian Caron Jake. Leivas grew up on the Colorado River Indian Reservation and began learning the songs in 1992. The songs reveal a cultural and spiritual connection to numerous sites in a large circular area that encompasses parts of Southern California, Arizona, southern Utah, and western Colorado. The singer begins when he or she is travelling through the landscape. Madrigal describes: "[Traditionalists] begin a sing at dusk and will often sing all night. During the sing, the Song travels up the Colorado from the Bill Williams fork, north to Las Vegas, arriving there about midnight and continues delineating Chemehuevi territory, eventually arriving back at the Colorado River by dawn."[65] The songs link all thirteen bands of the Southern Paiute, or Nuwuvi, people. According to Leivas, "the songs show the connection and share our duty and obligation to protect Mother Earth."[66]

The plan to work with the NALC to preserve the areas in the songs as a Salt Song Trail issued from the recording project with the Cultural Conservancy's Storyscape Project, which focuses on preserving indigenous cultures and lands. The Cultural Conservancy and activist-educator Phil Klasky began it in 1998, following Klasky's ongoing work with the Chemehuevi, Quechan, Cocopah, and other tribes to stop the proposed nuclear waste dump at Ward Valley.[67] Klasky and the Conservancy researched traditional Mojave songs to assert the traditional territorial boundaries and significance of the site proposed for the waste storage. As Nelson recalled, "From that important environmental justice work, it became even clearer that the documentation of Native stories and songs is an important way to lay claim to ancestral lands."[68] When the Cultural Conservancy does recording and documentation, all intellectual property rights and the rights to the recordings remain with the traditional singers.[69]

The Salt Songs that the Conservancy has been collaborating with traditionalists to record are "oral maps" that knowledgeable listeners can follow through the landscape.[70] The singers are collaborating with the Cultural Conservancy and the NALC as part of a larger vision to protect the ecology and culture of their homeland: "Our goal is to make the connection between cultural preservation and environmental protection and to promote the relationship between cultural and biological diversity."[71] Singers from the thirteen bands of Nuwuvi (Southern Paiute and Chemehuevi) participated in the recording of the Salt Songs. They travelled from Arizona, California, Nevada, and Utah to sing and record their songs with Nelson and Klasky. The songs are extremely important, both because they describe the ancient landscape and because of their contemporary significance for the land's and the people's present and future.[72]

Storyscape Project Director Klasky created a map of the lands the Salt Songs travel through, and the goal is to preserve sites and establish access and use easements along this trail. Using cultural conservation easements, access and use easements, and direct land acquisition, singers could begin to restore traditional migration and harvesting cycles. This is the long-term vision of the collaboration between the Cultural Conservancy, the NALC, and the traditionalists.

The partnership between the Cultural Conservancy and the NALC began as early as 1999, when Dean and Theresa Mike invited Cultural Conservancy Executive Director Melissa Nelson to participate in planning meetings to form the NALC. Nelson calls the NALC "a perfect model of local tribes developing their own Native land trust for sites within their traditional territory and [for] collaboration with other tribes in the area."[73] As the NALC worked to obtain the Old Woman Mountains, the Cultural Conservancy was supportive, in part helping to coordinate the participation of Paiute Salt Song singers to sing to the cultural sites in the mountains. The Cultural Conservancy was impressed by the NALC's unique approach to "maintain[ing] [the Old Woman Mountains] as an eco-cultural preserve [and] healing landscape—a great concept that is unusual [in the] mainstream land trust movement."[74]

The Cultural Conservancy itself is a nontraditional "land trust" organization, because despite the term "Conservancy" in its name, it has chosen to not hold lands. Nelson described this position as an ethical stance that the organization took in the face of requests to hold lands for tribes and Native communities. Instead, the Cultural Conservancy focuses on documenting the cultural importance of the lands. It uses this information, along with the conservation and legal expertise of board members, staff, and affiliates, to negotiate the transfer of lands to Native entities. The Cultural Conservancy takes a firm stance regarding honoring the sovereignty of tribes and Native communities. As Nelson explained: "These are their lands, and they hold [them]. We won't be a third-party landholder. Preserving the cultural connection of the land underlies the ability to acquire the land . . . making that argument is so important."[75] However, the Cultural Conservancy also recognizes the importance of developing organizations that can hold lands temporarily or permanently for Native entities, when that is necessary.

When Nelson started working at the Cultural Conservancy in 1993, the organization, then led by Patricia (Claire) Cummings, was already pioneering the concept of cultural conservation easements. According to Nelson, Cummings developed private cultural conservation easements between Native communities and timber companies that owned northern California lands with sacred sites.[76] For the Cultural Conservancy, a cultural conservation easement simply applied the concept of "rare or endangered habitat or ecological value" to rare cultural value, which could take the form of an archaeological site or a place in a creation-story song or in oral history.[77] In the early 1990s, Nelson and Cummings began presenting the concept of easements for cultural purposes at the largely non-Native annual Land Trust Alliance (LTA) rallies. Nelson remembered this work as "a real uphill battle": it was difficult both to convince land trusts of the significance and importance of working with tribes and to build Native communities' trust in land trusts.[78] The two women began by building relationships between supportive individuals in land trusts and in tribes, but when either of these individuals left their positions, the larger alliances between the organizations and tribes tended to disintegrate. Cultural private conservation may have been an idea just slightly ahead of its time.

The lands sung of in the Salt Songs face numerous contemporary threats from OHVs, miners, vandals, and others. The traditional singers would like to see a protected area, with a learning center offering information on the Salt Songs, the attributes of the lands, and the need to protect them for contemporary and future cultural and natural well-being: "Now how on earth do you protect a song? By buying a place? By having an organization, electing a board? How do you protect a song when it's a part of an entirely differ-ent social imaginary? That's the challenge. Because it's not about economic growth, it's not about capitalism, it's not about ownership."[79] The NALC is working with the tribes participating in the project, including Chemehuevi and Paiute traditionalists, and the Cultural Conservancy, to help raise public awareness of these irreplaceable cultural sites and areas.

As Russo explained: "In order to protect the cultural resources associ-ated with the Salt Songs, you have to make a different map of the world. . . . There is a way the Salt Songs define the territory, not the reverse. You can't understand the territory unless you understand the Salt Songs."[80] Mapping the Salt Songs is part of the Cultural Conservancy's purpose of document-ing cultural importance in order to support acquisition. The NALC can use the map both to prioritize sites for protection, in collaboration with Chemehuevi and Paiute traditionalists, and to make an even greater case to outside funders, developers, and landowners regarding the importance of preserving these lands.

The Kumeyaay-Diegueño Land Conservancy

The Bands of the Kumeyaay Nation are working to establish a Kumeyaay-Diegueño Land Conservancy (KDLC). Over thousands of years, Kumeyaay honed a complex and sophisticated system of hunting, fishing, and horti-cultural stewardship across their desert, riparian, and coastal homelands.[81] Following a history of dispossession, resistance, and survival, Kumeyaay now live in thirteen bands in San Diego County and four in Baja Califor-nia. When California became a state in 1850, its boundary cut "through the heartlands" of Kumeyaay territory, which lies on both sides of the U.S.–Mexico Border.[82] Following the Senate's silent rejection of the 1852 treaties of Temecula and Santa Ysabel, settlers continued to appropriate Kumeyaay lands and to actively resist any federal government efforts to establish Kumeyaay reservations. In 1875, inland Kumeyaay were expelled from their ancestral homes, and President Grant responded by setting aside 52,400 acres for Indian people in San Diego County.[83] Currently, there are about 20,000 Kumeyaay descendants in San Diego County, which has more reservations than any other county in the United States.[84]

The KDLC seeks to preserve sacred lands throughout San Diego County and 60 to 70 miles south into Baja California. This area of interest embraces the traditional Kumeyaay lands as they were when the Span-ish first landed in present-day California.[85] The eastern boundary of the proposed Kumeyaay-Diegueño Land Conservancy would touch the west-ern boundary of the NALC's area of interest. In order for the KDLC to advocate for preserving Kumeyaay lands, they had to first define the extent and boundaries of Kumeyaay territory. Although the Kumeyaay know the extent of their homeland, "from a Western point of view, people were always asking us 'where is it written down,'" according to Louis Guassac, board member of the KDLC.[86] In response, Kumeyaay elders worked with researchers to examine archived journals of Spanish missionaries. The missionaries had carefully noted where language and culture changed as they traveled through Southern California seeking converts. The researchers' and elders' work resulted in a Kumeyaay-Diegueño map of aboriginal territory, which extends from the ocean through the mountains and into the desert.

For the Kumeyaay people, colonization introduced forced labor at the missions, genocide at the hands of incoming settlers, land seizures by the state and individuals, the introduction of disease, and the institution of boarding schools that served to divest Indian people of their culture and identity.[87] Recognizing that centuries of colonization had separated Kumeyaay groups—even those on the same side of the border—from one another, the member Bands of the Kumeyaay Nation organized the Kumeyaay-Diegueño Unity Bands. At these meetings, Kumeyaay-Diegueño tribal leaders had an opportunity to discuss issues of importance to all of the bands. The idea for the KDLC grew out of these meetings. So far, eight Kumeyaay bands have signed on to the KDLC. In both vision and action, the effort to form the KDLC is one of restoration—of culture, nationality, and relationships among people and between people and the land.

By obtaining and setting aside lands throughout their ancestral homeland for tribal use, the KDLC is reclaiming the Kumeyaay homeland and Kumeyaay knowledge and relationships to the diverse landscape. They will also be learning from one another across the modern U.S.–Mexico border—because Kumeyaay on each side have had very different experiences. For example, the Kumeyaay on the Mexican side were not subjected to the Native American boarding school system.[88] The two groups—which are really one people—speak the same language, with some dialectical differences. They are furthering their customary affinal ties as they work together on the KDLC.

The KDLC is proceeding with its organizational development at a pace in harmony with the will of its members. The fires that scorched San Diego County in 2007 interrupted this process. Now that tribal communities are recovering, the conservancy is back to work formulating its 501(c)(3) status. It currently enjoys a productive protégé relationship with the NALC. Thus far, the NALC has helped the Conservancy to apply for nonprofit status, form a board, acquire grants, and develop a strategic vision. As a result, the Kumeyaay-Diegueño Land Conservancy now has a board of directors, with an elected chairperson, vice chair, and secretary, and an acting executive director. The KDLC received nonprofit status in summer 2010.

Influenced by their cultural ties with the Kumeyaay and Dieguño, the NALC board members made a formal decision to work with the KDLC. This also clearly fit with the NALC's mission to assist other tribes and tribal communities with establishing land conservancies. Additionally, the Kumeyaay and Dieguño live in one of the most rapidly developing areas in the country, so it is particularly important to the NALC that it work to preserve the region's numerous natural and cultural heritage sites. These sites are critical to the identity and ancestral knowledge of these peoples.

Working in partnership with the KDLC, the NALC received a gift of a 37-acre parcel in Julian, California, a site that is significant for its contemporary and historic cultural value. The former owner of the site, Francis Mosler, willed that the property be provided to a nonprofit that would steward the land and asked that the Kumeyaay apply as one of several groups that might receive the land and $250,000 in accompanying funds. The NALC filed in partnership with the KDLC, as the KDLC was not yet a nonprofit. The title was transferred to the NALC for the KDLC in June 2009, and as of August 2010, the NALC was in the process of transferring the property and the funds to the nonprofit KDLC.[89] The KDLC plans to use the property to inaugurate a Kumeyaay learning landscapes program. The NALC is partnering with KDLC to raise additional funds for this cultural enrichment program.

In addition to the Julian property, the KDLC has also acquired 42 acres of the sacred mountain of Kuuchamaa (also known as Tecate Peak), which is central to Kumeyaay cosmology.[90] Although the top of the peak is recognized as a sacred site by the National Park Service, the many cultural sites located just below the peak were not protected. The KDLC will work to preserve and protect the cultural value of this landscape for present and future generations. The KDLC has been developing and distributing public information about its activities. As of summer 2010, the organization was finalizing a brochure containing information on both the Julian and Mt. Kuuchamaa properties, as well as a brief history of the KDLC and an outline of the organization's five-year strategic plan.[91]

The aboriginal territory of the Kumeyaay people is a vast and varied landscape that remains, to the present day, a source of identity for Kumeyaay-Dieguño communities. The board members of the KDLC, like those of the NALC, understand the challenge of protecting, conserving, and enhancing this landscape as a source of cultural continuity and enrichment.[92] They acknowledge that the long-term success of their endeavor will ultimately rely on the strength, perseverance, patient resolve, and resilience of the people throughout the Kumeyaay Nation.[93]

They also understand the importance of the Native land conservancy as a new tool for providing protective management for lands that are culturally and spiritually important to the Kumeyaay Nation.[94] Although commonly understood as multiple political and governmental units within a larger ethno-linguistic group, the Kumeyaay affinal communities are also related to each other through the landscape and by ancestral knowledge. According to Russo, who has been supportive of the KDLC's formation: "For these communities, their territory is a collective learning landscape and a framework for identity that resonates with ancestral knowledge, which contains ancient and time-tested understandings of the natural world. This 'ethnoscape' represents a learning landscape that can be used to transfer indigenous knowledge across generations, connecting people to the land and, through the land, to each other."[95]

Native American Land Conservancy: What Makes It Work?

The NALC is guided by a "belief in the power of vision married to intentional action," as Russo explained.[96] Organizational leaders realize that either action or vision alone is insufficient. By working with tribal leaders and elders, the NALC tries to bring these two elements together in each of its projects. For example, in its collaboration with the Salt Song singers, the NALC begins with the singers' strong vision for preserving the sites described in the songs. The NALC accompanies this vision by trying to organize events and take other actions that will help the singers to preserve the sites: "Everything we've done—from Horse Canyon to the Old Woman Mountains, to the Fish Traps—started as a vision, and NALC proposed very specific actions, and there are tangible outcomes."[97] The NALC shares its vision for protecting cultural landscapes in a way that attempts to reach the hearts of its constituents. Russo described a recent encounter with a Bureau of Indian Affairs employee, who came to an NALC event with a prepared speech, but he was so moved that he stood up and spoke extemporaneously about his grandmother's teachings on "lessons, learning, and the land" and how, for him, those teachings mirrored his understanding of the efforts of the NALC.[98]

The NALC is deeply committed to reaching out beyond cultural borders, as "experience shows that no one group or sector can protect the land," according to Russo.[99] The NALC builds cross-cultural and multisectoral partnerships between tribes, conservation groups, public agencies, private landowners, and the philanthropic community, in the general public interest of preserving endangered landscapes that are culturally and biologically rich. These partnerships build toward a goal of finding creative ways to meet tribes' needs to acquire, protect, and steward culturally, environmentally, and spiritually important sites.

In order to be an effective partner, the NALC has legal and technical expertise in its board members and independent contractors. Specifically, the board includes two lawyers, three historians, Native and non-Native traditionalists, businesspeople, civic leaders, and other people with strategic development and planning skills. The legal, organizational, and professional skills of these individuals help the NALC initiate and sustain successful land transactions and draft functional memorandums of understanding and governing and management documents. NALC board members are volunteers who donate their time to the organization. The NALC executive director is an independent contractor. The NALC also has a site monitor who monitors property the NALC owns. According to Russo: "It is not our goal to create a complex organization. Rather, it is to be in a position to act effectively, efficiently, and economically to address sacred site issues, with the majority of funds dedicated to acquisition, site monitoring, and management."[100]

Because of their challenging experience with forming a Native American land conservancy without any assistance from existing conservancies, NALC leaders underscore the importance of perseverance in working to establish Native conservation organizations: "Kurt and the Mike family . . . they just never gave up. They said, 'it will take time, and we will learn as we go.' You really do have to keep the faith, and believe in what you are doing, no matter how difficult. Just keep moving forward."[101] According to Trafzer, when the NALC was first getting started, they also invited other tribes to collaborate with them or to use the NALC's assistance to initiate projects. However, many of the tribes the NALC approached simply watched until the NALC had successfully brokered projects, like the Old Woman Mountains purchase. Now that the NALC has a proven record of successful projects and partnerships, and it is providing assistance to groups like the Kumeyaay, interest is growing. Trafzer sees this as a very positive development that meets the NALC's mission: "We can use the learning curve that was so hard for us to gain, to help [other tribes and organizations]. We can help them to get started, and [let them] know where to turn to for some help."[102]

To serve this mission, Executive Director Russo wrote the following chapter, on the "nuts and bolts" of how to form and sustain a Native American land trust. Russo's chapter is not meant to re-create the voluminous literature on forming and sustaining successful land trusts, which spans materials listed on the Land Trust Alliance Web site[103] to step-by-step texts, such as the Land Trust Alliance's workbook, *Conservation Easement Steward-ship*[104] and Byers and Ponte's sophisticated *Conservation Easement Handbook*.[105] Russo's chapter is unique because it provides an account of how a specifi-cally Native land trust, with extremely little assistance, managed to grow into a successful organization that is now helping other Native land trusts. Aside from Wood and O'Brien's suggested steps in their in-depth analysis of Native land trust models,[106] there is no how-to literature for Native land trusts. As such, Russo's chapter fills a void and provides a personal account of the NALC's development, with recommendations for emerging Native land trusts.

6

The Art and Science of Creating a 501(c)(3) Native American Land Conservancy

Kurt W. Russo, Executive Director,
Native American Land Conservancy

This chapter covers some of the basic considerations for establishing and maintaining a 501(c)(3) nonprofit, Native-controlled organization dedicated to land conservation. Creating a nonprofit organization is not the only, or always the best, approach for conserving lands important to Native people. It does, however, represent an important tool that is available to the Native American community, and one that has met with a good deal of success in organizations such as the InterTribal Sinkyone Wilderness Council and the Native American Land Conservancy (NALC). Information presented in this chapter draws heavily on the experience of the NALC, an intertribal, grassroots organization established in 1998 to acquire, preserve, and protect Native American sacred lands.

The topics covered in this chapter include the steps involved in applying for 501(c)(3) status, developing a board of directors, cultivating conservation financing readiness, positioning the organization, and engaging in a partnership process. The material represents a general introduction to each of these topics, and it is designed to help groups understand some of the basic challenges and opportunities associated with Native land conservancies.

Applying for 501(c)(3) Status

There are eight types of tax-exempt 501(c)(3) organizations: charitable, religious, educational, scientific, and literary; those that test for public safety; those that support national and international sports competitions; and those that work to prevent cruelty to children or animals. Many community and economic-development organizations have chosen to classify themselves as educational organizations. Additionally, 501(c)(3) public charities are supposed to receive at least one-third of their support from the general public. However, some organizations find themselves relying heavily on donations from founders or board members, or returning, year after year, to the same foundations or corporations for income, which may not count as "public" support.

Forming a new nonprofit involves two distinct steps. Generally, the organization's founders will need to file articles of incorporation with the appropriate agency in their state (usually the state's Secretary of State). Next, they will need to secure federal income tax exemption by filing the appropriate forms with the Internal Revenue Service (IRS). There are a few basic steps that need to be taken in preparing for 501(c)(3) status:

1. Budgeting for the $500 application fee. Organizations whose gross receipts have averaged, or will average, less than $10,000 per year currently pay $150. Larger organizations pay $500. The IRS announces and may raise the fees each January, so submitting your application late in the year (but before January 1) may have some financial benefit for the organization.
2. Designating a committee of "incorporators," who will be officers responsible for developing by-laws and preparing the other documents for the application.
3. Obtaining a Tax ID number using IRS Form SS4 (Application for Employee Identification Number).
4. Preparing by-laws and articles of incorporation.
5. Submitting IRS Form 8718 (User Fee for Exempt Organization Determination Letter Request).
6. Completing relevant parts 1–4 of IRS Form 1023 (Application for Recognition of Exemption).

Once IRS approves the organization's application, the tax-exempt nonprofit organization enjoys several federal, state, and local income, property, sales, and other tax exemptions. Your tax-exempt status increases your opportunity to receive numerous public and private grants, along with donations from individuals, because contributions are tax deductible to donors. Tax deductions inevitably encourage more individuals, corporations, and foundations to donate to your charitable cause, allowing your nonprofit organization to expand and further develop its activities. A number of corporations and foundations are typically required by their operating rules to donate their funds only to 501(c)(3) tax-exempt organizations, so obtaining tax-exempt status is key to receiving donations. Additionally, tax-exempt status opens doors to low-cost mailing, advertising, and purchasing rates, along with other discounts and preferences.

Creating a Board of Directors

One of the first, and most important, tasks to growing a 501(c)(3) is creating a board of directors and associates of the organization. Building a board is not a matter of luck; it requires careful consideration of what skills and expertise (and personal agendas) prospective board members bring to the effort in relation to the organization's vision and mission. The traditional three "W's" for nonprofit boards include wisdom, work, and wealth, as well as leadership experience and the ability to work as a member of a team. As one example, the board of the Native American Land Conservancy includes Native and non-Native directors with experience in accounting, law, fundraising, and strategic planning, as well as scholars in the field of Native American history. The NALC's Native board members are also familiar with the protocols for working with tribal governments and communities as well as cultivating broad-based contacts in the surrounding community. This breadth and depth of experience and expertise is critical to the success of the organization and its efforts to develop wide-ranging support networks in Native as well as non-Native communities.

The conventional approach to forming a board of directors includes appointing four officers: president (or chairman), vice president (or vice chairman), treasurer, and secretary, with other directors designated as members of the board. The organization's by-laws should describe the roles and responsibilities of these officers and their terms of office, as well as the terms of the other board members. It is also useful to keep in mind the board's three basic responsibilities: to cultivate donors, to donate money, and to hire and fire the executive director. In general terms, the board must not get involved in the administration of the organization. This can easily lead to micro-management and discontinuity of effort, leading to a negative impact on the morale of the organization.

Beyond these basics are other less tangible considerations. Board meetings often resemble a field of negotiation. The framework for the negotiation is the mission and vision of the organization. But the negotiation comes down to the personalities involved and their perspectives on how the organization should best achieve its mission. One of the more important issues is the question of control relative to the mission of the organization and the personalities of the board members. One example, taken from the NALC's experience, is the question of control relative to risk management. There is an old adage that organizations either grow or die. Yet growth cannot be achieved without an element of risk.

As mentioned in chapter 5, a group seeking to acquire a sacred site asked the NALC for a $100,000 loan—a sizeable portion of the conservancy's available financial resources—and it was not clear whether the loan would be repaid. Several board members felt that making the loan was too risky. Others argued that despite the risk, it would advance the mission of the organization. The NALC went forward with the loan, and two years later, the risk taking was rewarded when the land was secured and the loan paid back in full.

The question of control also plays out in the relationships among board members. In most organizations, the president or chairman of the board does not control how decisions are made. Her or his job is to guide and facilitate the discussion, not control it. It is imperative in forming and operating a board that members keep in mind that success is found in organizations in which the individuals—including the president or chairman— recognize that control should not rest in the hands of a few individuals. Far more can be accomplished when no one tries to take control or take the credit. It is crucial that a new board of directors take the time for board development—not only in the early stages but throughout its life cycle. For nonprofit organizations, many and often free opportunities and venues exist for board development. One source of training is the Chronicle of Philanthropy (http://philanthropy.com), which is also an excellent source for monitoring activity in the philanthropic community. There are also groups and organizations that offer these services for a fee, such as the Potlatch Fund in Seattle, Washington. The topics covered during a recent Potlatch training seminar for the NALC board of directors included:

1. understanding a board's life cycle and where the NALC is in terms of its own life cycle;

2. identifying the next steps for the NALC and verifying that these steps are consistent with the board's strategic plan;

3. identifying the differing roles for the board and management in terms of implementing those next steps;
4. clarifying roles for board and staff members;
5. sharing the message with other groups and organizations; and
6. fundraising.

The discussion, facilitated by the Potlatch Fund, included an evaluation of the NALC's strategic plan. Some of the topics, which should be germane to the development of many nonprofit organizations, included:

1. What does the NALC want to have in place in five years? The NALC identified developing a $250,000 endowment, greater internal and external education, expansion of land-acquisition efforts, more full-time staff, an interpretative center, greater board participation, and an enhanced public profile.

2. What are the roles and responsibilities of the board? Members concluded that their roles encompassed developing and enforcing the policies of the organization, sharing networks, raising funds, donating money, and helping to raise the public profile of the organization.

3. What is the ninety-day strategy? Considering its mission and its five-year plan, the board identified some concrete, realistic goals for a ninety-day period. These included updating the Web site, increasing public outreach to the local community, creating a database of donors, finalizing a template of priorities for a broad-based land acquisition strategy, and drafting a succession plan. All are important, but the succession plan is critical for the organization. All too often, a handful of visionaries found an organization but fail to look down the road to the day after their departure. Each board member is responsible for helping to identify successors who will provide continuity for the organization.

4. What are the most enjoyable aspects of being part of the NALC? It is possible for nonprofit organizations' members to take themselves too seriously, and in so doing, lose sight of each other and what brought them together and inspired their initial interest. Although growing a nonprofit is hard work, it should also be enjoyable. In the case of the NALC, the board members revisited their inspiration for being part of the organization and identified five favorite aspects of being part of the NALC: its mission and

vision, its outings to sacred landscapes, meeting with outside groups, board retreats, and learning more about the issue of sacred lands preservation.

Conservation Financing Readiness

Many nonprofits, including the NALC, grow out of informal discussions between a handful of individuals with a compelling vision. The tone and temper of these early stages of the organization's life cycle are conditioned by this overarching vision. In many cases, little thought is given during this initial stage of development to the details of how the organization will fund its activities. Additionally, visionaries often are not experts in fiscal management. As a consequence, when funding is secured, the organization can experience a disturbance in its field of vision. It is critical that the organization take into consideration—early and often—how it will finance its operation.

Three broad areas should be considered in the arena of financial readiness. First is the issue of fiscal control. It is important that someone in the organization be experienced and have expertise in tracking finances. Although this is important throughout the organization's life cycle, it is particularly important during the three-year advance ruling period for a 501(c)(3). Both the board and the staff should be familiar with the fiscal matters of the organization. The responsible officer should review the organization's key financial accounts at least once a month and submit a written summary at the monthly board meeting. Equally important are developing an investment strategy and retaining the services of a legitimate and reliable financial steward to manage the organization's portfolio.

The second consideration is opening doors and creating options for the organization. The key to success is creating a broad base of support within and beyond the immediate community. This means knowing the community and its interests and linking the organization's mission to regional and national networks. Developing these networks is both an art and a science. Like every art form, it requires creative thinking in both identifying networks and gaining their interest and support. The organization needs to tell its story from the inside out, in a narrative that embraces the interests of other groups and organizations. It also involves a careful inventory of other groups and organizations: their mission, areas of interest, their character and personality, and their sources of support.

The third consideration for a land conservancy is developing a financial plan for how the organization will implement a land transaction. The financial plan should map out every step of a transaction and should be an integral part of the organization's broader financial strategy. Every land transaction has multiple elements that need to be taken into consideration. These include but are not necessarily limited to:

1. A description of the project and its importance.
2. The desired rights to be acquired (ownership, easement, and so forth).
3. A desired interim and long-term ownership outcome (land trust, government, or private ownership).
4. An optimal vehicle for protection.
5. Desired sources of funding.
6. Backup sources of funding.
7. A detailed budget.
8. Implementation steps, benchmarks, and timelines.

It is important to consider conventional as well as alternative—and imaginative—fundraising techniques. In the case of the more conventional sources of funds, such as private or public grants, relationships are the key to success. Although it is necessary to write a clear, concise, and compelling grant proposal, that, in itself, is insufficient. It is also important to read about and understand not only the funder's mission and funding priorities but also its overall strategy, past funding history, and the composition of the board. In addition, the governing body of an organization can often be surprised when its members explore the network of contacts that each individual brings to the table. The exploratory process can reveal unanticipated, and oftentimes personal, relationships that connect the governing body to sources of support for the organization.

In addition, the organization should not strictly rely on outside sources. Remember that the philanthropic community is often interested in: (1) the question of long-term sustainability and (2) evidence of a broad-based and creative fundraising strategy. For example, the NALC has two annual fundraising events: a golf tournament and a fashion show. These events not only raise money, they also cultivate new friends, colleagues, and supporters in an ever-widening circle of association.

Positioning the Organization: The Importance of Studying Each Organization's "Case"

In the typical handbook on land conservancies, "positioning the organization" focuses on defining the niche of the organization and its place in the organizational and philanthropic landscape. But it is important to take a step back and broaden the focus, beginning with the question: Why should anyone care about what you care about? Time and money are always in short supply, and there are any number of charismatic organizations with unique and compelling visions. How can an organization position itself to garner interest and support? How can funders tease out the often-subtle connection between the organization's mission and the purpose of a potential source of funds? It all starts with the board of directors knowing their "case." Every board member must carefully critique and wholeheartedly believe in the mission of the organization. They need to be able to convey the organization's passion and, at the same time, be prepared to respond to individuals or organizations that may be skeptical or even openly critical of its vision.

This leads to the second step in positioning the organization: knowing the other person's or group's case. It goes without saying that individuals who fund land conservation care deeply about the land. It is incumbent on every board member to be actively engaged in outreach programs and to know in advance how these other organizations work and what they care about in terms of conservation. For example, a potential funding source might care most about bird habitat. However, it is important to understand not only what they care about but also *why* they care. What is it about wildlife—what is their "case"—that might inspire such an organization to fund a land conservancy whose primary focus is not on wildlife or wildlife habitat? This leads to the third element of positioning the organization: putting your case in their terms.

Take the case of the NALC, whose focus is the protection of Native American sacred lands. Several years ago, NALC applied to the National Fish and Wildlife Foundation (NFWF) for funding to help acquire a Native American sacred site. After reviewing the grant history of the NFWF and consulting with its director, the NALC submitted a grant request that made a case for protecting threatened and endangered species and critical habitat in the context of Native American cultural values as part of a unique ethnoscape. In securing the grant, the NALC not only helped preserve wildlife and promote the protection of a cultural landscape, it also helped educate members of the foundation about the relationship between their case and the NALC's case.

Making your "case" is not a straightforward process. It requires the application of creative thought, a willingness to stand at a critical distance from the organization and see it as outsiders might see it, and enter into their understanding of what your organization cares about. It is a delicate balance, but one that the board and key staff must master.

The Partnership Process

Volumes have been written about the importance of partnerships for the land conservation movement, much of it common sense. Predictably, these works discuss how to identify allies, develop joint board appointments, and share fiscal responsibility. Although all of this is necessary, it is insufficient for cultivating enduring partnerships. Once again, we will take a somewhat different angle of view, emphasizing the importance of the character of different organizational cultures.

As in any relationship, the endings are often in the beginnings, so it is important to start with true and effective communication. This is an especially important topic for Native-controlled land conservancies dedicated to preserving sacred lands and who often work with non-Native groups and organizations. Native land conservancies working with non-Indian groups will invariably encounter a number of critical cultural incidents. This is particularly true when the issue concerns the acquisition and protective management of sacred landscapes signified and sanctified by ancestral knowledge. When compared to non-Native belief systems, the Native view of the land traces back to an entirely different cultural narrative of why and how these lands came to be created, what powers animate the landscape, what constitutes learning and what is knowledge, and what is public or private information. The NALC has been fortunate to work with broad and open-minded groups throughout its history of land acquisition and protective land management. At the same time, the NALC has gone out of its way to impress on these organizations that the nature of "nature" for Native people is not identical with—and may even be contrary to—the conventional Western worldview of it.

One place to approach cross-cultural partnerships with individuals or groups is to use a mental map that depicts potential "domains of dialogue." These domains are presented in a highly simplified form, and they have been used extensively as a growing point for cross-cultural collaboration in the Pacific Northwest.[1]

The best place to start is with what you know, beginning in Domain A. What values do you and your potential partner share, and are you aware that you share them? It might be land preservation in general, or the protection of wildlife habitat in particular. Or it might be the value of strengthening communities and their connection to the land. This is the most fruitful place to begin the dialogue. The next move is to Domain B where, based on your shared awareness of common ground, you can identify ways in which you and your partner are aware of your dissimilarities. On the topic of communities, for example, Native communities are dissimilar from other groups and communities in at least one important way: they are communities of interrelated families that have lived side by side for many generations. That difference is often known, and even admired, by potential partners who come from more temporary and less historic (place-based) communities of common interest.

This avenue of communication opens up a dialogue in Domain C. Although people might have a general understanding that tribal communities consist of interrelated families, they might not know that tribal communities are not homogenous in their values but consist of a wide range of orientations. Compared to their fellow community members, some tribal members can be more individualistic than others, be more accommodating to change, and believe themselves masters of their fate rather than subject to forces beyond their control. Both Native and non-Native communities represent a tapestry of basic values represented by a range of outlooks and attitudes. Making room for difference includes appreciating that variation is the rule, not the exception, for all human groups and groupings.

Domain D is in many ways the most problematic for forming lasting partnerships. For example, tribal societies differ from their non-Indian counterparts in their place-based identity, which, in many cases, traces back to oral histories of Creation. One of the most prevalent obstacles to cross-cultural partnerships is a lack of awareness of the present-day significance for tribal cultures of traditional ways of knowledge (their ancestral "world-making" process). Outside groups often understand these histories as fictional, mytho-poetic stories. For the Native individual or group, however, this body of knowledge contains longstanding, literal truths about the landscape. It is critical that the Native participants understand that their non-Native counterparts and colleagues stand in a very different relationship not only to the past but also to past ways of knowing. In addition, it is incumbent on the non-Native group or individual seeking to partner with Native land preservation conservancies to appreciate this as true knowledge that is critical to the tribe's world-making process.

Conclusions on the Process

Creating and maintaining a Native-controlled process engages a very different world of history, interests, and values. On the one hand, an organization must take specific steps to file for 501(c)(3) status. Its board members and staff also must understand the strict conventions of fundraising and fiscal management. In that sense, we can say that this is a "science," with conventional rules and guidelines. At the same time, growing a nonprofit engages creative talent associated with artistic sensibilities. The act of creating a nonprofit—or being a vehicle for its creation—is a visionary moment and process. Similarly, understanding and taking advantage of opportunities, teasing out connections and relations—or composing them and making them real—is also a highly creative act. Every nonprofit needs a rich mix of talent, orientations, and skills to make it successful.

One of the most important aspects of every nonprofit is identifying, pursuing, and forming a number of partnerships. In doing so, it is sometimes necessary to partner with state or federal agencies that, in the past, have been complicit in the historical oppression of Native peoples. To overcome these barriers and equally significant obstacles, communication is the key— true communication, not one based on false stereotypes. It is our hope that this information might be useful to groups and individuals interested in forming, or working in partnership with, Native-controlled land conservancies. As one NALC board member, Theresa Mike, constantly reminds us in times of stress and uncertainty: "Remember, it's a process. It's all a process."

Collaborations between Tribes and Land Trusts

This section transitions from examining Native American land conservancies to looking at partnerships between tribes and non-Native land trusts. In the following cases, the tribe, a Native nonprofit, an individual, or in some cases, the non-Native land trust owns the land. Regardless of the situation, both the tribe and the non-Native land trust are essential partners to enabling the conservation agreement. Some of the tribes have not yet formed their own Native land conservancies, and others prefer to let non-Native land conservancies hold easements and perform other complementary functions to support their tribal and Native land management priorities.

Some of the agreements discussed in this section are complete and operational, whereas others are in various stages of formation, negotiation, and contestation. In the latter case, the elements being worked out include which parties can perform which actions on the land; which party is responsible for the monitoring and maintenance of the land; and which institutional arrangement is most likely to generate the most fundraising, conservation, environmental compliance, or other benefits.

The cases in this section are from five states in far-flung regions of the nation: Alaska, California, Michigan, North Carolina, and Washington. The cases also cover an array of tribal entities: federally recognized and unrecognized tribes, as well as those petitioning for federal recognition, Native allottees, and informal associations of Native practitioners. This range allows for a productive exploration of how different Native entities might work with non-Native land trusts to achieve mutually beneficial goals.

7

Mitigation of Tribal Development

Yocha Dehe Wintun Nation (California)

The Wintun have lived in and around rural Yolo County in California's Central Valley for thousands of years, stewarding rich landscapes like the oak woodlands and riparian corridors of the Capay Valley. In 1909, the Federal Government established the Rumsey Indian Rancheria of Wintun Indians,[1] creating a designated living area for Native people displaced by the incoming settlers and ranchers. In 1982, the Bureau of Indian Affairs purchased another 118 acres, expanding the rancheria to its present size of approximately 260 acres. This oak grassland is bisected by Cache Creek and largely dedicated to agriculture and grazing.[2]

The Yocha Dehe Wintun Nation recently became one of the nation's leading Native business entities. The tribe runs the popular and successful Cache Creek Casino Resort. The tribe also owns and manages numerous agricultural properties in the rural Capay Valley, totaling 7,300 acres.[3] It oversees real estate development in Springfield, Illinois, and Sacramento, California.[4] In response to California environmental regulations, and local opposition to Capay Valley casino development and expansion, the tribe has embarked on conservation and restoration partnerships with the Golden State Land Conservancy, Cache Creek Conservancy, Yolo County, and other partners. The Yocha Dehe Wintun Nation has gone beyond mitigation requirements for the development and expansion of tribal enterprises by investing a large tract of land in conservation and habitat restoration.

FIGURE 7.1. Whenever possible, established trees are left in place when land is developed. This large oak tree also provides a shady rest area for workers in the newly planted olive grove. (Photo courtesy of Lauren Silva)

Partnerships for Mitigation

Using revenues from tribal enterprises, Yocha Dehe has purchased thousands of acres of farmland in the ecologically and agriculturally rich Cache Creek watershed, which consists of a mosaic of small family farms and larger agricultural operations. The tribe engages in agricultural management, and it enhances habitat for culturally and ecologically significant species (fig. 7.1).

In 2004, the tribe began the environmental review process for locating a new golf course on land near the casino that is partially in tribal fee status and partially held by the Bureau of Indian Affairs (BIA) in federal trust for the tribe. The tribe had to go through a California Environmental Quality Act (CEQA) process to develop the fee land.[5] Analytical Environmental Services, a Sacramento-based environmental consulting firm that focuses on environmental work with tribes, completed the CEQA analysis. As the tribe's environmental consultant, Analytical Environmental Services identifies all of the requirements for permitting and land-use change, and it ensures compliance with environmental regulations, including those of CEQA. The firm fulfills the functions of a tribal environmental department.[6]

FIGURE 7.2. Yocha Dehe Golf Course. (Photo courtesy of Jennifer Kline)

Some of the fee land where the tribe planned to develop the golf course was under the Williamson Act, more formally known as the California Land Conservation Act of 1965. The Act requires that an agreement be reached between the landowner (in this case, the tribe) and the local jurisdiction (Yolo County) to maintain the agricultural use of the property for a designated length of time (ten years, renewed annually) in exchange for a lower property-tax rate.[7] Because a golf course is for a recreational, rather than an agricultural, use, the tribe had to undergo a process with Yolo County and the State of California to remove the land from the Williamson Act (fig. 7.2).

When land is removed from a Williamson Act contract, the Act's easement-exchange legislation (effective January 1998) and CEQA oblige the landowner to mitigate, or substitute, other lands. This requirement can be satisfied by creating a conservation easement on equivalent land of equal or greater size, located within 2 miles of the parcel being converted. The tribe mitigated the golf-course parcel by conserving 314 acres of prime agricultural land. The area planned for the golf course was also designated Swainson's hawk foraging habitat in the environmental review process. This designation required an additional 189 acres of mitigation. Overall, the tribe was required to set aside and manage 503 acres (314 for the Williamson Act removal and 189 for the hawk protection) of mitigation land.

The tribe already owned two large ranches across the street from the casino, totaling 1,321 acres. The parcels consisted of agricultural and pastureland with two creeks, along with one stretch going up from the valley floor into a canyon. The tribe has two wells on the ranches, as well as a drainage basin, both serving the Cache Creek Casino Resort. Since the California Department of Transportation (CalTrans) was in the process of improving Highway 16, which bisects the Capay Valley and is the main artery conveying visitors to the resort, the tribe set aside 77 acres for a CalTrans right-of-way. The tribe also set aside one acre each around each well, and it reserved 20 acres for an area that was a tribally operated equestrian center but is now serving as the headquarters for the tribal cattle operation.[8] The tribe agreed to place the remaining 1,222 acres of ranch land into a permanent conservation easement held by the Golden State Land Conservancy (GSLC). Of that, 189 acres between the creeks at the base of the hills was set aside for Swainson's hawk habitat.

Swainson's Hawk

On the 189 acres designated for the hawk, the tribe is required by the terms of the mitigation and the easement to maintain alfalfa and other dryland-farmed, low-lying crops for the hawk's foraging. They are not permitted to grow orchards or vineyards, as the hawk forages only in habitat consisting of certain crops.[9] The narrow focus of this part of the easement may make it easier to monitor its effectiveness.[10] Reflected in the terms of the conservation easement, the rest of the property combines agricultural land and unimproved rangeland, as determined by the soils, topography, and current farming activities.

Collaboration with the Golden State Land Conservancy

Bob Whitney, president of the GSLC, founded the land trust in 1999 as a specifically "landowner-friendly" organization.[11] It prioritizes conservation for habitat preservation and other environmental values, while simultaneously developing terms that work for landowners. According to Whitney, "We don't advertise or compete. We require endowments to cover the cost of monitoring and enforcing the conservation easement based on our actual cost. Our focus on being 'landowner friendly' does not imply that other land trusts are not, [but] we try to convey to landowners why they might want to do business with us."[12] The GSLC is a member of the Land Trust Alliance, which has developed standards and practices for land trusts across the United States. The GSLC currently holds more than 34,000 acres of conservation easements throughout California.[13]

Analytical Environmental Services coordinated the development of the easement between GSLC and the tribe. The environmental firm had worked with GSLC before, but the tribe had no preexisting relationship with the land trust and had never put land into easements before. The tribe approached the local Yolo Land Trust and the California Rangeland Trust before deciding to work with the GSLC. At that time, individual board members of the Yolo Land Trust did not support the casino's expansion, so the tribe perceived the organization, as a whole, to be unsupportive of the easement project. The tribe was unable to work with the California Rangeland Trust because the grazing operation on site was insufficient to meet that trust's criteria for a ranch under its conservation program. The GSLC was chosen as a partner because it held easements in nearby Mendocino, Napa, Sonoma, and Lake counties, and it had a good reputation with private landowners in the region.[14]

The GSLC was a willing partner, "not for purposes to expand the casino-resort or to conserve rangeland, but to prevent rural land fragmentation, protect productive agricultural lands, and to conserve wildlife habitat and water quality," according to Whitney.[15] Although landowners (including tribes) and land trusts generally agree that it is preferable to work locally, sometimes partnerships for mitigation can be built outside of the area. According to Deborah North, former Interim Executive Director of the Yolo Land Trust, landowners should have a choice about what organization will hold an easement on their property. She noted, "It's in everyone's interest to support efforts that result in the best conservation outcomes."[16] The Yolo Land Trust prioritizes local relationships, and it is working to build a rapport with the tribe to collaborate on future projects.[17]

Analytical Environmental Services did the environmental baseline assessment of the ranches to support the monitoring and enforcement of the conservation easement. This includes identifying existing uses and key riparian corridors and any threatened and endangered species, as well as establishing photo points for yearly monitoring. The tribe granted and the GSLC accepted and recorded the conservation easement on the tribe's fee title land. According to an Analytical Environmental Services employee, environmental consultant Pete Bontadelli, "The net result here is that we have an area the tribe can use beneficially, and we met the environmental requirements for developing the golf course by placing more than sufficient acreage into a permanent easement."[18] The GSLC conducts annual monitoring, including transmittal of a monitoring report to the tribe. Close collaboration with the ranch manager to resolve any issues has been the primary strategy to maintain the ranch's conservation values. In 2009, the GSLC reported that the tribe has initiated substantial ranch road remediation, erosion control, and stream-habitat improvements.

Fee-to-Trust Considerations

All of the ranch land held by the easement is in fee status owned by the tribe, and there are no current efforts to put it in trust. As Whitney noted, "The GSLC felt very comfortable because this is private land, owned by the tribe. But the reality of the world is that things change, and if the land ever went into trust, the easement would be invalid unless the BIA accepted it."[19] With years of experience working in collaboration with California Indian Legal Services in his former role as co-director of the Santa Barbara–based Environmental Defense Center and a staff person with the Santa Barbara Indian Center, Whitney said that if this ever became an issue, he would encourage the BIA to subordinate the trust status to the conservation easement, so that the easement would still hold.[20] According to Bontadelli, although the BIA does not like to take land into trust that has any encumbrance, once land is in federal trust status, tribes can enter into arrangements with other parties that serve the same purposes as an easement on fee land.[21]

Collaboration with Cache Creek Conservancy

The Cache Creek Conservancy is a 501(c)(3) restoration organization, dedicated to stewarding and enhancing the habitat and health of Cache Creek. The conservancy focuses particularly on the stretch of creek from the Capay Dam, just upstream from the town of Capay in Yolo County, to the settling basin where Cache Creek enters the Yolo Bypass and the Sacramento River. The Yocha Dehe Wintun Nation has been collaborating with the conservancy to eradicate exotic species (primarily tamarisk and also arundo) on tribal fee and trust lands bordering Cache Creek in the Capay Valley. The collaboration began with a friendship between former Executive Director of the Cache Creek Conservancy Jan Lowrey and former Rumsey Chairwoman Paula Lorenzo. The two leaders worked together through other organizations and developed a strong working relationship. Although there is no formal written agreement between the tribe and the conservancy, both parties have demonstrated an ongoing commitment to collaborate. The conservancy and the tribe also work together on the Cache Creek Conservancy's Tending and Gathering Garden (see chapter 15).

In 2003, Jan Lowrey, then the conservancy executive director, worked with the tribe to acquire a five-year, $250,000 grant from the U.S. Fish and Wildlife Service to eradicate invasive plants along Cache Creek, particularly tamarisk (also known as salt cedar) and arundo. Although the grant went directly to the tribe, the conservancy served as project manager and collaborated in its implementation.[22] These two plant species are extremely aggressive—they choke out native plants, reduce habitat for local wildlife, and absorb large amounts of water from the soil. Additionally, they are flammable when dry, creating a fire risk in the Cache Creek basin. Tamarisk also excretes salts into the soil, making the land inhospitable to other plant species.

The tribe took the lead on securing the necessary permits from the California Department of Fish and Game for doing nonnative plant removal in the basin. The conservancy manages the on-the-ground species removal by hiring and overseeing a trusted subcontractor that regularly completes restoration work. Methods used to eradicate the species include spraying, biocontrol with the tamarisk leaf beetle (*Diorhabda elongata*) to defoliate the trees, and mechanical removal. Yocha Dehe fee and trust lands also host test sites for tamarisk biocontrol using the beetle, which are starting to show good results.

Working to control invasive species on Yocha Dehe tribal lands is part of a larger, multiparty effort to remove nonnative plant species all along Cache Creek. In 2009, the tribe and the conservancy completed this five-year eradication project, which also included revegetation with native species. In 2010, the tribe's proposal for "Cache Creek Cultural Restoration Project—Phase II" was funded as a three-year project. The conservancy will again serve as project manager and the two parties will collaborate to continue eradication of invasive species and revegetation with native species. Phase II also represents a significant expansion of the project, as it will focus on a newly acquired tribal property just downstream from the golf course.[23]

Conclusion

The Yocha Dehe Wintun Nation has applied conservation tools and partnerships as an exercise of tribal sovereignty over land and resource management. For example, for the initial easement process to mitigate the development of a tribal enterprise, the Yocha Dehe selected a conservation partner (GSLC) and co-designed the terms of the easement to meet both mitigation requirements and its own needs. The result was an easement that goes far beyond mitigation requirements and involves a partnership between the tribe, as a sovereign government, and a regional, nonprofit land conservancy. In the second example given above, the tribe had a goal of habitat restoration along the creek that traverses tribal homelands, so it selected an able conservation partner with which it had an ongoing relationship, and the two parties have raised substantial funds and are working steadily to improve the riparian ecosystem. As these examples show, rather than infringing on tribal sovereignty, conservation easements and partnerships can serve larger tribal land management, cultural preservation, and community development priorities.

8

Senate Bill 18 (Burton) and Mitigation of Non-Tribal Development

Morongo Band of Mission Indians (California)

Morongo Reservation lands in the San Bernardino Mountains of Southern California were set aside by executive orders in 1876 and 1881.[1] Residents are primarily Cahuilla but also include Serrano, Cupeño, and Chemehuevi people.[2] The rolling hills of the reservation contain valuable streams, springs, and grazing lands. The land borders Interstate 10 and lies just 80 miles east of Los Angeles in Riverside County. Over the last twenty years, Morongo has created several economic enterprises that now capture tourists and commuters traveling between Los Angeles and Palm Springs, as well as drawing visitors from out of the area. The tribal government employs more than 3,500 people, and their largest venture is the $250 million, 44-acre Morongo Casino, Resort, and Spa. Another Morongo venture is a 383,000-square-foot water-bottling plant in Cabazon, operated by Arrowhead Spring Water and employing more than 200 people.[3]

Utilizing SB-18: Traditional Tribal Places Law

Morongo Reservation is 32,000 acres in size and located entirely in Riverside County. However, the historic tribal territories of Morongo members cross Riverside, San Bernardino, and Los Angeles county boundaries, so Morongo cultural and environmental personnel must be ready to consult on resource protection in a very large area. In 2004, Senate Bill 18 (introduced by John Burton), hereafter SB-18, mandated for the first time that cities and counties consult with tribes before amending their general plans.[4] SB-18 also designated tribes as one of the entities that can hold conservation easements, giving tribes more tools to protect cultural and natural resources. According to former Morongo Cultural Resources Director Britt Wilson, city and county general plans are extremely important "guideposts for development" in rapidly expanding areas like Riverside County.[5] In 2006, Riverside County was California's second-fastest-growing county.[6]

The SB-18 process in California begins when a general plan or specific plan action is contemplated in an area where tribes have historic and contemporary ties to the land. The project planner at the city or county level sends a letter to the tribes, which typically includes maps, information on any cultural resources surveys, and preliminary development plans.[7] The earlier the planner provides notification, the better, as most tribes are responding to multiple cities, counties, private landowners, and other parties regarding development and cultural resources protection. Morongo encourages cities and counties to impose standard conditions regarding protection of human remains[8] and cultural materials[9] and to engage in further consultation if discoveries are made.

In order to officially consult under SB-18, the resources or the site must be on or be eligible to be on the California Register of Historical Places or be defined as a "Native American sanctified cemetery, place of worship, religious or ceremonial site, or sacred shrine."[10] Morongo has been successful in protecting important sites, and no cities so far have asked the tribe to prove "sacredness," which has been a problem in the courts, as evidenced by the litigation over the San Francisco Peaks (*Navajo Nation et al. v. U.S. Forest Service et al.*, 2007), *Lyng v. Northwest Cemetery Protective Association* (1988), *Bear Lodge Multiple Use Association v. Babbitt* (2000), and other cases involving protection of sacred sites on public lands.

Rio Vista Specific Plan

In the case of a proposed plan for residential development in a hillside area, the SB-18 consultation began in the standard way: a formal letter to the Morongo Band from the project planner at the Riverside County level, and a response from Wilson requesting consultation. Then the planner, Wilson, and a representative from the archaeological firm consulting on the project took a field trip to the site and recorded all of the cultural sites on the property using a Geographic Positioning System (GPS).

The data on the site's location and characteristics were integrated into a Geographic Information System (GIS) map, allowing the project planner and other parties to virtually compare the location of features of the proposed development with cultural sites that need to be avoided. "If you look at the designs, there are ways to redesign to fulfill open-space requirements and resource protection requirements," explained Riverside County Archaeologist Leslie Mouriquand. "In so many cases, it's unnecessary to destroy sites; everyone can come out a winner."[11] The computerized mapping makes it possible to analyze whether or not sites can be preserved *in situ* or need to be relocated onto tribal lands. On this project, many of the features were large and difficult to move, so the options were either to avoid them during construction, partially or entirely remove them from the site, or let them be crushed during the grading process. The tribe offered to remove some of the features to tribal lands for use in cultural interpretation and education.

Following a second field trip and further communication between the tribe and county partners, Mouriquand requested a formal conclusion to consultation, which the tribe approved. She then began to craft the conditions of approval for the development, which included the agreed-upon points for preservation and monitoring of construction.[12] There is no legal mandate under SB-18 to create a formal written agreement between the tribe and the county and, although both parties would prefer one, issues of understaffing and workload make creating it difficult. "A written agreement would be ideal, because it would memorialize in a formal way the agreed-upon negotiations through the SB-18 negotiation process," said Mouriquand.[13] Although consultation on this project became less formal (moving from sit-down meetings to e-mails, phone calls, and site visits) as parties continued to work together, the results are still formally integrated into Riverside County's conditions of approval for the development. As such, the developer cannot proceed without meeting certain requirements, including those reflecting the tribe's interests.

St. Boniface Indian School

A housing development was slated for a parcel containing approximately 100 acres near the historic site of the St. Boniface Indian School, where ancestors of tribal members were forcibly educated during the Indian Boarding School era. On the site, there is a 1- or 2-acre cemetery. The project lies within the City of Banning, California, and SB-18 required tribal consultation with the city. Following notification, the Morongo Band negotiated with the developer for the cemetery and 5 acres of un-buildable land. In total, Morongo got 7 acres back through the SB-18 consultation process. However, with the general decline in the housing market, the building project is not currently moving forward, so the land conveyance to Morongo has yet to be completed.

Desert Dunes

The Morongo Band of Mission Indians and the Agua Caliente Band of Cahuilla Indians have collaborated to ensure protection of archaeological sites in a proposed housing development called Desert Dunes. Although the local jurisdiction (in this case, the county) is supposed to contact the tribe to initiate SB-18 consultation, in this instance, former Morongo Cultural Resources Director Wilson remembered initiating contact: "I became concerned because the site was slated for destruction," Wilson explained. "I contacted the county to ask about the site and that kicked off our negotiations."[14] The project is located in the Desert Hot Springs area near Palm Springs, and cultural resources on-site included polished disks, shells, and projectile points. Initially, the developer's archaeological consultant created a map of the previously recorded areas of the site and overlaid it with the planned housing tract maps so that the development could avoid areas that were important to the tribes. To protect the sites, the cultural resources map was kept confidential. Publicly available maps and other documents merely show the village area as "open space."[15]

Morongo and Agua Caliente negotiated for 5 acres of this "open space" to protect culturally important sites. These lands were selected based on several factors, including the archaeologist's map of known culturally important sites. The size of the area that contained sensitive sites was much larger, but saving 5 acres was a compromise the developer and the tribes could both accept. However, Agua Caliente Director of Historic Preservation Patricia Tuck became concerned when she learned that the entire project area had not been surveyed, creating a potential that unknown resources might exist between the recorded sites.[16] The developer agreed to a full survey. The tribes worked with the archaeologists, and they found several additional sites. As of mid-2010, the county and the tribes were waiting for the developer to select a mutually acceptable archaeologist to evaluate the significance of the newly identified sites.[17] The results of the evaluation will enable County Archaeologist Mouriquand to work with the tribes to determine how the sites should be mitigated.

As with the St. Boniface Indian School area, the decline in the housing market has led to a postponement of the project. However, Riverside

County supports the agreement designating the open space, and it has proposed that this be a condition of approval for the development. The tribe is relying on this county support, since there is no signed agreement with the developer.

Despite the postponement, the county is improving access around the project area, including widening roads and adding sidewalks. Morongo Cultural Heritage Program Coordinator Mike Contreras reported going out on the site in December 2009 with representatives from the county and the Agua Caliente Band of Cahuilla Indians, Ramona Band of Cahuilla Indians, Cabazon Band of Mission Indians, and Torres Martinez Desert Cahuilla Indians. The tribal representatives walked through the roads project with county representatives to make sure "everything was [being] done right" and cultural sites were being protected.[18]

The Process

In each of the above examples, the process for protecting cultural resources under SB-18 required working with the city or county in which the consultation was taking place, as well as directly with the developer. Although SB-18 mandates a government-to-government consultation process with tribes, ultimately, the developer will have to pay for or implement the actions agreed upon during the consultations. According to Wilson, the local government's involvement is still important, because the tribe asks that it place conditions on the project based on the agreements between the tribe and the developer.[19] The local government can also enter into three-party agreements with the tribe and developer to "ensure that the developer does what he says he will do."[20] Morongo has proposed this structure for the St. Boniface Indian School case.

Although SB-18 legislation has raised the awareness of local governments and developers about protecting irreplaceable cultural resources, development is still affecting lands of importance to tribes. The language in SB-18 calls for reaching an agreement between the city or county and the tribe "if feasible." "In a perfect world, Morongo would like the sites totally left alone but that is not always going to happen," said Wilson. "SB-18 is important as a 'first step,' because it requires cities and counties to officially consult with tribes in 'good faith,' giving the tribes a place at the table that they never had before."[21] Although Morongo has had several successes, they have still lost sites and features. For example, Wilson worked on behalf of the tribe to protect sites in an area proposed for a large housing tract. There were five or six boulders with milling features on them within the project area. The boulders were not eligible for the National Register of Historic Places, and although they were important to the tribe, elders did not consider them "sacred." According to Wilson, "Throwing around the 'sacred' word too much can [negatively] impact a site where you truly have a sacred feature, such as rock art or a burial or a ceremonial site."[22]

Each tribe has its own way of prioritizing sites. For the Morongo Band, the protocol usually involves taking a tribal historian or an honored elder to the site, where she or he will determine its importance and the appropriate level of use or protection. In this particular case, the site's lack of designation as sacred or historic place meant no legal mandate for consultation under SB-18 technically existed. In addition, the boulders were scattered throughout the project area, making it inconvenient for the developer to create open space around each one. Morongo requested monitoring around the boulders and the relocation of one of the most clearly marked ones to open space within the development. Wilson also recalled several examples involving other tribes in which the remains of Native people had to be moved for the development. "Tribes have won sometimes, but moving of graves is fairly common [even though it is] . . . offensive to Indian people," Wilson said.[23]

The City of Coachella

In some cases, the Morongo Band and other tribes used "capping" to protect cultural resources from being either pilfered or built on. When developments end up surrounding historic village and other sites, it becomes too easy for children and other local residents to unearth cultural resources, either accidentally or purposefully. In such a situation in Coachella, then–City of Coachella Archaeologist Leslie Mouriquand took the lead in negotiating with the developer to place Ye'wi'vichem Park (which translates from Cahuilla to English as "Ancient Ones") over a historic site. The developer gave up four lots out of 597 to create the park, capped the archaeological site, and made it into open space.[24]

In this case, tribal participation began with the California Environmental Quality Act (CEQA) process, during which the city sends project information to the tribes for review and comment. The sites uncovered by a cultural resources survey made the area eligible for nomination to the National Register of Historic Places. Mouriquand wrote the mitigation measure, following tribal input, and she recommended that the site be capped and made into a public park.

When the developer began work on the park nearly two years later, tribal representatives and Mouriquand reviewed his plans and commented.

Torres-Martinez Elder Ernest Morreo participated as a design consultant for the park, commenting on the appropriate animal motif for the area and the proposed plants, and supplying the translation for the plaques (one in English and one in Cahuilla) that were placed on a large boulder in the center of the concrete cap over the site. The park has space for the city or tribes to place statues and other public art related to Desert Cahuilla cultural heritage. At the park's completion, the Coachella city government held a dedication and invited dignitaries from all levels of government. During the ceremony, Mr. Morreo blessed Ye'wi'vichem Park and sang traditional bird songs.

The park won Coachella a Governor's Historic Preservation Award, the State of California's highest preservation award. "Tribes were involved from the front end of the CEQA process all the way through to the end, when they verified mitigation completion with their presence at the park blessing," said Mouriquand.[25]

Easements

Another important feature of SB-18 is that it expands the number of groups that can hold conservation easements to include both federally recognized and unrecognized tribes. The Morongo Band of Mission Indians has several easements pending, but no agreements have been finalized, due in part to the relative youth of the SB-18 process. SB-18 took effect only in March 2005, so the list of concluded consultations is short, whether they resulted in easements, open-space agreements, capping of archaeological sites, land transfers, or relocation of cultural resources to tribal lands.

Under SB-18, tribes may choose to negotiate conservation easements with developers or private landowners to protect important sites. Private landowners can get a tax credit if they grant conservation easements to tribes or other parties that can legally hold easements. Wilson encourages negotiating easements to guarantee access in perpetuity.[26] Easements may also need to include a cultural resource management plan for the site, detailing procedures such as capping the site or documenting or relocating cultural resources.

The Morongo Band is currently pursuing easements on ceremonial rock shelters and a route to access them.[27] Generally, landowners with projects affected by SB-18 are large homebuilders or commercial developers. An easement owned by the tribe protects sites in perpetuity and preserves access, which is particularly important when sites are located in gated communities with restricted access. Morongo has also worked to ensure that no buildings are placed on village or burial sites and that buffer zones are established around rock-art sites to prevent vandalism and to enable private visitation by tribal members. Although in the past, features left in open space were vandalized or removed by archaeologists, now tribes can be more proactive about placing easements on and around these features or having them moved to tribal lands. Although moving features off-site disrupts their historical location, sometimes it may be the best way to ensure they are under tribal control and not disturbed.

Proactive Strategies for Tribes, Cities, and Counties Using SB-18

Although the Governor's Office of Planning and Research has been doing ongoing SB-18 trainings around the state for counties, cities, tribes, and the general public, some cities and counties may not understand the SB-18 "consultation" process. According to Wilson: "Many cities are used to just getting letters from other agencies, and they put them in their files, and they may or may not address the issues in the letters. Some cities think they can do that with SB-18, but it is more than just receiving a letter from the tribe—it should involve face-to-face consultation."[28] To make the consultation agreements into binding actions that the developer must take in order to move forward with a project, Wilson stresses converting the consultation agreements into formal conditions for approval of the development. Then, the city or county is mandated to impose these conditions before the development is allowed to proceed, and the conditions stay with the land, even if the project changes hands.[29] "It gives tribes something to hang their hat on, and the city has to make certain the developer follows the conditions," Wilson added.[30]

In addition, before an SB-18 process is triggered, Southern California tribes are already acting, by collaborating to develop effective consultation procedures and by creating maps of their traditional territories. The tribes then provide these maps to counties and cities, and they request advance notification about projects that would impact traditional lands. Anthony Madrigal (Cahuilla) described such a process in his 2008 text on Cahuilla and Chemehuevi environmental and cultural programs, in which the Cahuilla cultural resources protection program included the development of a traditional lands map, drawn in consultation with tribal elders.[31] The map was provided to Riverside County planners.

The Cahuilla program has also developed a map of cultural, archaeological, and traditional gathering sites for use in tribal prioritization of sites for preservation. It contains sensitive information that the tribe is careful to protect, yet it also concentrates important cultural information in a spatial record that can be used for intratribal planning.[32] The cultural sites map is also a useful means of informing both tribal members and employees consulting with cities, counties, and developers on behalf of the tribe.

On the county side, Mouriquand has tracked the development of SB-18 over the three years that lapsed between its proposal and its approval in California, and she has been involved as an instructor training local jurisdictions in the law's procedures. One of the biggest needs she sees under SB-18 is training for personnel, particularly planners, about the intent and implementation of SB-18. Mouriquand also recommends inserting formal language from the law in project notification letters to tribes. "We're looking at other jurisdictions and finding that nobody is including language that cites the law that there is a ninety-day period that tribes have to request consultation," she said. "Make sure you have that language in letters going to tribes, so that the letter will hold up in court as a legal notice." Mouriquand also advised tribes to get to know the local government jurisdiction that is issuing these SB-18 consultation letters, so that the two parties can more effectively work together and meet deadlines.[33]

Intertribal Collaboration to Protect Cultural and Environmental Resources

The Morongo Band participates with several other Riverside and San Bernardino County tribes in an Intertribal Cultural Resources Working Group focused on tribal environmental concerns.[34] Participants include the Cabazon Band of Mission Indians, Soboba Band of Luiseño Indians, Twenty-Nine Palms Band of Mission Indians, Pechanga Band of Luiseño Indians, Pala Band of Mission Indians, Los Coyotes Band of Mission Indians, Ramona Band of Cahuilla Indians, San Manuel Band of Serrano Mission Indians, Agua Caliente Band of Cahuilla Indians, and Santa Rosa Band of Cahuilla Indians. Other interested neighboring tribes have also always been welcome to sit in.[35] Since 2005, the group has been meeting every two months, with meeting sites rotating between participant hosts.

The Working Group has decided to remain informal, so no notes are taken, and there are no formal committees and subcommittees, although sometimes a smaller group of representatives from the full Working Group will meet to focus on a particular issue. Because of distance and scheduling conflicts, not every tribe is represented at every meeting, but the primary purpose of the Working Group is to keep communication open and to share information. Its success has drawn visitors from as far away as Lone Pine Paiute-Shoshone Reservation, who were interested in using the Working Group as a model to form their own collaborative.

Meeting participants typically include one-to-three representatives of each tribe's cultural resource management programs (such as the Tribal Heritage Program Officer or THPO, archaeologist, and other staff). The Working Group may invite one or more guest speakers to give an update on specific projects or to present their consultation protocols and get some feedback from the tribes. Past guests have included tribal liaisons from CalTrans, the Bureau of Land Management, and the U.S. Forest Service. After the guest leaves, focused, confidential discussions can ensue among the tribal representatives about sensitive issues, such as concerns regarding the Native American Graves Protection and Repatriation Act (NAGPRA) and strategies for working with various agencies and programs. According to Mike Contreras, "This is probably the best little group that there is to address cultural resources."[36]

Conclusion: Effectively Applying SB-18

The Working Group and tribes' proactive development of maps identifying priority sites for protection are examples of strategies that will make bills like SB-18 more effective. SB-18 is not as strong as proponents initially had hoped. For example, the bill mandates only that local jurisdictions offer consultation to tribes, but it does not require the jurisdictions to comply with tribes' requests. Still, with effective collaboration between city or county governments and tribes, the SB-18 consultations on general-plan and specific-plan amendments have enabled protection of cultural sites. By being both well informed on SB-18 and well prepared to negotiate firmly for site protection, tribes like the Morongo, Agua Caliente, Cahuilla, and others have applied SB-18 to improve tribal participation and leadership in local planning and development.

9

Developing Cultural Conservation Easements

Little Traverse Bay Bands of Odawa Indians (Michigan)

The Little Traverse Bay Bands of Odawa Indians is composed of Odawa people native to the area now known as the state of Michigan. Odawa traditional lands extend from the forested Upper Peninsula in the north to the lower and warmer lands of southern Michigan.[1] The tribe signed treaties in 1836 and 1855 that ensured them a 336-square-mile reservation in Charlevoix and Emmet counties, on the northern coast of Lake Michigan, 30 miles south of the Mackinaw Bridge.[2] Despite these treaties, American expansion and settlement throughout the late 1800s and into the early 1900s steadily eroded the Odawa rights to their lands (including hunting and fishing rights).[3]

In the 1930s and 1940s, Native people in Michigan united in several politically savvy groups—the Michigan Indian Defense Association (1933), the Michigan Indian Foundation (1947), and the Northern Michigan Ottawa Association (1948)—to advocate for fair adherence to their treaty agreements, including the right to recover funds promised by the federal government. Although the Northern Michigan Ottawa Association won their claim in 1971 and received some financial restitution for resources taken, the federal government refused to recognize their fishing rights in a 1980 court case because they were an organization and not a federally recognized tribe.

In 1982, Little Traverse Bay Bands, which had comprised Unit 1 of the Northern Michigan Ottawa Association, formed a nonprofit corporation to pursue reaffirmation of its federally recognized tribal status through the U.S. Congress. The tribe called for reaffirmation rather than recognition because its federal recognition as a party to treaties had never been formally terminated.[4] In 1994, President Clinton signed Public Law 103–324, reaffirming the Little Traverse Bay Bands of Odawa Indians as a federally recognized tribe. Today, the tribe has more than four thousand members, and tribal government employs 175 full- and part-time employees. Tribal enterprises (a casino, gas station, fish market, hotel, and so forth) employ more than nine hundred people.[5]

Through their comprehensive governing code, the tribe established innovative guidelines for holding, negotiating, and enforcing conservation easements, cultural preservation easements, and traditional use easements. The tribe also has corporation codes that allow for tribally owned corporations and nonprofit corporations under tribal law.[6] The tribe's Conservation and Cultural Preservation Easement Act, for example, along with the corporation code enabling tribal nonprofits, allows the tribe to develop its own land conservancy under tribal law, according to former Tribal Chairman Frank Ettawageshik.[7]

The Little Traverse Bay Bands of Odawa has not yet developed a conservancy, and it does not hold any conservation or traditional-use easements, but it has long-term plans to do so. Since 1999, the tribe has also been in the process of collecting baseline data on tribal natural resources, including water quality and wetlands. These data will assist the tribe in developing effective resource management plans and identifying priorities for conservation. As the following narrative describes, the tribe has already created nature preserves by resolutions and in cooperation with other entities, such as the Little Traverse Conservancy.

Little Traverse Conservancy

The Little Traverse Conservancy was founded in 1972 to protect the natural diversity and beauty of northern Michigan by preserving significant land and scenic areas and fostering appreciation and understanding of the environment.[8] Described as the "oldest regional nonprofit land trust in Michigan," the conservancy has more than 4,200 members and has protected over 40,000 acres,[9] including more than 105 miles of shoreline along lakes, rivers, and streams.[10] The conservancy began using conservation easements as a tool for land protection in 1986, and today it holds 208 conservation easements protecting 18,575 acres.[11] The state of Michigan has been friendly to land conservation, as evidenced by a 2006 law (SB-1004) that eliminates tax increases at the time of sale on properties that are protected with conservation easements.[12] By eliminating reassessment during land transfers, the new law creates property-tax breaks for landowners with conservation easements. However, unlike California's Senate Bill 18, Michigan state law does not specifically name Indian tribes as potential holders of conservation easements. However, it also does not exclude them.[13] The act reads: "A conservation easement [is] granted to a governmental entity or to a charitable or educational association, corporation, trust, or other legal entity." According to the Little Traverse Bay Bands' Attorney James Bransky, tribes would presumably fall into the category of "governmental entity."[14] In the context of the Taimi Hoag easement discussed in this case study, the tribe owned the property and granted the easement to the Little Traverse Conservancy, so this statute was not tested.

Although the tribe is discussing forming its own land trust, its current primary mechanism for utilizing conservation easements is through existing land trusts, like the Little Traverse Conservancy. The conservancy works in five northern Michigan counties—Emmet, Mackinac, Chippewa, Cheboygan, and Charlevoix—and it is supported by the collective efforts of individuals, families, and businesses. In 2008, members donated more than $730,000 to the Little Traverse Conservancy (LTC).[15] Volunteers and staff work to monitor easements, steward natural lands, build trails, and provide interpretive signage in cooperation with landowners. One of the conservancy's many partners over the years has been the Little Traverse Bay Bands of Odawa Indians (LTBBOI).

The LTC and the Little Traverse Bay Bands of Odawa Indians: Developing a Partnership

The Little Traverse Conservancy and a nonprofit organization representing the Little Traverse Bay Bands of Odawa Indians began working together in the 1980s, before the tribe received reaffirmation of tribal status in 1993. According to Tom Bailey, executive director of the conservancy: "A tribal elder came in and said, 'We've been watching you, and for non Indians, you get it with regards to the land business—in terms of respecting land and working for conservation instead of development.' Then another elder came in and said the same thing."[16] Bailey and former Tribal Chairman Frank Ettawageshik,[17] who also currently serves on the Little Traverse Conservancy Board of Directors, developed a working relationship and began looking for areas of possible collaboration. At that point, the conservancy was just getting into conservation easements, and Bailey and Ettawageshik began developing the idea of cultural conservation easements.

Cultural Conservation Easements

Bailey and Ettawageshik see two classes of cultural conservation easements: traditional ceremonial use and traditional medicinal gathering. The first class encompasses lands with burials, areas of cultural or spiritual importance, and ceremonial sites. These easements are intended to accommodate and encourage continuation of use. The second class fosters continued traditional gathering, with appropriate landowner notification.[18] As Bailey explained, "These two classes involve use, such as conducting ceremonies on the property. If I have a stone circle on the back forty of my farm, and I enact a cultural conservation easement with the tribe, on solstice, tribal members would be there for ceremony. If my land has tobacco or sweetgrass, a [cultural conservation] easement would affirm tribal members' right to enter my property at certain times to collect these herbs and medicines."[19] Ettawageshik agreed, adding that private landowners may be concerned about certain cultural uses, such as harvesting birch bark, but if these are done correctly by knowledgeable tribal members, the resource will last for hundreds of years and may even be enhanced: "Some see nature as wild, but Native people have been working the landscape and modifying it for millennia. People marvel at all of the berries that grow along our trails, never thinking that we carried the seeds there so that the plants would grow and we would have food as we walked along."[20]

Ettawageshik knows that the Odawa homeland is not "wild"; his ancestors altered it, creating the resources that tribal members still work to steward and gather today: "We would burn savannas to keep them grassy for certain animals, and burn berries to keep them from getting overgrown. [An organization like] The Nature Conservancy would create 'natural areas' in bogs where we have gathered forever, making criminals out of our grandmothers that gathered there and that transplanted the plants there hundreds of years ago."[21]

Although many conservation easements simply preclude development, cultural conservation easements allow certain types of physical access and use by tribal members at particular times. Like a conservation easement, the concept of the cultural conservation easement relies on the "bundle of sticks" metaphor for property ownership, in which each stick is a property right that can be separated from the others. Sticks, or property rights, include mineral rights, development rights, and the right to declare war.

The federal government reserves some sticks, such as the last example, and state governments reserve others. As Ettawageshik explained, "We separated out the concept that there are ceremonial sites on different properties—on a site there may be a 10-acre portion with a sacred stone where every year or every five or ten years you have a ceremony. The cultural easement is a property right to hold a ceremony."[22] A cultural conservation easement even includes elements of a conservation easement, in that a property with a cultural conservation easement on it could not be developed in a way that would preclude carrying out a ceremony. Cultural conservation easements can be between tribes and private landowners or between the tribe and a quasi-public entity, such as a land conservancy.

According to Bailey, several private landowners in Michigan were excited about the potential for cultural conservation easements, and they stated that they would feel honored to have ceremonies happening on their lands and to help ensure that gathering and traditional land management would continue.[23] In case property changes hands and the next landowner is not as friendly to tribes, cultural conservation easements allow gathering and other specific access or ceremonial rights to continue in perpetuity. Cultural conservation easements also create a mechanism for the tribe to collaborate formally with the Little Traverse Conservancy to establish and retain specific rights to conservancy properties.

In late 2003, Ettawageshik asked Rachel Smolinski with the Tribal Environmental Services Department to draft a cultural conservation easement. Beginning in 2004, the draft entered a process of review and refinement in both the tribe's legal department and with the conservancy's lawyers. The formal cultural conservation easement is still a work in progress. In a 2008 interview, Ettawageshik expressed his desire to implement the cultural conservation easement, but he noted that the tribe has been busy on a variety of other fronts.[24] Although the cultural conservation easement has yet to be formally tested, the tribe and the conservancy are poised to utilize it as a tool for land access and preservation.

The Conservation Easement Supplemental Agreement

By developing a supplemental agreement, the Little Traverse Bay Bands of Odawa Indians and the Little Traverse Conservancy found a way to address the issue of placing restrictions, such as conservation easements, on tribal lands slated to go into trust. The federal government reviews parcels for "unacceptable encumbrances" on the title before taking land into federal ownership or trust.[25] Conservation easements may be seen as encumbrances or liabilities. The Conservation Easement Supplemental Agreement looks like a conservation easement but is actually a specific agreement with the tribe, which establishes certain uses and prohibitions on the property. The tribe also signed a limited waiver of sovereign immunity, allowing the conservancy to enforce the terms of the agreement. Developing the agreement also laid the groundwork for cultural conservation easements.

In 2000, the tribe was seeking to offset their development activities by protecting land. A federal National Oceanic and Atmospheric Administration (NOAA) grant became available through the Michigan Coastal Management Program, administered through the Michigan Department of Environmental Quality (DEQ). Governmental entities could apply for up to $500,000 through the state to acquire land, and partnerships between multiple entities were encouraged. The tribe's nascent Environmental Department contacted the Tip of the Mitt Watershed Council for technical assistance with local watershed planning, and the council recommended contacting the Little Traverse Conservancy. The tribe partnered with both the council and the conservancy and received $250,000 in 2001 to buy a 55-acre property within the Little Traverse Bay watershed that met all three entities' objectives, as well as those of the grant. "We have a lot of the same goals as the conservancy, but one that stands out for the tribe is protecting culture," said Smolinski.[26]

The 55-acre parcel includes traditional gathering areas; is within the boundaries of the Little Traverse Bay Bands' historic reservation; is located on the coast, crossed by a stream, and includes a wetland; and was under development pressure. Because the land is along the U.S.-31 corridor between Traverse City and Petoskey (one of the conservancy's priority areas for land protection) and located within an existing 200-acre conservancy preserve, the Little Traverse Conservancy was also able to contribute funding. The total cost of the 55-acre parcel was $340,000. The conservancy leveraged funds from private foundations to purchase the property with the understanding that the tribe would buy it from them as soon as the grant funds came in. Although the tribe received the $250,000 grant in 2001, the purchase was not completed until 2004 because the conservation easement supplemental agreement had to be developed prior to the purchase. The conservancy made up the $90,000 difference between the grant and the purchase price. In 2004, the tribe acquired the 55-acre parcel, and in 2005, it dedicated the land as the Taimi Lynne Hoag Natural Area (figs. 9.1 and 9.2). Hoag was Smolinski's supervisor and colleague in the Tribal Environmental Department, and she passed away of cancer before the property was purchased.

This was the first official collaboration between the tribe and the conservancy. Conservancy staff member Kieran Fleming noted that the process

FIGURE 9.1. The beginning of the trail at the Taimi Lynne Hoag Natural Area. (Photo courtesy of Little Traverse Bay Bands of Odawa Environmental Services Department)

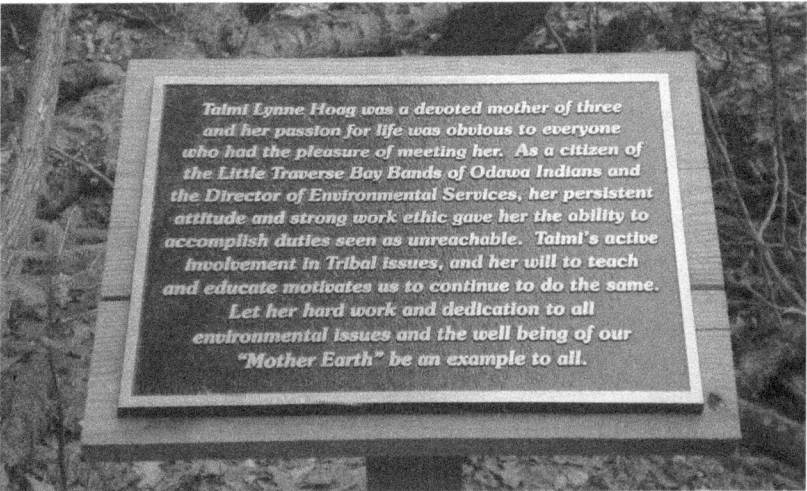

Taimi Lynne Hoag was a devoted mother of three and her passion for life was obvious to everyone who had the pleasure of meeting her. As a citizen of the Little Traverse Bay Bands of Odawa Indians and the Director of Environmental Services, her persistent attitude and strong work ethic gave her the ability to accomplish duties seen as unreachable. Taimi's active involvement in Tribal issues, and her will to teach and educate motivates us to continue to do the same. Let her hard work and dedication to all environmental issues and the well being of our "Mother Earth" be an example to all.

FIGURE 9.2. The dedication plaque at the trailhead in the Taimi Lynne Hoag Natural Area. (Photo courtesy of Little Traverse Bay Bands of Odawa Environmental Services Department)

was aided by willingness and creativity on the part of the conservancy, the tribe, and their respective attorneys. "We wrote the book as we went; it was hard to find people who had been through this before," said Fleming.[27]

Many legal uncertainties arose when the tribe received reaffirmation of sovereign status. For example, one of the grant requirements was that a conservation easement be placed on the property, but there were few models nationally for an easement structure that would be enforceable against a sovereign nation and would still allow the land to go into trust. The conservancy and the tribe spent more than a year researching, developing, and refining a Conservation Easement Supplemental Agreement, a unique document that serves the purpose of a conservation easement for land held in trust by the federal government for a tribe. There are two agreements in place on the property, a Primary Conservation Easement that was in force while the land was in fee status, and the Conservation Easement Supplemental Agreement, which went into force when the land went into trust in 2005. If the land goes out of trust and back into fee status, the Primary Conservation Easement goes into effect again and the conservancy retains its interest in the property.

The Conservation Easement Supplemental Agreement recognizes the legal precedents for conservation in tribal, state, and federal statutes, and it establishes that the terms of the easement can be upheld in either the state or tribal jurisdiction. Both agreements set aside the land from development, restrict uses on site, and are binding in perpetuity. The Conservation Easement Supplemental Agreement enables the conservancy to enforce the tribe's compliance with the terms of the easement: "Our current tribal administration is very supportive of the land being protected, but would the next administration be the same? It's in all of our best interests, and in the best interest of the next seven generations."[28] The Conservation Easement Supplemental Agreement does not cover chain in title, like a typical conservation easement. Addressing chain in title is not necessary because the land is held in trust for the tribe and will not be changing hands. Although the conservancy negotiated directly with the tribe, the tribe's attorney focused on communication with the Bureau of Indian Affairs to place the land in trust, while maintaining the development restrictions.

The Conservation Easement Supplemental Agreement ultimately brought all parties, including the Department of the Interior, the Michigan Department of Environmental Quality, the tribe, and the Little Traverse Conservancy, to a consensus. The Bureau of Indian Affairs now holds the land in trust for the tribe, and the Little Traverse Conservancy holds a Conservation Easement Supplemental Agreement on the property. "It couldn't have turned out any better, although maybe a little quicker," said Smolinski. "You don't realize how long these things take."[29] The tribe continues to manage the Taimi Lynne Hoag Natural Area in cooperation with the conservancy.

According to its staff members, the conservancy treats the property like an easement, in terms of monitoring and stewardship activities done in collaboration with the tribe. The grant requires the tribe to allow public access to the parcel, and the tribe and the conservancy have been working on an interpretive trail system since 2005, with the latter providing materials and technical assistance to the tribe for building trails and boardwalks (fig. 9.3). Both parties have worked side by side to create a linkage between the trails on the tribe's 55-acre preserve and the conservancy's neighboring 200-acre preserve. The tribe and the conservancy have weekly contact when the tourist season starts and also communicate frequently on land and invasive-species issues.

The development of the Conservation Easement Supplemental Agreement built good communication between the two entities. "We know we can contact each other now and that it's going to be a positive relationship," said Smolinski.[30] Similarly, according to Fleming, "Our goal is to do more with [the tribe]. They have an interest in lands within their historic tribal boundaries for things other than casinos, and there is a potential for future collaboration. This one paved the way. Collaboration works great as long as people aren't afraid to do it."[31] Indeed, the tribe and the conservancy continue to collaborate on the latter's preserves.[32] For example, the conservancy recently acquired an approximately 400-acre parcel adjacent to tribal land. In summer 2009, the tribe collaborated with the conservancy to inventory the property for invasive species and determine future management options, and the tribe is also working to connect trails from its property to conservancy trails, in order to allow access for recreation, hunting, and gathering.

Words of Wisdom

Smolinski offered several pieces of advice for other tribes developing agreements with land trusts. First, she encouraged tribes to gather baseline land data and information on possible partnerships on projects before making decisions. In order to form partnerships, it is helpful to identify local (Native and non-Native) entities with similar land-protection goals. When working with multiple players, despite how close goals may be, each entity has its own requirements and priorities that must be negotiated with the other participating entities. In this complex collaborative process, maintaining

FIGURE 9.3. Little Traverse Bay Bands of Odawa Environmental Services staff, Little Traverse Conservancy staff, and volunteers resting after carrying in lumber and materials for construction of boardwalks on a trail in the Taimi Lynne Hoag Natural Area. (Photo courtesy of Little Traverse Bay Bands of Odawa Environmental Services Department)

open communication and a "positive attitude" are key. With the Taimi Lynne Hoag Natural Area, for example, players included the Bureau of Indian Affairs, the Tip of the Mitt Watershed Council, the Little Traverse Conservancy, the Michigan Department of Environmental Quality, and multiple tribal departments, including the cultural preservation and natural resources departments. "Everyone had to know what was going on with the property," said Smolinski.[33] In addition, because of the decision to dedicate the site to Ms. Hoag, it was necessary to involve, include, and honor the Hoag family. Smolinski advised: "Include as many people as you can. It's going to be a lot of hard work and there are going to be bumps in the road, so make sure you get people on board, involve them from the beginning, and give yourself plenty of time. It can take years, but it's well worth it because the end product can be something really wonderful."[34] The tribe also believes that future collaborations will be easier, given all of the groundwork that was laid in the process of creating the Taimi Lynne Hoag Natural Area.

Native Nonprofits and Petitioning Tribes

Tsi-Akim Maidu (California)

Tsi-Akim Maidu tribal members are descended from Mountain Maidu in Plumas and Lassen counties, as well as Concow and Nisenan Maidu in Placer, El Dorado, Butte, Yuba, and Nevada counties in California. The Tsi-Akim have mapped some of this complex descendancy in an "Ancestral Nexus" map that is in progress and available from the tribe on request.[1] "Tsi-Akim" refers to a historic village site just outside the town of Quincy in Plumas County.[2] The Tsi-Akim Maidu are petitioning for federal recognition as the descendants of those who lived on the Taylorsville Rancheria, just to the north of Quincy.[3]

Taylorsville Rancheria

Following a series of funding appropriations to purchase lands for "homeless California Indians,"[4] in 1923, the Bureau of Indian Affairs (BIA) purchased the Taylorsville Rancheria from the heirs of Indian allottee Old Allick. Allick had originally been allotted the parcel in 1897.[5] The BIA believed the allotment was an ideal place to establish a rancheria, because it was adjacent to the town and employment and Indian people were already living on the site.[6] As Greenville Indian Industrial School Superintendent Edgar K. Miller wrote to the Commissioner of Indian Affairs on July 26, 1923: "Several Indians have homes on this land, and that is one reason I wanted to purchase it. Some of these Indians have camps, some houses. There are now three frame Indian homes upon it. . . . It is very desirable for Indians and has been used a great many years only by Indians."[7] The Taylorsville Rancheria was established and settled in the mid-1920s. In 1952, however, it was condemned, ostensibly due to lack of adequate water.[8] Because it was condemned before Termination, people who had lived there were ineligible to join the Tillie Hardwick lawsuit.[9]

The record is scant on whether people were forced off the Rancheria, or were away working at seasonal jobs, when it was declared abandoned. One elder remembered walking to her friend's house at the rancheria as a young girl—the friend's aunt was in tears when they arrived, reporting that people had come and told her that she had to move from her home.[10] In general, the site is remembered throughout the Maidu community as "something that was taken" from the Maidu.[11] The BIA sold the rancheria to Plumas County in the early 1960s for approximately $30,000. Because the Taylorsville Rancheria was never reinstated as tribal trust land, the descendants of the individuals who lived on this land remain unrecognized by the federal government.

Tsi-Akim Cultural Activities

Today, the Tsi-Akim Maidu are a growing tribe, with a tribal council composed solely of tribe members and a nonprofit arm that has Native and non-Native people on its Board of Directors. Under the leadership of Tribal Chairman Don Ryberg, the Tsi-Akim Maidu are actively petitioning for federal recognition. The tribe is involved in numerous community and cultural activities in Plumas and Nevada counties. In Nevada County, for example, the tribe coordinates the multiday Indigenous People's Days celebration in mid-October, celebrating it near the date formerly known as Columbus Day.

The tribe also offers educational events and panels throughout the year, participates in a group to address intergenerational trauma and healing from unresolved grief, is active in collaborative land and water restoration, and runs a successful thrift store to help support office staff and expenses involved in the work to gain recognition. In Plumas County, the tribe hosts an annual Big Time, and tribal members conduct traditional ceremonies, including the Bear Dance[12] and "coming-of-age" dances, held at the Taylorsville Campground—the site of the historic Taylorsville Rancheria.

Nevada County Land Trust

The Nevada County Land Trust (NCLT) was formed in 1991 to conserve the unique and varied natural and cultural landscapes of Nevada County,

California. With a board and staff composed of ranchers, farmers, environmentalists, and community-minded citizens, the NCLT has successfully protected 5,000 acres of forest, farm, natural, and recreational land from development through conservation easements and fee-title transactions.[13] The efforts of the land trust include preserving local agriculture, building trails, and conducting environmental education outings and camps for adults and youth. The NCLT thrives on partnerships—with private landowners, tribes, community groups, schools, and local, state, and federal government entities, as well as other land trusts and conservancies.

Tsi-Akim and Nevada County Land Trust: Building a Collaboration

The Tsi-Akim Maidu tribe and the Nevada County Land Trust (NCLT) are cooperating to manage a property rich in cultural resources. The two parties are also working to create an agreement so that tribal members can have access to other NCLT properties with cultural resources. The collaboration began informally, as many do in small communities. Tribal member Wendy Olenick was a caretaker for longtime community resident and local librarian Francis Burton.[14] At her death, Burton's will gift deeded her 38-acre parcel to the NCLT, stipulating that she wanted to see a "children's park" on the site. The Burton Homestead was the NCLT's second property acquisition, according to former NCLT board member John Taylor.[15]

On a visit to the Burton Homestead during an NCLT event, Tribal Chairman Don Ryberg saw the grinding rocks on the property and told the land trust he thought the land "should have been given back to the Indians."[16] According to Taylor, "[Tribal members] were really taken by it because there was a village there at one time."[17] The NCLT wanted to work with the tribe on the Burton Homestead. A series of conversations between the tribe and the land trust led to the development of the Maidu Active Cultural Center, or MACC, described below. The NCLT invited Ryberg to become an advisor to the board, and Ryberg also became a friend of NCLT Director of Conservation Programs (and former Executive Director) Dan Macon. The 38-acre Burton Homestead hosts several joint tribe–land trust events, including a two-week, two-session kids' camp, workshops, birding inventories, the annual NCLT picnic, annual Indigenous People's Days events, and the tribe's own ceremonial and cultural events.

According to Macon, the Tsi-Akim Maidu and the NCLT support each other—in 2006, the land trust adopted a resolution supporting federal recognition for the tribe.[18] In turn, the tribe has participated in NCLT

events and efforts, such as a 2007 panel discussion on traditional stewardship, which involved tribe members and members of the Tsi-Akim Maidu
nonprofit's board of directors. The panel was held at the Nevada County
Library, as part of the "Armchair Treks" series that the NCLT hosts when it
is too rainy or cold to hold their regular Treks hiking program. According to
NCLT Executive Director Marty Coleman-Hunt, the tribe's 2007 panel was
"the best attended event we've ever had—standing room only."[19] The tribe
also supports the NCLT Summer Kids Camp by teaching Native American
Studies for one full week of the two-week camp.

On June 4, 2007, the tribe and the NCLT negotiated and signed a
Memorandum of Understanding (MOU), establishing their commitment
to work together to develop a formal agreement on the Burton Homestead.
On June 1, 2008, the tribe and the NCLT signed a final agreement, which
leases a 3-acre section of the 38-acre homestead to the tribe for ten years
for $10 per year. This 3-acre section is the site of the Maidu Active Cultural
Center. According to Ryberg, this arrangement ended up being expensive
for the unrecognized Tsi-Akim Maidu Tribe, because the actual annual cost
is approximately $800, including the $10 to the land trust, Nevada County
property taxes,[20] and $400 for a portable toilet near the MACC.

What's Happening on the Land?

Along with Chairman Ryberg, Tsi-Akim Cultural Director Grayson Coney
and others began work to create a "living village." The first step was to
thin the dense vegetation in the area around the grinding rocks. Then,
in May 2006, they constructed the first large, wheelchair-accessible traditional house of cedar, pine, and oak. In 2007, they completed a second
bark house, and in 2008, they added two excavated pit houses, for a total
of four structures (fig. 10.1). The two bark houses are located on either side
of the newly constructed Chee Bee Likum Stage, named for one of Chairman Ryberg's ancestors. These houses are used as staging areas for dancers
and performers. The Chee Bee Likum Stage has seating for three hundred
people, and the tribe used it for the first time during the 2008 Indigenous
People's Days. The tribe also has plans to build a sweathouse, shade structures, and a roundhouse on the site. In collaboration with the NCLT, the
tribe will also assist with raising funds to build a classroom and restrooms
on the Burton Homestead, moving the land further toward the uses Burton
wanted to see there—education and cultural activities.

The tribe has also constructed acorn granaries, and on another area of
the property outside of the living village, they have established a healing
grounds, which can be used for dances, ceremonials, and other healing

FIGURE 10.1. A bark structure at the Maidu Active Cultural Center. (Photo courtesy of Michael Ben Ortiz)

activities. "We have built a place where people can come and heal from some of the wrongs that have been done in this county," Coney explained.[21]

The dance ground itself is an example of a type of healing. It is built on a reclaimed mine-tailings site. Tailings are crushed rock, sand, and gravel that were leached with mercury and cyanide to remove gold. Although most of the materials left from mining have already washed farther downstream, the tribe was very careful not to cause further erosion of the possibly contaminated soil and rock when they worked on the site. "We reseeded all of the areas that we had disturbed down to dirt, then covered them with leaves and pine needles to encourage the new growth," Coney described.[22] The tribe planned this mitigation with the seasons—grasses and flowers are already growing on the disturbed sites and will hold the tailings in place during the winter rains.

Before the tribe worked on the site for the dance ground, Coney remembers that the land had "big deep scars" in it from tailings and hydraulic mining: "We put it all back together the best that we could and made a place for the community to come together to heal. It has got the [healing] energy in it already."[23] Healing, in the sense Coney describes it here, was achieved in the process of creating the healing grounds and the Maidu Active Cultural Center. The tribe consciously worked to repair the damaged land and re-create a place for a traditional society to flourish, in a unique partnership with a non-tribal land trust. "How often is it that people ask the Indians to come back to their land," Coney asked, recognizing the land trust's forward-thinking actions in building a collaboration with the tribe.[24]

Of course, collaboration is not always easy, especially because the tribe has only a limited lease on the property and must meet the landowner's guidelines for use and management. The irony of this situation is not lost on Coney, who sees himself as helping to "put the land back together" following the disrespect of miners and settlers, yet he has to be very cautious in everything he does. As he explains, "Had it been completely opposite, the gold miners would have asked permission to gently lift gold nuggets out of the creek, assuring [the Indians] that they wouldn't muck up the water. That is how I'm feeling now putting it back together."[25] Despite the difficulty of trying to build people's understanding about the tribe's goals for the land and techniques for its management, Coney is guided by a larger vision: "You don't have a choice—the Creator expects you to put [the land] back together because you are a human being. In order to get through it and do it properly, you have to finesse sometimes and not upset people. . . . You don't want to upset the balance that made it possible for you to be there in the first place."[26] The tribe has proceeded carefully with creating and expanding the Maidu Active Cultural Center and many of the members are proud of how it looks and what it is used for: "If the tribe owned that property outright I can't imagine that one [of the improvements] would have been done differently than we have done now. That is how conscientious we have been."[27]

Tribal members are currently using the bark houses for meetings, hand games, other cultural events, and public education and outreach. "From a perspective of active cultural use, any form of tribal events can be held out there," Coney explained.[28] In the lease agreement with the NCLT, the tribe has the right to exclude others from the Active Cultural Center: "If the public wants to cooperate with the tribe and the land trust, they can ask to have events out there with the tribe or the land trust or both, but it shouldn't be expected. It should be respected. It's not a state-run or county-run facility; it's a privately owned facility."[29] Although NCLT board member Taylor similarly articulated that no one could go inside the MACC structures without a tribal member being present, he added that when people have requested a visit to the village, tribal members have been "quite willing to give tours and explain what it is all about."[30] Coney, for example, is on the site almost daily and regularly shares the area with visitors. He wants the public to know that an active cultural center is quite different from other entities that they may be used to. "It is not an interpretive center," Coney said. "You are pulling up on Indian land, it's the real thing."[31]

The Maidu Active Cultural Center and the innovative agreement with the NCLT to use the property have attracted a lot of attention. People have been inspired by the tribe's activities, and many have appreciated the chance to experience a Native village that is a place of living cultural practice. Olenick, providing a tribal member's perspective, said she was pleased that children would be able to experience the feeling of a bark house and thereby gain a greater respect and understanding for Native people or for their own Native heritage. "The kids need to see what [a bark house] looks like," she explained. "They need to see what it really was like, instead of looking at a book."[32]

Aside from the MACC, the entire property (which includes two ponds and a hilly area in addition to meadowland) will remain in a natural state for use in environmental and Native studies, hiking, and other recreation. Wildlife on the property includes 175 species of birds,[33] as well as coyotes, bobcats, bears, mountain lions, hawks, and gopher snakes.

Formalizing Collaboration

The structure of the collaboration consists of the MOU between the NCLT and the tribe, signed in 2007, and a lease, signed in 2008, which makes explicit which portion of the property will be used by the tribe and what can be done on it. Macon, who was the NCLT Executive Director when the MOU was being drafted, envisioned long-term coordination with the tribe, in order to inventory cultural resources on NCLT properties and jointly develop plans for cultural resources protection.[34] The MOU states that the "NCLT and the tribe will work together to permanently conserve lands of mutual interest in Nevada County."[35] To this end, Ryberg has walked NCLT properties with Macon and others to inventory cultural resources. Although the MOU does not provide tribal access to all NCLT easements, as that is largely up to the landowner's specifications, the NCLT has brought the tribe and landowners together when there is interest on the part of both parties. The MOU also enables tribal members to join NCLT technical advisory committees, "as appropriate," to advise the NCLT board on projects and approaches to conservation.

The MOU articulated the tribe's and the land trust's joint commitment to develop a plan for the Burton Homestead, collaborate to preserve other lands in Nevada County, and support one another's efforts. The MOU also called for the formation of a Steering Committee, which included Ryberg,

Macon, and others, to work on the lease agreement for the homestead. Developing the MOU and then the lease agreement (including a plan for the site) was an ongoing process of communication and compromise. For example, it is important to the tribe that the MACC is available for their use in perpetuity. "It is very important for what we are doing," Ryberg said. "The land trust may at some point donate or sell the property to a state park or another nonprofit, and we don't want the village to be transferred as well."[36] Although the MOU acknowledges that the tribe is investing substantial time, funds, and labor into creating the Maidu Active Cultural Center, neither that document nor the lease guarantees perpetual access.

Coleman-Hunt, the current NCLT executive director, did not recall any conversations addressing use "in perpetuity."[37] She explained that the NCLT has the right to transfer the Burton Homestead to another entity, although the NCLT would retain (and continue to enforce) the conservation easement in accordance with Burton's wishes for the land. The NCLT does not currently have plans to transfer the parcel, but if it were considering a transfer, "the tribe would be involved in those discussions," according to Coleman-Hunt. She also noted that Ryberg has expressed a desire to assume ownership of the Burton Homestead, and the NCLT is willing to continue to explore this. However, currently, there is no plan to transfer ownership to the tribe, and the lease is for just ten years.[38] Tribal members are working to negotiate the lease for up to ninety-nine years, in part so that they can apply for funds to build an office space and create more programs on the property. According to Taylor, the NCLT is willing to partner with the tribe on fundraising.[39]

The Burton Homestead is structurally unique among NCLT's properties, as it is the only property with a formal steering committee because of its cultural importance. The grinding rocks and other resources there opened an opportunity for the NCLT to work with the tribe, according to Macon, the NCLT director of conservation programs.[40] The tribe is similarly enthusiastic about its collaborations with the land trust. From Ryberg's perspective, the partnership with the NCLT will help to provide employment, educational opportunities, and grant funds, and it will draw speakers and audiences, all of which will help to support the Tsi-Akim Maidu bid for federal recognition.[41]

What Makes It Work?

The tribe and the NCLT communicate frequently and support one another's events within the small, foothill community of Nevada City. NCLT volunteers and tribal members have developed relationships by collaborating over time on projects ranging from reducing the harmful effects of mercury in fish to supporting the annual Indigenous People's Days. The NCLT is also fortunate to have had administrators with experience in negotiating formal and inclusive agreements and board members who are open to innovative collaborations. For example, before joining NCLT, Macon was the coordinator for the High Sierra Resource Conservation and Development Council, where he gained valuable experience in creating MOUs for collaboration between the council's multiple and diverse partners. According to Macon, the development of the NCLT–Tsi-Akim Maidu MOU and subsequent lease agreement "grew out of how we had been working together and a desire to formalize it."[42]

Alaska Native Lands

Kachemak Heritage Land Trust (Alaska) and Nushagak–Mulchatna Wood–Tikchik Land Trust (Alaska)

Alaska's Native homelands form a complex and unique mosaic of land ownership. Alaska is over 60 percent federally owned (238 million acres), with the largest agency landowner being the Bureau of Land Management, which has 82.5 million acres under its control. In comparison, the State of Alaska owns 89.8 million acres, and Native corporations own 39.3 million acres.[1] The federal government still owes land to both the State of Alaska and Native corporations, based on the agreements associated with Alaska's statehood (1959) and the Alaska Native Claims Settlement Act (ANSCA, 1971).[2] Alaska Native regional and village corporations were formed under the 1971 Act, and they are the largest private landowners in the state.[3] There are also many individual Indian allotments, distributed to heads of household under the Alaska Native Allotment Act of 1906.[4]

Despite its millions of acres of protected national parks, wildlife refuges, and wilderness areas,[5] some of Alaska's open spaces (particularly those in the more populous southwestern and southeastern areas of the state) are being subdivided and developed. When lands are developed, access may be reduced for Native cultural and subsistence needs. At the same time, Native corporations are some of the largest businesses and developers in Alaska, and they need to maintain their ability to develop revenue-generating opportunities on their landholdings. Developing lands poorly can block wildlife corridors, reduce recreational and tourism opportunities, and compromise streams important for salmon migration. However, utilizing lands responsibly by following principles of traditional stewardship can actually enhance ecosystems and wildlife.[6]

Although there are numerous threats to Alaska's resources, both Native Alaskan and non-Native conservation leaders encourage a balanced approach that includes enhancing culture, economics, and ecology, and building communication between Native and non-Native landholders. According to regional Native corporation Cook Inlet Region, Inc. (CIRI) Director Margie Brown, who serves on the national board for the Trust for Public Land and the state board for the Alaska chapter of The Nature Conservancy, "I have tried to discourage the 'sky is falling' approach when describing the need for conservation in Alaska and instead encourage a more thoughtful discussion of 'opportunity' to get things done before conservation is in a crisis mode."[7]

This case study will describe the efforts of two Alaska land trusts—the Kachemak Heritage Land Trust and the Nushagak–Mulchatna Wood–Tikchik Land Trust. Another important, emerging Native Alaska land trust, the Native Conservancy Land Trust led by Dune Lankard, is not discussed here, but some information is available in Wood and Welker's *Tribes As Trustees Again: Part I*[8] and online, in Lankard's own words, during a presentation to Bioneers 2008.[9] Lankard's work to ensure that the shareholders in Alaska Native corporations can vote on conservation decisions speaks to the pressures facing Native Alaska corporations, shareholders, and allottees trying to balance conservation, development, and cultural sovereignty.[10]

Alaska's Conservation Context

According to Kachemak Heritage Land Trust (KHLT) Executive Director Marie McCarty, there are currently five regional land trusts in Alaska that have adopted the twelve standards of the Land Trust Alliance (LTA), each of which has a list of associated practices.[11] The five LTA-member land trusts in Alaska gather every eighteen months to develop and coordinate conservation strategies.[12] Because Native corporations are the largest private landowners in the state, and because Native allottees face immediate development threats, this group has focused some of its meetings on developing procedures for doing outreach to Native communities and corporations. This effort aims to build trust in order to encourage collaboration. As former KHLT Director Barbara Seaman explained, there is a need for constructive information exchange between the land trusts and Alaska Native individuals, communities, and corporations: "They [Native people] have a tradition of being good stewards, and they don't necessarily trust that we are going to do as good of a job. We are clear about being a nonprofit and doing this for the benefit of the future. We respect traditions and property rights."[13] Still, without funds to purchase lands, land trusts may be hard-pressed to convince tribes and Native corporations to collaborate. Even within this context, the KHLT has been involved in several partnerships with Native entities; continues to send information to corporations, village councils, and families; and works to keep communication open and resources available.[14]

The informal Alaska association of land trusts created a brochure for distribution to Alaska Native corporations, tribes, nonprofits, and allottees, which describes natural resource protection concerns and conservation easement options. The brochure urges keeping Native lands in Native hands, and it describes some ways to do that using conservation tools. For example, the KHLT or another land trust can facilitate land transfers between private, non-Native parties back to Native individuals or corporations and hold conservation easements on the properties as a way to ensure that the land will not be developed. For landowners, including Native corporations, who transfer conservation easements to the KHLT, "it is not [a matter of] giving up property rights—just some of the development rights."[15]

Most private landowners have a tax incentive to donate or sell a conservation easement. However, Alaska Native individual allotments are exempt from taxes because they are held in federal trust for allottees by the Bureau of Indian Affairs. As such, these allotment landowners have no tax-based fiscal incentive to donate or sell a conservation easement. On the other hand, land-owning Alaska Native corporations are not exempt from taxes, so they can receive a tax deduction if they donate land or an easement for conservation. However, they may not have the resources to benefit from the deduction. "The crux of the issue is not that we cannot use tax incentives, it is that people or corporations have to have large tax burdens to be able to take advantage of these provisions," explained Brown, CIRI Director. "Alaska Natives, by and large, are not wealthy people, and if someone is not earning enough income to pay taxes, a tax deduction is meaningless."[16]

Another fundamental problem in Alaska with using conservation easements is that they seem contrary to the purposes of a corporation, which include generating revenue for shareholders. As former Seldovia Native Association (SNA, an Alaska Native village corporation) Chairman (1972–2003) and current SNA board member Fred Elvsaas explained:

> We've got an obligation to shareholders, and that obligation runs beyond the boundaries of Seldovia. We have shareholders all over the lower forty-eight states and overseas. . . . Your remote shareholder is not concerned where his dividend comes from, as long as he gets it.

He doesn't have a direct relation with the land anymore, [he's] not using it for subsistence purposes or lifestyle. In fact, [he is] far removed from the corporation and the culture of the tribe. . . . The obligation of the company is first to preserve the company and along with that, to grow the company and to be able to pay meaningful dividends to shareholders, and land trusts don't allow that. . . . Probably there is some way you could use land trusts as a way of saving on taxes, but . . . if you put lands in trust, then you've lost the ability to do things, and [lost] your competitive edge in the business world of the area.[17]

Conservation easements have become nationally known as a tool that *can* bridge business and conservation interests, by using business principles to place values on conservation outcomes. The first half of this chapter will explore initial collaborations between the KHLT and Alaska Native allottees and regional and village corporations to use conservation easements for mutual benefit. The second half of this chapter will focus on the Nushagak–Mulchatna Wood–Tikchik Land Trust, including discussion of proposed legislation that would extend tax incentives for conservation to Alaska Native corporations. The challenges of using conservation easements in an Alaska Native corporate context, as posed by Elvsaas and other Alaska Native corporation leaders, continue to call for creative solutions.

Kachemak Heritage Land Trust

The Kachemak Heritage Land Trust (KHLT), Alaska's first land trust, was established in 1989 to preserve Kenai Peninsula lands with natural, recreational, and cultural value. The KHLT area of service includes the cities of Kenai, Soldotna, Seward, Homer, and many small communities on the peninsula.[18] The KHLT was formed in response to a multiyear land-use conflict involving the Kachemak Bay State Park, a popular recreation destination, the Seldovia Native Association (SNA), and the CIRI.

The conflict dates back to the years immediately following the 1971 passage of ANCSA, when Alaska Native regional and village corporations began making land selections. Since the land freeze had been lifted following the settlement of Alaska Native land claims, the state was simultaneously selecting lands pursuant to the Alaska Statehood Act of 1959.[19] SNA selected lands that the state had previously selected as "Mental Health Lands," following Public Law 84-830 (1956).[20] The SNA interpreted ANCSA to read that all land around the village itself was available to the Native village corporation for selection. However, the state interpreted the law as saying that state-selected "general" (that is, non–Mental Health Lands) land was available for selection by village corporations, whereas Mental Health Lands were not. This was not clarified, but the SNA learned that the state had selected the Kachemak Bay State Park (designated as a park in 1970) as general land, so the SNA amended its request and selected land within the park instead. "Then the state came unglued," remembered Elvsaas.[21]

After Elvsaas led the SNA in securing nearly 30,000 acres of the park, he asked if the state would like to do a land trade with the SNA, so that the state could get the parkland back. The SNA wanted to trade for land that had market value and the ability to generate revenue. The SNA met resistance from the state and local constituencies near lands the Native corporation selected. This struggle began in the early 1970s, under Alaska Governor William Egan, and did not come to full resolution until the beginning of the second term of Alaska Governor Walter Hickel in the early 1990s. At this time, local conservationists were concerned because SNA owned timber rights (as well as land rights) on large inholdings within the park, and they had sold rights to clear-cut to Koncor Forest Products, Inc., an Alaska Native timber management company.[22]

Rather than exacerbating the conflict through opposition, the KHLT began to work with the SNA, recognized their property rights, and helped to bring the parties together. The SNA is located within the region of the Alaska Native regional corporation CIRI, which was asked to step in and facilitate the agreement with the SNA, the timber company, and the state. However, negotiations to have the state buy the land stalled. When the CIRI agreed to sell its subsurface estate to the state (Alaska Native regional corporations own subsurface rights to lands that Alaska Native village corporations own surface rights to), the negotiations were completed just in time for legislative approval. In addition to the CIRI sale, the state purchased SNA's surface rights, including the timber.[23] The state used funds from the Exxon Valdez oil spill settlement to make these purchases.[24]

Ultimately, the SNA received revenue from the land while still protecting the resource. According to Elvsaas, the SNA also benefitted from the increase in value on their private land when the park went into permanent protection:

> Putting that land back in the park made more of [Kachemak] Bay open to recreation, but [it meant that there was] less private land, so the value of the remaining private land went up. As the largest landholder in Kachemak country, [SNA's] values went instantly up.... A trust such as Kachemak Bay State Park gave us an instant benefit.... Our people have full use of the parkland, too, so we haven't lost a thing, but yet managed to enhance our values.[25]

Both the CIRI and the KHLT were essential to making this deal happen. "Although we played a small role, we did help bring the [SNA] to the table," said Seaman.[26] She attributed the land trust's success to its size and character: "Land trusts are usually small, regional organizations—we know each other in the community and people tend to trust people they know."[27] Elvsaas confirmed the land trust's very helpful role in the transaction.[28] This community work won the KHLT the 1991 Allen Morgan Award from the Land Trust Alliance (LTA), which honors land trusts for excellence in membership development.

Cook Inlet

In 2000, owners of a successful construction company offered to donate a 43-acre parcel on Cook Inlet to the KHLT. The company had already developed the surrounding property into high-end homes. This remaining piece afforded these homes a scenic view of the inlet and mountains beyond. The company owners realized that the view was an asset to the neighborhood, and they could receive a tax benefit from donating the parcel to the land trust, which would protect the land from further development.

Because the KHLT covers a large area with a small staff and operates under strategic planning guidelines, the organization takes time to research every parcel it is offered. "We don't want to be haphazard," Seaman explained. "We want to be strategic, and this piece popped out as significant."[29] Ecologically, the parcel was wetland, with beachfront habitat that was good for moose and other animals. Noting that the parcel bordered Kenaitze Indian Tribe (Dena'ina) land, KHLT staff contacted the tribal offices and found that the site was culturally important as a place for gathering beach greens and fish. Dena'ina people return to the site, known as Neli Gheli or "waterfront," in the springtime to gather food and fish (fig. 11.1).[30]

The KHLT accepted the company's land donation and began working with the tribe to craft the terms of the conservation easement. The tribe wanted to ensure that traditional uses could continue, and the KHLT wanted to be certain that open spaces and habitat could be protected. In a trade, the KHLT transferred ownership of the parcel to the tribe, and the tribe turned a conservation easement over to the KHLT. The easement prohibits development or commercial use. In lieu of any payment, the tribe made an endowment to the KHLT's stewardship fund to enable ongoing monitoring of the parcel and to provide for legal defense. The KHLT preserves the principal and uses the interest from these funds to cover the costs of monitoring and maintaining the easement.

FIGURE 11.1. Robert Fulton (Dena'ina) on the 43-acre parcel on Cook Inlet owned by the Kenaitze Indian Tribe and protected by a conservation easement held by the Kachemak Heritage Land Trust. (Photo courtesy of Wild North Photography, Kachemak Heritage Land Trust)

Monitoring is a cornerstone of the KHLT's activities, just as it is with most land trusts. When the KHLT acquires an easement, it commits to ongoing monitoring to ensure compliance with the terms of the easement. At the time the easement is assigned, the land trust begins with baseline documentation of all aspects of the parcel (soils, wildlife, vegetation, history, and so forth). This is often done in coordination with the landowner. As part of this baseline information gathering, KHLT staff members produce detailed maps of the site and establish photo points where they will take photographs annually. If the KHLT is ever challenged in court, the maps and photo documentation provide important evidence of changing conditions on the site. When the KHLT visits a site (annually or more often, as needed), the land trust invites the landowner to participate in the site visit. Afterwards, the KHLT sends the landowner a detailed report of the monitoring results. If the landowner initiates any changes on the site, such as building trails or structures (as might be allowed under the easement terms), he or she notifies the KHLT first, and the land trust may visit and monitor development.[31]

KHLT former Executive Director Seaman remembered the Cook Inlet land transfer as one of her happier memories of a successful land transaction: "We went in to [the tribe's] board meeting and offered them a piece of land that was important to their culture. They were thrilled, and we were thrilled—everyone was happy."[32] This was an important land acquisition for the tribe, since this land had been out of Native ownership for many years. According to Rita Smagge, then executive director of the Kenaitze Indian Tribe, "The preservation and perpetuation of our tribal culture and traditions cannot be separated from the preservation of our ancestral lands and natural resources."[33] The land was effectively returned. "The trust was there," added Seaman.[34]

Because of the unique cultural, scenic, and recreational values of this parcel, the KHLT's conservation easement has more restrictive terms. Most KHLT easements balance conservation with development of one or more residential elements. In Alaska, property that has a covenant disallowing the construction of any features does not have a high resale value. "We want people to be able to live on and enjoy their property and still protect conservation values," Seaman explained.[35] The easement on Cook Inlet, however, allows only traditional uses, recreation, and educational activities.

Seeking Conservation Options for Allotment Lands: Spotlight on Ninilchik Lake

Alaska Native corporations and tribes, conservationists, developers, timber and oil companies, and others are all concerned with the status of Native allotment lands, which compose a large number of individual, 160-acre parcels throughout the state. As Alaska develops and Native allottees consider their property rights, some are selling their lands. Overselling of allotment land will fragment the habitats that make Alaska unique. The KHLT continues to make itself available to explore conservation options with these landowners, as well as to make presentations to Native communities, villages, and corporations that may be interested in forming their own land trusts. On allotments held in trust by the Bureau of Indian Affairs (BIA), the land trust and the allottee must contact the bureau early on in the process so that the agency can be involved in and approve or disapprove of any changes.

A former KHLT board member, Bruce Oskolkoff, is now director of Land and Resources for the Alaska Native village corporation Ninilchik Natives Association, Inc. Oskolkoff, his parents, aunts, uncles, and brothers and sisters are the heirs to a 160-acre parcel surrounding Ninilchik Lake, the only major lake in the central Kenai Peninsula. The lake is critical wetland habitat for cranes, swans, moose, and other animals. Oskolkoff and his family hope to work with the KHLT on a potential conservation easement.

The Oskolkoff parcel has been in probate for more than thirty years and is just now being deeded into separate parcels (each held in trust by the BIA for an individual heir), despite some heirs' wishes to keep the parcel in one piece. The allottees' will was not clear, and the BIA divided the property so that all twelve legal heirs (Oskolkoff's parent's generation) have a 2.5-acre slice of lakefront property, as well as equal shares in the remaining acreage, which is split into 10-acre tracts.[36] The twelve heirs each have between two and five children, so each of the subdivisions constitutes a tenancy in common for the second generation of heirs.

Oskolkoff and other family members are concerned that it will be tempting for heirs to take their smaller, subdivided parcels out of federal trust and sell them, thereby fragmenting the original allotment. "It's a unique situation," Oskolkoff said, because most land is removed from trust and then subdivided, but in this case the land was subdivided and then put into trust. He believes that his grandparents meant for the property to remain undivided. "They always said they wanted to see it protected and kept in one piece," he said. "They assumed that everyone would get a user right, and the property would stay intact."[37]

Many of the other allotments in this area of the central Kenai Peninsula have been sold—largely to non-Native interests. There are only six remaining allotments, including the Oskolkoff parcel. As he began looking around the state at options to protect the property, Oskolkoff met Seaman, who was thinking about how conservation tools could be used to protect Native lands. Oskolkoff served on the KHLT board from 2001 through 2003, hoping to learn more about easements and other tools. "There is a lot more work to do in terms of making progress to protect Native allotments," he said. "In the Homer area, [land trusts] haven't really broken through to Native interests."[38] This may be because this particular area has a higher overall population and a lower number of allotments than other parts of the state.

Another reason Oskolkoff feels that there has not been much success with applying conservation tools to Native allotment lands is that there have been other pressing conservation concerns for land trusts in Alaska, such as protecting riverfront lands that directly affect salmon habitat. From the viewpoint of allottees, although they want to protect their lands, it can be difficult to resist high offers from prospective buyers. Oskolkoff's family has been offered millions for the whole parcel, and one of his relatives has been offered more than $800,000 just for her own 2.5-acre lakefront piece. "Everyone knows the lake, and they ask me how we will ever protect it," Oskolkoff said. "In reality, there may be no way to get owner agreement to do that."[39]

As Oskolkoff looked at the conservation tools available, he decided that easements would be the most appealing to the family. The forty-some heirs met and discussed this option, and some raised concerns about placing restrictive conditions on valuable property that they may need to sell one day. They also discussed selling the property to a land trust, but many felt that the land was just too valuable not to sell to the highest bidder. Ultimately, many family members were not opposed to finding a way to protect the property, if they could agree on a strategy that did not take away all of their ownership rights, including the right to sell.

Contrasts and Similarities: Alaska Native Corporation Conservation Options

The property rights situation is different for Native corporations vis-à-vis allotment lands. Oskolkoff was president of the Ninilchik Natives Association, Inc. (NNAI), an Alaska Native village corporation that, along with the Cook Inlet Region, Inc. (CIRI), owns much of the central Kenai Peninsula. The NNAI's property is developable, with good timber and riverfront acreage. Land around the NNAI's holdings is being subdivided steadily, and the corporation is also developing some of its own lands. On lands they have set aside and will not develop, the corporation faces the same "temptation," as Oskolkoff terms it, as Native allottees: to sell the land for large sums of money.[40]

As president of the NNAI, Oskolkoff worked to set up a land trust, which was later incorporated into the NNAI as the Two Rivers Trust. It was a joint venture between the tribe and the corporation, both of which had balanced representation on the trust's board. The Alaska State Branch of The Nature Conservancy (TNC) supported the formation of the Two Rivers Trust, and TNC State Director Randy Hagenstein served on its board. The trust's goal was to think about conservation alternatives for corporation lands. Following nearly two years of regular meetings, a leadership change occurred, the trust's board stopped meeting, and the trust became inactive.

Under the Alaska Native Claims Settlement Act, corporations have the power to let their land "sit," thereby "banking" land assets in a nontaxable status, which effectively preserves resources. However, if land is not actively managed, key habitats may change, altering the land's value for wildlife and subsistence. There is a balance between leaving land alone and allocating the resources to manage it. Leasing or selling the land for development could result in numerous habitat impacts. Alaska Native corporate shareholders have diverse interests, which include but are not limited to protecting land for subsistence users. However, the driving interest remains the bottom line—shareholders must benefit from how the corporation manages its holdings. Oskolkoff draws a contrast with land trusts, which he says have "a lot of tools but one main direction: to protect resources and interests in land itself."[41]

Oskolkoff was hoping that a land trust and conservation easements would be able to place protective covenants on allotment and corporation land to take it out of developable status. Corporations have to think about these related management, financial, and preservation issues on a very large scale—the NNAI, for example, has about 160,000 acres, with more to be added, and the CIRI is even larger. "The magnitude of the holdings is staggering—in the middle of highly developable property," Oskolkoff said. "They can protect it if they plan on it."[42] Although Oskolkoff initially thought that a land trust would be a way to keep land intact, he and other Native landowners are concerned about the possible lack of safeguards for land trust management. They are concerned that landowners could sell to a land trust expecting perpetual protection, and then the land trust could sell the land.

According to former KHLT Director Seaman, that sort of sale is extremely rare and can be avoided with an array of legal mechanisms to ensure that the land trust complies with the landowner's mandate to protect land in perpetuity. These safeguards include transferring the land with deed restrictions on it, transferring the conservation easement to another entity for double protection, or going to a county recorder's office and recording the land trust board's resolution accepting the property. "It would be really unusual to see a land trust receive a piece of property and dispose of it in a way that didn't fit the landowner's wishes," she said.[43]

Current KHLT Director McCarty said that the land trust, for example, works to avoid miscommunication with landowners by maintaining two categories of land donations: conservation lands and trade lands.[44] The KHLT board agrees to provide permanent protection to conservation lands by either retaining direct ownership or by accepting and holding a permanent conservation easement. The KHLT, like many other land trusts, was not formed to become a landowning organization; instead, its larger purpose is to enable landowners to conserve their properties while retaining ownership. To this end, the KHLT will accept and enforce easements in perpetuity, but it may not want to own property in perpetuity. In deciding whether to hold the land or the conservation easement, the KHLT always gives priority to the owners' wishes. "We wouldn't sell something that the landowner did not want us to sell," Seaman said.[45]

The second category, "trade lands," are parcels that the KHLT and the donor have mutually agreed have no conservation value. The KHLT is authorized by the landowner to sell trade lands to benefit work to conserve other properties. As indicated above, the KHLT also accepts donations of conservation easements, which empowers the land trust to enforce development restrictions on property even when it changes hands.

Nevertheless, Oskolkoff feels that the potential for abuse exists. He described but did not name a land trust that was founded solely to gain ownership of land. "It's disappointing," he said, and it leaves Native landowners with the question of whom to trust when they are trying to conserve their lands. "Tribal people want to know: if we convey the land to a land trust, what assurance is there that it will be there forever?"[46] According to Seaman, the LTA and its member land trusts would have a very negative response to a land trust that obtained property simply to sell it.[47] Oskolkoff also voiced concern over alienating tribal lands: "Land trusts are trying to use all available tools to protect lands, but Native people are saying, 'Why shouldn't I just stay in power, and control this land, rather than give it to a land trust that may sell it later?'"[48]

Both Seaman and TNC State Director Hagenstein felt that Native landowners can simultaneously conserve and retain ownership of their lands. "We know Native people are proven stewards of the land, and [using conservation easements] is a way they can protect their heritage," Seaman explained.[49] According to Hagenstein, TNC encourages land trusts and conservation organizations to give priority to acquiring conservation easements on Native lands, thereby leaving most of the property rights in Native hands. Hagenstein also envisions Native land trusts becoming the entities that hold the easements on Native lands, ensuring that no part of the chain of title leaves Native ownership.[50]

In developing relationships with land trusts, Native and non-Native landowners alike need to use available legal safeguards to hold land trusts accountable. As Seaman notes, "[Land trusts] are supposed to keep [the property] in a certain condition forever via a conservation easement—they are making a promise that the land will be protected. The law is pretty well established. It would not be worth the land trust's while to break the landowner's trust."[51] In addition, land trusts—and particularly land trusts that adhere to the Land Trust Alliance's standards and practices—are quite watchful of the practices of other trusts. This is because just one unethical organization can ruin a landowner's perception of the public interest goals of most land trusts.

Building a Bridge

The KHLT recently completed an updated conservation prioritization strategy, and it recognizes that Native lands in its region are the most valuable and contested parcels, in terms of habitat, open space, and access. The trust plans to work to build communication and collaboration with Native communities and corporations, to assist them in setting up Native land trusts or to find incentives to establish conservation easements on their land.

The KHLT has had Alaska Native representation on their board and hopes to have more representation in the future. As a smaller land trust, one of its constraints is it cannot purchase easements; instead, it receives all of its easements by generous donations from willing landowners. Native corporations have to produce revenue for their shareholders and therefore need to realize a profit from land transactions, so they cannot simply donate lands or easements. Native corporations have offered to sell easements to land trusts, and larger trusts like The Conservation Fund and The Nature Conservancy have purchased them. Although smaller land trusts like the KHLT may not be able to afford to buy easements and parcels that corporations put up for sale, they might play a key role in mediating these transactions if they have good relationships with both the Native corporation and the large conservation organization.

The Nushagak–Mulchatna Wood–Tikchik Land Trust

An Alaska Native corporation, Choggiung Limited, initiated the formation of the Nushagak–Mulchatna Wood–Tikchik Land Trust (NMWTLT) in 2000 in response to the rate of sale of Alaska Native allotment lands.[52] The NMWTLT works in southwestern Alaska in the Bristol Bay region, encompassing six major watersheds (the Nushagak, Wood, Igushik, Togiak, Goodnews, and Kanektok Rivers), America's largest state park (the 1.6 million-acre Wood-Tikchik State Park), the U.S. Fish and Wildlife Service's 4.8 million-acre Togiak National Wildlife Refuge, 1.4 million acres of Alaska Native corporation land, and hundreds of individual Native allotment parcels ranging in size from 30 to 160 acres.[53] Because Native allottees selected lands based partially on subsistence (and thereby habitat) value, these parcels are under development pressure and represent key priorities for conservation.

Alaska Native Corporations and Allotment Inholdings

Many Alaska Native individuals applied for allotments just before ANCSA passed in 1971 and extinguished the 1906 Alaska Native Allotment Act. Some applied for lands that their families had been using for centuries, and others simply applied for available lands to ensure that they had rights to some property within their homeland. The BIA holds all Alaska Native allotments in trust for individuals. With BIA approval, individual owners or groups of owners who are heirs to a single parcel can take lands out of trust and sell them.

When Alaska National Interest Lands Conservation Act (ANILCA) passed in 1980, nearly 8,000 pending allotment applications were approved, many of which were within existing land-use designations, such as national parks, wilderness areas, and lands selected by Alaska Native corporations. This created a patchwork of land ownership, preventing large land managers (such as parks and Native corporations) from managing all of the lands within their boundaries. Today, twenty-five years after the approval of many allotments and with the growing popularity of sportfishing concessions in the Bristol Bay region, individual allotment owners are coming under increasing financial pressure to sell.

Although some Native allotment holders have offered to sell their land to the surrounding Native corporation, the typical practice is to sell to non-Natives who want to develop lodges or sportfishing businesses. As Tim Troll, former chief executive officer of Choggiung Limited and current executive director of the NMWTLT, explained: "This was undermining the ability of Native corporations to manage their lands. The policy of the corporation was to manage its land in a manner that did not compromise shareholder use of the land for hunting, fishing, and continuing their subsistence lifestyle. That lifestyle and the resources that support it are harder to manage if a hunting or fishing lodge is built in the middle of corporate lands."[54]

In addition, if Native allottees sell their lands within this patchwork of Native corporation and allotment lands, it can affect the corporation's economic development. For example, Native corporations own property on both banks of the Nushagak River, where they have developed revenue-generating, seasonal sportfishing camps. As Randy Hagenstein, Alaska state director of The Nature Conservancy (TNC), said: "They are selling an exclusive experience in an environment that is stewarded well and without permanent structures. If one of the allotments goes on the market, and a commercial lodge developer buys it and puts in a camp or a lodge, then the Native corporations lose their exclusivity, and the experience they want to provide their clients is degraded."[55] This business-based reasoning would provide a viable justification for a Native corporation to allocate funds to purchase an individual allotment, but the mere threat that an allotment might be sold to a developer cannot justify spending corporate funds to buy isolated parcels.

As Elvsaas explained: "When you look at conservation easements you have to look at, 'How does it affect your bottom line? How does it affect your shareholders? How does it affect your company's ability to grow?'"[56] A corporation must also treat shareholders equitably, and purchasing one shareholder's allotment but not another's, when both would willingly sell to the corporation, could be seen as unfair dealing.[57] The corporation could justify using corporate resources to buy parcels for development, which would generate funds for all shareholders, but it is more difficult to justify buying parcels in remote areas to protect stewardship and subsistence values.

FIGURE 11.2. Aerial photo of the Agulowak River. The Nushagak–Mulchatna Wood–Tikchik Land Trust worked with The Conservation Fund to negotiate a $10 million conservation deal with Aleknagik Natives Ltd. and the Bristol Bay Regional Corporation. The easement protects both surface rights owned by Aleknagik Natives Ltd. and subsurface rights, owned by the regional Bristol Bay Native Association. (Photo courtesy of The Conservation Fund)

Faced with this challenge, Choggiung Limited began conversations with The Nature Conservancy (TNC) and The Conservation Fund (TCF) about supporting conservation on Native lands. TCF is an environmental nonprofit focused on conserving American landscapes and building sustainable conservation leadership. In one historic transaction, a Native corporate shareholder had an allotment on the Agulowak River, a world-class trout-fishing stream in the Wood Tikchik State Park, which he offered to sell to Choggiung Limited (fig. 11.2). There was no business justification for purchasing the parcel, and it was not an inholding on corporate lands. However, the allottee was able to sell the land to TCF. This was the first significant conservation purchase by a nonprofit conservation organization in the area.

Choggiung Limited asked TCF if it could facilitate purchasing other allotments, but TCF has to consider each potential acquisition in light of its national conservation goals. Instead, the organization suggested that

Choggiung Limited consider forming a nonprofit land trust that could acquire parcels of local conservation interest and manage them for their subsistence value. Choggiung took the suggestion seriously, and with the help of TNC, the corporation sent employees to the national LTA Rally in 1998 to find out about land trusts. It subsequently formed the NMWTLT, which eventually took a conservation easement on the parcel acquired by TCF.

TNC has also purchased allotments for conservation, but the organization prefers transactions in which Native entities retain title. The board of trustees and staff for TNC in Alaska compiled a set of guiding principles for engaging with allotment holders. The principles established tiers of action, in which fee-simple acquisition is the least appealing option because it constitutes erosion of Native title. Conservation easements, on the other hand, were a much more acceptable mechanism for land conservation. Similarly, the NMWTLT prefers acquiring conservation easements. As Troll explained, "We don't want to take land out of Native ownership. If we purchase the development rights, the owner can retain the property for subsistence."[58] This strategy has had mixed outcomes for keeping Native land in Native ownership, but it has left the decision-making power in Native hands. Two allotments on which TNC has easements were later sold by the Native owner to a non-Native.[59]

The Alaska Dilemma: Tax Incentives for Conservation Easement Donations

The NMWTLT is striving to develop ways that Native landowners can protect habitat and subsistence while still obtaining revenue from their lands. Alaska Native corporations pay taxes on all income, including income generated by lands they hold,[60] yet these Native entities are not currently included in the proposed temporary or permanent conservation tax incentives. Like the farmers and ranchers who are eligible for these incentives, Alaska Native corporations also own ecologically significant land, but in contrast to the farmers and ranchers, the corporations often receive limited cash income from that land.[61] Many Alaska Native corporation shareholders are also involved in traditional subsistence for livelihood and survival,[62] but the benefits received from these uses are not quantified in the same ways as farmers' and ranchers' revenue. As U.S. Senator for Alaska Mark Begich has noted, with development pressure increasing in Alaska,

> population growth and the pressure to pursue cash-generating activities have increased the desire for substantial development. . . . Without permanent protection, [Alaska Native] land could be developed in a

manner that would destroy its ability to support the traditional ways and subsistence lifestyles crucial to Alaskan Native communities. Making use of tax incentives available to other Americans will make it easier for Native communities to make the right decisions for their shareholders.[63]

Under Alaska statutes, Alaska Native corporations may place easements on their lands.[64] However, if a corporation were to donate an easement today, it would be able to deduct just 10 percent of its income over five years. For example, if the donated easement was worth $1 million,[65] and the corporation's taxable income was $1 million, it could write off only 10 percent of that income, or $100,000 every year for five years, for a total of $500,000, just half of the value of the gift. In contrast, under the 2006–2009 conservation tax incentive, qualified farmers and ranchers could deduct up to 100 percent of their income over fifteen years, until they reached the value of the gift. This makes sense for donors who are relatively cash poor but rich in land assets and who want to continue ownership and uses permitted under a conservation easement. Although the temporary conservation tax incentive expired on December 31, 2009, an effort is underway to make it permanent, via House Resolution 1831 and Senate Bill 812. Conservationists expect that Congress will renew the incentive for another temporary period before possibly ratifying the bills.[66] If these bills, and the proposed Senate Bill 1673 and House Resolution 3568 (discussed below), are passed, Alaska Native corporations will also benefit from the conservation tax incentive by being able to deduct the full value of their donated easements.

Activists like Harris, Troll, and others are advocating for policy makers to accept that Alaskan lands are productive, in terms of producing salmon and wildlife, for example. They would like conservationists to recognize that the Native corporations stewarding land are economically dependent on it, and that they are providing important and unpaid conservation services, just as farmers and ranchers do.[67] This concept is particularly important for Native corporations because land is their primary asset, and under corporate principles, assets must be converted into monetary value. "If the federal income tax incentives given to farmers and ranchers for conservation easement donations were the same for Native corporations who own vast tracts of land, it would make it easier to protect these lands," Troll explained.[68] As will be discussed later in the chapter, the value of the conservation easement extends far beyond the tax benefit for Native corporations, but it would still be useful and would provide a financial justification for conservation. According to Harris, the Tyonek Native Corporation has pledged to put any tax savings from easements back into conservation.[69]

On September 15, 2009, Senator Begich introduced Senate Bill 1673 and U.S. Representative for Alaska Don Young introduced House Resolution 3568 to amend the Internal Revenue Code 170(b)(2) to extend the conservation tax incentives to Alaska Native corporations so that they will be eligible for a tax deduction from donating qualified conservation easements. The donations must qualify under Section 170(h)(1), be made by a Native corporation, or be ANSCA land. Section 170(b)(2) states the length of time for which the deduction is valid and the percentage of income that can be deducted. The two proposed bills are collectively referred to as the Alaska Native Conservation Parity Act of 2009. As of early 2010, SB 1673 was in the Senate Finance Committee and HR 3568 was in the House Ways and Means Committee.

TNC, the LTA, and the Alaska Federation of Natives (AFN) support the Parity Act.[70] The AFN resolution argues that the act would enable Alaska Native corporations to simultaneously protect significant habitat and meet their fiduciary responsibilities to shareholders. The resolution also notes the inequality inherent in having incentives that are available to land-rich but cash-poor farmers and ranchers but that exclude Native landowners, whose primary asset is land and who are facing significant conservation pressure.[71] The Tyonek Native Corporation and the Native Village of Tyonek submitted the successful resolution to the AFN, were instrumental in the development of the act itself, and have a plan for its implementation.[72] The corporation has defined an 8-mile stretch of its land along the Chuitna River that it would like to see covered by a conservation easement held by a federally recognized tribe, the Native Village of Tyonek.[73] TNC is currently working with the tribe to do baseline documentation for the easement and to develop a monitoring plan.[74]

Although government entities like the tribe can hold conservation easements, will the easement donor be eligible for a tax deduction? This question is also being asked in the lower forty-eight states, and the answer has largely been positive. Tribes are qualified recipients of donated easements under IRS Code 170(h)(3), which mentions states and political subdivisions, and IRS Code Section 7871, which notes that tribes may be treated as states for determining when contributions (of conservation easements, for example) may result in tax deductions. Further, the Indian Tribal Government Tax Status Act (1982) and Section 1065 of the Tax Reform Act (1984) establish that Indian tribal governments are to be treated as states or as political subdivisions for specified federal tax purposes, including deductions based on charitable donations. However, these provisions have yet to be tested. If the Alaska Native Conservation Parity Act of 2009 is made into law, the Native Village of Tyonek may be the first tribe to hold a conservation easement, and the Tyonek Native Corporation may be the first entity to receive a tax deduction for donating a conservation easement to a tribe.

Significance of the Chuitna Easement

For the Tyonek Native Corporation, which has spearheaded the effort to extend the conservation tax incentive to Alaska Native corporations, the value of the conservation easement goes far beyond tax incentives.[75] The Chuitna River is particularly important to Tyonek Native Corporation's members, the Tebughna people, because it is important habitat for five species of salmon, including king salmon. The salmon are not only important for the tribe's subsistence, but they also support the declining Cook Inlet beluga whale (*Delphinapterus leucas*). This whale population has been dropping so rapidly that the National Marine Fisheries Service has proposed to make Cook Inlet critical habitat for the beluga. The inlet is the site of projects, commerce, and development that would all be impacted by this designation.[76]

Harris and Elvsaas both noted that the whale is declining because the salmon have declined due to destruction of salmon spawning habitat in rivers and streams that feed the inlet. The Tyonek Corporation's proposed conservation easement would enhance and restore salmon habitat, thereby helping the salmon, the beluga, and the people—particularly the traditional Tebughna people who have always relied on the beluga for subsistence. As Harris explained:

> The Chuitna River is the last river between Anchorage and our village that still has its traditional run of king salmon. We want the whale to survive because this village is a whale-hunting community. We are the only Athabascan whale-hunting community in the world, and this generation is the first generation since the beginning of time that will not be a whale-hunting generation, because there are no king [salmon]. This effort we are attempting on this river is to rebuild the king salmon for the survival of this species of beluga whale, and to encourage the rest of the community to restore their rivers [where] king salmon [spawn].[77]

The conservation easement would cover 2,700 acres of land along the Chuitna. The river is threatened by both overfishing and regional economic development, including the proposed Beluga coal projects.[78] A video by the Tyonek Corporation, entitled "For the Benefit of All," indicates that sustainable energy projects (including hydroelectric, geothermal, and coal-to-gas-to-liquid projects) can co-exist with sacred site protection and conservation activities along the river.[79] However, the local tribe—the Tebughna of the Native Village of Tyonek—may not be as convinced. An April 2010 editorial in the *Bristol Bay Times* noted that the tribe opposed the Beluga coal projects, citing concern for the health of their subsistence resources on surrounding lands and waters.[80] The terms of a conservation easement that would protect the resource, yet still allow some development, access, and stewardship, have yet to be finalized.

Harris sees the easement as an assertion of relationship to and respectful management of the land. He is concerned about the general decline in Native Alaskan wildlife, and, in turn, the decline in the ability of Native Alaskans to acquire traditional healthy foods and engage in intergenerational subsistence practices. He feels strongly that conservation practices that have closed land to any management and subsistence hunting have caused imbalances and decline in wildlife populations:

> Those who think they know what's best will put out all forest fires as soon as they occur, and, as such, there is no new growth. . . . Wildlife are forced to migrate to areas where there is harvesting and new growth, usually in areas near people, predators follow them . . . then a policy came down, 'thou shalt not kill wolves,' and . . . we had a 98 percent moose calf mortality because of predators. Predators are so abundant, but they are starving; the balance has been disturbed. . . . We are very shocked with what has happened, and very anxious.[81]

Harris sees conservation easements as a useful strategy that allows limiting destructive use, but enabling stewardship and subsistence. "When we talk about a conservation easement, we are not wanting to conserve what is, we are wanting to conserve for what will be," he added, differentiating active conservation from hands-off conservation.[82] Extending the conservation tax incentives to Native corporations like Tyonek will enable them to begin using easements as a tool to protect and restore critical habitat.

Nushagak–Mulchatna Wood–Tikchik Land Trust: Governance and Partnerships

Although the NMWTLT was initiated by a Native corporation, the land trust recognized that funding to run the land trust and accomplish conservation goals would most likely come from outside the Native community and outside the region. As such, the trust established a board that could draw on broader interests, resources, and skills. Currently, there are four Native board members, one of whom serves as board president, and five non-Native members, including representatives of sportfishing and commercial fishing industries. According to Troll, board members share a common focus on habitat protection, and no board decisions have generated internal controversy.

The NMWTLT has also thrived through critical partnerships with TNC and TCF. These two conservation giants are focused on preserving southwestern Alaska because it is the largest remaining wild salmon run in the world. In what Troll describes as a "symbiotic relationship," the TNC and TCF raise funds to acquire parcels and then turn them over to the NMWTLT.[83] In turn, the NMWTLT raises stewardship funds to monitor lands it receives for conservation and to provide resources for potential litigation.

The NMWTLT has also been expanding its work into water conservation, in partnership with TNC and the Southwest Alaska Salmon Habitat Partnership, which is now part of the National Fish Habitat Partnership Initiative. The NMWTLT has been monitoring streams to determine the distribution of salmon, and then nominating streams for inclusion in the *Catalog of Waters Important for the Spawning, Rearing, or Migration of Anadromous Fishes*.[84] After a stream is accepted, any proposed actions on it must be permitted by the Alaska Department of Fish and Game. The NMWTLT has also been examining water-rights procedures under which individuals and organizations can apply to the Department of Natural Resources to reserve water in streams for fish. This is important for Native corporations because, while corporate lands include waters, corporations do not own the water or the riverbeds.[85] However, these corporations may be able to use environmental statutes to expand regulation and control over culturally and economically important waters that cross corporate lands.

Trust Land and Easement

Currently, the NMWTLT owns two parcels in fee and holds the conservation easements on another two parcels. The funds to purchase the land or the easement for all of these parcels were initially raised by TNC or TCF. The NMWTLT owned the Chythlook easement on land held in federal trust by the BIA, located in the Silver Horn Fiord of Lake Beverly. However, it took that land out of federal trust and sold it, but the easement remains in effect.

The question of whether or not the BIA can be held legally responsible if an easement is violated on trust land has not been tested. Troll believes that the easement remains an enforceable right, even if the land is in federal trust. In his opinion, federal sovereign immunity does not apply if there is a contractual arrangement to which the Native allottee agreed and the federal government assented.[86]

The federal government, through the Bureau of Indian Affairs (BIA), does not substitute its judgment for that of the Native allottee; it merely takes measures to assure the Native allottee is not defrauded. When the land trust negotiates to buy a parcel or a conservation easement from a Native landowner who has his or her land in federal trust, the BIA's responsibility is to appraise the land. The allottee cannot sell the land for less than the land's fair market value, as determined by the BIA appraisal.

Challenges

Faced with the sheer number of Native allotments situated within key habitat and cultural sites, the biggest challenge facing the NMWTLT is raising funds to purchase lands or easements. According to Troll, most available federal or state grants are for doing restoration work, rather than acquisitions.[87] The NMWTLT is focused on protecting habitat on Native allotment lands that are surrounded by either Native corporation lands, or non-conservation lands owned by the state and designated for "general public use." These two land management arrangements pose the greatest challenges for fundraising because of the impossibility of guaranteeing large-scale conservation. For example, if a Native allotment comes up for sale inside a state park, funders know that if they support the purchase, all of the land around the allotment is protected. On private lands, however, the land around the allotment is not protected, so purchasing the allotment parcel does nothing to stop development from occurring in surrounding areas. Rather than helping to guarantee a 160-acre (or even smaller) island of protection, funders typically prefer to contribute to larger projects. However, the parcels most vulnerable to development are these individual allotment lands within general-use state land and corporate landholdings, particularly along the Nushagak River. Corporations must go through lengthy procedures to make land use and management decisions, but individual Native allottees can decide very quickly to alienate or develop their lands.

Strategy

The NMWTLT developed a prioritization process for Alaska Native allotment and Native corporation lands along the Nushagak River, using a database of traditional ecological knowledge (TEK). The TEK database contains local Native knowledge of plants, landscapes, waterways, animals, and other natural resources. Working with a local tribal watershed council, NMWTLT staff members visited the Native villages in the region and completed mapping sessions with Native elders and other village residents to identify areas important for subsistence hunting gathering and fishing. Elders have been willing to share this information in order to protect the sites.

Working with GIS staff at TNC, NMWTLT staff used this TEK information to create a digitized, searchable TEK database. TNC digitized the spatial TEK data (which consisted primarily of lines and points noting important habitat, traditional use locations, and place names) and merged them with other data layers available from federal and state agencies identifying important wildlife habitat. Combining diverse data sets enabled NMWTLT to prioritize Native allotments for protection based upon where multiple values and uses converged.

The TEK database has also been the basis for collaborations between NMWTLT and Native corporations, associations, and tribes. NMWTLT recently used it to prioritize conservation on Native allotments along the Nushagak River. There are nearly 350 allotments in this area alone, and they have varying degrees of habitat and cultural value. TNC overlaid the TEK GIS layer (including the spatial files and linked database) with information on fish distribution and habitat and used all of the resulting information to rank allotments for conservation.

In addition to serving as the executive director for the NMWTLT, Troll is also the Southwest Alaska Program Director with TNC, and TNC has an MOU with the NMWLT to produce the TEK layer and database. The data in the TEK layer belong to the Bristol Bay Native Association (BBNA), a nonprofit tribal consortium composed of thirty-one tribes in the Bristol Bay area. BBNA is underwriting the costs of the project, with the help of a USFWS grant to the Curyung Tribe. TNC has also partially underwritten the project with grant funding it received from the Gordon and Betty Moore Foundation. TNC has the rights to use the information to prepare land prioritization plans but cannot share the information in the database without BBNA's permission.

In October 2009, Koliganek Natives, LTD, an Alaska Native Village Corporation in Koliganek, Alaska, and also a member of BBNA, established an MOU with the NMWTLT and TNC to develop a conservation land management plan by mapping culturally and ecologically important sites. The plan will help Koliganek to responsibly guide future development. Koliganek has been involved in cultural/conservation planning since at least 2005, when it participated in a traditional-use conservation area plan, eventually published by the Nushagak Mulchatna Watershed Council in 2007.[88] In 2009, Koliganek designated 98,000 acres of corporate holdings as a salmon reserve, an interim status pending the results of the land prioritization process.[89]

Possible Scenarios and Considerations

Tribes in Alaska are considered nonprofits and as such, they can hold conservation easements on Alaska Native corporation lands, in addition to being able to hold them as tribes. One possible scenario is that land trusts like NMWTLT could raise the money to purchase an easement from the Native corporation, which would then turn it over to the tribe to manage. One challenge in this scenario is creating the incentive for the corporation to divest itself of the easement. Another challenge is that the transfer of either the easement or the land to the tribe could put the tribe and the Native corporation in competition. As Elvsaas explained, "If the tribe was to have some land . . . deeded over or purchased or gifted, then the tribe could generate revenues also, which would help the same people. That is a wonderful thing, except that now you have taken your resource or asset from the corporation and given it to the tribe to use . . . to generate revenue, in direct competition with what your corporation is able to do."[90] If the corporation did pass the easement to the tribe, the tribe could focus on ensuring that traditional land uses could continue. The corporation would still own the land, without the development rights, but those rights are of critical importance for the corporation in terms of generating revenue from the land.

Concerned about Native lands remaining in Native hands, Hagenstein suggested the formation of regional Native land trusts composed of tribal governments who elect a board of representatives to guide the organization. Then, the corporation or allottee could still hold the property and the Native land trust would hold the development rights, constituting no erosion of Native title, just "rearrangement of title among Native entities."[91] Although the NMWTLT is rurally based and has Native representation on the board, it is not a Native organization. In contrast, if tribes came together in each region and elected a board to run their land trust, it would be a Native organization. Hagenstein suggests that tribes develop the land trusts rather than Native corporations, as corporations stand to gain from the sale of development rights.[92]

The Big Picture

Native corporations and allottees own more than 40 million acres of land in Alaska, including lands with high habitat value that have been used traditionally for centuries. According to Troll, "land trusts and conservation easements are tools that can make a big difference up here in the next fifty years if they are used right and if people want it."[93] Having watched how quickly Native allotment lands were sold and developed in the lower 48 states, Alaskans are eager to make sure the same pattern does not occur in the north. "We're trying to get ahead of the game," Troll explained. "For those who really want to protect traditional and subsistence use, the allotment lands are the biggest threat they face."[94] In order to prevent the development of numerous small allotment lands that are vitally important for habitat and subsistence, the NMWTLT is working on education, fundraising, and partnerships. Their focus is to keep these Native lands in Native ownership, with covenants that can protect them for future generations.

Like the KHLT, the NMWTLT will continue to conduct outreach and build trust with the array of Alaska Native entities—including Alaska Native village and regional corporations, federally recognized Alaska tribes, and Alaska Native nonprofits—that have deep interests in both the subsistence resources and economic development potential of their lands. Although business and conservation may seem antithetical in the Alaska Native corporate context, and business and culture may clash in the relationships between Alaska Native tribes and Alaska Native regional and village corporations, conservation easements and Native land trusts can be one of the many tools that can bridge these differences. In order to successfully apply conservation easements and land trusts in Alaska, conservation tax incentives must be made available to Alaska Natives, and opportunities for communication between conservationists and Alaska Native entities must continue to increase.

12

Land Purchases and Fee-to-Trust Considerations

Jamestown S'Klallam Tribe (Washington)

The Jamestown S'Klallam Tribe is located on Washington State's forested and marine Olympic Peninsula, along the Strait of Juan de Fuca. The tribe's livelihood historically revolved around salmon, shellfish, and other natural resources.[1] Fishing and hunting continue to be important to tribal citizens. Although the reservation is only 13 acres, the Jamestown S'Klallam Tribe retains fishing rights in a large area, based on the 1855 Point-No-Point Treaty.[2] This area consists of both unadjudicated rights to hunt and gather in lands and waters ceded in the treaty and designated "usual and accustomed areas." Federal court decisions in the 1970s defined and adjudicated these areas, which now stretch from the entrance of the Strait of Juan de Fuca, eastward through the Strait, including the San Juan Islands, extending through Admiralty Inlet and Hood Canal, to encompass all of the basins that flow into these marine areas.

In order to protect the quality, quantity, and extent of surrounding natural resources and habitat, the tribe must engage in multiple partnerships. In the last three decades, and under the twenty-five-year leadership of Tribal Chairman Ron Allen, the Jamestown S'Klallam Tribe has grown tremendously, in both services and land base. For example, it now owns more than 200 acres of both fee and trust land. The tribe uses its acreage for education, natural resources protection, and tribal operations. The tribe is the coleader of the Dungeness River Management Team, which coordinates management and monitoring of that river's watershed.[3] The tribe also plays a prominent service and economic-development role in the community, by running medical and dental clinics, a casino, a nature center, and multiple government departments, making it the fourth largest employer in Clallam County.[4]

Jamestown S'Klallam Tribe: Land Protection and Collaboration

The Jamestown S'Klallam Tribe has collaborated extensively with the North Olympic Land Trust (NOLT), Clallam County, the Clallam Conservation District, state and federal agencies, private landowners, and other entities. These collaborative efforts have resulted in environmental restoration, protection, enhanced recreation, and public-outreach opportunities. The tribe began exploring the use of conservation easements in 1990, when a property that was suspected of causing marine-water-quality problems came on the market. The tribe was unable to acquire the property until 2001, when it used its own funds combined with state and federal grant monies to buy it. It is now part of the large Jimmycomelately Estuary restoration project discussed below. In easement collaborations, the tribe typically purchases the property, and the other partners, such as the North Olympic Land Trust (NOLT), hold the easement.

NOLT was created in 1990 as part of a local effort to utilize national land-conservation tools to conserve priority lands in Clallam County. As of 2009, the land trust had protected 1,811 acres using fifty-seven conservation easements and five land acquisitions.[5] The land trust works to preserve biodiversity, natural resources, and cultural heritage. According to Executive Director Greg Good, NOLT protects habitat for salmon and wildlife, and preserves farmland, sustainable timberland, clean water and air, scenic vistas and open space, and cultural heritage. "For the land trust to be successful in achieving its mission, collaboration with the local tribes, government agencies, and other local nonprofits is essential," Good explained.[6]

Although there are no formal memorandums of understanding (MOUs) or written agreements between the NOLT and the tribe, they have been collaborating to protect lands for more than twenty years. The tribe and the land trust worked together to protect over 100 acres of Dungeness riparian lands through a state riparian-habitat grant. The tribe's successful grant-writing staff helped secure the funding and identify important parcels for protection, and then NOLT implemented the program. NOLT and the Jamestown S'Klallam Tribe also both serve on the Dungeness River Management Team, and they share field-monitoring resources (for example, tribal field staff assists with maintaining the integrity of NOLT conservation easements). Tribal staff members also assist NOLT as technical advisors when needed, and the tribe and the land trust support one another in public-outreach efforts, such as annual stream festivals, presentations, and field trips.

When properties along the Dungeness River and associated tributaries are inappropriately farmed, developed, or otherwise used, this negatively affects water quality and fish habitat throughout the watershed. The tribe, Clallam County, NOLT, and the Washington Department of Fish and Wildlife (WDFW) have worked together to purchase and protect, in perpetuity, about 70 acres of floodplain near the mouth of the Dungeness River. This began in 2003 when the land trust purchased a conservation easement on two vacant parcels, and the tribe purchased the properties encumbered with the easement. This initial investment by NOLT, with the tribe providing matching funds, enabled Clallam County and WDFW to utilize state and federal grant funds to purchase an additional 14 acres and 45 acres, respectively, at the mouth of the river. In this case, the parties purchased homes built in the floodplain outright from willing sellers, demolished the houses, and restored the properties to productive habitat for salmon and other wildlife. With the homes out of the floodplain, the size and location of the river channel can fluctuate, as it would in a restored ecosystem.[7]

The tribe itself does not hold any conservation easements, which is an explicit decision based on at least two factors: "Holding a conservation easement entails a responsibility to uphold and monitor the parameters of the easement. So far, the tribe has not been interested in accepting this responsibility, and the NOLT was created for this purpose exactly."[8] Through the tribe's partnership with NOLT, both entities can maximize their skills and resources to protect critical habitat. As of 2010, the tribe and NOLT continue to collaborate, and they are currently negotiating a conservation easement on one of the last remaining privately owned parcels along the Jimmycomelately Creek, which is key habitat for summer chum salmon.[9] The easement would cover approximately 64 acres and offer permanent protection to a .93-mile section of the Creek.[10] In 2009, NOLT received a $527,693 grant from the Salmon Recovery Funding Board to purchase the easement.[11]

The tribe also participates in several multiparty land-and-water protection efforts, including the Dungeness River Management Team. That entity has served as the local "watershed council," gathering natural resources data and implementing and monitoring watershed projects for more than twenty years. According to former Jamestown S'Klallam Environmental Planning Manager Lyn Muench, "It takes decades to do this stuff, but we finally just forged all of these partnerships. We prioritize habitat needs and pinpoint areas where outright purchase is preferable. Then whoever has the cash makes the purchase."[12] The tribe and partners often use the 2003 *Recommended Land Protection Strategies for the Dungeness Riparian Area* to prioritize properties in the watershed based on their salmonid habitat value and level of threat from development (fig. 12.1).[13] The 2003 report, authored by the tribe, is based on interviews with biologists familiar with the river and fish needs and Clallam County's zoning and development regulations. In order to protect high-quality river habitat and allow for needed restoration, the principal recommended actions were purchasing lands, placing conservation easements on them, and stewardship. The tribe also relies on Geographic Information System expertise to merge data and create maps and graphics, which greatly assist with planning and monitoring land preservation and restoration projects.

The Dungeness River Audubon Center

The Dungeness River Audubon Center (henceforth, the River Center) is a regionally acclaimed facility located in a public park on tribal trust land. The tribe comanages the River Center with three other partners—the Olympic Peninsula Audubon Society, the River Center Foundation (a local nonprofit that spearheaded the establishment of the park and the center), and Audubon Washington (the state office of the National Audubon Society). The tribe is represented on the River Center Foundation's board of directors and a formal MOU details the terms of the partners' relationships.

The River Center's story began in 1984, when a railroad traversing the community closed, and a group of citizens tried to turn it into a trail. The citizens' group was unsuccessful in raising the money and political support to create a trail, and the railroad began to sell pieces of the 45-mile-long right-of-way to adjacent property owners. When a critical section—including a bridge over the Dungeness River (a main fishery artery for the tribe)—went up for sale, the tenacious citizens' group contacted the Seattle office of the Trust for Public Land (TPL). This situation exemplifies the critically important role that the TPL often plays in brokering successful land acquisition and protection.

The TPL bought one-half mile of trail and the bridge in 1990 and sold it to the Washington Department of Fish and Wildlife (WDFW) for management by the Clallam County Parks and Recreation District. Most of the local citizens working to create the trail and save the bridge were Audubon Society members who had been involved in creating and managing a local natural history museum and education center, the Sequim Natural History Museum. Around the same time that TPL and WDFW purchased

FIGURE 12.1. A view of the Dungeness River from the River Center. Gravel bars provide necessary substrate for fish spawning. (Photo courtesy of Randy Johnson)

the bridge and trail, the school district needed the building housing the museum, forcing the museum's relocation. There was land for sale adjacent to the bridge parcel, so the citizens' group got the support of a legislator, and they applied for and received two state grants totaling $400,000. One, from the Washington Department of Natural Resources Aquatic Lands Enhancement Account, was used to purchase the land, and the second, from the Washington Department of Community, Trade, and Economic Development, funded the construction of a building to house the natural history museum and education center.

Meanwhile, the Clallam County Parks and Recreation District had an election, and turnover on the board of directors changed the district's priorities from the natural history museum and trail project to a community pool. The district decided not to accept the $400,000 in grant funds to buy the parcel of land and build the center, so the citizens had to find another sponsor to oversee the funding. After unsuccessfully approaching Clallam County and the City of Sequim, the citizens broached the subject of the project with the Jamestown S'Klallam Tribe. They spoke directly with the tribal chairman, a visionary who saw the opportunity to be involved in managing 10 acres of land on the Dungeness River, where the tribe had no landholdings. In 1995, Chairman Ron Allen agreed that the tribe would be the fiscal agent for the grants, overseeing the purchase of the land and the construction of the building.

The local citizens formed a nonprofit organization called the Rainshadow Natural Science Foundation (RNSF), which eventually became the River Center Foundation. When the tribe and the RNSF began planning the building, the only place suitable for construction was on a part of the trail still owned by the WDFW and managed by the Clallam Parks and Recreation District. The tribe asked the district for a small part of their right of way. Instead, the district and the WDFW transferred the entire one-half mile and the bridge to the tribe at no cost. The tribe put the land into tribal trust status, a process in which the U.S. Bureau of Indian Affairs assumes title to the land for the benefit of the tribe. The tribe and three other partners now manage the Railroad Bridge Park there, on tribal trust land. Despite this parcel's complex ownership and its distance from the tribe's reservation at the head of Sequim Bay, the fee-to-trust process "was not any more difficult than other fee-to-trust applications."[14]

The Jamestown S'Klallam Tribe is a government entity immune to suit, so when the WDFW turned the land over to the tribe, the tribe issued a limited waiver of sovereign immunity. By leaving itself open to a lawsuit should it ever deny public access to the site, the tribe was, in essence, guaranteeing that access in perpetuity. This waiver is limited to that particular property for that specific purpose. As Leo Gaten, Governmental Policy Advisor for the Jamestown S'Klallam Tribe, notes, "When you issue the waivers, you are subjecting yourself to a jurisdiction you ordinarily wouldn't want to be subject to; but you have to issue them sometimes in order to accomplish what you want to do."[15] In nearly all of the collaborations described in this chapter, the tribe has been willing to issue a limited waiver of sovereign immunity.[16] These waivers are included in an easement document, which is enforceable by both parties.

Today, Railroad Bridge Park is 26 acres in size, with numerous riparian and forest trails. Clallam and Jefferson Counties, several cities, and the tribe at its reservation on Sequim Bay are now collaborating to develop the rest of the historic railroad right-of-way into a 100-mile regional trail. Each governmental entity will manage the portion of the trail that passes through its jurisdiction, and the local Peninsula Trails Commission will provide overall coordination and communication.

The tribe and the other partners oversaw the construction of the Dungeness River Audubon Center, which was completed in 2001. It became one of seventy-five Audubon centers in twenty states. The center's facilities and programs continue to expand, and in 2007, it had over twenty thousand visitors, and more than one-hundred thousand people visited Railroad Bridge Park. The River Center hosts classes for fourth through eighth graders, birding classes for adults, several summer camp sessions, and numerous other events and activities. Drawing on private local donations, fundraising events, private foundation grants, and additional state and federal grants, the tribe, the River Center Foundation, and the Olympic Peninsula Audubon Society raise most of the funds for the center's day-to-day operations.

Collaboration with Jefferson Land Trust to Protect Tamanowas Rock

To the east of Jamestown S'Klallam Tribe's headquarters, across the Clallam County line in Jefferson County, Tamanowas or Chimacum Rock rises 150 feet out of the surrounding forest. The Rock is an important spiritual site to the S'Klallam bands, including Jamestown S'Klallam, Elwha, and Port Gamble S'Klallam. Port Gamble S'Klallam spiritual leader Gene Jones's grandfather, also a spiritual leader, led people to the Rock for prayer and fasting and, today, Jones is also taking people to the Rock for traditional spiritual practices. Jones is also active in cleanup and stewardship of the site, which gets a lot of non-tribal use.[17] Tamanowas Rock is much beloved by the surrounding population, including rock climbers, hikers, and local teens. So, when the property was threatened by development in 2005, the local community was deeply concerned.

Specifically, an approximately 86-acre parcel to the north of the Rock, 66 acres of which is known as the Nicholsen Short Plat, went up for sale, and those parcels included an access easement across the Tamanowas Rock parcel. The Nicholsen Short Plat, and an adjoining 20 acres just to the south, were being eyed for development, and there was "great concern that someone might buy it and exercise the right to use the easement across the Tamanowas Rock property," according to Jefferson Land Trust Executive Director Sarah Spaeth.[18] The Jamestown S'Klallam Tribe stepped in to buy the Nicholsen Short Plat and the 20 acres, offsetting the cost by placing a conservation easement on the 20-acre parcel, using the Jefferson County Conservation Futures Fund. A percentage of property tax and timber tax dollars are deposited into the fund, which is used to purchase conservation easements on selected properties.[19] In February 2008, the tribe received a grant from the county to purchase a conservation easement on the 20-acre parcel, to be held by the Jefferson Land Trust. Tribal members and staff and Jefferson Land Trust staff have long known one another and interacted, according to Spaeth, so this seemed like a natural collaboration.

The county rejected the tribe's subsequent application to purchase a second conservation easement on the remaining 60 acres of the Nicholson Short Plat property. The tribe considered trying to place the 80-acre parcel into federal trust in 2007, but, at that time, the BIA was not open to taking into trust any property that was not contiguous with existing tribal trust property. According to Jamestown S'Klallam Staff member Leo Gaten, "[the Bush] administration [was] hostile to fee-to-trust transactions."[20] This may change under the Obama administration, and the land trust is aware that the tribe is likely to apply to the BIA to place some of the property into trust status, most likely the 20-acre parcel with the conservation easement and the north 20 acres of the Tamanowas Rock property, thereby creating a 40-acre sanctuary for the Rock.[21] According to Spaeth, the land trust is confident that the conservation easement will remain viable if the land is converted into trust status.[22]

Tribes have a number of incentives to try to place acquired lands into trust status. For example, once lands are in trust they are exempt from property taxes. However, the tribe does contribute funds to Clallam County, where all its existing trust and reservation land is located, to offset county costs for police and fire protection. Trust property that is not used for gaming is also subject solely to federal and tribal oversight. Trust properties must meet federal regulations (including the Clean Water Act, the Endangered Species Act, and so forth), but tribes have more freedom to meet these requirements in culturally appropriate ways. Before placing a property in trust, the Bureau of Indian Affairs (BIA) requires that loans are paid off and taxes have been paid. Once it is in trust, the BIA has to approve subsequent leases and other transactions on the land.

Conservation easements and other encumbrances can make the process of transferring fee land into BIA-held trust land more difficult. Depending on the interpretation, conservation easements can represent a type of restriction and a liability on the land. However, according to Gaten, the BIA has recently taken into trust tribal fee properties with conservation easements on them. He differentiates conservation easements from other encumbrances that the BIA typically does not allow on lands they accept into trust, such as mortgages or covenants, conditions, and restrictions (CC&Rs).[23] The decision to accept certain encumbrances, such as conservation easements, is based partially on a determination of the likelihood of potential liability for the federal government, which holds title to trust land for the benefit of a tribe or allottee. According to Gaten, the federal government has determined that conservation easements, like easements for utilities and roads, present a minimal threat of liability. However, he also cautioned that understanding the details of this determination requires further clarification from BIA national and regional officials, as determinations vary by region.[24]

In recent years, the Tamanowas Rock site has been the locus of increasing activity for the Jamestown S'Klallam Tribe, the Jefferson Land Trust, and other partners. In 2008, the owner of the Tamanowas Rock site, who had previously been unwilling to sell, put the property up for sale, eventually agreeing to the appraised price of $600,000.[25] Washington State Parks, which owns the adjacent Anderson Lake State Park property, took the lead on negotiating with the landowner, in communication with the Jamestown S'Klallam Tribe, the Jefferson Land Trust, and the Northwest Watershed Institute. Washington State Parks and the Jamestown S'Klallam Tribe were concerned about the challenge of buying the property up front, and then trying to get a grant to reimburse the purchase cost. Land trusts have more flexibility to take on risk to make conservation purchases, so the Jefferson Land Trust stepped in and acquired a $480,000 loan from the Bullitt Foundation that covered 80 percent of the purchase price. Meanwhile, to share the risk with the land trust, and purchase a stake in the property, the Jamestown S'Klallam tribe put up some of its own funds, and took out loans from local community members to cover the remaining 20 percent ($120,000) of the purchase price. That 20 percent is also a non-refundable option on the property, so the tribe has the first right to buy the property from the land trust.[26] With this combination of funds, the Jefferson Land Trust purchased the 63-acre Tamanowas Rock parcel in December 2009.

In 2010, both Washington State parks and the Jamestown S'Klallam Tribe were working to raise funds from federal appropriations, private grants, low-interest loans, and the local Conservation Futures Fund, in order to purchase the parcel from the land trust.[27] On April 19, 2010, the Conservation Futures Citizen Oversight Committee recommended that the Jefferson County Commissioners grant $200,000 from the Fund to three co-applicants: the tribe, the Jefferson Land Trust, and state parks.[28] The Commissioners will make a decision within the year. Some citizens groups, such as rock climbers, are advocating for public access if public monies support the tribe's purchase of the site. Although challenges remain in terms of balancing public access and spiritual practices on the site,[29] the land trust and tribal partners are proud of their efforts to protect the important Rock from desecration and development: "The partnership has worked really well so far, in that we've had a lot of coordination between various groups," said Spaeth. "We just had a wonderful celebration [in March 2010] with tribal members and the land trust, just appreciating how far we've come."[30]

Partnerships with Local and Federal Agencies:
Jimmycomelately Estuary Restoration

The Jimmycomelately Creek is the largest tributary stream flowing into Sequim Bay from the 15.4-square-mile Jimmycomelately watershed. The creek and the bay are important habitat for more than seventy species of birds, and historically, they have provided the tribe with abundant fish, shellfish, and wildlife.[31] The creek was a priority for restoration, particularly because of its declining run of summer chum salmon, a threatened species under the Endangered Species Act.[32] In 1999, only seven chum came up the creek to spawn.[33] The poor condition of the watershed had also resulted in flooding in south Sequim Bay, affecting both human and fish populations. A flood closed Highway 101 in the late 1990s, blocking access to the North Olympic Peninsula.[34] In a 2002 *Peninsula Daily News* article, Jamestown S'Klallam Habitat Biologist Byron Rot described how the fast and high flows move gravel and destroy salmon "redds," or nests, along the creek bottom.[35]

Extensive logging, dredging, development, and transportation on roads and rails degraded Jimmycomelately Creek and its estuary. Undoing more than two hundred years of damage (the S'Klallam people of this area were first contacted in 1790)[36] required an extensive, multistage, multiparty restoration effort. Beginning in the early 1990s, the Jamestown S'Klallam Tribe built partnerships with Clallam County, the Clallam Conservation District, the Washington State departments of Transportation and Fish and Wildlife, and three private landowners.

The ten-year, $7 million project involved twenty-seven partners,[37] and it included a four-step plan that began with constructing a meandering stream channel along one of the creek's historic channels, a job completed in 2003. The next steps were restoring the estuary and replacing a bridge to accommodate the new channel. Finally, the creek was diverted into the new channel in 2004.[38]

Among the diverse funding sources for the project, the Washington Aquatic Lands Enhancement Account under the Washington Department of Natural Resources provided a grant to buy a conservation easement to accommodate the new alignment of the Creek. Initially, the landowner did not want to sell the land but was willing to have a conservation easement put on the section traversed by the creek and the buffer. The tribe eventually used the grant to buy the development rights from the landowner and place

FIGURE 12.2. Ceremonial salmon release following the restoration of Jimmycomelately Creek. In 1999, only seven summer chum salmon came up the creek to spawn. By 2004, following restoration, that number had jumped to 1,700. (Photo courtesy of Jamestown S'Klallam Tribe Natural Resources Department)

a conservation easement on the property. The tribe purchased the property in June 2006, and in 2007, it put it into federal trust. The conservation easement was in place before the Jamestown S'Klallam Tribe purchased the property, and when the tribe requested that it be converted to a trust, the federal government accepted the encumbrance. The tribe and its partners also got a ten-year designation under the Natural Resources Conservation Service's Conservation Reserve Enhancement Program (CREP) to protect the property, which was a flower farm, while they rerouted and revegetated the creek. CREP funds paid for all of the riparian vegetation planting and maintenance. A 2005 article in the *Peninsula Daily News* described workers planting "8,000 trees and shrubs and a field of lilies and camas."[39]

Among its goals for the project, the tribe planned to "monitor and evaluate the project as a model restoration program."[40] The monitoring was split into ecological, habitat, and biological components, and the last included keeping track of changes in fish behavior and survival. Summer chum counts showed significant improvement following the restoration (fig. 12.2). "We are now getting lots of summer chum," said Hals. Indeed, in 2003, 460 chum returned to the creek to spawn.[41] With the help of many volunteers and a brood-stock program at the Dungeness Hurd Creek Hatchery, the 2004 chum run saw 1,700 fish[42] and the 2005 return was 1,698.[43] The Jimmycomelately Creek restoration project continues to be an extensive restoration and monitoring effort. Tribal natural resources staff emphasized the positive returns the tribe has seen from the project for the environment and the community.

Conclusion: Caring for What Sustains Us

Based on treaties negotiated more than 150 years ago, tribes like the James-town S'Klallam have rights to harvest fish and other resources from their "usual and accustomed places," even if those places are now owned by federal, state, or private entities. These tribes have a stake in lands out of their ownership, similar to an easement holder's stake in the land covered by the easement. These tribes must work with landowners to ensure that their treaty rights are not breached, including ensuring that the environ-ment is not degraded to the point that resources are in decline. In this context, conservation purchases in partnership with land trusts and other entities have become an accepted method for tribes to obtain fee or trust ownership of properties. Having a conservation encumbrance complements the tribes' goals of restoring riparian areas to improve fisheries and other habitat. When the Jamestown S'Klallam tribe applies to the BIA to put lands into trust, the agency may recognize the low risk and comply with the tribe's conversion requests, even though the trust land is encumbered with a conservation easement and a tribal limited waiver of sovereign immunity to enable enforcement.

Despite its historic treaty rights and collective tribal land ownership on the Dungeness since 1874,[44] the Jamestown S'Klallam Tribe regained federal recognition only in 1981. It has been slowly and steadily working to rebuild its land base. According to the 2008–2009 *Report to Tribal Citizens*, the tribe had about 130 acres in fee and trust status.[45] When culturally and ecologically important lands become available, the tribe has found it helpful to partner with entities like the Jefferson and North Olympic land trusts and state and federal agencies.

In sum, this chapter illustrates some of the range and complexity of the partnerships forged by one Pacific Northwest tribe to access and sustain a tribal homeland that is no longer solely owned by the tribe. Visionary lead-ership and creative leveraging of resources has enabled the tribe to partner with seemingly incongruous entities in order to achieve land acquisition and restoration goals, which ultimately serve the entire regional ecosystem, as well as the tribe's spirit and culture.

13

Land Purchases and Fee-to-Trust Considerations

Eastern Band of Cherokee Indians (North Carolina)

Qualla Boundary, the Eastern Band of Cherokee reservation, is located on the forested eastern flanks of the Great Smoky Mountains in North Carolina. The Cherokees believe that they have always lived in western North Carolina, and archaeological evidence corroborates their presence there for more than 11,000 years.[1] In the 1500s, Cherokees controlled some 140,000 square miles throughout the present-day southern United States.[2] For the first two hundred years of contact with Europeans, the Cherokees traded with the newcomers. Increasing land pressure from settlers, miners, and land speculators, however, led to the land cessions in the Cherokee treaty of 1819.[3] In it, the Cherokee agreed to live within their reduced area in western North Carolina, northern Georgia, southeastern Tennessee, and northeastern Alabama or to move west to Indian Territory.[4] The treaty also offered Cherokees the option of remaining on their lands (outside of the reserve) if they applied for and were granted a 640-acre individual reservation. Those who made the latter choice would renounce their Cherokee citizenship and become citizens of the state where they resided. As such, they became known as "citizen Cherokees."[5]

As competition with settlers over land continued, President Andrew Jackson began to increase pressure on the Cherokee to move out of their homelands to Indian Territory in present-day Oklahoma. The Cherokees resisted removal and received acknowledgment of their limited sovereignty from the Supreme Court in *Cherokee Nation v. Georgia* (1831) and *Worcester v. Georgia* (1832).[6] However, these rulings were ultimately ineffective against Jackson's 1830 Removal Act, and the 1835 Treaty of New Echota.[7] In 1838, more than 17,000 Cherokees were marched to Oklahoma on the deadly "Trail of Tears."

Members of the Eastern Band of Cherokee Indians (EBCI) in western North Carolina are descended from "citizen Cherokees," who chose individual reserves following the treaty of 1819. When Cherokees were being rounded up from reservation lands to be marched out west, the citizen Cherokees pointed to their distinct legal status, and they called upon the services of sympathetic white lawyers and landowners to assist them.[8] Drawing on these alliances, the Eastern Band of Cherokee Indians has a long, ongoing tradition of working to buy back and protect lands lost during the removal.

The Eastern Band's 51,000-acre reservation was officially defined by the Temple Survey in 1876 and then formally placed into federal trust in 1924.[9] In the 1930s, the federal government created the Great Smoky Mountains National Park adjacent to Cherokee lands and began construction of the 469-mile-long Blue Ridge Parkway, whose southern terminus crosses Cherokee lands. This brought a bustling tourist economy. Today, more than two hundred businesses are located on the reservation—most of them owned by Eastern Band citizens. Economic activity includes the 75,000-square-foot Harrah's Cherokee Casino and Hotel in Cherokee. In addition to other hotels, the tribe also runs logging companies, ranches, construction enterprises, aquaculture companies, garment and textile factories, and a drinking-water bottling company.[10] Thousands of visitors come to Cherokee each year to learn about the history and culture of the region and to enjoy the Great Smoky Mountains that helped to shelter the Cherokee from removal just 150 years ago.[11]

Land Trust for the Little Tennessee

Since its formation in 1997, the Land Trust for the Little Tennessee (LTLT) has worked in the Southern Blue Ridge to conserve the ecologically diverse waters, forests, and farms, and the unique history and culture of the rural Upper Little Tennessee and Hiwassee River Valleys in western North Carolina and northern Georgia. The LTLT envisions a rural landscape and quality of life that includes a healthy ecosystem, a sustainable economy, and a strong sense of community.[12] LTLT leadership also recognizes the importance of past and current Native land stewardship. According to the baseline report on the Cowee Mound property, prepared by LTLT Land Stewardship Coordinator

Dennis F. Desmond, the Little Tennessee River Valley "is one of the most archaeologically significant regions in North Carolina."[13] Sites in the valley include Native American settlements that date back to 8,000 BC, including many major sixteenth- through eighteenth-century Cherokee towns.[14]

One of twenty-four local land trusts in North Carolina, the LTLT purchases lands, accepts land transfers, holds conservation easements, and offers educational and outreach activities, as well as engaging in direct land restoration and stewardship with private landowners. The LTLT partners with local governments, developers, tribes, public agencies, and private landowners to protect lands and resources that are given priority because of their ecological, scenic, and cultural values.

Eastern Band of Cherokee Indians and Land Trust for the Little Tennessee: Partnering for Historic and Cultural Preservation

The relationship between the LTLT and the Eastern Band began through the introductions and encouragement of Tom Hatley, then–Sequoyah Professor of Cherokee Studies at Western Carolina University and an advisor to the LTLT since its inception. As a historian and forester, Hatley knows the importance of the Little Tennessee Valley in both U.S. and Cherokee history. Having been involved in land protection for over twenty-five years, Hatley is also familiar with the depth of engagement required for a conservation transaction: "The human dimension is primary in a lot of cases. Owners are giving an easement or selling it in some preferential way to a conservation group or a tribe. It's a reconciliation process as well as a land transaction."[15]

Hatley began to work with LTLT Director Paul Carlson, who had a deep commitment to cultural conservation as a result of his years directing forestry projects with indigenous communities in the Andes Mountains of South America.[16] Hatley advised the LTLT team as it was developing a protection strategy for the Little Tennessee River Valley, and he worked as a consultant for the Cherokee Preservation Foundation to develop strategies for bridging the Native and conservation communities. "We eased into it," Hatley explained. "It took a bit of an effort to meet each other, but a bit of informal vision developed between key staff people in the tribe and other leaders."[17] One of the first projects the tribe and the LTLT worked together on was managing rivercane stands.

In 1999, the LTLT acquired Tessentee Farm, located along a historic trade route linking the Mississippi Valley to the piedmont and plains. The farm includes rivercane in thick stands called canebrakes, and the LTLT sought the advice of Cherokee traditionalists to steward the rivercane. Eventually, the two parties developed a legal agreement to regulate rivercane harvesting. Following this interaction, the tribe passed a formal resolution supporting the LTLT's role in conserving the Needmore Tract, a large piece of culturally and ecologically rich land owned by Duke Energy. The LTLT and numerous other partners helped to facilitate the state's purchase of the Needmore Tract for conservation in 2004. "[The tribe] didn't directly benefit from it," said Hatley, "except in knowing that sites were protected."[18]

In 2005, the LTLT invited Cherokee traditionalist Freeman Owle to join its board. Owle served until 2007, when the Cowee deal was in the final stages of negotiation between the tribe, the LTLT, and funders. "For the LTLT to have the kind of foresight to ask [Owle] to be part of their board is a big plus for them," said EBCI member Juanita Wilson.[19] Wilson was the tribe's deputy administrative officer during the Cowee transaction and was assigned by the chief to be the tribe's point person for the project.

The EBCI had some familiarity with the conservation community through the Trust for Public Land's (TPL) Tribal Lands Program. In 2005, TPL worked with the Cherokee Nation of Oklahoma and, to a lesser extent, with the EBCI to acquire the Chief Vann House, a large Cherokee plantation in Georgia. The complexity of most land conservation transactions provides roles for local and national conservation groups to partner with tribes. Although some tribes may hesitate to partner because of the potential impact of joint transactions on tribal sovereignty, multiple parties are often necessary to acquire lands that have been alienated from tribal ownership. According to Wilson, who was instrumental in maintaining the partnership between the LTLT and the tribe as they worked to acquire Cowee Mound, sovereignty can be productively applied to strengthen "government-to-government" relationships with numerous outside entities. "Although you have your own laws and government, you have to work with others and give and take," she explained. "You have to be able to reach out."[20]

Hatley acknowledged the importance of tribes' working with regional, state, and national conservation groups, as well as funders and politicians, but he underscored the need to form partnerships with local land trusts: "There may be reasons for long-distance help and expertise, like a tribal lands program that can break the ice with the tribal council, but a local land trust may be the best long-term ally."[21] Although forming a partnership takes ongoing, mutual education and trust building, working locally offers opportunities for daily collaborations to acquire funding, create programs, build regional support, and perhaps most importantly, take steps toward reconciling historical wrongs.

FIGURE 13.1. The Cowee Mound, with the Cowee Mountains in the background. The Land Trust for the Little Tennessee selected this photo for the cover of its 2006 annual calendar. (Photo courtesy of Ralph Preston)

Collaboration to Protect Cowee Mound

The ancient Cowee Mound and community of Cowee are located along the Little Tennessee River near the town of Franklin in rural northern Macon County, North Carolina. The Cowee Mound property consists of 52.77 acres of floodplain, rolling pastureland used in hay cultivation and grazing, and forested upslope (fig. 13.1). According to Paul Carlson, executive director of the LTLT, "the Cowee Mound is the most intact Mississippian-period archeological site in western North Carolina."[22] Although the site has never been excavated, surveys reveal continuous agriculture and other uses of the mound, dating back at least 1,400 years. According to Cherokee language instructor Tom Belt, the Creator wanted the Eastern Cherokee to stay behind to make sure the tribe's homeland remained protected, and "returning the mound to its people fulfills that prophecy."[23]

In the 1700s, Cowee was an important civic and commercial center for the mountain Cherokee. It was attacked three separate times between 1760 and 1776 by British and colonial forces seeking control of an Appalachian trade route. Until the late 1770s, nearly eight hundred Cherokee lived in Cowee.[24] In the 1830s, the mound and surrounding property were converted into a private parcel owned by Joseph Welch. He owned the parcel for ten years before he sold it to the Hall family, in whose possession it remained for nearly 175 years. The Hall family never allowed any excavation of the mound. "Most of the other Cherokee town mounds, which were [Cherokee] sacred and civic spaces, were excavated by gentlemen archaeologists in late nineteenth century, or, in other words, looted. [The Halls] protected the land."[25]

In 1973, the Hall descendants agreed to add the Cowee Mound and Village Site to the National Register of Historic Places. Although this is a nationally significant designation, it does not restrict use of the site, in the way that a conservation easement does. When Hall descendant Katherine Bowden Porter died in 2002, the land was transferred to her husband, James Porter, who wanted to see the parcel go into Cherokee ownership. Mr. Porter worked with LTLT Land Protection Coordinator Sharon Taylor to arrange a win-win solution that would ensure both Cherokee ownership and perpetual conservation (fig. 13.2). "Katherine Porter left a wonderful legacy of conserving the Mound, and it was James's desire to have the Mound return to tribal ownership," Carlson said.[26]

At least three departments of the Eastern Band of Cherokee Indians were intimately involved in the transactions that led to the tribe's ownership of the Cowee Mound: the legal department focused on land purchase negotiations, the Museum of the Cherokee Indian provided advice on the historical significance, and the Tribal Historic Preservation Office (THPO) advised the tribe on archaeological protection and how to construct protective covenants and easements that would maintain the resources in perpetuity (fig. 13.3). "Our job . . . was to bring this to the chief and to the Land Acquisition Committee, and make them recognize the value of that archaeological site and the danger it was faced with should a developer purchase the land. We really had to sell the tribe on spending that money on a site that they could not ever develop themselves. They were very excited to do it."[27] Although the THPO often works to develop long-term mechanisms to protect cultural resources, Townsend noted that the Cowee transaction was different because of the extent of the partnership with the LTLT: "A land trust that is about preserving the land and protecting that land from development partnering with an Indian tribe that is also interested in protecting their archaeological sites from development—that is unique. It shouldn't be, but I don't know of another situation where that has happened."[28] Townsend particularly credits Wilson and Annette Tarnawsky, then with the tribe's legal department, for their hard work to build the partnership with the LTLT.

In 2006, the LTLT received funds from the North Carolina Clean Water Management Trust Fund (CWMTF). Because LTLT staff and Wilson had worked on previous grants together, there was a high level of trust between

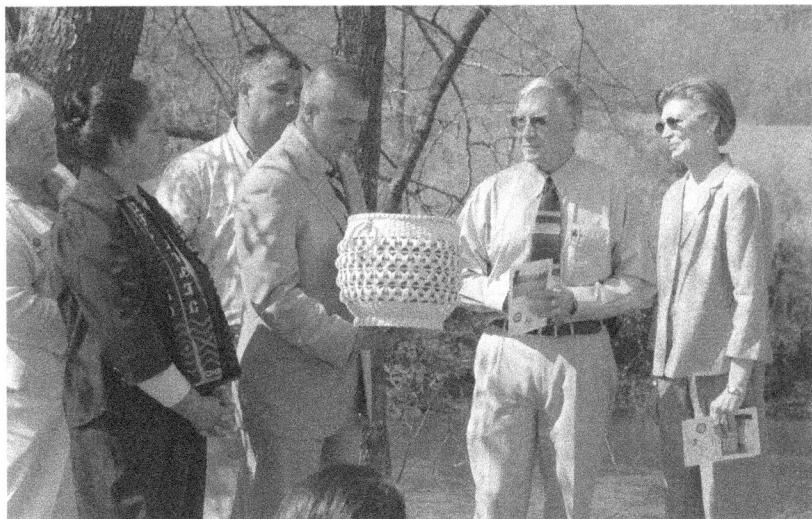

Figure 13.2. Chief Michell Hicks presenting a Cherokee basket to Dolores and Lloyd Porter. Lloyd is a nephew of Katherine and James Porter, descendants of the non-Cherokee family that owned the mound for nearly 175 years before selling it to the tribe with a conservation easement held by the Land Trust for the Little Tennessee. (Photo courtesy of Ralph Preston)

Figure 13.3. Chief Michell Hicks and the Warriors of AniKituhwa at the Cowee Mound Ceremony on April 23, 2007. Also present is tribal elder and singer for the Warriors, Walker Calhoun. (Photo courtesy of Ralph Preston)

the two entities. In 2003, through the Cherokee Preservation Foundation, LTLT received a grant to establish management strategies to restore and enhance natural resources, such as rivercane for Cherokee artisans. In fall 2007, LTLT received a grant to assist in conserving an ancient landscape and to expand Cherokee artisan resources in the upper Little Tennessee River Basin. "We know the LTLT inside and out, because of working with them [on these grants]. We had to know how high a level of fidelity they could demonstrate toward the mission of the foundation. The LTLT is high profile, very transparent."[29]

The CWMTF monies are designated for the protection of federally designated critical habitat for water quality and floodplain maintenance. Although the tribe was able to partner with the land trust to benefit from these funds, Native land access and management needs are often left out of state, federal, and local master plans for bond acts and other initiatives. To remedy this, Hatley is currently working with the LTLT and the EBCI to insert tribal land protection interests and concerns into the visioning processes that lead to public funding initiatives, such as the CWMTF.[30]

Ultimately, for the administrators of the CWMTF, the Cowee site was significant for its 3,138 feet (0.6 mi) of Little Tennessee River frontage, which is part of the nearly 27 miles of river corridor identified by the North Carolina Natural Heritage Program as Nationally Significant Aquatic Habitat. The specific 0.6-mile riparian area near the mound is federally designated as a critical habitat for a threatened fish, the spotfin chub (*Erimonax monachus*), and an endangered mussel, the Appalachian Elktoe (*Alasmidonta raveneliana*). The stretch is also part of the Little Tennessee Flyway, utilized by migrating waterfowl, and it is home to other federally endangered and state-designated "special concern" plant and aquatic species, including rare patches of giant rivercane (*Arundinaria gigantea*), one of only two native bamboo species in the continental United States.[31]

The state CWMTF monies allowed the LTLT to purchase the 70-acre Cowee Mound and town site, which covers land in two parcels on opposite banks of the Little Tennessee River. The mound was a priority parcel for the LTLT because of its historic and riparian values and its location between two tracts that have already been conserved—one by the LTLT (the historic Hall Farm) and the other by the State of North Carolina (the Needmore Tract). The EBCI purchased both properties associated with the mound (the 52.77-acre Cowee Mound parcel and the 17.19-acre Carter Branch parcel) from the LTLT, receiving title on April 23, 2007. In total, the Eastern Band contributed $880,000 and the state CWMTF contributed $421,000 for the project, in addition to some transaction costs.

The Eastern Band now holds title to the parcels. The State of North Carolina holds the conservation easement on the Cowee Mound and Carter Branch properties to protect them from further development, and the LTLT monitors the easement. As Michell Hicks, chief of the Eastern Band of the Cherokee, said in a statement to the press: "Cowee Mound in Macon County is an important historical and cultural site to the Cherokee people. The collaborative opportunity presented to us by the Land Trust for the Little Tennessee, which includes our ownership of the property, is unprecedented."[32] With the oversight of their respective legal counsels, the LTLT and the tribe based these easements on a LTLT template. The tribe currently holds the land in fee simple status, but it may eventually want to put the land into trust. "The way you word the easement is critical to moving towards trust status," said Wilson.[33] Representatives from the tribe and the LTLT did not express concern over potential barriers to putting a property with an easement on it into trust, but both parties were careful to work with knowledgeable legal counsel in order to ensure that their respective interests were protected. "In the end, all of these legal devices are designed to assuage fears of what could go wrong. You need to have a certain amount of trust, so not so many layers of restriction are necessary to make these deals work."[34]

Currently, the parcels can be used for educational purposes and traditional agriculture, and they are being managed for hay cultivation. The LTLT applied for a grant from the Revitalization of Traditional Cherokee Artisan Renewable Resources (RTCARR) initiative to help manage the Cowee Mound property for at least one year. "We're pleased to partner with the tribe for management because we're in the community," LTLT's Taylor explained.[35] Although the easement ensures that the area will never be commercialized, the Eastern Band, the LTLT, and the state of North Carolina as the easement holder plan to collaborate to increase interpretive signage and educational programs on the site. Specifically, the Eastern Band plans to install educational kiosks and to restore traditional Cherokee agriculture. Wilson underscored the importance of placing this important acquisition within the EBCI's larger efforts to develop a master plan, which will prioritize lands for protection and education, development, and other tribal needs.[36]

Conclusion: Looking Forward

The Cowee Mound is neither the end nor the extent of the collaboration between the LTLT, the EBCI, and other partners: "I think it sets a valuable precedent for future land preservation purchases and initiatives because if other land preservation organizations know that the tribe can be a good partner [for preservation] it opens the doors for pooling resources in other settings."[37] Since the purchase, the tribe and LTLT have discussed expanding the Cowee purchase, by purchasing another mound. "The Cowee purchase set up these other opportunities," Townsend added.[38]

As of 2010, the tribe and the land trust were working to cooperate on a purchase of another parcel, a 108-acre tract overlooking Cowee Mound. The site contains the pinnacle of Hall Mountain and old-growth holly trees, according to Taylor.[39] For several years, the land trust had worked with the developers who owned the property to reach a conservation option. In 2009, a bank took title to the land from the developers in lieu of foreclosure, and then the Land Trust took out a loan to buy the land from the bank. The Land Trust worked with the tribe to write a grant to raise funds so that the tribe could buy the land from the LTLT, thereby enabling repayment of the loan. The tribe applied for the one-to-one matching grant from a new federal Community Forest and Open Space Conservation Program, which has been authorized under the Farm Bill but not yet fully funded. If the tribe is able to purchase the property from the Land Trust, it would establish the parcel as a community forest, which would include tribal management of artisanal resources (such as basketry materials) and educational opportunities in sustainable forest management. The parcel might also lend itself to interpretation of the Cowee Mound, since it provides an excellent view of the site.

The LTLT received title to the land in 2010, but the fate of the grant for the tribe's potential purchase will not be known until the program is funded. At that point, decisions will be made about what conservation restrictions and agreements are needed. Although the collaboration is in a preliminary phase, if the success of the Cowee Mound purchase is any indication, the tribe and the land trust have the necessary experience and mutual trust to make this land acquisition beneficial for all parties, including future generations.

In the meantime, the tribe may be strengthening its own conservation program. As Hatley explained, "While there is a lot of overlap between the reasons tribes and land trusts protect land, there will be some land that won't interest the land trust, or they won't be able to participate. So it's better for the tribes to develop some capacity within their own government or nonprofit world to form a tribal land trust."[40] This land trust structure may begin as informally as having an employee familiar with real estate and conservation law, who can connect state, federal, tribal, and private funding streams to acquire and protect lands for the tribe.

14

Watershed Protection

Nisqually Indian Tribe (Washington)

The Nisqually, or Squalli-Absh, homeland is located along the Nisqually River in western Washington, 10 miles east of the city of Olympia, at the southern end of Puget Sound. In 1854, Washington territorial Governor Isaac Stevens and representatives of Nisqually, Puyallup, Steilacoom, Squaxin, and other tribes negotiated the Treaty of Medicine Creek. The Treaty ceded tribal lands, established three reservations, and confirmed ongoing fishing rights in the "usual and accustomed places."[1] The proposed Nisqually reservation was a 1,280-acre upland, forested parcel west of the Nisqually River.[2] Nisqually leader and orator Leschi and his brother Quiemuth reportedly refused to sign the treaty unless the Nisqually could get land along their Nisqually River. Stevens denied this request, but X's were placed by Leschi and Quiemuth's names anyway, indicating their acceptance.[3]

The Puget Sound Indian War ensued 1855–1856. Indian Agent Michael Simmons had all "friendly" members of the Nisqually and other tribes interned on Fox Island in Puget Sound, while the Washington Territorial Volunteers and U.S. soldiers pursued Leschi and other resistors.[4] Despite widespread sickness, interned Indians remained on Fox Island because Stevens had authorized shooting Indians on-sight on the mainland.[5] Leschi's surrender, and the ongoing costs of providing food and medical care to the internees, contributed to Stevens' desire to make peace with the Indians. In August 1856, Stevens renegotiated with the Nisqually and established a 4,717-acre reservation including land on both sides of a 4.5-mile stretch of the Nisqually River.[6]

Following this partial victory, the Nisqually reservation would be subject to future reductions. In 1884, the land was divided into thirty family allotment parcels, and, in 1917, on the eve of World War I, Pierce County (the jurisdiction surrounding eastern Nisqually reservation lands), had the opportunity to attract an army base to the region. The War Department and the county agreed that if the latter provided the land, the base would be built. Pierce County voters approved the condemnation of 84,000 acres, including 3,300 acres of land held in trust for the Nisqually tribe, displacing all of the Nisqually on the north bank of the river. The reservation was reduced to one-third of its former size.[7] There were reports that the displaced people did not receive payment for the seized land, and some tribal members left the area.[8]

The next fight was asserting the tribe's rights to fish from the Nisqually. The Treaty of Medicine Creek confirmed that right, but it was ignored by sportfishermen, the state, and industry. Activist Bernie Whitebear, also known as Bernard Reyes or Sin-Aikst, recalled bloody confrontations on the Nisqually River as the Nisqually people fought for the right to fish in the river as they had for centuries.[9] In 1974, *United States v. Washington*[10] found that the Washington State tribes did indeed have fishing rights, based on the Medicine Creek and other treaties. The tribes were entitled to half of the "harvestable number of fish," and non-Native fishers were entitled to the other half.[11] This decision placed Washington tribes, like the Nisqually, in a key position as fisheries' stewards.

Leaders and Partners

Over the last twenty-five years, the tribe has aggressively pursued land restoration and acquisition. It now owns more than 1,000 acres of the former reservation, and it has added additional acreage outside of original reservation boundaries. The tribe employs more than 350 people in government departments and enterprises, including the Red Wind Casino near Olympia, a convenience store, and in fish and shellfish harvest operations.[12] It also operates two fish hatcheries, on Clear Creek and Kalama Creek.

The Clear Creek Hatchery is on former tribal lands that now belong to the Fort Lewis Army base. The process of establishing a tribal hatchery on Army land took years of negotiation and fundraising. Natural springs on the Fort's land were an ideal site for salmon spawning, but the Army was concerned about having a nonmilitary operation within its boundaries. Eventually, Fort Lewis agreed to the tribe's proposal, and the tribe raised approximately $12 million in federal funds between 1987 and 1989 to build the hatchery. Operation and maintenance funds come from a settlement between the tribe and the City of Tacoma.

Tacoma Power built its first dam on the Nisqually River in 1912.[13] Dam management (including releasing flows at alternate times for power generation) disrupted fish habitat and salmon survival downstream. Following the Boldt Decision, the tribe and other local partners formed the Nisqually River Coordinating Committee (NRCC), which did a study to develop minimum flow requirements for salmon survival.[14] The tribe sued the city for damages to the salmon population, and in 1988, the tribe's Business Council approved a settlement with the City of Tacoma.[15] The city made a commitment to maintain the minimum flows determined in the NRCC study and to pay the Clear Creek hatchery's operating costs. The hatchery opened in 1991.[16]

The Nisqually Tribe has off-reservation fishing rights and historic cultural and subsistence ties to the salmon and other marine resources in the region.[17] The tribe is recognized locally, regionally, and nationally as a leader in protecting and restoring Nisqually Basin fisheries. As part of its ongoing work to improve and maintain the health of a watershed threatened by pollution, development, and over-harvesting, the tribe has forged collaborations with two basinwide organizations, the Nisqually River Council and the Nisqually Land Trust.

In 1985, the Washington State Legislature approved Substitute House Bill 323, directing the Department of Ecology to develop a management plan for the Nisqually River, which flows from Mt. Rainier National Park to the Nisqually National Wildlife Refuge at Puget Sound. The Department of Ecology convened a Nisqually River Task Force with representatives from numerous basin interests, including all levels of government (federal, tribal, state, local), resource managers, agriculturalists, and environmentalists. Farmers and timber operators, who were concerned that the tribe and environmental interests were going to shut down their operations, initially resisted. According to a *Frontline* report on the Nisqually, trust was built largely due to the efforts of tribal leader Billy Frank Jr. (Nisqually), who, after a particularly contentious session, called for an end to the in-fighting and recognized the importance of all parties—farmers and timber companies included—and the need to find a lasting solution. As Frank recalled, "I never gave up on any of these people, I never gave up on . . . any of our leaders up and down the watershed. I said, you know, 'We, we have to be together.'"[18] The task force developed a coordinated plan recognizing the river's ecological, economic, and recreational values, and it created two implementation organizations: The Nisqually River Council, comprising the interests represented on the initial task force, and the Nisqually River Citizens Advisory Committee, which ensured citizen representation.[19]

According to Nisqually Tribe Salmon Recovery Program Manager Jeanette Dorner, who grew up in the basin, the tribe was very active in the formation of the council, under the leadership of Billy Frank Jr.[20] Frank was known nationally for his activism to maintain tribal fishing rights in the Northwest.[21] The initial task force developed the Nisqually River Management Plan, which was approved by the state legislature in 1987, and council members have been meeting monthly to coordinate watershed efforts ever since. Several affiliated organizations developed out of the council, including the Nisqually Land Trust. Relationships built on the state-sanctioned council assist the tribe's efforts to influence management of off-reservation hunting, fishing, and gathering areas. "We want to work with people involved in the whole watershed," said Nisqually Tribe member and Natural Resources Program Manager Georgiana Kautz. "If we can work through issues and come up with solutions, it's much better than going to court."[22]

Where the tribe has full ownership, they are careful to practice sustainable management. On non-tribal lands, the tribe encourages landowners to follow environmentally friendly practices. "We want people living along the river to continue to do the things they are doing—fishing, farming, etc.—but to find a balance, and to be aware of the habitat and what we have to do to keep it in good condition," said Kautz.[23] When the Nisqually River Council was first formed, some agribusiness owners were very concerned about the possible impacts to their property rights and economic viability. One large agricultural landowner was particularly opposed, but through Frank's continued outreach, and many meetings, field trips, and discussions with other council members, the landowner came to the table and eventually became one of the council's strongest supporters. The council's updated 2005 Stewardship Plan explicitly embraces the principle of sustainability in all areas of the watershed, including economic aspects.[24]

Partnerships in the Nisqually Basin between the tribe and other parties have caught national attention for their successful environmental and community outcomes. Kautz credits strong leadership at every level and continued communication between parties. For example, while the relationship was not always so good between the tribe and the Army at Fort Lewis, now working agreements are in place. "They have changed some of the way they do things," she said. "They have a goal to protect everyone in the United States, and I told them I have a goal, and that's to make sure I'm a Nisqually tribal member forever."[25]

In order to improve and maintain the health of a watershed threatened by pollution, development, and overharvesting, the tribe has forged collaborations with many parties, including the Nisqually River Council and the Nisqually Land Trust. As Kautz continued:

> We're telling people to take a look at watersheds that have tribes on them; there [is] a lot of collaboration . . . because in order for us to get to salmon recovery, it's not going to be just us alone, it's going to take everybody within the watershed: the agencies, the farmers, the tribes, and Fort Lewis! Sometimes I do get angry about what happens, but I also know that I want to be positive, I want to move forward, and I want my children to have these same type of beliefs that you can do whatever you want, accomplish whatever you want, and that we'll be able to exist as Nisqually tribal members, today, tomorrow, and forever.[26]

The tribe does educational activities and outreach with numerous basin communities and reminds all parties of the vital importance of salmon to the region's economy, culture, and subsistence.

At the Mouth of the River: Nisqually Indian Tribe and the USFWS

Through participation on the Nisqually River Council, a relationship developed between the tribe, which is doing ongoing salmon recovery work, and the U.S. Fish and Wildlife Service, manager of the Nisqually Wildlife Refuge at the mouth of the Nisqually River. Drawing on federal funding and extensive coordination with a landowner, the tribe purchased the last large privately held parcel in the Nisqually estuary, a 300-acre farm. It was a high priority for habitat restoration, as dikes built by pioneer farmers on the land to keep saltwater out of pastures were preventing fish passage. Based on lessons learned from previous restoration successes, plans were made to breach the dikes and create a salt marsh for salmon habitat. The tribe began doing restoration on the land in 1996, and it took the last dike down in 2006, resulting in improved fish and wildlife habitat.[27] Because the parcel is within the boundaries of the refuge, the tribe developed an agreement with the USFWS to cooperatively manage the land. Employees work for either the tribe or the refuge, coordinating efforts to manage, restore, monitor, and improve public access to the estuary.

The two entities applied for funding jointly, working with Ducks Unlimited and others to raise over $4 million to complete a process that culminated in November 2009 with 762 acres of restored estuary habitat on the USFWS-owned section of the refuge. Since salmon are born in freshwater, live as adults in the ocean, and then move through the estuary (undergoing a major physiological change) before they return upstream to spawn, estuaries are essential habitat for both young and mature salmon. The tribe's modeling efforts showed that the estuary was a place where restoration could have the greatest regional benefit. As Salmon Recovery Program Manager Jeanette Dorner noted, "The model indicated that by doing the restoration we're doing on Tribal property and will do on the refuge, we can expect to see a doubling of naturally produced Chinook. It was the most significant step we could take to improve overall abundance."[28] According to a November 12, 2009, *King 5 News* report on the restoration, "This single project increases what's left of such places in Puget Sound by 50 percent."[29] The project represents the largest estuary restoration effort in the Pacific Northwest.[30]

Nisqually Land Trust

The Nisqually Land Trust (NLT) was formed in 1989 in response to rapid population expansion in the Nisqually River watershed. In 2008, the NLT embarked on a strategic planning process for 2009–2011, and it defined its organizational vision and mission: "to protect, restore, and manage the natural and essentially wild aspects of the Nisqually River basin while cooperating with watershed communities to support an ecologically sustainable way of life. Our mission is to acquire and manage critical lands to permanently protect the water, wildlife, natural areas, and scenic vistas of the Nisqually River watershed."[31]

As of 2009, the NLT has conserved more than 2,800 acres of the watershed, with thirteen conservation easements and the acquisition of fee title to 2,804 acres.[32] Funding for land conservation and acquisition comes from donations, mitigation funds, and grants. One of the NLT's largest sources of funds has been the Washington Salmon Recovery Funding Board, a state agency that distributes state and federal funds to protect and restore salmon habitat. Mitigation funds have come primarily from several private corporations and from hydroelectric utilities, as well as from special events, such as the NLT's annual dinner and auction. The tribe also donates to the land trust and lends its field crew to help with plantings and maintenance.[33] According to NLT board member and Nisqually Tribe Environment Program Supervisor George Walter, the NLT is "an important tool for building a stewardship ethic and a permanently protected land base."[34] The NLT is part of a larger vision of the Nisqually Basin as "a watershed community that is caring for each other and working on long-term sustainability," he added.[35]

NLT and Nisqually Indian Tribe: Conditions for Collaboration

The Nisqually Tribe has had to build partnerships to protect its off-reservation, traditional land base and fishing rights. The stated mission of the tribe's Environmental Management Program is "to protect habitat that support the Nisqually Tribe's treaty rights by working with government agencies and private landowners."[36] The tribe has rights to harvest salmon throughout the river corridor and tributary streams. Because the NLT and other long-term property owners in the watershed affect the salmon population, and therefore, the treaty right, the tribe is very concerned with coordinating resource protection with these other landowners. "We don't care who protects that waterfront, as long as it is protected forever," said Kautz.[37] In addition to participating on the Nisqually River Council, the tribe does strategic planning to determine where to allocate fiscal and other resources to protect key areas in the basin.

The tribe and the NLT have worked together to raise funds for land protection. However, the tribe does not help the NLT prioritize parcels for protection but instead coordinates with the trust to ensure, and sometimes control, access to parcels. Moreover, if the tribe is able to purchase a parcel, the NLT will defer ownership to it. Part of Walter's job assignment with the tribe is to participate in some NLT activities. This is a natural for him since he also serves as president of the NLT board of directors. "The tribe recognizes that its goals and the land trust's goals coincide for land protection," Walter said.[38] The tribe is interested in protecting both the fish habitat and culturally important places on the land in their traditional territory. Under Walter's and the tribe's leadership, the environmental program monitors water quantity and quality, timber harvests, and other activities that can affect water resources; enforces environmental regulations; and engages in watershed planning. The tribe's objectives include collaborating with the Nisqually River Council and the NLT to protect the watershed in perpetuity.

The Nisqually Tribe and the NLT do not have formal terms of agreement for collaboration. However, the tribe has contributed matching funds, staffing assistance, and technical support, including GIS mapping services, aerial photos, information on salmon usage, and habitat restoration on NLT properties. For example, in 2006, the tribe contributed a $400,000 habitat migration grant to the purchase of the $1.2 million, 240-acre Powell Creek

FIGURE 14.1. Looking up the Nisqually River shoreline from the Nisqually Land Trust's Powell Creek property. With funds from the Nisqually Tribe, the Nisqually Land Trust purchased an old logging road that crossed Powell Creek, and it then worked to remove culverts and riprap to restore fish passage. (Photo courtesy of Nisqually Land Trust)

parcel on the Nisqually River that contains critical salmon-spawning habitat and a wetland and that links two existing NLT properties on either side (fig. 14.1). Tribal members and officials also attend the NLT events, and one of the tribal fishermen contributes salmon to the NLT's annual salmon bake and membership meeting.

Ohop Creek

One example of the collaboration between the Nisqually Tribe and the NLT is occurring on Ohop Creek, an important salmon tributary stream that has been degraded by channelization, silting, and pollution. Nearly ten years ago, the tribe began working on a plan to restore salmon productivity in this stream by returning the creek to its original channel. The NLT, using funding and support from a variety of sources including the tribe, has acquired more than 200 acres along the Ohop to support this collaborative restoration effort. The tribe, a local restoration nonprofit called the South

Puget Sound Salmon Enhancement Group, and other partners, including Pierce County, Pierce Conservation District, and state and federal fisheries agencies have been working to restore the creek, and, as the major land-owner, the NLT is responsible for the long-term stewardship of the land and the Ohop.

Like other areas of the watershed, the Ohop had been altered by pio-neer farmers who attempted to dry the valley for farming by using a steam shovel to deepen and narrow the historically meandering creek channel. This replaced marshes with grazing and agricultural lands and greatly reduced spawning habitat for salmon, as well as habitat for birds, frogs, and other animals.[39] Ohop Creek was chosen for restoration by the tribe following an analysis of salmon habitat in the watershed and a subsequent modeling effort. According to Dorner, the tribe looked at how salmon use the resources, and how the resources have changed over time, to see where projects would have the largest positive impact on salmon populations. Although there are many tributaries to the Nisqually, the Ohop is particu-larly important because of the number of salmon and the diversity of salmon species that use it, as well as its role in maintaining salmon "life-history diversity." The latter refers to having a range of viable options for salmon habitat, so that if there is a catastrophic event (for example, a chemical spill in the main stem of the Nisqually), the salmon will be in a range of locations, which ensures that the entire population will not be affected.[40]

Because of the large cost and scope of the Ohop restoration, the proj-ect is proceeding in phases: In fall 2009, partners had constructed a new, meandering channel, complete with forty-two engineered logjams to slow water flow and create habitat. In October 2009, partners—including the Nisqually Tribe field crew—and land trust volunteers, including local student groups, began planting the 400 acres along the new channel's banks. The restored Ohop Creek channel, which "has been lengthened from .6 miles to 1.1 miles," will be opened to flow in summer 2010.[41] According to Walter, "In a few years, Ohop Creek will be a wooded, meandering stream, with much better salmon habitat."[42]

Terms of Collaboration

According to Dorner, the NLT has also been an essential partner in the tribe's salmon recovery plan, because the NLT helps to ensure protection by obtaining either conservation easements in perpetuity or parcel ownership in fee. "If you just restore, you're losing ground that's not protected," said Dorner. "The NLT helps to ensure we are not losing ground."[43] The tribe and the NLT collaborate to get lands along the river into public ownership or private ownership with protective easements. The tribe and partners in the Nisqually River Council, including the NLT, have over 70 percent of the main stem of the Nisqually below the dam in protected ownership. The tribe's goal is to see 90 percent of the land in protected ownership. "This gives us security in knowing we can move forward with restoration knowing that significant portion of the river is protected," Dorner added.[44]

The tribe and the NLT maintain their relationship in part by clearly delineating their spheres of influence. The NLT works on private lands, not on tribal lands, which are the sole purview of the tribe. Lands located near the Nisqually Reservation also are within the tribe's sphere. All of the NLT's conservation easements are on private—not tribally owned—lands. The tribe does not hold any conservation easements, although tribal leadership is considering implementing them as one conservation strategy. In 2007, according to Walter, "There is only the vague recognition that conservation easements are possible tools available. There are no specific plans to use them, and [the tribe] has conducted no analysis regarding the relationship between conservation easement restrictions and fee-to-trust procedures."[45] The tribe and the NLT share a desire to steward the long-term health of the watershed. Their collaboration began slowly and grew over time, as the NLT built a positive reputation with watershed landowners, including the tribes. The neighboring Puyallup and Squaxin tribes have also made donations to the NLT, because they, too, recognized the NLT's role in helping to maintain the southern Puget Sound's largest river, which produces fish for everyone.[46]

Two of the nine current NLT board members are also employees of the tribe, although this is not required in the bylaws. In the past, tribal members have been involved in the NLT's governance, but no tribal members currently serve on the board. The NLT and the tribe strengthen their relationship by sharing staff and by communicating about watershed issues. Walter encouraged other land trusts and tribes: "Call each other. There should be a natural collaboration. From a land trust point of view, an Indian tribe should be a source of technical assistance, and from a tribe's point of view, a land trust can be one of the vehicles to accomplish long-term goals. You build the contact for mutual interests and mutual benefits."[47]

Partnerships for Native Land Management

Cache Creek Conservancy Tending and Gathering Garden (California)

The Cache Creek Conservancy (hereafter, the Conservancy) is a nonprofit organization formed in 1995 by a group of citizens that sought to promote restoration and improve the riparian corridor along Cache Creek. The creation of the Conservancy represents a long-awaited compromise between industrial, farming, environmental, and other factions, each with a strong interest in the health and productivity of the creek.

Restoring Cache Creek

Cache Creek begins in Clear Lake and flows through Lake and Colusa counties in California before traversing the agricultural Capay Valley in Yolo County. The lower reach of the Cache Creek channel was heavily mined in the 1970s and 1980s for aggregate—sand and gravel used in concrete and industrial construction. "Gravel wars" ensued between local stakeholders (including the miners) with an interest in the creek channel. "Competing interests and values . . . created fissures in the community," explained Conservancy Tending and Gathering Garden Steering Committee member Jacquelyn Ross (Pomo, Coast Miwok).[1] As Conservancy Executive Director Lynnel Pollock pointed out, efforts to remove mining from the creek channel had been ongoing for nearly twenty years, and "all partners realized that more needed to be done."[2]

In 1994, the leadership of Yolo County began to develop a plan that would balance mining with environmental and habitat values in the creek channel. In 1995 and 1996, the aggregate mining companies working along Cache Creek, the county, and other stakeholders were invited to participate in a process to develop a Cache Creek Area Plan. In 1996, the Yolo County Board of Supervisors adopted the plan, which has two components—the Off-Channel Mining Plan and the Cache Creek Resource Management Plan (CCRMP). The Off-Channel Mining Plan took aggregate mining out of the creek channel and instituted a mechanism whereby the industrial mining companies would provide funds for reclamation and restoration along the riparian corridor.[3] The CCRMP focuses on restoring that corridor, which includes the Jan T. Lowrey Cache Creek Nature Preserve. To support its infrastructure, projects, and programs, the nonprofit Cache Creek Conservancy relies on grants and other funding in addition to the amount it receives through the CCRMP.

The county, local private landowners, and other parties were concerned about who would oversee the restoration and management. Most of the land along the 14-mile corridor covered by the Resource Management Plan was privately owned, and it was unclear how landowners would become involved. As Ross and her coauthors describe: "The Conservancy was created as a vehicle for implementation of the Cache Creek Resource Management Plan. . . . [It] was the first organization in living memory dedicated to restoration of Cache Creek's riparian corridor in the area historically mined for gravel. Its mission is to promote the restoration, enhancement, and prudent management of the stream environment along Cache Creek."[4] The Conservancy served as a bridge between landowners, the aggregate industry, and county government, all of which are represented on the Conservancy's board of directors. The Conservancy developed and strengthened existing relationships with private landowners along the creek and has built a positive reputation for doing quality restoration projects that enhance habitat while simultaneously respecting landowners' values.

Jan T. Lowrey Cache Creek Nature Preserve

In 1999, the Teichert Land Company, one of the aggregate mining operations operating along the creek, donated 130 acres of upland and riparian land to Yolo County to establish the Cache Creek Nature Preserve, now the Jan T. Lowrey Cache Creek Nature Preserve, for habitat protection and preservation. Teichert specified that the land was to be managed by the Conservancy for habitat conservation, and the Conservancy created a separate agreement with Yolo County to establish the former's land management role. The entire 130-acre parcel is covered by a conservation easement, which is held by the Conservancy, with Yolo County as the landowner. The Conservancy was not initially going to hold easements, but as a nonprofit, they were in the best position to do so. Yolo County, Teichert, and the Conservancy discussed options for other easement holders, including the Department of Fish and Game, which would have involved an additional layer of bureaucracy. "As an organization, holding easements is not our primary purpose," explained Conservancy Executive Director and former Yolo County Supervisor Lynnel Pollock. "We do restoration work."[5]

The Conservancy's programs on the Nature Preserve include environmental education with school groups, ongoing environmental stewardship and restoration, and public outreach—partially through the Tending and Gathering Garden and by providing opportunities for Native people to steward and gather plant materials for traditional use.

The Tending and Gathering Garden

The 2-acre Tending and Gathering Garden is a unique partnership between members of the Native American community and the Conservancy to demonstrate traditional California land- and plant-management practices. The garden began as a demonstration project in 2000, initiated by Shannon Brawley, a graduate student in geography at the University of California, Davis; Kathy Wallace (Karuk, Yurok, Mohawk, member of Hoopa Valley Tribe), a traditional basketweaver, cultural educator, and cofounder of the California Indian Basketweavers Association (CIBA); and Jan Lowrey, the former executive director of the Conservancy.

As an undergraduate in 1999, Brawley was studying landscape architecture and restoration and working in garden maintenance for wealthy landowners. She read *Before the Wilderness: Environmental Management by Native Californians*,[6] a book that gave her a deep appreciation for Indian horticultural management. In her landscaping work, Shannon observed the offhand ways in which native plants were being improperly installed, neglected, and mismanaged: "I was dealing with native plants, but landscape architects were not utilizing them in the right way. I was stewarding someone's property, but they didn't value that you actually had to care for something. I related to what [traditional] weavers were experiencing."[7] Brawley found herself driven by a desire to share the importance of caring for local native plants, partly to ensure that weavers would have easy access to the plant materials they needed. The idea for the Tending and Gathering Garden grew out of

Brawley's undergraduate senior thesis. Later, it would be the focus of her work in graduate school, where she was a recipient of a Ford Foundation Community Forestry Research Fellowship.

UC Davis Landscape Architecture professor Dr. Rob Thayer suggested that Brawley contact the California Indian Basketweavers' Association. She called Sarah Greensfelder, then–executive director of CIBA, and explained the outline of her project to create a garden for the restoration of native plants that would also make them available to basketweavers. In 2000, at the suggestion of Greensfelder, Brawley and two of her professors met with Wallace to explore ways of incorporating Native values and practices into Brawley's thesis. "It began strictly on paper," Wallace remembered.[8]

Brawley followed another recommendation from a different professor to contact the Cache Creek Conservancy. She proposed creating the garden in the Conservancy's Nature Preserve, arguing that it would restore part of the property while providing a needed resource for Native people. The Cache Creek board of directors agreed and offered a 2-acre area near the center of the preserve, along the wetlands that were created by the restoration of gravel pits.[9] As Brawley recalled, "I came to Jan [Lowrey] at the right time. The Conservancy was just forming on that land. He was very open. . . . We had an empathetic ear in Jan."[10]

Lowrey was a unique and important supporter of the project because of his deep connections to the area. His family had owned land in the region for generations, and he had gone to school and worked with local Native people, including Paula Lorenzo, then–chair of the Yocha Dehe Wintun Nation (at the time, the Rumsey Rancheria). Lowrey also knew landowners, politicians, and other regional stakeholders, and he could help build the support and buy-in for the Tending and Gathering Garden.

Brawley took Wallace to the Conservancy to meet Lowrey. Wallace reflected on Lowrey: "In my experience of working to get people to recognize the validity of our traditional land-management techniques, I never met someone who understood what we wanted and was as open to these ideas without rejecting them out of hand."[11] A longtime advocate for weavers and a founder and former chair of CIBA's Land Access Committee, Wallace has extensive experience working with multiple parties to ensure Native American access to indigenous weaving materials. "There are not enough of us to do the job by ourselves," she said, referring to Native weavers. "I learned that collaboration is the only way to make changes."[12] But not just any collaboration—partnerships built between Native people and landowners or other parties must be equitable, respectful, and inclusive. Wallace emphasized the need to involve Native people from the ground up in the Tending and Gathering Garden. She noted that Lowrey was also "very adamant" about involving Native people from the beginning. "He constantly advocated for us because he felt we were the 'experts'—not docents or volunteers—but the experts."[13] Wallace suggested that Brawley meet with Chairwoman Lorenzo to discuss the project.

Brawley herself also continued to do research about the area and to meet local weavers. When she told Lowrey that she hoped to meet Wintun elder Bertha Mitchell, Lowrey mentioned Brawley's work and goals to a Public Relations Department employee for the Yocha Dehe Wintun Nation. That person helped Brawley set up a meeting with Mitchell and two other weavers. Brawley recalled that initial meeting: "I was scared. . . . I didn't know what to say, I had this idea, [yet] Bertha was so skeptical. . . . I continued to write her letters, to try to have a relationship with her, and now she is a good friend."[14] Wallace also remembered this initial meeting and noted that the Native ladies responded to the garden project "with a mixture of hesitancy and support."[15] Nevertheless, they offered ideas for making the garden as useful, traditional, and respectful as possible. According to Ross and her coauthors, one of the elders, a master basketweaver, suggested a shade structure "so weavers could retreat out of the sun when processing materials."[16] A structure for this purpose, combining traditional design with the requirements of contemporary building codes, was completed on the site in 2005.

After observing the progress, and feeling that she could trust Brawley and Lowrey to create an inclusive project, Wallace gave Brawley a list of other local Native weavers, teachers, council members, and others who might be interested in sharing their time and expertise. Wallace encouraged her to include everyone, whether they participated at the outset or not. "I told her it was very important to keep them informed," Wallace said. "They all have a stake."[17] She also advised Brawley to be extremely transparent with all of the project participants and to create an atmosphere in which people felt safe enough to voice their opinions. Meetings were designed to allow people to contribute their ideas and concerns, in a respectful environment, and food was always served.

In addition to an environment of respect, Wallace worked with Lowrey and Brawley to ensure that they understood the need for compensation of Native participants' time and shared knowledge. "People are always looking for the opinions of Native people, and they never compensate them," Wallace explained. "I think of all the people that I and other Native practitioners helped [with theses and dissertations], and then they are paid as being the 'expert' for the information that they were given by the traditional practitioners. This has happened time and time again. So, at least provide people with food and mileage so it's not an imposition for them to come to a meeting."[18] The garden project and the Conservancy always raised money to cover the costs of that compensation, as well as to pay weavers when they demonstrated or taught basket weaving at events. As Brawley recalled, this "set the example that we needed to pay for the expertise and knowledge."[19] Wallace also continued to be very clear about the importance of reciprocity: "I didn't want to get people involved if it was a situation of being taken advantage of. Some people were very skeptical of 'another student project,' and we weren't going to be successful unless people backed the project."[20]

Through the meetings with Native people at the Conservancy, Brawley also learned more about weavers' needs. It became clear that 2 acres was not enough to provide materials for one weaver, let alone many weavers. Nevertheless, it would be an ideal site for teaching about native plants, traditional stewardship, and traditional plant uses. According to Tending and Gathering Garden Steering Committee member Ross: "In that small space, we could create a demonstration garden and a living gallery where weaving teachers from various tribal traditions could bring their students to identify plants and learn to tend them."[21] The steering committee consisted of a core group of all of the individuals involved, and it created achievable goals for the garden. In the beginning, the group met as often as once per month, and those who lived nearby were on the site as often as once per week. Brawley worked with Lowrey, some steering committee members, the California Conservation Corps, volunteers, and workers on loan from local farms, who planted and watered the plants the steering committee selected. The garden now features multiple species native to the Cache Creek watershed, all of which have many traditional uses (figs. 15.1 and 15.2).

The garden is important to Native weavers because it represents a place where native plants are accessible for stewardship, teaching, and use. An essay analyzing the project, written by steering committee members Jacquelyn Ross (Southern Pomo/Coast Miwok), Don Hankins (Plains Miwok, Osage), Brawley, and Lowrey, reflects on the vital importance of access: "Access is necessary for traditional food gathering, hunting, and ceremony. It is required for the tending and harvesting of plants necessary for the creation of baskets, traps, cordage, and other uses."[22] In other words, access is essential for cultural sustainability. Although plants used in weaving were traditionally widely available throughout California "once-viable gathering areas are now overgrown, subject to chemical exposure, congested with invasive plants, and suffer insect predation. The garden has become a place to teach traditional techniques in a clean environment."[23]

FIGURE 15.1. The beginning of the Tending and Gathering Garden at the Cache Creek Nature Preserve, August 2003. (Photo courtesy of Cache Creek Conservancy)

FIGURE 15.2. The Tending and Gathering Garden at the Cache Creek Nature Preserve, March 2007. These two photos were taken from the same location, approximately three-and-a-half years apart. (Photo courtesy of Cache Creek Conservancy)

The garden expanded well beyond Brawley's initial project, which included understanding the effects of Native Californian plant stewardship on restoration and finding solutions to the inaccessibility of safe gathering areas for Native weavers. The steering committee overseeing the garden is composed primarily of Native people from fourteen tribes,[24] who provide guidance on practices, plants, and uses. Following traditional protocol, major actions regarding the garden are first presented to the elders and leaders of the local tribe, the Yocha Dehe Wintun Nation. Although the Conservancy board of directors approved the Tending and Gathering Garden as an organizational effort, it is not a separate easement.

Tending and Gathering Garden Steering Committee

The steering committee is composed of representatives with a variety of skills, experiences, and resources.[25] Meeting times are organized around members' schedules, to accommodate family and work responsibilities. In addition to communicating with the Conservancy regarding the garden project, the steering committee has worked internally to build communication and shared principles. "The committee members all come from different tribal nations, with separate ancestries, governments, and cultural legacies. Designing rules to govern the garden represents a dimension of international negotiation."[26] The import of this process of building communication and collaboration in the management of a shared resource owned by an external, public entity is not lost on the committee members. As Ross explained, "We are working across generational, tribal, and gender lines, to great effect. We seem to be enjoying this work."[27]

Brawley joined the Conservancy in 1999, when the Teichert Foundation first funded the research for and development of the Tending and Gathering Garden. She was a coordinator and facilitator for the garden's steering committee and functioned as a liaison between the committee and the board. Before the committee had a representative on the Conservancy board, Brawley would go to both meetings and coordinate the relationship between the two. Committee members, Lowrey, and other board members also spoke with one another directly, talking over concerns and working to deal with questions and issues across cultural lines.

As a facilitator for the Committee, Brawley acknowledged the depth of the process and worked to develop her own facilitation style: "The process of trying to create a safe place took a lot of time. . . . When you're dealing with people who have been hurt and ignored, you have to [take that time]. . . . It's a process that can't be rushed. . . . We all shared our experiences.

That's the difference . . . inclusion from the very beginning. That was a big emphasis for Kathy [Wallace] and the steering committee. In a small way, we could create a space for healing people and the land."[28] The committee developed slowly, with a lot of persistent outreach by Brawley and others. Some weavers watched what was going on at the Conservancy for a while before getting involved. During this process, Brawley came to care less about her academic work and more about the project: "It would have been easy for me to give up, but I really believed in the project, believed in what it was all about. In the end, I didn't really care about me and the dissertation. [That] was secondary."[29]

A Growing Collaboration

As the garden project grew, it gained national and international attention, and the steering committee members began giving presentations about it at regional, national, and international conferences—one as far away as the International Geographic Union Conference in Glasgow, Scotland, attended by Wallace and Brawley. According to Brawley, all of these presentations included at least two perspectives—that of the Conservancy and that of the steering committee—and sometimes more. "There was a real need for respect for all perspectives," Brawley explained.[30] Locally, the project had the support of the Yocha Dehe Wintun Nation tribal council members and UC Davis departments, faculty, and staff members.

Ranchers adjacent to the Conservancy sent their workers to the garden in slow times, and the Conservancy paid them to help with bed preparation and irrigation. The Yocha Dehe Community Fund provided funding for a garden coordinator and other aspects of the project; the Teichert Foundation, Yolo County, and Yocha Dehe Community Fund provided funding for native plants; and local growers and ranchers contributed plants and knowledge. Traditional basketweavers from the steering committee led tours of the garden and presented their skills and knowledge with the plants to numerous visiting groups, ranging from local schoolchildren and teachers to participants in international conferences.

Wallace calls the garden project "extremely successful," partially because it involved so many Native people.[31] Brawley reflected that the key elements for successful collaboration are time, inclusiveness, and building strong relationships: "Start from the beginning, take the time, create an atmosphere where people feel safe to share, and never discount someone just because they don't come to the first meetings. Always invite everyone, and then people start to feel comfortable and may end up getting involved."[32] When Brawley stepped out of her role as garden coordinator, noted cultural educator Diana Almendariz (Maidu, Wintun, Hupa, Yurok) was hired into the position as an enthusiastic partner in the cultural and ecological development of the garden and its outreach program. Lowrey and the steering committee worked with Almendariz to begin developing an interpretive brochure about the garden, which Pollock completed when she became executive director. Almendariz and the steering committee also worked with the Conservancy to create signs for the garden, which provide the plant names in three languages—Wintun, English, and Latin.

As their projects and commitments expanded, the steering committee and the Conservancy saw the need for a formal representative on the Conservancy board. The Conservancy Nominating Committee selected Don Hankins, who is now an Assistant Professor of Geography and Planning at California State University, Chico, and he began serving in 2007. Although Hankins had to resign from the board due to distance and scheduling conflicts,[33] he remains on the steering committee, which meets annually, and has offered to remain a technical advisor to the board.[34]

The Significance of Respectful Documentation for Co-Learning

Like Brawley, Hankins was also a graduate student in geography at the University of California, Davis. Part of his Ph.D. project focused on the Jan T. Lowrey Cache Creek Nature Preserve site, but on its riparian corridor rather than the garden. Working with Lowrey, the steering committee, and others, Hankins studied the effects of traditional burning as a vegetation management tool. Wallace remembered Hankins' first underburn in the riparian area along Cache Creek as a "historic moment."[35] As fire engines stood by waiting to respond, the fire crept through the riparian corridor so slowly that Hankins and his crew had to use torches to keep it going. He had prepared the site so well by clearing the ladder fuels and waiting for the right weather and wind conditions that the fire remained under control.

Wallace felt that the burn was so important because it illustrated the value and the safety of traditional indigenous burning. As a weaver who had been working for years to get federal agencies and private landowners to allow underburns for the health of native plants used in traditional basketry and for overall ecosystem health, Wallace was grateful for Hankins' dissertation that documented the burning process. "To have all of the information about fire written down scientifically was so important," she said. "Since then we've gotten a lot of cooperation."[36] Wallace also cited Lowrey's work as key to making Hankins' underburn project possible.[37]

In the meantime, the steering committee helped to convince Brawley to extend her master's project into a doctoral dissertation on the garden that would document both the process of creating the garden and the effects of the weavers' traditional management of the plants. Brawley agreed. The documentation of the weavers' stewardship was important to the steering committee because it would help to answer the question of whether a heavily mined and impacted site like the Cache Creek Nature Preserve could be restored "to a Native Californian standard of ecological health."[38] This standard encompasses sustainable, integrated human stewardship and use. "I feel that we have helped to set a higher standard for restoration as the cultural uses of the natural resources require an extremely healthy, managed landscape," Ross wrote in 2003.[39]

Ultimately, however, family needs made it impossible for Brawley to complete the dissertation. However, she wrote up all of the protocols and original goals for the project and left them on file at the Conservancy. These records, along with meeting notes and copies of Brawley's original letters inviting participants to join the steering committee, are available for public review. In addition to these documents, there are photographs and slides cataloguing the entire garden implementation process.[40] In a 2009 interview, Brawley emphasized that, although the process and goals documented in these archives may be helpful for other groups creating their own collaborative projects on the land, "process and goals should be developed as each group and site feels [they] should unfold."[41]

Garden Management

All of the Cache Creek Nature Preserve, including the Tending and Gathering Garden, is managed as a nature preserve—not a park with public access. The gates to the preserve are open during the day when staff is on site, and school groups can make reservations for field trips. Managing the preserve as private property helps maintain the integrity of the garden. As Pollock observed, the garden is near the center of the site, in a semi-protected area, and although vandals and trespassers sometimes enter the reserve during non-operating hours, the garden itself has never been disturbed.[42]

All traditional gatherers are asked to notify the project coordinator and make an appointment if they would like to visit the site. The garden is not a primary gathering site for any one person but rather a place for Native American students to come and gather plants for the first time, for example.

To assist with site monitoring, the Conservancy board approved a gathering protocol, which among other things, asks gatherers to fill out a form describing how much they gathered, when, and what type of material.[43] Gatherers can also request permission from the Conservancy to gather species that grow on the preserve but outside the garden, such as tule and willow.[44]

Beginning in 2001, the steering committee developed a series of guidelines that include the vision for the garden, steering committee membership principles, gathering guidelines, a protocol for protecting intellectual property rights, and a termination agreement were it ever necessary to discontinue the garden project. The intellectual property rights policy focuses on the garden, and specifically on cultural programming with the Tending and Gathering Garden Steering Committee. The policy recognizes and respects that Native American individuals, families, and communities have intellectual property rights over their knowledge. Any knowledge shared with the Conservancy in the development of the garden, in educational activities, or in other restoration on the site, "is shared with permission for the purposes of nonprofit education at the Cache Creek Nature Preserve."[45] According to the policy, cultural presenters associated with the garden and the steering committee should also be personally attentive to protecting their intellectual property by not sharing private information.[46]

All of the policies were discussed and refined until the Conservancy's board of directors adopted them in April 2008.[47] One reason the process took so many years was that the steering committee met less frequently beginning in 2006, and it had to adapt the guidelines to changing circumstances and needs. The garden currently operates under the guidelines, which include respect, notification, and communication about visiting and using the site. So far, supply has not been an issue, as there are more plants in the garden than the gatherers are utilizing. "It renews itself," said Pollock.[48]

Changes in the Garden

Brawley and Lowrey both played the roles of facilitator and liaison between the Conservancy and the Tending and Gathering Garden Steering Committee. Because of Lowrey's history in the area and ability to negotiate and partner with diverse parties, he was a skilled ally for the project, sometimes providing a buffer between the steering committee and any parties who were less enthusiastic about the garden's presence at the Cache Creek Nature Preserve. Wallace described Lowrey as key to the project's success.[49] His untimely death in 2006 resulted in several transitions, and "the project changed," she explained. For example, she felt that there were fewer formal meetings of the steering committee,[50] due to scheduling conflicts and changes in communication between the Conservancy and the committee. "This is pretty common when there is turnover in relationships," Hankins said, noting that the new director, Lynnel Pollock, "recognizes the importance of the project and has advocated for continued engagement and support."[51]

The steering committee has always taken seriously its responsibility to exemplify a collaborative, inclusive, and productive process. According to Ross and others, participants worked steadily to write the protocols that govern their work and to serve as a model for other partnerships: "We knew that it would be helpful to have some ground rules in place to manage interactions that could easily become unwieldy. While I have felt some frustration with the delicacy of the language we must employ to keep everyone involved and satisfied, we are setting an example for other projects."[52]

Wallace's only regret was that more of the process of developing the garden and the protocols was not thoroughly documented. "When you are working with someone you trust, you think it's okay, but [protocols] should be written down."[53] Nevertheless, the protocols and documentation of much of the garden's development are on file at the Conservancy, and future actions may involve synthesizing this information or ensuring that each steering committee member has a copy. Wallace still retains faith in the project and the land: "It doesn't matter what happens because the plants are there, the land is there. We developed this relationship with the plants there and the land there. Native people know that people come and go."[54]

The garden, as well as the willows in the preserve's riparian area along Cache Creek, were valuable resources for Wallace in her role as a traditional educator. Numerous basketry materials were concentrated in these two locations within the preserve. She and other weavers could take students there to learn about plants and to care for and collect them. "I miss taking my students to the Conservancy—it was right there," she said.[55] Wallace believes the preserve is not currently an ideal site for master basketweavers to take their students, primarily because the riparian area has not been recently burned. An underburn there would revitalize plants that are important for traditional basketweavers.[56]

The riparian area was burned only in 2002 and 2004, during Hankins' study, and in a 2006 wildfire.[57] Several planned burns never occurred because of time conflicts. Hankins and UC Davis Professor of Wildlife, Fish, and Conservation Biology Deborah Elliott-Fisk plan regular burns in the riparian area starting in 2010. They will use an adaptive management and research framework for long-term monitoring, which will involve CSU Chico and

UC Davis undergraduates. Hankins describes the Conservancy board and management as being "in full support of burning," and he noted that the Conservancy is actually working with the Yocha Dehe Wintun Nation to burn on tribal land for the health of the riparian area along Cache Creek.[58]

As for the Tending and Gathering Garden, its maintenance and monitoring are now part of the preserve restoration ecologist's scope of work. According to Hankins, "Molly [Ferrell, staff restoration ecologist] and other staff contact me regularly regarding input about management needs and intents. The staff are fully intent on doing what is both ecologically and culturally appropriate [in the absence of] a traditional cultural practitioner present to manage the site."[59] In November 2008, Ferrell implemented a burn in the garden, revitalizing several California Native grass species.[60] She has also been working to improve soil health by mulching in the sedge bed. Ferrell and other Conservancy staff are eager to see if sedges gathered this year will have longer roots, preferred by basketweavers, due to this management action.

Sharing the Garden

The Tending and Gathering Garden has grown and flourished as an environmental education site for visiting schoolchildren, according to Pollock.[61] More youth than ever are visiting and experiencing curricula, some of which is based on traditional Native uses of plants. For example, in 2009, there were at least three cultural events at the Cache Creek Nature Preserve that involved demonstrations by steering committee members. In 2010, Pollock began talking with California Indian Basketweavers' Association about the possibility of bringing Native youth to the garden on educational field trips.[62]

The various concerns about the garden site may also resolve with time, as the garden is still quite young and was created on a site that had been used industrially prior to its restoration. As Brawley explained, "It will take years for it to come up to some kind of ecological standard, because there was nothing on the land. . . . We were learning what it meant to restore a site that had been taken down to stone."[63]

In addition to being a place that weavers can visit and use, the garden has become known as a site for the broader public to learn about contemporary Native land use and stewardship. Along with education for school groups, the Conservancy uses the site to offer trainings on land management. The garden also led to an institutional relationship between weavers and the Conservancy that now manifests in both the committee structure and in the protocols agreed upon between the committee and the Conservancy board.

It is also possible that a steering committee member might again serve on the Conservancy board.

In sum, the garden project served as a catalyst for Native inclusion in the Conservancy's planning, land stewardship, and governance. Now participants can continue to build on that relationship and work to maintain and expand the communication protocols developed during the first six intensive years (2000–2006) of garden development and interaction. Although the work of the Steering Committee is less heavy now than it was at the beginning of the project, both the Conservancy and the committee have a long-term vision for the garden and the partnership. As Pollock noted, "We hope to be here forever, and [we hope] that the garden is here forever."[64]

Tribes and NRCS Conservation Tools

A discussion of U.S. Department of Agriculture's Natural Resource Conservation Service (NRCS) programs is particularly germane to a book on tribal participation in private conservation. It is NRCS's mandate to work with landowners interested in implementing conservation and restoration programs on private or tribal lands. NRCS funding for conservation can be an important resource for Native and non-Native land trusts and conservancies implementing restoration programs on parcels they own outright or on which they hold conservation easements. By providing conservation easements in exchange for funds to enable restoration, the NRCS also helps private and tribal landowners (federally recognized and unrecognized) undertake restoration and other projects on fee or trust lands.

After a brief discussion of tribal resource conservation districts that are being formed, this chapter provides a glimpse of two collaborations between the NRCS and California tribes.[1] The first, the Coarsegold Resource Conservation District (RCD), discusses a non-Native RCD that is particularly active in its area of focus in Madera County, California. The Coarsegold RCD is working on Native homelands, and its board realizes both that there are opportunities for collaboration between local tribes and the RCD and that the RCD has much to learn from Native land stewardship. Two tribes have engaged at least partially with the RCD's land management activities—Picayune Rancheria and North Fork Rancheria—but the RCD and the tribes do not yet have a formal or extensive partnership.

The RCD is taking steps toward formal collaboration with local tribal governments by encouraging landowners to invite tribal participation on easements in Madera County. The original idea was to ensure that engagement and consultation with tribes was part of every conservation easement. However, Native and non-Native landowners balked at language that would confer blanket land access to Native peoples, thereby impacting their private property rights. In response, the RCD is experimenting with language that will encourage landowners to work with tribes and tribal members on a site-specific and individual basis. A discussion of this preliminary process lets us examine how one particular non-Native RCD is working to develop this language. Both the process and the language itself may provide points of reflection for other RCDs and tribes embarking on similar collaborations.

The second example focuses on the Susanville Indian Rancheria (SIR) in northeastern California. The tribe used the NRCS Wetlands Reserve Program to assist in land acquisition, restoration, employment, and educational programs. This mini-case offers a brief and straightforward example of how tribes and the NRCS can collaborate to achieve mutually beneficial goals. SIR accepted a limited easement on the parcel it acquired, leaving open the opportunity to develop it in the future when the easement expires. Whether or not the tribe chooses to place this land into trust or leave it in fee status, the NRCS easement holds firm for its thirty-year duration because it is a federal easement and, therefore, effective on trust land.

Tribal Resource Conservation Districts, the Coarsegold Resource Conservation District, and the Susanville Indian Rancheria (California)

Resource Conservation Districts

Soil and water conservation districts are local-level, formal civic institutions that have state and federal mandates to identify and address local conservation needs. The 1930s "Dust Bowl" crisis, when millions of acres of cropland were destroyed by drought and attendant soil loss, led the federal government to pass legislation in 1937 establishing the Soil Conservation Service, predecessor to the Natural Resources Conservation Service, housed under the U.S. Department of Agriculture (USDA). Conservationists quickly realized that a centrally governed, federal agency in Washington, D.C., could not be responsive to all local needs, so local counterparts of the service were set up under state law to be controlled by local boards of directors.[1] This was the birth of the "Soil Conservation District," a concept that quickly spread throughout the continental United States.

Soil conservation districts collaborate and coordinate with numerous federal, state, and local agencies. District foci have broadened to include soil health, water, air, plants, and animals, in addition to an original focus on erosion. Projects can include forest-fuels reduction, watershed restoration, research, demonstration or pilot projects, training on conservation methods for erosion control, invasive weed removal, riparian area fencing, and environmental education for youth and adults, among other activities. Depending on local priorities, districts may also purchase or manage property or conservation easements on lands that are in need of conservation, restoration, or protection. Conservation districts are funded through a variety of mechanisms and may raise funds through tax assessments or charitable donations, or by applying for competitive state, federal, or private grants and loans. In California, soil and water conservation districts focus on a variety of environmental issues and are generally termed "Resource Conservation Districts" (RCDs) to reflect the broad scope of the natural resources they steward.

The relationship between conservation districts and the Natural Resources Conservation Service has been longstanding. In 1994, a Memorandum of Understanding, originally signed over fifty years ago, was revised "to modernize and reinvent their historic partnership" and to add state conservation agencies to the agreement. To assist conservation districts, each NRCS field office has a district conservationist who helps the local district with project planning and technical implementation. The conservationist serves as a liaison between the local district and federal and state resource management and conservation agencies, as well as with funding programs.

Conservation districts can also be formed under tribal law and are another route to working with USDA agencies and their numerous programs. For the USDA to recognize tribally formed conservation districts, a three-way MOU is signed between the tribe, the tribal conservation district, and the secretary of the Department of Agriculture. This MOU helps maintain the government-to-government relationship between the USDA and the tribes, while enabling local control of priorities. Tribal conservation districts allow tribes to gear district services toward culturally meaningful concerns, such as promoting sustainable fisheries management, respectful use of wildlife, and other practices that may not be priorities in a state-formed conservation district.

As of 2010, California has 103 state-formed districts, and one tribal conservation district, the Klamath Trinity Resource Conservation District. Three other California tribes (North Fork Rancheria of Mono Indians, Picayune Rancheria of the Chukchansi Indians in Coarsegold, and Fort Independence Indian Reservation) have signed tribal resolutions to create tribal RCDs. These three tribes are in the process of developing and finalizing the required MOU. The Indian Nations Conservation Alliance (INCA) provides a handbook for tribal conservation districts and information about existing tribal districts throughout the United States. NRCS–California American Indian Liaison Reina Rogers is also a resource for tribes working to establish tribal RCDs.[2]

Non-tribal, state-organized conservation districts interface primarily with the NRCS and state-level conservation agencies and programs. In contrast, tribal conservation districts interface at the federal level with USDA though the three-way MOU. Elevating the interface to a federal department level is more congruent with respecting the government-to-government relationship and the federal government's trust responsibilities. A 1988 MOU, signed by the U.S. Department of the Interior, Bureau of Indian Affairs (BIA), the NRCS, and the Farm Service Agency, established the ability to create tribal conservation districts. This MOU recognizes the need for tribes to be able to work directly and cooperatively with these agencies. Prior to the 1988 MOU, tribes had to work through the BIA to receive services from USDA, NRCS, and the Farm Service Agency. A tribal conservation district enables funds to be channeled toward tribal resource stewardship priorities, as well as providing a structure to collaborate with neighboring non-tribal districts. Such collaboration can be vital to accomplishing watershed conservation projects that cross tribal and non-tribal jurisdictions. According to Rogers, "the main difference between tribal and non-tribal conservation districts is which body of government provides the enabling legislation. In practical terms, tribal districts provide insight and priorities on the land in Indian country, and who better than the local people to do that? Building communication and partnerships between tribal and non-tribal conservation districts in California is essential, however, because their interests or service areas often overlap."[3]

As the following example will show, building a relationship of mutual respect and inclusion between local Native Americans and the Coarsegold Resource Conservation District is resulting in some conservation easements that productively include tribal concerns and priorities, in the current absence of a local, tribally formed conservation district.

Coarsegold RCD

Partnerships

The Coarsegold RCD has formal MOUs with eleven entities, including nonprofits, seven continuing education high schools (through the Conservation Opportunities Resource Education, or CORE, Program), federal resource management agencies, and local fire-safe councils. The goal is to establish cooperation in local conservation and education programs. The Coarsegold RCD also has established formal partnerships with more than thirty-eight parties. The RCD has not yet developed formal MOUs with any of the local tribal governments: North Fork Rancheria of Mono Indians, Picayune Rancheria of the Chukchansi Indians in Coarsegold, or Big Sandy Rancheria Band of Western Mono Indians in Auberry. The RCD has a contract with the Mono Nation to do fire-safe thinning around the homes of tribal elders and to provide education on fire-safe thinning for all landowners. It also has an agreement to hold three 2010 workshops or demonstrations on thinning for fire safety on tribal lands.[4] During the past three decades several Native American landowners have participated in major Coarsegold RCD conservation programs.[5]

The Coarsegold RCD and the local Native people first began discussions in the mid-1980s, according to board member Neil McDougald, when the county sprayed the vegetation and Native people who collected it got sick. The Coarsegold RCD asked local Native Americans in North Fork and Oakhurst to identify culturally important plants. In partnership with the elders and other culture keepers, the Coarsegold RCD then began an information campaign. They developed programs, produced educational videos, and held workshops about Native plant use. As McDougald explained, "Native people came and talked about the vegetation, what they used it for, and how important it was. We took a situation where the people spraying didn't know what they were doing or how it affected others and created communication."[6] Since that time, some local Native people have led RCD workshops about plants native to the area, traditional gathering methods, basketry materials, and conservation measures. As part of the general public, tribal members have also attended tours and workshops on fuels-reduction and other ecological projects. They have then often requested and completed similar work on their individual properties.

Coarsegold RCD also produces educational brochures on conservation topics, such as "Living in the Foothills," and it is planning to make a brochure identifying plants that Native people use for food and fiber. "We've always wanted to make some kind of flyer to show people what kind of plants [Native people] use so the plants are managed," Coarsegold RCD Board Chairman and County Supervisor Tom Wheeler explained.[7] According to NRCS Tribal Liaison Rogers, it is important to identify the plants and the general areas where Native people tend and gather them in order to advise Native and non-Native ranchers, farmers, and other land managers to avoid these areas, but the sharing of this information, particularly about gathering areas, is also "a big issue in Indian county with many points of view."[8] Through its partnerships, the CRCD hopes it will be attentive to these points of view and to the protection of traditional ecological knowledge.

A Respectful Resource Management Philosophy

The landscape where the Coarsegold RCD works consists of oak woodland, brushy foothills interspersed with grassland, and coniferous stands at higher elevations. When RCD board member Larry Ballew and his wife, Christine, a tribal member, look at the land around them, they see a landscape that has been managed by both Indians and non-Indians, and it continues to require tending and maintenance. They think about Christine's Chukchansi relatives using fire to create grasslands for wildlife forage, increased water, and open space. Christine recalled turn-of-the-century photos of nearby Yosemite, for example, in which Yosemite Valley had few conifers because of the Native management that occurred there.[9] According to Larry, maintaining similar grasslands west of Yosemite requires an understanding of how they were created and maintained.[10] The Ballews also consider the fact that the Native people got everything they needed from this landscape: "They made their baskets and tools off of the land . . . [but] if you look at a solid brush stand, there are no tools there. They don't grow under those conditions. When you thin brush, you get more sun [and] increased water, and that generates more diverse plant, animal, and aquatic species that can be used for tools, basketry, and household requirements."[11]

Larry recognizes that local Native management practices are as intensive as the RCD's million-dollar fuels reduction, biodiversity enhancement, and conservation projects.[12] He and the other RCD board members compare Western science-based practices to techniques derived from a Native management philosophy. In 1990, for example, they thinned an oak woodland and then took satellite photos for five years to see what changes, if any, resulted: "We found that our trees suddenly became much larger. We ended up with more crown closure than before the trees were thinned, and acorn production increased five- or sixfold."[13] Larry underscored that these improvements were achieved by thoughtful management, rather than by "protecting or isolating" the resource by setting it aside. "The whole management scheme that I'm reusing is no different than [that used by] my wife Christine's great-great-grandfather," he said.[14] Observing these projects and doing similar management on their own land, the Ballews have seen an increase in biodiversity, particularly of culturally important plants and wildlife. "Management is using common sense, science, and experience," Larry explained. "I think it's tremendous that we don't leave people in a state of ignorance when it comes to conservation. You can see why the Native Americans manage the resources the way they did and still do."[15]

Christine agreed that many of the philosophies of the Coarsegold RCD's work are the same as traditional Native management, but she does not think that enough Native landowners are aware of the RCD's programs. Although she recognizes that RCD board members have done a lot of work to reach out to the Indian community, she knows that much more outreach and collaboration are needed.[16] Sometimes the issue is one of building trust between the RCD and Native landowners. "We've all logged and ranched together for generations, so there is that community connection," she said, noting the longstanding relationships between the families of RCD board members and local Native Americans. "The issue is making everyone aware of what's available through the conservation district," she said.[17]

As one way of formalizing their cooperative activities with Native people, the Coarsegold RCD is working to encourage landowners with easements in Madera County to work with tribal members who would like to access their lands to steward particular culturally important plants. Currently, the RCD has negotiated the right (via a formal Madera County Board of Supervisor's resolution) to inspect any conservation easements that go through the county. This means that sometimes the RCD is the easement holder—it oversees 3,000 acres in Coarsegold already—and sometimes it just reviews easements before they are approved. The RCD board includes two registered foresters as well as other members with a range of areas of expertise. Wheeler believes that the RCD board has used its right to review easements to successfully help manage local rangeland and other habitat.[18]

In 2008, the RCD board began working to develop language to assist Native access to gather and steward culturally important plants and other resources on lands protected by conservation easements in Madera County. The goals of inserting the language were to "reflect our respectfulness" of the local Native people, according to McDougald, and to "provide an opportunity" for private landowners and Native Americans to continue and expand working together, in a way that legally enables Native people to utilize those resources.[19] Originally, it read in part: "It shall be permissible for grantor to dedicate appropriate areas on the property for access and use by local California Indians who have prehistoric ancestral or cultural ties to the property. Such access and use shall be for traditional noncommercial cultural purposes."[20] However, Native and non-Native property owners alike resisted the idea of being told to allow people on their property. Provisions regarding access in order to plant certain species and remove others also generated concern. In response, Ballew and RCD board members are "toning down" the freedom-of-access provisions and focusing on encouraging people to develop voluntary written agreements for access to specific places, for named purposes, at certain times. To make this happen, the RCD is working on a mechanism to bring together willing landowners and Native individuals seeking access to properties for gathering, ceremonial purposes, and other uses. The RCD is modifying the access language to encourage communication and access and simultaneously protect property rights.[21]

Of course, on its own easements, the RCD can encourage indigenous use and access. The RCD manages a 200-acre conservation easement in North Fork, which serves as partial mitigation for the development of a new high school. The RCD worked with the school district, the Army Corps of Engineers, and the U.S. Fish and Wildlife Service to develop the easement. The RCD emphasized the importance of the site as cultural land, and it wants to include Native American use as part of the management, according to McDougald.[22] Currently, the RCD is mitigating impacts to a culturally important species—elderberry, which is also home to an endangered insect, the Valley Elderberry Longhorn Beetle. Youth were out on the land in 2009 planting elderberry. The high school is a charter school for environmental studies, making it an ideal place for cross-cultural learning opportunities. Wheeler described plans for a course in which the students will learn how to negotiate with the county, the state, developers, and others to create conservation easements.[23]

Next Steps

The Coarsegold RCD's inclusive language for conservation easements is still under development and being reviewed by RCD partners. Once it is complete, the RCD will submit it as a resolution to Madera County. By developing this language and then applying it to easements throughout the county, the RCD is working to acknowledge the scope and importance of historic and ongoing Native stewardship of the land, as well as respect for current Native and non-Native private property rights. The delicate process of developing this language exemplifies the RCD's complex and important mission to build stronger relationships between diverse local people and to enhance natural resource knowledge.[24]

Utilizing NRCS Tools for Acquisition and Restoration: Susanville Indian Rancheria

We now turn from the southern Sierras to northeastern California, for an example of how one tribe has harnessed NRCS programs for a cultural land-acquisition and restoration project. The Susanville Indian Rancheria (SIR) is a federally recognized tribe composed of Paiute, Maidu, Washoe, and Pit River members. It is located adjacent to the town of Susanville in the Honey Lake Valley, where the Sierra Nevada and Cascade ranges meet the Great Basin.

The BIA purchased the original 30-acre Susanville Rancheria in 1924 under the 1921 Rancheria Act, which authorized the bureau to create homesteads for "homeless California Indians."[25] In 1978, the BIA acquired an additional 120 acres for the Susanville Rancheria. The rancheria has been steadily growing and working to purchase additional lands and put them into trust. Today, it has a land base of 1,340 acres and a population of 698.[26] The Rancheria employs tribal members and other local people in housing, education, environmental, and other government departments, as well as in the expanding Diamond Mountain Casino Hotel and Mini-Mart.

Cradle Valley Property

In 2003, the rancheria purchased the Cradle Valley Ranch, a 160-acre parcel in northeastern Plumas County, with pine forest, aspen stands, and a riparian corridor. Clarks Creek bisects the property and is surrounded by 28 acres of wet meadowlands with willows and native grasses. Cattle were damaging the creek and riparian zone, and the SIR wanted to protect it by keeping them out. The tribe applied and received funding from the NRCS Wetlands Reserve Program (WRP) and other partnering sources (including the U.S. Fish and Wildlife Service, the Environmental Protection Agency, and North Cal–Neva Resource Conservation and Development Council) to fence the area. Susanville Indian Rancheria plans to steward the Cradle Valley property to reach a precontact ecological condition, establish a cultural center, offer educational programs to demonstrate traditional management, and host cultural gatherings.

Wetlands Reserve Program

The WRP is a voluntary program that works with landowners to support the restoration, protection, and enhancement of wetlands for the benefit of migratory birds and other wetland-dependent species. In California, the WRP targets marginal agricultural land subject to flooding and saturation, where it is easier to restore wetland functions and values. It offers landowners permanent or thirty-year easements and cost-share programs in which the landowner agrees to restore the wetland but does not place an easement on the property. Under either the permanent or thirty-year easement, the NRCS pays the landowner some or all of the value of the easement and then provides both technical and financial assistance for restoration. Under the restoration cost-share agreement, NRCS will pay up to 75 percent of restoration costs, and the agency and the landowner agree on certain practices and management of the parcel for a defined length of time.[27] If the landowner just wants to do some restoration of the parcel but not place an easement on it, a cost-share agreement is the preferable option. Although an easement results in a payment to the landowner as well as funds to support restoration, landowners must enter a competitive application process to interest NRCS in purchasing an easement. Therefore, it may behoove the landowner who is considering placing a future NRCS-held conservation easement on his or her property to work with NRCS on a cost-share agreement first, thereby establishing a relationship with the agency.[28]

Leveraging Funding Sources

The tribe put about 65 acres of the Cradle Valley property into a thirty-year WRP conservation easement, with the NRCS as the easement holder. The terms of the easement require that the land be maintained primarily as habitat for wetland birds and other riparian species. An appraiser calculates the agricultural value of the land, and the NRCS pays the tribe 75 percent of that in exchange for the easement.[29] If the easement had been in perpetuity, the SIR would have received a payment for the full agricultural value of the land.

The tribe used the NRCS WRP funds for thinning and pruning for fire safety and forest health. These were used in combination with funds from the U.S. Forest Service, Plumas National Forest, under the national Secure Rural Schools and Community Self-Determination Act of 2000. Susanville Rancheria crew members pruned trees and burned piles of fuel to increase the amount of sunlight coming into the forest, strengthen the aspen stands, and remove unhealthy concentrations of young trees and underbrush. NRCS WRP monies were also matched with funds from the U.S. Fish and Wildlife Service Tribal Landowner Incentives Program. The Cradle Valley project—with its combination of funding sources, employment of tribal members, habitat protection, and fuels reduction components—was highlighted by the U.S. Department of the Interior Office of the Inspector General, which had been asked by the Environmental Protection Agency (EPA) Administrator to look at how tribes were using EPA funding. As a result, the publication *Tribal Successes: Protecting the Environment and Natural Resources* highlights the Susanville Indian Rancheria's Cradle Valley project.[30]

Moving Land from Fee-to-Trust Status: Considerations

The SIR owns the Cradle Valley property in fee simple but may want to put the land into trust status in the future. The tribe has found it more efficient to do forest thinning and other activities while the land is still in fee status. For example, on trust land, thinning may require a lengthy forest-management plan, a forest officer's report, and a BIA permit if forest products are going to be sold.[31] On fee land, the tribe still has to meet California Environmental Quality Act (CEQA) and Timber Harvest Plan guidelines, but the process can go much faster. However, having an easement on the property was a concern for the tribe, in that an encumbrance could hamper a future fee-to-trust process. This made the ability to have a short-term easement an attractive option.

Conclusion: The NRCS and Tribes

The NRCS programs discussed in this chapter range from tribal and non-Native RCDs to restoration-incentive programs that can provide would-be purchasers with considerable property stewardship funds. NRCS responds to private landowners, yet it also has a substantial tribal outreach program, which focuses on work with Native nations as well as with individual allottees. It is perhaps the only federal agency that offers Native (fee and trust) landowners cost-share programs and other opportunities for conservation land management. Other case studies in this text, such as the Jamestown S'Klallam Tribe, also used NRCS program funds to do restoration on properties it helped to acquire and protect along the Dungeness River. As tribes and Native entities explore private conservation tools, NRCS resources available to tribes are both a key funding source and a useful institutional mechanism (tribal RCDs) through which to attract more funds and build larger networks with other tribes engaged in restoration, acquisition, and stewardship.

17

Conclusion

Returning ancestral lands to Native people has power. Power to educate about historical injustices that still affect us all, whether Native or non-Native. Power to inform non-Natives about how Native people live today, on or off reservation. Power to understand why a landscape is important—not just for its beauty but also for its history, culture, and ability to sustain and transform lives.

—Bowen Blair, Founder, Tribal and Native Lands Program,
Trust for Public Land[1]

Tribes and Native organizations are using conservation tools in innovative ways to conserve cultural resources and to regain a stake in the stewardship of their traditional homelands. Using easements, land trust structures, and other conservation mechanisms to achieve indigenous goals increases the range and relevance of these tools, which were previously limited to protecting natural ecosystems (such as forests, prairies, riparian corridors) and the livelihoods that depend on those ecosystems (such as farming, ranching, sustainable timber harvesting). Tribal use of conservation mechanisms broadens their applicability to include cultural resources, maintenance of cultural knowledge, subsistence, wildlife maintenance, community development, and environmental justice; strengthens their appeal to diverse constituencies, including landowning business entities; enables partnerships between tribes, conservation districts, land trusts, and public conservation agencies; and encourages the development of Native land trusts and conservation districts.

The chapters in this book have traveled through some diverse ecosystems, institutional arrangements, and relationships to place. What can readers take with them as they begin (or continue) to apply these tools to develop a more equitable and historically conscious conservation landscape? This conclusion offers reflections on the range of examples of indigenous applications of "private" conservation tools and partnerships described in the book. The following chapter is divided into three sections, which follow the key inquiries set forth in the Introduction: (1) Lessons Learned: what are best practices that can be gleaned from the case studies? (2) Challenges: what are some of the hardships organizations and tribes addressed during development and implementation of conservation tools and institutions? (3) Encouraging Native (Private) Conservation: how might these conservation tools be amended to work better in Native contexts and Native institutional arrangements? Each of the three sections features information from a range of the case studies, which are analyzed along two principal axes. The first is application, which is discussed in the three main sections. The second is institutional arrangements—Native land trusts, collaborations between tribes and land trusts, and collaborations between tribes and the NRCS. The theoretical thread of environmental justice runs through each section.

Lessons Learned

Native Land Trusts

Drawing on legal precedent in private conservation and public support for conservation, tribes can harness land conservancy structures to access, protect, steward, and set aside lands that are no longer tribally held. Native American land conservancies affirm tribal sovereignty by recognizing and reaffirming tribal members' rights to their homelands. The land conservancy structure has provided a useful way for some tribes to organize, build alliances with other Native and non-Native groups, and raise funds for the protection of sacred sites. Tribes can adapt the basic format of a conservancy to fit their own cultural, social, and political patterns of organization, or to address a particular land-based struggle or need. The two examples in this book—the InterTribal Sinkyone Wilderness Council (henceforth, the Council) and the Native American Land Conservancy (NALC)—are nonprofit land trust structures that have been able to raise money to purchase culturally important lands. The two organizations are different in their board composition and their mode of operation, and they therefore offer a range of lessons for readers.

Both the Council and the NALC formed largely in response to an external stimulus, although the stimuli differed. The Council formed out of a battle to protect culturally and ecologically important land from a proposed timber harvest. The NALC formed in response to an offer of culturally significant, isolated desert that held deep resonance for several regional tribes. Native land trusts often were also often spurred by ongoing, internal efforts to increase unity, cultural perpetuation, and collaboration. For example, the Kumeyaay-Diegueño Land Conservancy (KDLC) built upon the foundation of the Kumeyaay-Diegueño Unity Bands, and the NALC grew from the Twenty-Nine Palms Culture Committee.

Each of these Native land trusts grew beyond an initial project to become an innovator and leader in the field of Native conservation. The Council became one of the first organizations to establish a conservation easement with a non-Native land trust on lands owned by a Native entity, and it has become a leader in collaborative watershed planning with neighboring landowners, including the California State Parks. The NALC is helping grow Native land trusts (like the KDLC) from San Diego to New York to Alaska. And the Nushagak–Mulchatna Wood–Tikchik Land Trust (NMWTLT), while not a self-described Native land trust, focuses on Alaska Native lands and is exploring the application of environmental-protection statutes to increase Alaska Native sovereignty over waters that cross Native corporation lands.

Both the NALC and the Council had to pass through a difficult period of "proving themselves" to outside entities. Although each organization's internal vision for cultural and ecological restoration may have been strong and in place, the format of the organization itself was so new that it required much external education and demonstration to convince observers (both Native and non-Native) of its purpose and abilities. The Council was initially operating in a hostile climate, with its environmental allies diametrically opposed to the timber interests that initially had more powerful influence over the county government. Several parties were vying for the Sinkyone "upland parcel," and the Council had to show why it was the best candidate. It earned this support over time, and the Council's proactive strategy of initiating restoration projects on the land established its capacity, programs, and relationship to the place. It was also extremely skilled in public relations and built a broad network of supporters. All of these factors ultimately led to relationships that enabled the Council's collaborative conservation easements and connections to funders for the land purchase.

The NALC, although it was not beset by competition for the parcel, had to similarly establish itself as a viable entity that could take title to the land and serve Native interests. As the NALC chapter explains, the emerging conservancy received no advice or support from other conservation organizations. When it figured out how to form and was able to purchase the Old Woman Mountains parcel, it became passionate about offering its expertise to emerging organizations. However, other organizations and tribes wanted to observe the NALC's progress before accepting help or becoming involved. As the NALC's suite of successful projects grew, other groups increasingly sought its help to accomplish similar goals by using Native land trust structures and developing cooperative agreements. To facilitate more of these arrangements, the NALC has applied a strategy of holding conferences that bring numerous parties and stakeholders together to share strategies, target areas, and connect funders and groups.

Both the NALC and the Council faced questions about how to organize. This was uncharted territory because there were virtually no Native land trusts. The Council chose a model whereby members of regional federally recognized tribes elected representatives to serve on the Council's board of directors. This formal structure established an organization that reflects the participation of ten sovereign Native nations; in a sense, a United Nations of regional tribes. In contrast, the NALC has embraced a much less formal model with a board composed of Native and non-Native people who share various business and community ties, as well as an interest in cultural and land preservation, particularly in the Southern California desert region. The NALC board includes representatives from several Southern California tribes, including the Kumeyaay, Cahuilla, and Chemehuevi. In this populous part of the state, the NALC found that a strategy of including non-Native board members would help to bridge understandings of place and make a case for why everyone should care about Native sites. In rural Alaska, the NMWTLT embraced a similar strategy in order to deal with the numerous stakeholders in rural Alaska allotment lands, who might also bring funding and partnerships to the table to make it easier to protect those lands. Ultimately, both the formal intertribal and Native and non-Native board membership models have been successful, illustrating that there is more than one way to develop governance of a Native land trust.

Both the NALC and the Council emphasized the time and work it takes to build both internal and external cohesion. Internally, each group had to choose a mode of organization that worked for its members and that met state and federal nonprofit law. Externally, each group also needed to estab-lish relationships with legal allies that could help negotiate the processes of attaining nonprofit status and acquiring parcels for conservation. Each group also needed to build relationships with funders based on common interests in a parcel of land. These relationships take maintenance over time and ongoing communication to build trust and cross-cultural understand-ing. This is clear particularly with the fight to protect the Sinkyone, which began with the 1985 *EPIC v. Johnson* case (the land was not transferred to the Council until 1995). As of 2010, the Council's work, partnership building, and education on the land continues. These are long-term processes that take a high degree of investment.

The operation of these conservancies takes place at a fertile legal intersection that requires parties to become somewhat versed in property law, conservation law, nonprofit law, traditional cultural laws, and federal Indian law. The array of legal factors that affect a site make partnerships with other organizations even more appealing, because each partner may bring different expertise to the table. The Council has ongoing relationships with legal allies who have been supporting the tribes' work since the initial 1985 lawsuit. Both it and the NALC have developed strong internal and external partnerships that enable them to traverse the legal intersections of operating a Native American land trust. Rather than an obstacle, the legal pluralism inherent in Native private-land conservation provides a prime location for innovating new structural arrangements that enable multiple goals—cultural, environmental, scientific, and recreational, for example—to meet on a single parcel.

As one example of this, the Council formed a nonprofit organization composed of federally recognized sovereign tribes, each with a formal government-to-government relationship with the United States. As a nonprofit, the Council is subject to state law, and easements held by land trusts on the Council's land are enforceable under that law. In contrast, the NALC is not composed of formal representatives of sovereign recognized tribes, but it also interfaces with multiple jurisdictions on its projects. To protect the Cahuilla fish traps, for example, the NALC helped coordinate purchasing the land and donating it to the Anza Borrego State Park, based on a formal MOU between the park, the Torres Martinez Desert Cahuilla Indian Tribe, and the NALC. The MOU ensures Native protective management and monitoring of cultural resources on the site. On the Old Woman Mountains Preserve, the NALC used federal U.S. Fish and Wildlife Service monies to do biological surveys and monitoring on the site, and it leveraged other funds to develop cultural educational programs. The Native land trusts discussed in this volume are characterized by multiple cross-sectoral partnerships that enable unique land transactions.

Whether it is preferable to develop cooperative management or to attain full ownership depends on the characteristics of the site, the group or groups involved, and the financial resources available. Even when a tribal conservation organization buys a parcel, cooperative ownership is still a vital part of management. In the case of the Council, for example, it worked closely with the two non-Native land trusts that own easements on the parcel. As the cases in the book show, the tribes either had a role in deciding what would happen to their sites or regained full ownership of them. This is restorative and healing given the history of federal Indian policy.

In applying conservation easements on culturally important lands, tribes and Native land trusts are not limited to just one easement. Instead, they can stack easements on a parcel. The Council, for example, has effectively done that by having two conservation easements for related purposes but held by different land trusts. A property can also have both a conservation easement and a cultural easement. The landowner would be eligible for the conservation-easement tax incentive, and cultural preservation and access would be ensured by the cultural conservation easement. The latter is a relatively new concept (see chapter 9). Although many of the conservation easements highlighted in the text mention culture, they are still largely simple conservation easements. Stacking easements may be a way for tribes and land trusts to experiment with developing and applying cultural conservation easements, with an existing "safety net" of a standard conservation easement.

Although challenges will be discussed more in the next section, the two principal Native land trusts discussed in the book have overcome difficulties largely because of visionary founders, legal and political creativity, and skillful leadership. As Rosales and Hunter described in chapter 4, the Council was able to maintain its focus on getting culturally and ecologically important land back, which eventually set a precedent of culturally based management. The NALC, in turn, has been particularly successful at "telling its story," and then putting its story in "someone else's terms" in order to share the group's vision with partners and funders.[2] Both the Council and the NALC have benefitted from sophisticated executive directors and strong board participation and leadership.

Tribe and Land Trust Collaborations

The diverse cases in this section are linked by a common institutional relationship between a Native entity—that is, a tribe, Native nonprofit, or informal Native association—and a land trust or conservancy. Other partners may include local, state, and federal agencies; legal counsel; and non-Native citizens' groups. The cases differ in scale, time frame, land status, partners, goals, and other characteristics. This diversity in the sample allows for an examination of the many different possibilities for one general institutional relationship.

• *Agreements.* Because collaborations between tribes and private conservation organizations are a relatively recent phenomenon, they are generating unique and new legal arrangements. The characteristics of the partners

—which may include sovereign tribal governments and state and federal agencies—and the land status—which may be private, trust, or public—create the arrangements. Each of these categories invokes a separate area of legal analysis. Arrangements that cross multiple jurisdictions and legal categories can give rise to new legal tools. Two of the cases exemplify particularly unique public–private–Native legal configurations: the Jamestown S'Klallam Tribe's role in the Dungeness River Audubon Center and the Little Traverse Bay Bands of Odawa/Little Traverse Conservancy's Conservation Easement Supplemental Agreement.

The Jamestown S'Klallam Tribe is concerned with the stewardship and protection of the Dungeness River. As a sovereign tribal government and a major employer in the region, they are also an important institutional presence. When a citizens' group needed a government entity to sponsor a grant to build a nature center along the river, they eventually turned to the tribe, which agreed to help because of their interest in acquiring, restoring, and protecting watershed lands. The tribe entered into a complex, multiparty arrangement in which it became the landowner, and now the land is held in trust for the tribe. There may not be another example of such a partnership in the United States, in which the tribe works with three environmental nonprofit organizations to comanage an environmental education center on tribal trust land. The tribe provided a limited waiver of sovereign immunity, as many tribes do when an easement or other environmental interest has a stake on tribal land.

In the case of the Little Traverse Bay Bands of Odawa and the Little Traverse Conservancy, the tribe also provided a limited waiver of sovereign immunity and worked with the Conservancy and legal counsel to develop an additional layer of protection for a conservation easement on tribal trust land. Both the tribe and the Conservancy had an interest in finding ways to ensure the protection of the natural area in perpetuity. The partners created a Conservation Easement Supplemental Agreement, which serves the purpose of a conservation easement on tribal trust land. If the land were to go out of trust, the regular conservation easement would take effect. The supplemental agreement is a unique legal tool prohibiting development on trust land. The partners set a precedent in designing this agreement, although it may not be necessary if the BIA releases guidelines regarding conservation easements on trust land. In any case, it protects the parcel from development whether the land is in trust or fee status.

Formal protocols and agreements were not vital in every case, but in some situations, they made the difference between a partnership working or falling apart. Even in collaborations without formal terms of agreement, there were tacit protocols governing the interaction. The Nisqually Indian Tribe, for example, does not have a formal relationship with the Nisqually Land Trust, but the two entities follow general principles of respecting one another's spheres of influence. Notably, the land trust does not work in or directly adjacent to tribal lands—that area is the purview of the tribe—and the tribe leaves the acquisition and holding of conservation easements up to the land trust. The tribe and the land trust share some staff and expertise, and they attend and support one another's events. The Jamestown S'Klallam Tribe also does not have a formal agreement with the North Olympic Land Trust. However, both the Nisqually and Jamestown S'Klallam tribes are involved with their local land trusts in formal collaborations—via the Nisqually River Task Force and the Dungeness River Management Team, respectively—and they have formalized relationships on particular properties, where the tribe may own the land and the land trust may hold the easement.

Before the Tending and Gathering Garden Steering Committee and the Cache Creek Conservancy had a formal relationship, frequent communication and board liaisons guided their interactions. Over time, these developed into formal protocols for collaboration and garden management. The relationship between Tsi-Akim Maidu and the Nevada County Land Trust also began informally and grew into a formal MOU, final agreement, and steering committee for the Burton property. Most of the relationships between land trusts or conservancies and Native American tribes, nonprofits, or organizations in the sample started informally, which fits with Wood and O'Brien's observation that "the tribal trust movement to date has manifested a 'growth by handshake' process whereby formalized transactions are preceded by perhaps years of informal understandings between conservation managers and neighbors."[3]

An additional way to move toward formalizing a relationship is through representation. For example, Cherokee traditionalist Freeman Owle served on the board of the Land Trust for the Little Tennessee during the Cowee Mound transaction, and he actively participated in that process. Similarly, the Feather River Land Trust has consistently maintained Native representation on its board of directors. Although many of the organizations discussed in the book did not have Native leadership on the land trust board nor non-Native involvement with the tribe, the parties involved in these cases were able to establish common ground by engaging in frequent communication with one another.

• *Common Ground.* Both land trusts and Native entities may seek to remove sites from potential development, but with different objectives. A land trust following a preservationist ideal[4] may want to shield a property from any human management, whereas a tribe may want to steward the land, by enhancing and harvesting culturally important plants and animals and holding ceremonial events on the site, for example. The tribes and conservation organizations had to find shared points of interest, in order to focus their collaboration on an achievable point of common ground.

Finding common ground often grew out of building trust by collaborating on smaller projects. The Eastern Band of Cherokee Indians (EBCI) and the Land Trust for the Little Tennessee (LTLT), for example, worked together for a few years on developing management protocols and raising funds for traditional Cherokee management of culturally important plant resources on LTLT lands. Although the LTLT could exclude the tribe from the trust's lands, working with the tribe enhanced the resource, supported social justice by enabling the tribe to reestablish a relationship with a traditional resource, and increased the amount of funding to accomplish goals on the land.

When the acquisition of the Cowee Mound became a possibility, both the LTLT and the tribe saw mutual benefits to working together: the tribe knew that placing a conservation easement held by the LTLT on Cowee property would help raise the funds to acquire the culturally important parcel. And the LTLT knew that by working with the tribe, it could increase the range of conserved land along the Little Tennessee River. Now that the EBCI and the LTLT have accomplished the Cowee purchase, there is talk of future large-scale collaborations to purchase other mound sites, as well as EBCI's formation of its own Native land trust, which would coordinate with the LTLT.

Similarly, when the Kachemak Heritage Land Trust and the Kenaitze Indian Tribe were willing to collaborate on the acquisition of the Cook Inlet parcel, they achieved common ground with relative ease. Following initial conversations and planning, a developer donated the land to the trust, and it then transferred the property to the tribe, while retaining a conservation easement. In this case, the trust was able to protect the land from development, and the tribe was able to reacquire a culturally important parcel.

In several of the collaborations described in this section, the tribe may have had the goal of acquiring lands in its ancestral territory rather than specifically seeking to place it in conserved status. If the tribe was willing to have a conservation organization hold title to the development rights on a parcel, that often made it possible for the tribe to place the land back into tribal ownership. This was the case in the collaborations between the EBCI and the LTLT and between the Little Traverse Bay Bands of Odawa and the Little Traverse Conservancy, for example. In a twist on this concept, the Yocha Dehe Wintun Nation already owned the land, but it needed a land trust to hold a conservation easement on it in order to satisfy a mitigation requirement. This met the land trust's goal to protect California habitat, and the tribe conceded to a land trust having a stake on tribally owned land in order to meet its dual goals of mitigation and tribal conservation.

In the Nisqually and Jamestown S'Klallam cases, the tribe and its conservation partners found common ground in their wish to protect and restore the watershed. The Jamestown S'Klallam Tribe and the North Olympic Land Trust collaborated with county, state, and federal conservation agencies to purchase, restore, and place easements on shoreline properties. On the Nisqually, the tribe and partners followed a similar tack, working together to protect the watershed for the health of the entire ecosystem. Sometimes the clarity of this goal resulted in uncommon partnerships—between the Nisqually Tribe and the U.S. Army at Fort Lewis, for example, and between the Jamestown S'Klallam Tribe and numerous entities to establish the Dungeness River Audubon Center.

In order to find common ground, conservation organizations must learn to recognize tribes as partners. Tribes should not be lumped in with interest groups such as rock climbers[5] or hard-rock miners.[6] Conservationists must be attentive to a history in which tribal rights were disregarded and tribes were violently dispossessed of their lands. Further, tribes are sovereigns that predate the creation of the United States, and they have historical and cultural relationships with lands that preexist European arrival.

• *Monitoring.* The process of monitoring is part of a conservation easement. Land trusts described going out on the property at least once each year, often with tribal partners, to monitor resources and ensure that the terms of the easement were being upheld. In the cases of the Eastern Band of Cherokee and the Land Trust for the Little Tennessee and the Little Traverse Bay Bands of Odawa and the Little Traverse Conservancy, this face-to-face time on the land may have provided additional opportunities for strategizing on joint projects, including building trails, traditional-management efforts, and education ventures.

Monitoring protocols were also created with respect for Native cultural privacy, making them unique from typical monitoring procedures between land trusts and non-Native owners. Working with the InterTribal Sinkyone Wilderness Council, the Pacific Forest Trust and Sanctuary Forest both monitor in a way that specifically respects cultural confidentiality. The land trusts and the Council communicate and agree that the principles of the easements (such as the ban on commercial harvesting) will be upheld, but the small-scale harvest of a particular resource for cultural purposes, for example, is not challenged. The two parties monitor together, and, as Rosales described, "sovereignty is built into the easement."[7] This respects tribal autonomy, and the collaboration to protect the property is entered into by two willing parties, not by one party that is "policing" another.

Monitoring efforts by tribes and their conservation partners also help to underscore the positive impact of the collaborative action. For example, monitoring by the Jamestown S'Klallam Tribe has shown the extremely positive impact of restoration on the degraded Jimmycomelately Creek. This project took place over ten years, with more than twenty-seven partners, and it involved a process of acquiring easements and parcels along the creek and obtaining funding in stages for restoration. In this long process, fatigue might have set in, but tribal monitoring helped to keep morale up by showing the positive impacts of ongoing work in the watershed.

• *Roles.* As noted above, partnerships often thrive when clear roles are established. Particularly in cross-cultural work, both parties are going to have different interests in the land and different areas of expertise. Successful projects in the sample built on these differences to create productive partnerships. In the Jamestown S'Klallam case, for example, the tribe purchased lands and the North Olympic Land Trust held the easements. Each playing their role, the two parties (and other partners) leveraged funds to acquire key properties affecting the health of the watershed. In the Nisqually watershed, the tribe works on restoration to improve watershed health. For that restoration to last, it knows that the land must be in protective ownership, so tribal members encourage purchase and acquisition by the Nisqually Land Trust. In addition to having well-defined roles, partners can also support one another. For example, the Eastern Band of Cherokee formally supported transfer of lands to the land trust, even in locations where the tribe did not directly benefit.

• *Trust.* In order to work together, diverse partners had to build trust in one another. In several cases, trust developed based on an individual who had relationships with both tribal members and members of the land trust or conservation organization. The Eastern Band of Cherokee and the Land Trust for the Little Tennessee, for example, benefitted from the encouragement of Tom Hatley, a professor who worked with both entities. He foresaw numerous important outcomes from collaborative land transactions, not the least of which was some restitution for historical wrongs. In the case of the Cache Creek Conservancy Tending and Gathering Garden, Jan Lowrey had relationships with tribal members, conservationists, and other parties. The trust each of those entities had in Lowrey built the institutional capacity for the project to move forward. In addition to Lowrey's bridging role, Shannon Brawley and others worked to build trust based on frequent communication, inclusion, and personal engagement, as well as the development of protocols to formalize mutual respect. Finally, the Trust for Public Land Tribal and Native Lands Program also played an introductory and mediator role in several of the partnerships, in terms of assisting with real estate transactions and clarifying how conservation easements could be applied for Native purposes.

• *Prioritizing.* Another lesson from the successful collaborations between tribes and land trusts is the importance of prioritizing projects. Tribes in the sample took the lead on developing methods to strategize about where conservation or restoration would have the greatest possible impacts. The Morongo Band of Mission Indians, the Nushagak–Mulchatna Wood–Tikchik Land Trust (NMWTLT), the Eastern Band of Cherokee Indians, the Jamestown S'Klallam Tribe, and the Nisqually Tribe all set priorities for land acquisition and protection before or during partnerships. Often, this planning had a spatial component, which involved mapping and then comparing culturally significant areas with areas of ecological importance. This made it possible to focus efforts on parcels where multiple values converged. For example, Cahuilla engaged in this process in urban Southern California, developing maps of traditional territories, which helped cities and counties determine which tribe they should contact if a public works or development project might have an impact on traditional lands.[8]

The NMWTLT developed a prioritization process for parcels based on building a traditional ecological knowledge database and comparing that with other ecological data, so that limited funds could be spent on preserving the most threatened allotment parcels. A similar prioritization was underway between the NMWTLT and the Koliganek Natives Corporation, so that the latter could structure its development appropriately. The Jamestown S'Klallam Tribe drew on the expertise of its tribal natural resource staff and other staff to prioritize parcels in the watershed, creating a resource used by several parties. The Nisqually Tribe's modeling efforts have been essential to restoration of the Ohop Creek and the estuary, because it made it possible to pinpoint where restoration would have the greatest impact. The Nisqually's follow-up monitoring proves that impact and builds faith in the tribe's leadership for future restoration and land protection efforts.

• *Business.* A final lesson learned is in the category of business. Nearly all of the tribes in the sample are business leaders locally, regionally, or nationally. As mentioned in the Introduction, we should not view this business acumen as an enemy of conservation. Because of their business success, the tribes often could afford to have staff members focus on developing prioritization tools, monitoring plans, and environmental studies that enabled sound conservation decision making and the creation of strategic partnerships for broad conservation outcomes. As business entities, tribes can also cultivate a balanced approach to resource use among neighboring nontraditional conservation partners, such as large agriculturalists in the Nisqually Delta. Led by tribal Chairman Billy Frank Jr., the Nisqually tribe expressed a desire to see all of the economic players on the river be successful, and the tribe also asked that these players collaborate to ensure the river's health. As the section on Challenges will show, it takes creative thinking and partnerships to bridge divergent business and conservation goals.

Natural Resources Conservation Service (NRCS) Tools

The NRCS can work with tribes on restoration whether the property is in fee or trust status. NRCS programs and staff, particularly NRCS tribal liaisons, can serve as allies for tribes working to place lands in conservation status or to raise funds for purchase and restoration. The Susanville Indian Rancheria (SIR), for example, had a very specific goal to restore a newly acquired parcel. The SIR partnered with the NRCS Wetlands Reserve Program (WRP), which provided restoration funds. SIR environmental staff secured additional grants to pay a tribal work crew to complete the restoration work. The SIR decided to do various land management actions while the land was still held in fee, because proposing actions on trust land may entail time-consuming bureaucratic procedures. The Cradle Valley parcel offered opportunities to meet many of SIR's goals, including employment and training of tribal members, cultural revitalization, land acquisition, and tribally led restoration. As a public agency with programs that include conservation easements, NRCS embodies the dichotomy of public-private that characterizes "private conservation."

Challenges

Native Land Trusts

Both the InterTribal Sinkyone Wilderness Council (the Council) and the Native American Land Conservancy (NALC) emphasized that the process of using private conservation tools was new for them and involved a steep learning curve. As such, newly forming land trusts should be patient with themselves, but they should also seek out partners like the Trust for Public Lands' Tribal and Native Lands Program, the Council, and the NALC. These entities are willing to assist nascent Native conservancies and perhaps even those non-Native conservation organizations that want to understand how they can better partner with tribes to protect sites of importance to Native communities.

• *Governance.* Structuring governance is one of the biggest challenges when forming a new organization with few existing models. State law determines the requirements for electing officers and a board of a nonprofit organization, but the actual selection of board members may be a major decision within a community. For example, the NALC and the InterTribal Sinkyone Wilderness Council each made distinct choices about how to organize their boards. The Council chose to have board members formally representing local federally recognized regional tribes, whereas the NALC board members are Native and non-Native activists and do not formally represent tribal governments or other constituencies. Both boards have met with questions as to why they chose these particular organizational forms, yet both have been very successful and are now providing leadership to other organizations. There is no single model that fits all Native land conservancies. In addition, by-laws can be amended over time and organizations can change their structure and board composition as needed.

• *Cross-Cultural Communication.* This key challenge simply comes with the intersectional work of tribal conservation. Native land trusts often have multicultural leadership if representatives are from multiple tribes or Natives and non-Natives sit on the board. In addition, Native land trusts often collaborate with external organizations, including land trusts, conservation funders, and state and federal conservation agencies, which are all largely non-Native. In order to establish the common ground underscored in the Lessons Learned section above, partners have to agree on a common vocabulary and become aware of their different assumptions about project goals, including varying definitions of conservation, access, cultural and natural resources, and other terms. It can take a great deal of time to build communication and trust, and Native land conservancies and their partners should be prepared for a multiyear effort, including several small projects and cooperative endeavors (such as joint fundraising), before embarking on a larger land acquisition.

Over many years, the Council gradually established its partnership with the two non-Native land trusts that hold easements on the InterTribal Sinkyone Wilderness. The land trusts and the Council had to develop a shared understanding in order to develop easements that were respectful of tribal members' relationship to the land and cultural privacy and that simultaneously met the land trusts' requirements for resource protection. The Council had to be sure that the land trusts had a basic understanding of protocols for the protection of traditional ecological knowledge and of cultural and archaeological sites. As former Sanctuary Forest Executive Director Eric Goldsmith came to realize, his organization's ethic of virtually hands-off preservation differed substantially from tribal members' ethic of respectful stewardship. The Council and land trusts had to first identify these cultural differences and find a middle ground in order to develop agreements.

Cross-cultural challenges can even occur in subtle ways not involving direct communication between partners. For example, even the action of using conservation easements and land trusts, tools derived from both English common law and European-derived economic principles, which place a value on undeveloped land, are cross-cultural within a Native context. In working to establish the Salt Song Trail, for example, NALC Director Russo underscores that the NALC and partners in the Cultural Conservancy and the Salt Song Project are encouraging a different way of seeing the land and interacting with the desert. Yet, in order to preserve the land and share this vision, they are using private, market-based conservation tools, such as conservation easements, that define land conservation in a very narrow fashion—that is, as falling beneath its highest and best use (development). Herein lies the creativity and resistance in the Native conservation movement: conservative conservation tools for private land, which have a history of supporting wealthy non-Natives, are being used productively and innovatively to assert Native rights to and understandings of place.

• *Fear of Casinos.* Related to the challenge of cross-cultural communication is the relatively recent plague of "casino fear." It is based on a dim understanding of the regulations that enable tribes to establish tribal-state compacts and develop gaming facilities on tribal trust lands. The concern is that tribes will acquire lands meant for conservation, put them in trust, and then negotiate to build mega-casino resort complexes where conservationists had planned open space. In nearly every tribal conservation effort, partners have raised the fear that tribes might search for loopholes to build casinos. For example, when they tried to assume management of a closing army base, the Kumeyaay-Diegueño Unity Bands were accused of planning to build a casino there.[9] The NALC has also encountered casino fear in some of its plans, and tribes trying to participate in the Pacific Gas and Electric land divestiture process reported questioning about their intentions to establish casinos on trust land.[10]

When the BIA holds land in trust for a tribe or an individual, conservation easements may not be able to be enforced unless the tribe issues a limited waiver of sovereign immunity regarding the specific easement. However, creative agreements and arrangements—like the Conservation Easement Supplemental Agreement (chapter 9)—can ensure that conservation easements or similar covenants will be enforced on trust land.

Regarding Native land trusts and conservancies, the BIA holds land in trust only for tribes or Indian individuals but not for Native nonprofits.

As nonprofits under state law, Native land trust cannot have lands held in trust for them by the BIA, and thus they cannot negotiate compacts with states to develop casinos on their lands. The BIA holds lands in trust for the member tribes of the InterTribal Sinkyone Wilderness Council but not for the Council itself, which owns the Sinkyone Wilderness in fee. Similarly, the NALC's Native board members may have individual trust lands or may belong to tribes that have lands held in BIA trust, but the NALC itself is a nonprofit, so the BIA cannot hold the organization's lands.

In partnership with other non-Native entities, several tribes discussed in this book purchased land for conservation purposes and then placed it in trust with the BIA. These properties have conservation easements prohibiting development. The parties have assumed that the easement remains in force with the BIA as owner, and they have issued limited waivers of sovereign immunity, or in the case of the Little Traverse Bay Bands of Odawa and the Little Traverse Conservancy, the parties have created an additional layer of protection in the form of a Conservation Easement Supplemental Agreement, which functions like a conservation easement on trust land.

• *Competition.* Native land trusts are an emerging phenomenon, and state, federal, and private sources of funding may not yet have targeted resources for them. This may put these trusts in the unenviable position of competing for funding for cultural and environmental work with neighboring tribes. This can be particularly problematic in times of lean funding. The NALC tries to avoid such competition by applying for grants with clearly different emphases from those sought by member or partner tribes.

• *Capacity.* Given the scope of Native land loss and the sheer number of culturally important sites that need to be protected on non-Native lands, the need for Native land trusts is great. Yet how can emerging nonprofit organizations, with little precedent, take on this challenge? The Native land trusts profiled here formed around specific, local projects, which typically took several years. During that time, the land trust cemented its structure, operations, and goals. Following a successful acquisition, the land trust either focused on enhancing that project, perhaps by developing trails or educational events, or it began to expand into other related efforts at varying distances from the initial acquisition. For example, the Council has largely focused on the InterTribal Sinkyone Wilderness, but more recently, it has been sharing its process and advising other groups. In 2009, the executive director of the Council and a board member attended the international Ninth World Wilderness Conference, and they were active in developing resolutions on protection of old-growth forests for cultural values. This activity speaks to the ways in which the important work of Native American land conservancies is gaining national and international attention. The work of Native land conservancies also aligns with similar efforts by indigenous organizations outside of the United States.

After it acquired the Old Woman Mountains parcel, the NALC began developing mentor-protégé relationships with emerging Native conservation efforts and organizations in Colorado, Alaska, California, and Washington, among other states. It is a decentralized organization with one principal contracted employee, the executive director. How can it take on these diverse commitments and partner with entities in various locations, far from its base in Southern California? Energy and passion for the work, strategic alliances with funders, and coordinating conferences that focus on particular efforts have allowed the NALC to be remarkably successful with few human resources.

A final capacity challenge, shared by all land trusts, is the day-to-day management of acquired properties. When land trusts accept ownership of or easements on properties, they accept the responsibility to monitor to ensure that easement terms are being upheld. This takes time, expertise, travel funds, and manpower. The NALC's largest property, the Old Woman Mountains Preserve is more than 2,500 acres in size and located in the remote Mohave Desert. It contains priceless rock art and other cultural sites, as well as endangered species. The NALC has contracted with a passionate steward and caretaker who previously lived on the property full time. This is a unique situation, however. The challenge of stewardship capacity remains a key question for emerging land trusts, who may unwittingly accept responsibility for properties that are actually quite difficult to regularly monitor and protect.

Tribe and Land Trust Collaborations

Collaborations between tribes, Native nonprofits, or Native corporations and non-Native nonprofit conservation organizations must be acknowledged as nothing short of miraculous. These collaborations not only cross cultures; they cross jurisdictions and institutional forms that may—at least on the surface—appear to be diametrically opposed. One example of the latter are Alaska Native corporations, which must develop land to achieve benefits for shareholders while working with conservation organizations accustomed to purchasing development rights in order to keep properties pristine. The two parties are finding opportunities to work together that are mutually beneficial, even as they also struggle when little overlap exists in their respective missions. This subsection will touch on the challenges of power dynamics, institutional "fit," sovereignty, and incentive structures, which arise when tribes work with land trusts.

• *Power Dynamics.* Several factors, including who owns the land, influence power dynamics. In the Yocha Dehe case, the tribe is the landowner, and it sought a conservancy or land trust to serve a very specific function. The procedural and distributive aspects of environmental justice had already been achieved to some extent, in that the tribe owned some of its ancestral land. Although it must satisfy mitigation requirements for the land's development, the tribe can determine the entity with which it will work to meet those requirements.

On the other end of a spectrum of ownership and control of the process are the Tsi-Akim Maidu Tribe and the Tending and Gathering Garden Steering Committee, an intertribal group of weavers united by a common interest rather than a single tribal affiliation. Although very different entities, both the Tsi-Akim and the steering committee are not federally recognized and are undertaking similar efforts to structure access agreements with a conservancy landowner. It is each conservancy's commitment to social justice and the trust built between individual members of both parties—the Nevada County Land Trust (NCLT) and the Tsi-Akim Maidu (chapter 10) and the Cache Creek Conservancy and the Tending and Gathering Garden Steering Committee (chapter 15)—that brought the conservancy to the table. Although procedural environmental justice is partially achieved because some Native entities with a stake in the land are included in the conservation organization's discussions about how to manage its land, distributive justice is limited because the Native entity does not have a formal stake in the ownership of the land. This has improved in the Tsi-Akim case, in which the tribe and the NCLT negotiated a lease and final agreement.

In the Tsi-Akim Maidu and NCLT collaboration, building the rapport, communication, and trust to establish a formal Memorandum of Understanding and a ten-year lease on the site took several years. The formal agreement has been important for defining the tenure and scope of the tribe's stewardship of the property. Creating an agreement is also important for the land trust's long-range planning on the site. However, thus far, the tribe has not been able to get the NCLT to agree to a lease beyond ten years, which is not enough time for the Tsi-Akim Maidu to be able to fundraise and complete more projects on the property. In addition, unexpected property taxes created a financial burden for the unrecognized tribe, whose funding comes exclusively from grants to its nonprofit arm, loans, fundraisers, and its tribal thrift store in Grass Valley, California. If the land trust decides to sell the property (and retain the conservation easement, of course), it has committed to involving the tribe in those discussions. However, the amount of power the tribe would have in establishing a relationship with the new owner is uncertain. So, too, is its role after the ten-year agreement expires, despite the level of investment the tribe has made on the property. In sum, although the collaboration between the Tsi-Akim Maidu and the land trust has been extremely productive for both parties, the latter appears to retain the upper hand as a property owner.

The process of achieving environmental justice in conservation arrangements between tribes and private conservation associations is a shifting continuum, in which each party's advantages and disadvantages must be analyzed with reference to larger institutional structures. For example, lack of recognition is an injustice that leaves Native Americans like the Tsi-Akim Maidu without sovereign status or a tribal land base. Collaborating with a land trust may help an unrecognized tribe to regain at least a stake in land ownership, as well as raise its profile as a tribal entity that is engaged in formal agreements with other entities. This moves toward justice, within a situation of injustice.

The current agreement between the Tsi-Akim Maidu Tribe and the NCLT may also be seen as a "trial period." When the InterTribal Sinkyone Wilderness Council and the Pacific Forest Trust (PFT) developed their initial conservation easement, it included a five-year trial period, after which both parties could evaluate the partnership and decide whether the PFT would continue holding the easement. At the end of the five-year period, the Council requested that the PFT continue in its role. Although this situation's power dynamic is different because the Native entity is the landowner, the point to note is that the Tsi-Akim Maidu Tribe and the Nevada County Land Trust may choose to reevaluate their agreement after the initial ten-year period, leaving open the possibility of establishing a longer-term agreement.

Another challenge involving an imbalance of power can be seen in the Morongo case, where Southern California tribes have drawn up agreements with the county and developers under California Senate Bill 18 (SB-18). Although many real estate developments have the potential to harm cultural resources, SB-18 requires the county to notify the tribe only if the general or specific plan is amended. When consultation takes place, tribes can negotiate protection for culturally important sites not in tribal ownership. However, the tribe must have the support of the county in order to make these agreements binding.

Although some SB-18 consultations have resulted in informal agreements to protect sites, if projects are not completed right away and personnel change, these agreements cannot be enforced. However, if the agreements are developed into formal conditions of approval for development, they will hold for the parcel even if the land changes hands.[11] Although the Morongo Band has a productive relationship with Riverside County, the economic slowdown caused development projects, and the attendant cultural mitigations developed in the SB-18 consultation process, to stall. When projects are delayed or cancelled, the conditions of approval for the development may not be completed, leaving sites vulnerable to future development proposals.

Ultimately, no formal rules for collaborations between tribes and land trusts exist. This condition may leave room for creativity and innovation, if both parties are willing to work together. New partnerships may be developed that expand tribal oversight and involvement in land management far beyond the strictures of federal-tribal collaboration. However, at the same time, conservation organizations working on private lands have no mandate to work with tribes, which may be completely excluded. Addressing this concern or challenge was one of the impetuses for this book.

• *Institutional "fit."* As noted above, land trusts and Native tribes, nonprofits, and corporations are communicating across individual and institutional cultural differences. Sometimes the conservation tools just cannot be applied in a way that completely "fits" with the goals of one or both entities. There were several examples of this in Alaska. Partially to try to address the issue of earning the trust of Alaska Native allottees and Alaska Native corporations, Alaska land trusts developed a plan to support keeping lands in Native hands. Land trusts would purchase conservation easements from Alaska Natives, rather than buy the lands, thereby keeping the fee title or trust ownership in Native hands. However, the Nushagak–Mulchatna Wood–Tikchik Land Trust (NMWTLT) reported instances of these Native landowners selling lands to non-Natives after the land trust bought the easement.

Although an exploration of the landowner's decision on these properties is beyond the scope of this book, the outcome makes for interesting discussion. The conservation tool "worked" in that lands were conserved, the Native landowner received revenue for both the value of not developing the land and the sale of the land, and the land trust retained the easement. However, the tool was unsuccessful in terms of structuring the arrangement so that some land title stayed with the Native entity. The most successful aspect was the Native landowner's retaining the choice to make decisions about the property and to gain some revenue from it, even with a conservation restriction.

The NMWTLT also faced challenges in fitting the conservation needs for allotments into both conservation agencies' and Native corporations' funding priorities. Regarding conservation funding priorities, conservation funders typically want to invest in properties that will have large-scale impacts on conservation, rather than paying to conserve isolated parcels surrounded by developable lands. Ongoing challenges in conservation funding are exacerbated when priority parcels are 160-acre islands amidst other properties with different designations. The NMWTLT sees itself in a "race against time" to preserve these parcels, but it takes far longer to build partnerships and raise funds for acquisition than it does for an allottee to decide to sell. Thus, the limitations of the conservation tool (here, funding needs) do not "fit" with funders' priorities for conserving large tracts of land.

In terms of Native corporations' funding priorities, it is obviously difficult to have conservation tools address a key purpose of a Native corporation: obtaining profits for shareholders from land assets. Although the Kachemak Heritage Land Trust (KHLT) believes that the habitat, resources, and subsistence values on Native corporate and allotment lands are a priority, they are not an organization flush with funds. The KHLT typically receives easement donations and, currently in Alaska, a Native corporation or allottee has little or no incentive to donate an easement to a land trust, which would keep an asset (land) from generating revenue through development. Even if allottees or Native corporations wanted to sell or donate their land, why would they work with a non-Native land trust? Native entities are asking some of the same questions as land trust critics, specifically, what guarantees that a small, nonprofit, non-Native land trust will be able to preserve land in perpetuity? What will guarantee that this type of land trust will not turn around and sell donated land for its own benefit? Land trusts like KHLT offered a host of possible safeguards, including deed restrictions, secondary holders, resolutions, and pressure from the national Land Trust Alliance, but Native allottees continue to raise these questions, which may only be legitimately answered by continued communication between Native entities and non-Native land trusts, as well as ongoing observation of these land trusts over time.

• *Sovereignty.* A key institutional factor that affects tribes' and land trusts' willingness to work together is tribal sovereignty. Tribes retained their inherent powers of self-government as America expanded. Although a seminal court decision rendered tribes "domestic-dependent nations,"[12] they are still recognized as distinct governments that oversee their own affairs. Legislative and judicial attempts to erode tribal sovereignty have sought to reduce tribal control[13] over tribal lands, resources, and tribal members, but tribes continue to resist incursions against their sovereignty.

When tribal entities form a binding partnership with an outside entity, such as a land trust, they may have to waive their right of sovereign immunity from suit in order to make the contract enforceable. Some tribes and tribal legal counsel see the limited waiver of sovereign immunity (for a specific purpose and between specific parties) as a necessary and expected step to get business done, while others are concerned about a waiver's possible effect on diminishing overall tribal sovereignty.

Although a waiver of sovereign immunity makes the tribe liable for upholding the terms of the conservation easement, who is responsible if the easement is on land held in trust for the tribe by the BIA? When the tribe and the land trust enter into a conservation easement agreement, the land may still be in fee status, owned by the tribe. Tribes have often chosen to apply to the BIA to put land into trust after the conservation easement transaction is complete. The fee-to-trust process can take time, and there may be time constraints on the easement transaction (for example, grant funds may need to be spent).[14] Still, whether or not the BIA is involved at the outset or after the conservation transaction, if the land is put into trust with the BIA and a land trust holds the easement, and there is a breach of terms, is the easement enforceable against the BIA? Some parties in the cases believed that that agreement was, indeed, enforceable, and others, as noted above, developed supplementary agreements to function like conservation easements specifically on trust land.

• *Incentives and Disincentives.* Incentives for tribes to participate in private conservation include increased access to conservation funding sources, engagement in watershed-wide work, and opportunities to acquire land that would otherwise likely remain out of tribal ownership. Disincentives include possible infringement on tribal sovereignty, the challenges of building cross-cultural communication and partnerships, and the lack of applicability of many of the tax incentives available for other landowners.

Tribes are eligible for the conservation tax incentive only if they donate conservation easements on land they own in fee (private) status. It appears that tribes can accept conservation easements from donors and allow the donor to get a tax write-off for the value of the donation. By holding a conservation easement, the tribe obtains a formal stake in the land. No examples of tribes accepting and holding easements are currently known. If the donor offers a cultural conservation easement to the tribe, however, the tax code is even less clear as to whether a deduction for the value of the gift can be taken. Thus, continuing to emphasize the conservation values of such donations is "safer" than emphasizing the cultural values. Tax codes should be amended to include a cultural conservation tax incentive, to renew the conservation tax incentive, and to make all Native entities eligible for both.

In Alaska, the conservation tax incentives are either not applicable or not allowed. They are not applicable for Alaska Native allottees, who already do not pay land taxes. Alaska is unique in that allotments are still a major concern. Many allotments were approved as recently as 1981, under the Alaska National Interest Lands Conservation Act (ANILCA).[15] There are many 160-acre allotment parcels that are now facing development pressure from tourism and other uses. The two Alaska land trusts discussed in-depth in the text—KHLT and NMWTLT—are both making themselves available as conservation-planning partners with allottees. However, the latter face complex choices because they have the option of taking the land out of trust and selling it. Allottees need to ensure that they can get a fair price for their lands if they decide to sell, and when second-home buyers or tourist concessionaires are making exorbitant offers, it may be difficult for an allottee to choose the land trust as the buyer.

Although Alaska Native corporations could benefit from the conservation tax incentive, they are not eligible for it, even though (1) many shareholders depend on the land for subsistence, (2) the corporation manages the land for diverse public benefits, and (3) land is the corporation's principal asset. If they were eligible, they could use conservation-easement donations as write-offs against their overall income taxes, which would reduce revenue loss for shareholders. Proposed in 2009, Senate Bill 1673 and House Resolution 3568 call for extending these benefits to Alaska Native corporations.

Amending tax laws to make Alaska Native corporations eligible for incentives will help encourage conservation, but it will not reduce the many choices facing Native corporations about their lands. Currently, their best justification for buying allotments, according to Tim Troll, occurs when an allottee is about to sell to a non-Native business that would disrupt the corporation's enterprises by fragmenting market share and control over the land. In the absence of this situation, it is easier for Native corporations to justify purchases for development (for future revenue) than for conservation. Other conservation statutes that can help Native corporations gain further control over their inholdings may also be attractive options. For example, NMWTLT's efforts to list streams in the Anadromous Waters Catalog, thereby protecting the water for fish and increasing Native jurisdiction over waters that cross corporate lands, is an emerging area of Native conservation application that will be explored in future research.[16]

Finally, conservation statutes and conservation tax incentives do not explicitly apply to tribal entities, Native corporations, and Native allottees, which is a key indicator that easement-enabling statutes and incentives need to be reformed to enable tribal participation. As one example of how changes can occur, NRCS programs were not developed with tribes in mind, yet the NRCS created tribal outreach programs and enabled the formation of tribal RCDs so that tribes can specifically access NRCS programs in order to meet tribal needs. The initial situation was one of discrimination by default—the

NRCS programs were not designed to exclude tribes, but because they did not actively work to include tribal priorities or to address the unique tribal land status and government-to-government relationship, the programs actually ended up excluding tribes. NRCS took steps to remedy the situation. Now, the proponents of conservation need to do the same in order to make private conservation more accessible to tribes.

NRCS Conservation Tools

The mini-case on the attempted collaboration between the non-tribal Coarsegold RCD and local tribes illustrates several challenges. We should applaud the Coarsegold RCD's efforts to develop inclusive language, but the lack of any formal agreements between it and surrounding tribes indicates that those partnerships have yet to be deepened, broadened, and formalized. Creating MOUs and other agreements would allow the RCD to actualize its commitment to tribal resource-management philosophies, and it would let surrounding tribes collaborate with and receive the services of the Coarsegold RCD.

Encouraging Native Applications of "Private" Conservation Tools

Finally, how can easement law, statutes, and conservation organizations collaborate with tribes and Native nonprofits, allottees, and corporations to make private conservation tools more useful for these entities and for Native applications? Some of the groups profiled in this book, such as the Native land trusts—the InterTribal Sinkyone Wilderness Council and the Native American Land Conservancy—see themselves as helping to seed a liberating movement of Native-led conservation in Indian country. They have committed to helping others form land trusts and apply conservation tools to achieve Native goals of access, cultural site protection, stewardship, healing, and restoration. This section examines a few of the key points of leverage for enhancing the applicability of these tools in Indian Country.

Mitigation

At least two of the tribes began using these tools as part of mitigations. The Yocha Dehe Wintun Nation was required to mitigate golf-course development by setting aside a certain amount of land for the Swainson's hawk. The tribe surpassed the requirement, establishing a large reserve with an easement held by a regional land conservancy. The Little Traverse Bay Bands of Odawa was also seeking land to mitigate for the development of tribal enterprises. It was able to partner with the Little Traverse Conservancy and obtain federal funds through a state agency to purchase and create a tribal preserve with an easement held by the land trust. The preserve protects resources, provides recreational opportunities, and supports cultural perpetuation.

The majority of tribes in the book are strong business entities, so it is likely they will face mitigation requirements at some point in their business expansion. Easements and partnerships with land trusts can be an attractive tool for mitigating development, and this can initiate relationships that may lead to future conservation and cultural projects. Mitigation through private conservation enhances tribal sovereignty because the tribe is taking the lead in the process of deciding the terms, the extent, and partnerships for the mitigation. Conservation achieved through mitigation also provides a public benefit by setting aside land for wildlife and possible recreational, educational, and cultural programs.

Tribes may also have economic opportunities to provide mitigation services by accepting funds from companies or agencies to set aside areas of tribal land for conservation. This "carbon credit" program would serve to offset those companies' pollution elsewhere. Similarly, the government recognizes the value of farms for sequestering carbon and maintaining habitat and makes them eligible for conservation tax incentives. As argued in chapter 11, Alaska Native entities should be eligible for these same incentives, because Alaska Native conservation provides similar, if not greater, ecological benefits. In the future, short-term climate easements (perhaps modeled on the NRCS short-term Wetlands Reserve Program easements) could be created to allow polluting entities to buy climate allowances on Native lands as they phase into zero emissions.[17] This concept speaks to the need to use conservation tools for economic benefits. As both business leaders and conservationists, tribes may find this area of inquiry particularly useful.

Tribal Statutes

Tribes have asserted their sovereignty by developing codes to enable the formation of particular business entities, practices, or services within the Native nation.[18] U.S. states assert a similar type of sovereignty through the Uniform Conservation Easement Act (UCEA): to enable the use of easements, the state must either formally adopt the UCEA or develop their own similar statute, describing allowable designs and purposes for easements. Similarly, at least one tribe in the sample, the Little Traverse Bay Bands of Odawa Indians, established the ability to form a Native land trust in its tribal code. The tribe has not yet formed a trust, but having a code outlining how such a trust could be developed and would function was a forward-thinking move that allows it to create such an organization under tribal law. With this arrangement, an easement's terms would be enforceable in tribal court, which supports the sovereignty of tribal judicial systems.

Making Conservation Tools Native

This conclusion has emphasized the importance of ensuring that conservation-incentive regulations and statutes are amended to take into account tribal restrictions, opportunities, and goals. In addition to the importance of amending tax law, the rules governing appropriations for conservation should also be changed to make those funds available to tribes, not just to states or nonprofits. These appropriations should also take into account tribal interests, such as restoration for cultural perpetuation. The Eastern Band of Cherokee and the Land Trust for the Little Tennessee, for example, received funding from the Clean Water Management Trust Fund to help purchase the Cowee Mound, but this funding was not directly accessible to the tribe without a partnership with the land trust. The tribe has continued to work on inserting Native land access and management needs into public funding initiatives.

Land trusts and tribes are also collaborating so that the latter know which lands the trust is purchasing. This lets a tribe determine if these lands contain cultural resources. The respective morality and vision of the partners should not be the sole reason for this communication. Instead, the Land Trust Alliance (LTA) should formally encourage its members to include the land's first peoples in their leadership, land prioritization, land selection, and land management. Some land trusts have argued that this should occur only with the consent of the landowner, but a trust could make it a policy directive to work with tribes on conservation planning, stewardship, monitoring, and other tasks, in addition to determining specific involvement on individual parcels on a case-by-case basis.

The LTA standards and practices,[19] which all LTA member land trusts adopt, have not included any guidelines for relationships with indigenous peoples. However, at the annual LTA Rally in 2009, Native leaders from the Trust for Public Lands (TPL) Tribal and Native Lands Program and the InterTribal Sinkyone Wilderness Council offered a seminar on tribal conservation. Participants split into small groups and then worked as one large group to develop a list of standards that the LTA could adopt regarding how land trusts should relate to tribes. These draft standards include identifying aboriginal tribal boundaries in the land trust's service area and working with leaders from those tribes, as well as ensuring that conservation purchases are not excluding traditional uses. Because the LTA is such a large organization with so many members, having standards that address relationships with Native people and Native lands could make a significant difference in private conservation.

The seminar's initiator, Kawika Burgess, TPL's native lands program officer in Hawaii, is working on a follow-up article for the LTA publication *Saving Land Magazine*. According to Burgess, the goal of further developing the proposed standards and practices is to, first,

> just [develop] more awareness about Native and indigenous interests in land, and conservation, and culture on the land. In a way, reminding people that the history of people and land on Hawaii and on the continent goes back prior to Columbus and Captain Cook. [And a second goal is] just growing awareness and understanding and collaboration with tribes and other indigenous groups as far as their interests, culture, ties, connection to the land, and having land trusts look at that aspect in their project work. [20]

Burgess also sees great value for the land trusts in collaborating with indigenous people who have multigenerational relationships to and interests in the land. Indigenous partners may be able to assist land trusts with management and planning and increase the diversity of what has been a largely Anglo land trust movement. As he added, "having generational and traditional knowledge of the land only adds to conservation."[21]

Wood, Welcker, and O'Brien also offer some examples of how land trusts and the conservation movement in general can encourage tribal participation, such as involving tribes in monitoring easements, developing comanagement plans on conserved lands, creating coholding agreements with tribes on easements and conserved lands, hiring tribal members to do stewardship, and ensuring that land management plans receive tribal approval.[22] All of these joint actions could also serve as training opportunities for tribes considering forming their own land trusts.

NRCS Tools

The NRCS has already enabled an innovative partnership structure, through which tribes can access NRCS tools for private-land conservation. There is a precedent already for tribal RCDs, and for tribes using NRCS programs to achieve tribal goals. The NRCS is included in this text because it is specifically focused on private land and has adopted and developed programs to work on tribal land. The text allows a limited exploration of how some of these programs can be used to support tribes' use of private conservation mechanisms and partnerships. Further research should be done on these programs, as well as on programs specific to other agencies that provide funding to help private and tribal landowners preserve wildlife and natural resources. An example of one agency providing such funding is the U.S. Fish and Wildlife Service, which has partnered with several of the organizations and tribes discussed in this text.[23]

The NRCS has moved closer to environmental justice by creating a structure through which it could focus resources and work on tribal conservation priorities. Although tribes can now access NRCS services, assistance, and funds, and form tribal resource conservation districts (RCDs), the process of education and technical assistance required to establish a tribal RCD is continuing slowly. According to a list of tribal RCDs from the Indian Nations Conservation Alliance (INCA),[24] there are approximately twenty-two tribal RCDs in the United States and several more are forming. Of the states included in this book, California, Washington, and Michigan each have one tribal RCD, Alaska has two, and North Carolina has none. With the encouragement of the INCA, which holds an annual conference in Las Vegas where tribal RCDs and other conservation and resource enhancement strategies on tribal land are discussed,[25] tribes are developing more RCDs.

Conclusion

Most cases in this book, including Native and non-Native conservation partnerships and Native land trusts, show some degree of success in building communication with partners and taking action on the land, but that was achieved only with a struggle. The coalitions and organizations described are on the cutting edge of a new movement that unites cultural and political sovereignty with the ecological and economic opportunities inherent in emergent conservation policy and market-based conservation opportunities. Uniting these two very different spheres can be fraught with conflict, when divergent goals and means are juxtaposed to find common ground.

This book began with the hypothesis that tribal engagement in private conservation, as exemplified through a range of institutional arrangements, can and does achieve environmental justice and lights the way toward new legal mechanisms. The fourteen cases reveal that this intersection of conservation statutes, tribal jurisdiction, and Native and nonprofit institutional arrangements strengthens easements as a tool, by making them useful to more stakeholders and for more purposes. To achieve procedural and distributive justice, conservation incentives and enabling statutes must be modified to specifically include tribes and Native landowners as valued participants in the market for conservation easements. Tribes and Native entities must specifically be eligible for the tax and other benefits available to many non-Native fee landowners. Some new legal tools have emerged or are emerging, such as the conservation easement supplemental agreement, cultural conservation easements, and Alaska Native conservation incentives.

Much current scholarship on conservation easements is critical of their security, their adaptability to changing situations, and the potential for abuse in their valuation and enforcement. This text acknowledges these important criticisms, but it focuses on the concern that easements serve a narrow group of stakeholders and functionally exclude many indigenous landowners and stewards. This book looks at easements from the perspective of how they might better interface with tribal priorities.

Ultimately, we cannot continue to live in a world where "the perpetuation of injustice is acceptable"[26]—whether that injustice is to the first peoples of this land, many of whom still do not have access to their homelands, or to the plants and animals that all humans have the opportunity and the responsibility to steward. A productive engagement between land trusts and tribes to focus private conservation tools on Native land restitution and conservation outcomes is the wave of the future. It is also part of a very positive trend of changing narrow conceptions of "environment" and "conservation" to embrace multiple cultural experiences of place.

Although land trusts are generally accountable to their members—individuals who donate to support the goals of the organization—and to their funders, land trusts have heretofore not been accountable to tribes. This is despite the fact that trusts are operating on lands taken from tribes just a century ago and often have some common goals for the management of these parcels. The tribes, land trusts, and Native organizations profiled in this text offer a range of possible model partnerships and suggestions for improved collaboration. By engaging more deeply with tribes, land trusts have the potential to be at the forefront of a movement for justice and environmental protection, bringing the most important characteristics of each separate movement together.

Appendix

Interviewees

I am deeply grateful to many people and organizations for their generous cooperation in sharing their stories. Please note that the cases may not include quotes from or reflect the views of everyone acknowledged here.

Preface
Paul Hardy, Executive Director, Feather River Land Trust
Jason Moghaddas, Conservation Director, Feather River Land Trust
Marvin Cunningham
Trina Cunningham
Farrell Cunningham

InterTribal Sinkyone Wilderness Council (California)
Hawk Rosales, Executive Director, InterTribal Sinkyone Wilderness Council
Priscilla Hunter, Chairperson, InterTribal Sinkyone Wilderness Council
Luwana Quitiquit, Board Secretary, InterTribal Sinkyone Wilderness Council
Atta Stevenson, Board Member, InterTribal Sinkyone Wilderness Council
David Edmunds, Board Member, InterTribal Sinkyone Wilderness Council
Fred "Coyote" Downey
Ricardo Tapia
Richard Gienger
Laurie Wayburn, President, Pacific Forest Trust
Rachael Katz, Program Associate, Pacific Forest Trust
Neal Fishman, Deputy Executive Officer, California Coastal Conservancy
Jonathan Remucal, Stewardship Manager, Pacific Forest Trust
Eric Goldsmith, Executive Director, Sanctuary Forest
Sharon Duggan, Legal Counsel

Native American Land Conservancy (California)

Kurt Russo, Executive Director, Native American Land Conservancy

Clifford Trafzer, Professor, University of California, Riverside, and Board Member, Native American Land Conservancy

Louis Guassac, former Executive Director, Kumeyaay-Diegueño Land Conservancy

Larry Kinley, acting Executive Director, Kumeyaay-Diegueño Land Conservancy

Lisa Lang, Xaadaas Kil Kuyaas Foundation

Melissa Nelson, Executive Director, Cultural Conservancy

Tom Askew, Land Steward, Native American Land Conservancy

Yocha Dehe Wintun Nation (California)

Al Vallecillo, former Facilities Director, Yocha Dehe Wintun Nation

Jim Etters, Director of Land Management, Yocha Dehe Farm and Ranch

Bob Whitney, Executive Director, Golden State Land Conservancy

Pete Bontadelli, Analytical Environmental Services

Deborah North, former Interim Executive Director, Yolo Land Trust

Lynnel Pollock, Executive Director, Cache Creek Conservancy

Lauren Silva, Porter Novelli

Morongo Band of Mission Indians (California)

Mike Contreras, Cultural Heritage Program Coordinator, Morongo Band of Mission Indians

Britt Wilson, former Project Manager for Cultural Resources, Morongo Band of Mission Indians

Leslie Mouriquand, Riverside County Archaeologist

Carmen M. Manriquez, Community Development Director, City of Coachella

Patricia Tuck, Director of Historic Preservation, Agua Caliente Band of Cahuilla Indians

Little Traverse Bay Bands of Odawa Indians/Little Traverse Conservancy (Michigan)

Frank Ettawageshik, former Tribal Chairman, Little Traverse Bay Bands of Odawa Indians

Rachel Smolinski, Environmental Services Director, Little Traverse Bay Bands of Odawa Indians

James Bransky, General Counsel, Little Traverse Bay Bands of Odawa Indians

Thomas Bailey, Executive Director, Little Traverse Conservancy

Kieran Fleming, Director of Land Protection, Little Traverse Conservancy

Tsi-Akim Maidu/Nevada County Land Trust (California)

Don Ryberg, Chairman, Tsi-Akim Maidu
Grayson Coney, Cultural Director, Tsi-Akim Maidu
Wendy Olenick, Tsi-Akim Maidu
Dan Macon, Director of Conservation Programs, Nevada County Land Trust
John Taylor, Board President, Nevada County Land Trust
Marty Coleman-Hunt, Executive Director, Nevada County Land Trust
Stephanie Lorensen, Volunteer Coordinator, Nevada County Land Trust

The Kachemak Heritage Land Trust and the Nushagak–Mulchatna Wood–Tikchik Land Trust (Alaska)

Margaret Brown, President and Chief Executive Officer, Cook Inlet Region, Inc.
Tom Harris, Chief Executive Officer, Tyonek Native Corporation
Tim Troll, Director, Nushagak–Mulchatna Wood–Tikchik Land Trust, and
      Director of Southwest Alaska Programs, The Nature Conservancy
Bruce Oskolkoff, Director of Land and Resources, Ninilchik Natives
      Association, Inc.
Barbara Seaman, former Executive Director, Kachemak Heritage Land Trust
Randall Hagenstein, State Director, Alaska Chapter, The Nature Conservancy
Marie McCarty, Executive Director, Kachemak Heritage Land Trust
Mary Frische and Tom Collopy, Wild North Photography
Roger MacCampbell, District Ranger, Kachemak Bay District, Alaska State Parks
David Case, Attorney, Landye, Bennett, & Blumstein, LLP

Jamestown S'Klallam Tribe (Washington)

Hansi Hals, Environmental Planning Manager, Jamestown S'Klallam Tribe
Lyn Muench, former Environmental Planning Manager, Jamestown S'Klallam Tribe
Leo Gaten, Governmental Policy Advisor, Jamestown S'Klallam Tribe
Scott Chitwood, Director, Natural Resources, Jamestown S'Klallam Tribe
Greg Good, Executive Director, North Olympic Land Trust
Bob Boekelheide, Dungeness River Audubon Center
Sarah Spaeth, Executive Director, Jefferson Land Trust

Eastern Band of Cherokee/Land Trust for the Little Tennessee (North Carolina)

Sharon Taylor, Land Protection Coordinator, Land Trust for the Little Tennessee
Juanita Wilson, Board Chair for the Oconaluftee Institute for Cultural Arts (OICA)
Russell Townsend, Tribal Historic Preservation Officer, Eastern Band of
      Cherokee Indians
Tom Hatley, former Sequoyah Professor of Cherokee Studies, Western
      Carolina University
Paul Carlson, Executive Director, Land Trust for the Little Tennessee
Ralph Preston, Photographer

Nisqually Indian Tribe (Washington)

George Walter, Environmental Program Supervisor, Nisqually Tribe, and
  Board President, Nisqually Land Trust
Georgiana Kautz, Natural Resources Program Manager, Nisqually Tribe
Jeanette Dorner, Salmon Recovery Program Manager, Nisqually Tribe
Constance Bond, Programs Manager, Nisqually Land Trust
Linda Kunze, Stewardship Coordinator, Nisqually Land Trust

Cache Creek Conservancy (California)

Lynnel Pollock, Executive Director, Cache Creek Conservancy
Shannon Brawley, former Executive Director, California Indian Basketweavers
  Association (CIBA)
Diana Almendariz, Cultural Educator
Kathy Wallace, Cultural Educator, CIBA cofounder
Don Hankins, Assistant Professor, California State University, Chico

Susanville Indian Rancheria (California)

Tim Keesey, Environmental Manager, Susanville Indian Rancheria
Melanie Johnson, Cultural Director, Susanville Indian Rancheria

Coarsegold Resource Conservation District (California)

Tom Wheeler, Coarsegold RCD Board Chairman
Neil McDougald, Coarsegold RCD Board Member
Larry Ballew, Coarsegold RCD Board Member
Christine Elam Ballew, Native Landowner

Natural Resources Conservation Service

Reina Rogers, American Indian Liaison
Rob Roy, District Conservationist

Notes

Foreword

1. Lt. James Doty, Bureau of Indian Affairs, "Minutes of the Walla Walla Council, 1855," in *Report on the Source, Nature and Extent of Fishing, Hunting and Miscellaneous Related Rights of Certain Tribes in Oregon and Washington* (Los Angeles: Office of Indian Affairs, Division of Forestry and Grazing, 1942).

2. Ibid.

Preface

1. The Sierra Institute for Community and Environment is a nonprofit research and educational organization in the northeastern Sierra Nevada. Through its Forestry Center, the Institute offers outdoor learning and networking opportunities. See http://www.sierrainstitute.us for more information.

2. Marvin Cunningham, telephone communication, December 28, 2009; Paul Hardy, executive director of the Feather River Land Trust, agreed that this must have included 120 acres in Hungry Creek and three parcels in the valley of 80, 120, and 160 acres (telephone communication, January 8, 2010).

3. Farrell Cunningham, tour of Heart K Ranch, May 16, 2009.

4. Marvin Cunningham, personal communication, Genesee Valley, California, December 20, 2009.

5. According to Marvin Cunningham, not all of the heirs in the Davis family knew of the transfer of the land until after it had occurred (personal communication, Genesee Valley, California, December 20, 2009).

6. Paul Hardy, telephone communication, December 7, 2009.

7. Ibid.

8. Ibid.

9. For example, the Feather River Land Trust mission is general enough to amply accommodate cultural preservation. The mission is "to conserve, restore, and manage land in the Feather River region in cooperation with willing

landowners for the benefit of current and future generations." In a discussion entitled, "Why We Believe in Our Mission," the land trust notes that "the Feather River region . . . contains critical wildlife habitat, as well as historic ranches, Maidu cultural sites, scenic open spaces, and important recreation areas." See http://www.frlt.org/whoweare.html.

10. Jason Moghaddas, Feather River Land Trust conservation director, e-mail message to author, January 7, 2010.

11. Plumas County Health Department. Parcel 008–160–0–20. Sewage system red tagged, November 10, 1987. On file with the author.

12. Paul Hardy, telephone communication, January 8, 2010.

13. The FRLT has since expanded to a staff of seven. The organization has helped conserve fifteen properties, totaling nearly 30,000 acres in the Feather River region.

14. Trina Cunningham is still the representative, but her tenure is almost up, and it is unclear whether another Maidu person will replace her on the board.

15. Trina Cunningham, presentation at the "Cultural Conservation Easements Workshop," Public Interest Environmental Law Conference, Many Nations Longhouse, University of Oregon, Eugene, Oregon, February 27, 2009. Transcript on file with the author.

16. Wood and O'Brien, in one of two seminal works by Wood on tribal engagement in the land trust movement, note the important role of Native board members for Native land trusts. This can be extended to Native participation on non-Native land trust boards as well: "Board members act as spokespersons for the organization and can educate the public about the Native approach to restoration." Mary Christina Wood and Matthew O'Brien, "Tribes as Trustees Again (Part II): Evaluating Four Models of Tribal Participation in the Conservation Trust Movement," *Stanford Environmental Law Journal* 27, no. 2 (2008): 531.

17. Paul Hardy, personal communication, Quincy, California, 2003.

18. Trina Cunningham, telephone communication, May 2009.

19. Chad L. Hoopes, *Domesticate or Exterminate: California Indian Treaties Unratified and Made Secret in 1852* (Loleta, CA: Redwood Coast Publications, 1975).

20. Greenville Rancheria (Maidu, Wintun) is in Plumas County, Susanville Rancheria (Maidu, Paiute, Pit River) is in Lassen County, and Mechoopda, Enterprise, Mooretown, and Berry Creek (Concow Maidu) rancherias are in Butte County. Rancherias are small reservations that were established in the early twentieth century for "homeless" California Indians following the nonratification of treaties with California tribes. The people who lived on these lands and their descendants became federally recognized tribes, often comprising multiple tribal groups. Some rancherias were canceled within a few decades of their establishment. Taylorsville, for example, was declared "abandoned" (its residents may have been forced off or were away working) and the land was put up for sale. The 1953 Congressional Resolution 108 removed tribes from federal supervision in order to assimilate members into the general public, which eliminated many

rancherias. California passed its own version of termination legislation (Public Law 85–671) in 1958, terminating sixty-one California tribes and bands. In 1983, Tillie Hardwick (Pomo) brought suit against the U.S. government on behalf of seventeen California rancherias, alleging that Congress had not lived up to its termination agreements to provide terminated tribes with improved roads, water systems, sanitation facilities, and vocational schools. The suit was victorious and all the rancherias were reinstated as federally recognized tribes. Other terminated tribes have achieved recognition by other means, including seeking Congressional support for tribe-specific recognition legislation or going through a lengthy process with the Office of Federal Acknowledgement. For more on termination and re-recognition, see Carole Goldberg and Duane Champagne, "Status and Needs of Unrecognized and Terminated California Indian Tribes," in *A Second Century of Dishonor: Federal Inequities and California Tribes* (UCLA: Native American Studies Center, prepared for the Advisory Council on California Indian Policy, Community Service/ Governance/ Census Task Force Report, March 27, 1996); Donald Fixico, *Termination and Relocation: Federal Indian Policy 1945–1960* (Albuquerque: University of New Mexico Press, 1986); Allogan Slagle, "Unfinished Justice: Completing the Restoration and Acknowledgement of California Indian Tribes," *American Indian Quarterly*, Special Issue, "The California Indians" 13, no. 4 (Autumn 1989); *Tillie Hardwick et al. v. United States*, Civil No. C-79–1910-SW (N.D. Cal. 1983).

21. See, for example, Kimberly Johnston-Dodds, *Early Laws and Policies Related to California Indians* (Sacramento: California Research Bureau, California State Library, 2002), http://www.library.ca.gov/crb/02/14/02-014.pdf; and George Harwood Phillips, *Indians and Indian Agents: The Origins of the Reservation System in California, 1849–1852* (Norman: University of Oklahoma Press, 1997), 131. One exception is Greenville Rancheria, which was initially an Indian boarding school. After the school burned down in 1921, it was opened up for Indian settlement. See, for example, Juliann Elizabeth Giles-Rankin, "An Ethnohistorical Reconstruction of the Greenville Indian Industrial School" (Master's Thesis, California State University, Chico, 1983).

22. For example, Farrell Cunningham ruefully remembered an incident with a state agency, in which the agency planned to expand a road over a cultural site. He went to the agency and advocated for the protection of the site, but the agency was not legally mandated to work with him because he is a member of an unrecognized tribe. Instead, the agency was mandated to consult with the Rancheria, and its representative at that time was unaware of the cultural site on the property. Therefore, despite Farrell's information, the agency could continue with its road project (Farrell Cunningham, personal communication, Greenville, California, 2006).

23. See, for example, Kat Anderson, *Tending the Wild: Native American Knowledge and the Management of California's Natural Resources* (Berkeley and Los Angeles: University of California Press, 2005), 39; Stephen Powers, *Tribes of California*

(Berkeley and Los Angeles: University of California Press, 1976) [Reprint of 1877 *Contributions to North American Ethnology, III* (Department of the Interior: U.S. Geographical and Geological Survey of the Rocky Mountain Region)].

24. Hafen was a founding FRLT board member and former executive director of the Roundhouse Council. Paul Hardy cited Hafen's and Trina Cunningham's assistance in outreach to Native constituents (e-mail message to author, January 6, 2010).

25. Jason Moghaddas, e-mail message to author, January 7, 2010.

26. Anonymous Plumas County residents, personal communications, 2006–2009.

27. Paul Hardy, telephone communication, December 7, 2009.

28. Ibid.

29. Ibid.

30. Ibid.

31. See Beth Rose Middleton, Chapter 5: "Cosmology," in "'We Were Here, We Are Here, We Will Always Be Here,'" in "A Political Ecology of Healing in Mountain Maidu Country" (PhD diss., University of California, Berkeley, 2008).

Chapter 1

1. Chuck Sams III, presentation at the "Cultural Conservation Easements Workshop," Public Interest Environmental Law Conference, Many Nations Longhouse, University of Oregon, Eugene, Oregon, February 27, 2009. Transcript on file with the author.

2. See, for example, how in 1836 the Eastern Band of Cherokee retained William Thomas, a white lawyer who had grown up among the Cherokee. The Band instructed Thomas to represent them in court, collect any payments owed to them, and use the majority of these funds to purchase back lands for them. John R. Finger, *The Eastern Band of Cherokees 1819–1900* (Knoxville, TN: University of Tennessee Press, 1984), 17. For a 2009 piece about Indian tribes' efforts to buy back their homelands across the United States, see Timberly Ross, "Indian Tribes Buy Back Thousands of Acres of Lands," Associated Press, December 27, 2009.

3. See, for example, *United States v. Washington* 506 F. Supp. 187 (W.D. Wash. 1980). Tribes pushed the state of Washington to protect salmon habitat in order to maintain availability of the amount of salmon that the tribes were entitled to in treaty agreements. In *Klamath Tribes v. United States Forest Service* No. 96–381-HA (D. Or. Oct. 2, 1996), the court ruled that the federal government had "a substantive duty to protect 'to the fullest extent possible' the tribes' treaty rights, and the resources on which those rights depend." Judith V. Royster and Michael C. Blumm, *Native American Natural Resources Law* (Durham, N.C.: Carolina Academic Press, 2002), 545. The court mandated that the USFS consult with the Klamath tribes before harvesting timber on lands where the tribes had rights to hunt, in order to ensure that their treaty-guaranteed resources would be protected. In *Sohappy v. Smith* (302 F. Supp. 899, 1969), the U.S. District Court in Oregon

interpreted *Puyallup Tribe et al. v. Department of Game, et al.* (391 U.S. 392, 1968) to mean that "the state cannot so manage the fishery that little or no harvestable portion of the run remains to reach the upper portions of the stream where the historic Indian places are mostly located."

4. Mary Christina Wood and Zachary Welcker, "Tribes as Trustees Again (Part I): The Emerging Tribal Role in the Conservation Trust Movement," *Harvard Environmental Law Review* 32, no. 2 (2008): 429.

5. Bowen Blair, "Introduction," in *Restoring Native Homelands: An Anniversary Project Gallery* (San Francisco: Trust for Public Land, 2009).

6. Wood and O'Brien, "Tribes as Trustees," 543.

7. The Trust for Public Land's Tribal and Native Lands Program Coordinator for Hawaii Kawika Burgess organized a seminar entitled, "Collaborating with Tribes and Native Communities" at the 2009 LTA Rally. Speakers included Hawk Rosales, executive director, InterTribal Sinkyone Wilderness Council, and Charles Sams III, then-executive director, Trust for Public Land's Tribal and Native Lands Program (now executive director of the Indian Country Conservancy). In the 1990s, Melissa Nelson, executive director of the Cultural Conservancy, organized panel sessions on cultural conservation easements, well before the concept was in use by land trusts and tribes throughout the United States.

8. See Wood and Welcker, "Tribes as Trustees," for more on the threat of climate change.

9. Charles F. Wilkinson, *American Indians, Time, and the Law* (New Haven, CT: Yale University Press, 1987), xi.

10. Vine Deloria Jr., *Custer Died for Your Sins* (London: Collier-Macmillan Limited, 1969), 35–36.

Chapter 2

1. Rob Aldrich and James Wyerman, eds., "Land Trust Alliance: 2005 National Land Trust Census Report," http://www.lta.org.

2. Land Trust Alliance, "Frequently Asked Questions: Land Trusts," http://www.landtrustalliance.org/conserve/faqs/faq-land-trusts.

3. Mary Ann King and Sally Fairfax, "Public Accountability and Conservation Easements: Learning from the Uniform Conservation Easement Act Debates," *Natural Resources Journal* 46, no. 1 (Winter 2006): 115.

4. Victoria Edwards, *Dealing in Diversity: America's Market for Nature Conservation* (Cambridge: Cambridge University Press, 1995), 139.

5. In a 1990 brochure, the Land Trust Alliance cited the existence of "village-improvement societies" to "improve the quality of life and of the environment" in nineteenth-century New England. Land Trust Alliance, "Land Trusts: Finding the Answers that Save the Land" (Washington, DC: Land Trust Alliance, 1990). See also Edwards, *Dealing in Diversity*, 47.

6. Sally K. Fairfax et al., *Buying Nature* (Cambridge, MA: MIT Press, 2005), 1–2, 31.

7. Including Fairfax et al., *Buying Nature*; Edwards, *Dealing in Diversity*; Randee G. Fenner, "Land Trusts: An Alternative Method of Preserving Open Space," *Vanderbilt Law Review* 33, no. 5 (1980): 1039, 1042; and Frederico Cheever, "Public Good and Private Magic in the Law of Land Trusts and Conservation Easements: A Happy Present and a Troubled Future," *Denver University Law Review* 73, no. 4 (1996).

8. Fairfax et al., *Buying Nature*, 5.

9. Ibid., 39.

10. See http://www.landtrustalliance.org/policy for information on relevant policies that increase conservation incentives, and how supporters can pressure their representatives to renew these incentives.

11. This draft list was compiled by workshop organizer Kawika Burgess, Trust for Public Land's Tribal and Native Lands program coordinator in Hawaii.

12. King and Fairfax, et al., "Public Accountability," 69.

13. Nancy A. McLaughlin, "Rethinking the Perpetual Nature of Conservation Easements," *Harvard Environmental Law Review* 29, no. 2 (2005).

14. Uniform Conservation Easement Act 1(1), 12 U.L.A. 170 (1996).

15. Wood and O'Brien, "Tribes as Trustees."

16. King and Fairfax, "Public Accountability."

17. Ibid.

18. William Whyte, "Securing Open Space for Urban America: Conservation Easements," *Urban Land Institute Technical Bulletin no. 36* (1959). See also Duncan M. Greene, "Dynamic Conservation Easements: Facing the Problem of Perpetuity in Land Conservation," *Seattle University Law Review* 28, no. 3 (Spring 2005), 890. According to Fairfax, et al. *Buying Nature*, 156, Whyte's enthusiasm for easements only increased with experience. After being involved in a conservation program for the Great River Road in Wisconsin, Whyte "concluded that conservation had reached the limits of regulation, and advocated working 'with the people who own most of the landscape so that private interest will be coupled with public interest.'" See also William Whyte, *The Last Landscape* (Garden City, NY: Doubleday, 1968).

19. UCEA 1996.

20. Cheever, "Public Good and Private Magic," 5.

21. According to Edwards, prior to the passage of the Uniform Conservation Easement Act, some states would not recognize conservation easements as perpetual unless the easement owner held neighboring, or appurtenant, lands that would benefit from the easement. Edwards, *Dealing in Diversity*, 70.

22. Dominic P. Parker, "Land Trusts and the Choice to Conserve Land with Full Ownership or Conservation Easements," *Natural Resources Journal* 44, no. 2 (Spring 2004): 483.

23. See, for example, Cheever, "Public Good and Private Magic."

24. See, for example, Charles Geisler, "Property Pluralism," in *Property and Values: Alternatives to Public and Private Ownership*, ed. Charles Geisler and Gail Daneker (Covelo, CA: Island Press, 2000).

25. Cheever "Public Good and Private Magic."

26. Elizabeth Byers and Karin Marchetti Ponte, *Conservation Easement Handbook* (Washington, DC: Land Trust Alliance and Trust for Public Land, 2005), 189.

27. Ibid.

28. For a discussion of similar questions as to whether restoration work serves areas most in need of restoration, see Juliet Christian-Smith and A. Merenlender, "The Disconnect between Restoration Goals and Practices: A Case Study of Watershed Restoration in the Russian River Basin, California," *Restoration Ecology* 17, no. 7 (2009). For an examination or whether conservation easements meet goals of increasing biological diversity, see Adena Rissman and Adina M. Merenlender, "The Conservation Contributions of Conservation Easements: Analysis of the San Francisco Bay Area Protected Lands Spatial Database," *Ecology and Society* 13, no. 1 (2008): 40.

29. Edwards, *Dealing in Diversity*, 42.

30. Fairfax et al., *Buying Nature*, 175.

31. A qualified appraiser cannot be related to or employed by either the donor or the easement holder, for example. See Byers and Ponte, *Conservation Easement Handbook*, 89 for the characteristics of a qualified appraiser.

32. Byers and Ponte, *Conservation Easement Handbook*, 108–13.

33. As listed in California Civil Code 815.3.

34. Byers and Ponte, *Conservation Easement Handbook*, 81.

35. In 2003, for example, fourteen states (including California) offered tax credits for landowners donating easements. Ibid., 94.

36. For more on HR 1831 and S812, see http://www.landtrustalliance.org/policy/taxincentives/federal.

37. Byers and Ponte, *Conservation Easement Handbook*, 94–98.

38. IRC 170(h)(1)(2006); and Lawrence R. Kueter and Christopher S. Jensen, "Conservation Easements: An Underdeveloped Tool to Protect Cultural Resources," *Denver University Law Review* 83, no. 4 (2006): 1058.

39. Title 26 (Internal Revenue), Chapter 1 (Internal Revenue Service, Department of the Treasury), Part 1 (Income Taxes), 1.170A-14 (Qualified Conservation Contributions), subpart (a), http://edocket.access.gpo.gov/cfr_2003/aprqtr/pdf/26cfr1.170A-14.pdf.

40. See, for example, McLaughlin, "Rethinking;" Julia D. Mahoney, "Perpetual Restrictions on Land and the Problem of the Future," *Virginia Law Review* 88, no. 4 (2002).

41. Cheever, "Public Good and Private Magic."

42. For some examples among many, see Cheever, "Public Good and Private Magic;" Fairfax et al., *Buying Nature*; McLaughlin, "Rethinking"; Mahoney, "Perpetual Restrictions;" and King and Fairfax, "Public Accountability."

43. According to Cheever, "[client's] lawyer's . . . paint a picture of the Local Area Land Trust as a clique of local landowners who have manipulated the state conservation easement statute and federal tax law for their own personal ends

and financial gain—private land use control to achieve private ends." "Public Good and Private Magic" 9. See also Ray Ring, "Write-Off on the Range," *High Country News*, May 30, 2005; and David B. Ottaway and Joe Stephens, "Big Green: Inside the Nature Conservancy," *The Washington Post*, May 4, 2003.

44. McLaughlin, "Rethinking," 426.

45. Ibid., 429

46. Greene, "Dynamic Conservation Easements," 885.

47. Ibid., 902–903.

48. Byers and Ponte, *Conservation Easement Handbook*, 185–86, for example, recommends having an "amendment policy" which carefully examines the justification for amendments to the conservation easement.

49. Cheever, "Public Good and Private Magic," 10.

50. McLaughlin, "Rethinking," 428.

51. Gerald Korngold, "Privately Held Conservation Servitudes: A Policy Analysis in the Context of In-Gross Real Covenants and Easements," *Texas Law Review* 63, no.3 (November 1984) Cheever, "Public Good and Private Magic," 11.

52. Edwards, *Dealing in Diversity*, 61–62.

53. Cheever, "Public Good and Private Magic," 9; Jeffrey A. Blackie, "Conservation Easements and the Doctrine of Changed Conditions," *Hastings Law Journal* 40, no. 6 (1989): 1187; Korngold, "Privately Held Conservation Servitudes," 484–86.

54. Wood and O'Brien, "Tribes as Trustees," 526.

55. For example, see Byers and Ponte's chapter, "Dealing with Change: Amendments and Termination," for suggestions (*Conservation Easement Handbook*, 183–97).

56. Cheever, "Public Good and Private Magic," 12.

57. Byers and Ponte, *Conservation Easement Handbook*, 169–73; Wood and O'Brien specifically encourage land trusts to designate tribal backup holders (see Wood and O'Brien, "Tribes as Trustees," 491–92).

58. Winona LaDuke, *All Our Relations: Native Struggles for Land and Life* (Boston: South End Press, 1999).

59. Malcolm Margolin, "California Indians and Conservation," *News from Native California* 11, no. 2 (1997/1998). See also Anderson, *Tending the Wild*, the seminal text on California Indian land stewardship.

60. Hawk Rosales, presentation at the "Cultural Conservation Easements Workshop," Public Interest Environmental Law Conference, Many Nations Longhouse, University of Oregon, Eugene, Oregon, February 27, 2009. Transcript on file with the author.

61. See, for example, Wood and Welcker, "Tribes as Trustees"; Vine Deloria Jr., *God Is Red: A Native View of Religion* (Golden, CO: Fulcrum Publishing, 1994).

62. Sams, Cultural Conservation Easements workshop, February 27, 2009.

63. Wood and Welcker, "Tribes as Trustees." This terminology is a nod to the

concept of the "public trust," which makes the federal government responsible for holding the resources necessary for public survival (land, air, water) in trust and overseeing their sustainability, as a good trustee would. As Tsosie argues, the "public trust" is a general concept referring to the "public's interest in wise stewardship of common resources," as opposed to the tribal trust doctrine, which is a specific and lasting treaty relationship between the federal government and an Indian tribe. Rebecca Tsosie, "The Conflict between the 'Public Trust' and the 'Indian Trust' Doctrines: Federal Public Land Policy and Native Nations," *Tulsa Law Review* 39, no. 2 (2003): 281.

64. Dune Lankard, Bioneers 2008, available at http://www.youtube.com/watch?v=YemB5BU17u4.

65. I.R.C. 170(h)(4)(a) 2006; Kueter and Jensen, "Conservation Easements."

66. As Byers and Ponte note, the value of the tax benefit depends on the landowner's income, the value of the conservation easement, and the landowner's other deductions, among other variables. Byers and Ponte, *Conservation Easement Handbook*, 81.

67. Hawk Rosales, Cultural Conservation Easements workshop, February 27, 2009.

68. Ibid.

69. See, for example, Andrew Gulliford, *Sacred Objects and Sacred Places: Preserving Tribal Traditions* (Boulder: University Press of Colorado, 2000); Deloria Jr., *God Is Red*.

70. The Stewardship Council is charged with divesting Pacific Gas and Electric Company lands for conservation and public benefit purposes. For more on the Council, see http://www.stewardshipcouncil.org.

71. Farrell Cunningham, *Maidu Summit Land Management Plan*, 4. On file with the author.

72. Hawk Rosales, Cultural Conservation Easements workshop, February 27, 2009.

73. UCEA 1996.

74. Kueter and Jensen, "Conservation Easements."

75. Senate Bill 18 (Burton) 2004.

76. N.M. Stat. Ann. 47–12A-2 (2006).

77. Kueter and Jensen, "Conservation Easements," 1063.

78. Wood and O'Brien, "Tribes as Trustees," 518; Curtis Berkey, e-mail message to author, November 19, 2009; Chuck Sams, e-mail message to author, November 12, 2009.

79. IRC 170(h)(4)(b).

80. Kueter and Jensen, "Conservation Easements."

81. Ibid., 1066.

82. See, for example, Dean Suagee's description of Traditional Cultural Properties and how they are determined and then nominated for protection in the National Register of Historic Places. Dean Suagee, "The Cultural Heritage

of Indian Tribes and the Preservation of Biological Diversity," *Arizona State Law Journal* 31, no. 2 (1999): 522–23.

83. See IRC 170(c)(1).

84. Legal precedents include the Archaeological Resources Protection Act (1979), the Native American Graves Protection and Repatriation Act (1990), and the National Historic Preservation Act (1966). See also Wood and O'Brien, "Tribes as Trustees," 520.

85. Ibid., 519–20.

86. Kueter and Jensen, "Conservation Easements," 1062.

87. Wood and O'Brien, "Tribes as Trustees," 522.

88. Fairfax et al., *Buying Nature*, 42.

89. Edwards, *Dealing in Diversity*, 8.

90. Byers and Ponte, *Conservation Easement Handbook*, 98.

91. Sams, Cultural Conservation Easements workshop, February 27, 2009.

92. See, for example, *Lyng v. Northwest Indian Cemetery Protective Association*, 485 U.S. 439 (1988), in which the U.S. Forest Service's right to put a logging road through a sacred area on National Forest land was affirmed because the tribal right to worship on that area could not be allowed to trump other uses of the land. Similarly, *Bear Lodge Multiple Use Association v. Babbitt* (2 F. Supp. 2d 1448, D. Wyo. 1998, aff'd 175 F.3d 814, 10th Cir. 1999) affirmed that the spiritual value of the rock formation known as Devils Tower National Monument could not override a climber's right as a member of the public enjoying the site. For more on the significance of Devils Tower, see Gulliford, *Sacred Objects*, 162–67.

93. Code of Federal Regulations, Part 151, Section 13, "Title Examination." Also according to one BIA employee, a conservation easement would likely be included in the Exhibit B page of a Title Report, which the U.S. Department of the Interior (DOI) BIA Solicitor would review in a fee-to-trust application. If the tribe had accepted the conservation easement "it might be acceptable for the U.S. DOI." One consideration for the BIA is the possibility that a future tribal administration would disregard the easement "because of new tribal priorities," and then the BIA might be held responsible (e-mail message to author, May 4, 2010).

94. For example, see the Kumeyaay-Diegueño Land Conservancy (KDLC) section in the Native American Land Conservancy case. This point of view was expressed by Louis Guassac, first executive director of the KDLC (telephone communication and e-mails to author, September-October 2008).

95. According to Deloria Jr., the exemption of Indian land from taxes "is a general right of Indian tribes based upon their cessions of land in the last century." Further, "Most Indian tribes feel that they paid taxes for all time when they gave up some two billion acres of land to the United States." Deloria Jr., *Custer Died for Your Sins*, 39.

96. See, for example, Cheever, "Public Good and Private Magic."

97. Paul VanDevelder, *Coyote Warrior: One Man, Three Tribes, and a Trial that Forged a Nation* (New York: Little, Brown, and Company, 2004), 152.

98. Land Trust Alliance, "About Land Trusts" page, http://www.landtrustalliance.org/conserve/about-land-trusts.

99. For more background on The Nature Conservancy, see Edwards, *Dealing in Diversity*, 38–46.

100. According to an article by former California Indian Basketweavers Association Executive Director Sara Greensfelder, TNC is open to working with basket weavers to increase their access to resources on TNC's preserves. Sara Greensfelder, "The Nature Conservancy," *News from Native California* 6, no. 1 (1991/1992): 28.

101. See the Trust for Public Land Web site, http://www.tpl.org.

102. Blair, "Introduction."

103. Ibid.

104. Ibid.

105. Trust for Public Land, description of the Tribal and Native Lands Program, http://www.tpl.org/tier3_cdl.cfm?content_item_id=1180&folder_id=217. For more on the Program's mission, see http://www.tpl.org/tier3_cdl.cfm?content_item_id=13224&folder_id=217.

106. Sams, Cultural Conservation Easements workshop, February 27, 2009.

107. Ibid.

108. Ibid.

109. Ibid.

110. Stephen Cornell and Joseph Kalt, "Sovereignty and Nation-Building: The Development Challenge in Indian Country Today," *American Indian Culture and Research Journal* 22, no. 3 (1998); Stephen Cornell and Joseph P. Kalt, eds, *What Can Tribes Do? Strategies and Institutions in American Indian Economic Development* (Los Angeles: American Indian Studies Center, University of California, Los Angeles, 1992); Robert A. Williams, "Why Are Some Native Nations More Successful than Others?" lecture presented at the University of California, Berkeley, September 26, 2006.

111. Sams, Cultural Conservation Easements workshop, February 27, 2009.

112. I use the term "articulate" here in the sense of joining together two different elements, drawing on the work of Stuart Hall. "Race, Articulation, and Societies Structured in Dominance," in *Critical Race Theories: Text and Context*, ed. Philomena Essed and David Theo Goldberg (Malden, MA: Wiley-Blackwell Publishers, 2001); and James Clifford, *On the Edges of Anthropology (Interviews)* (Chicago: Prickly Paradigm Press, 2003).

113. "The Indian Country Conservancy: Conserving Land, Water, and Air to Make Indian Country Whole Again" (brochure produced by Indian Country Conservancy, 2010, http://www.indiancountryconservancy.org).

114. Wood and Welcker, "Tribes as Trustees," 58.

115. For an overview of the treaty-making period and individual treaties, see Francis Paul Prucha, *American Indian Treaties* (Berkeley and Los Angeles: University of California Press, 1994).

116. Joanne Barker, "For Whom Sovereignty Matters," in *Sovereignty Matters*, ed. Joanne Barker (Lincoln: University of Nebraska Press, 2005).

117. See, for example, the treaties negotiated between Governor Isaac Stevens and tribes in the Pacific Northwest. A December 26, 1854, treaty made at Medicine Creek, with the Nisqually, Puyallup, Steilacoom, Squaxin, and other tribes, includes this language: "The right of taking fish, at all usual and accustomed grounds and stations, is further secured to said Indians" (see Prucha, *American Indian Treaties*, 252, and Appendix B: Ratified Indian Treaties). That was repeated in subsequent treaties, such as the Treaty of June 9, 1855, with the Yakima Tribe (12 Stat. 951) and the July 16, 1855, Hell Gate Treaty with the Flathead, Kootenai, and Upper Pend d'Oreille.

118. Deloria Jr., *Custer Died for Your Sins*, 28.

119. Ibid., 35–36; Gulliford, *Sacred Objects*, 111.

120. *Lone Wolf v. Hitchcock* (187 U.S. 553, 23 S. Ct. 216, 47 L. Ed. 299 [1903]), for example, upholds Congressional plenary power over tribes to "abrogate the provisions of an Indian treaty." See David H. Getches, Charles F. Wilkinson, and Robert A. Williams, Jr., *Cases and Materials on Federal Indian Law*, 4th ed. (St. Paul, MN: West Group, 1998), 183.

121. See Tsosie, "'Public Trust' and 'Indian Trust,'" for a comprehensive discussion of the conflict between preserving tribal treaty rights and the government's trust responsibility to Indian nations and its responsibility to preserve public access and rights on public lands. See also Dan Tarlock and Holly A. Doremus, *Water War in the Klamath Basin: Macho Law, Combat Biology, and Dirty Politics* (Covelo, CA: Island Press, 2008).

122. Gulliford, *Sacred Objects*, 111.

123. See, for example, Wood and Welcker, "Tribes as Trustees"; Farrell Cunningham, "Take Care of the Land and the Land Will Take Care of You: Traditional Ecology in Native California," *News from Native California* 18, no. 4 (2005); Margolin, "California Indians and Conservation."

124. Suagee, "Cultural Heritage of Indian Tribes," 533.

Chapter 3

1. Dorceta Taylor, "American Environmentalism: The Role of Race, Class, and Gender in Shaping Activism, 1820–1995," *Race, Gender, and Class* 5, no. 1 (1997).

2. Ibid.; Robin Turner and Diana Pei Wu, *Environmental Justice and Environmental Racism: An Annotated Bibliography and General Overview Focusing on U.S. Literature, 1996–2002*, Berkeley Workshop on Environmental Politics Bibliography No. B 02–7 (Berkeley: Institute of International Studies, University of California, Berkeley, 2002), 4.

3. See, for example, Alfred L. Kroeber, *Handbook of the Indians of California* (Berkeley: California Book Company, 1925); Robert Heizer, *Languages, Territories, and Names of California Indian Tribes* (Berkeley and Los Angeles: University of California Press, 1966); Anderson, *Tending the Wild*.

4. Environmental justice is defined by Senate Bill 115 as "the fair treatment of people of all races, cultures, and incomes with respect to the development, adoption, implementation, and enforcement of environmental laws and policies." Senate Bill 115 (introduced by Senator Solis) 1999, http://info.sen.ca.gov/pub/99-00/bill/sen/sb_0101-0150/sb_115_bill_19990909_amended_asm.html.

5. See M. K. Heiman, "Race, Waste, and Class: New Perspectives on Environmental Justice, *Antipode* 28, no. 2 (1996); S. L. Cutter, "Race, Class, and Environmental Justice," *Progress in Human Geography* 19, no. 1 (1995); and Turner and Wu, *Environmental Justice and Environmental Racism*, 10–12.

6. Turner and Wu, *Environmental Justice and Environmental Racism*, 10.

7. William H. Rollins, "Imperial Shades of Green: Conservation and Environmental Chauvinism in the German Colonial Project," *German Studies Review* 22, no. 2 (1999): 187.

8. See, for example, Karl Jacoby, *Crimes Against Nature: Squatters, Poachers, Thieves, and the Hidden History of American Conservation* (Berkeley and Los Angeles: University of California Press, 2001); Mark Spence, *Dispossessing the Wilderness: Indian Removal and the Making of the National Parks* (New York: Oxford University Press, 1999).

9. Roderick P. Neumann, "Ways of Seeing Africa: Colonial Recasting of African Society and Landscape in Serengeti National Park," *Ecumene* 2 (1995): 161f.

10. Rollins, "Imperial Shades of Green," 18.

11. See Anderson, *Tending the Wild.*

12. Ibid., 2.

13. As legal scholar Rebecca Tsosie explains, "Native peoples have a unique [legal, moral, political, and cultural] relationship with their ancestral homelands, which were forcibly taken by the U.S. government during the nineteenth century for use as 'public lands.'" (Tsosie, "'Public Trust' and 'Indian Trust,'" 271).

14. Although the National Park Service was not established until 1916, the first acquisition that it now manages was the Hot Springs reservation in Arkansas, set aside in 1832 (Fairfax, et al., *Buying Nature*, 36.

15. Jacoby, *Crimes Against Nature*, 151.

16. See, for example, ibid., 169: "The ultimate goal of conservation, however, remained not the elimination of industrial capitalism but its reformation." Gifford Pinchot, the first chief of the U.S. Forest Service, argued that conservation would ensure the supplies that underlie business stability. "Conservation meant predictability" for industry.

17. Ibid., 187.

18. Steven J. Crum, "Pretending They Didn't Exist: The Timbisha Shoshone Tribe of Death Valley, California, and the Death Valley National Monument up to 1933," *Southern California Quarterly* 84, nos. 3/4 (2002).

19. Robert J. Paton, "Back into the Park: California Desert Protection Act Offers Hope to Timbisha Shoshone," *News from Native California* 8, no. 4 (1995).

20. Marina Drummer, "Endangered Cultures, Endangered Species, and the Law," *News from Native California* 15, no. 2 (2001/2002): 33.

21. Fairfax et al., *Buying Nature*, 99.

22. For an example of this in northern California, see Beth Rose Middleton, "Seeking Spatial Representation: Mapping Mountain Maidu Allotment Lands," *Ethnohistory* 57 (3) (Summer 2010): 363–88.

23. "The Treaty of September 30, 1854, with the Bois Forte Band of Chippewa affirmed subsistence rights to an area including what is now the Boundary Waters Canoe Wilderness Area." Eric Freedman, "When Indigenous Rights and Wilderness Collide," *American Indian Quarterly* 26, no. 3 (2002): 281.

24. Ibid., 378.

25. Fairfax et al., *Buying Nature*, 103–32.

26. Fairfax et al., *Buying Nature*, 113. Fee title is a designation of land ownership that refers to owning the greatest possible number of rights to land. A fee title owner has the right to use and dispose of his or her land, subject only to state and federal laws, applicable taxes, eminent domain, and escheat (the process by which property reverts to the state if the owner dies without heirs).

27. Jeff Romm, "The Coincidental Order of Environmental Justice," in *Justice and Natural Resources: Concepts, Strategies, and Applications*, ed. Kathryn Mutz, Gary Bryner, and Douglas Benner (Washington, D.C.: Island Press, 2002).

28. With the exception of the Antiquities Act of 1906 (16 USC 431–433). The Antiquities Act enabled the President to set aside historic sites in order to protect them from pot-hunters, and to enable archaeologists to study them. Tribal members were not mentioned as beneficiaries. For a comment on this point, see Gulliford, *Sacred Objects*, 100.

29. Tsosie, "'Public Trust' and 'Indian Trust,'" 301.

30. Suagee, "Cultural Heritage of Indian Tribes."

31. Mary Ann King, "Co-Management or Contracting? Agreements between Native American Tribes and the U.S. National Park Service Pursuant to the 1994 Tribal Self-Governance Act," *Harvard Environmental Law Review* 31, no. 2 (2007).

32. See, for example, the MOUs described in chapter 5, "Native American Land Conservancy"; and Lawrence M. Lesko and Renee G. Thakali, "Traditional Knowledge and Tribal Partnership on the Kaibab National Forest with an Emphasis on the Hopi Interagency Management," in *Trusteeship in Change*, ed. Richmond Clow and Imre Sutton (Norman: University of Oklahoma Press, 2001).

33. 36 CFR Part 800: Protection of Historic Properties, http://www.achp .gov/regs-rev04.pdf/.

34. Suagee, "Cultural Heritage of Indian Tribes," 531.

35. Patricia Parker and Thomas King, "National Register Bulletin 38: Guidelines for Evaluating and Documenting Traditional Cultural Properties," http:// www.nps.gov/nr/publications/bulletins/nrb38/ (1990, revised 1992, 1998). Some non-Natives, including Congressman Wally Herger of northern California, became concerned that these sacred-site protections would be misused by tribes to block development: "The idea of being able to look at a site, form a cultural

tie to it, and then somehow draw a line around it is a practice that could get out of hand," he told the *Mt. Shasta Herald* in August 1994 (see Michelle Alvarez, "Mount Shasta: A Question of Power," *News from Native California* 8, no. 3 (Winter 1994–1995): 4–7.

36. See, for example, Crum, "Pretending They Didn't Exist."

37. Konrad Liegel and Gene Duvernoy, "Land Trusts: Shaping the Landscape of Our Nation," *Natural Resources and Environment* 17, no. 2 (2002).

38. For example, Rissman and Merelender found in their study of conservation easements in the San Francisco Bay Area that properties held by land trusts were less likely to allow for recreation and access than public conservation lands ("Conservation Contributions").

39. Edwards, *Dealing in Diversity*, 161.

40. *Bear Lodge Multiple Use Association v. Babbit* 175 F.3d (10th Cir. 1999); *The Access Fund v. U.S. Dept. of Agriculture, U.S. Forest Service*, 499 F.3d 1036 (9th Cir. 2007); and regarding the judge's decision to uphold the U.S. Forest Service's right to protect historic and cultural resources at Cave Rock, see http://www .washoetribe.us/content/view/24/2/.

41. Beth Rose Middleton, "Soda Rock/ChuChuYamBa," in Middleton, "'We Were Here.'"

42. Tsosie, "'Public Trust' and 'Indian Trust,'" 300.

43. Ward Churchill, "The Earth Is Our Mother," in *The State of Native America*, ed. Annette Jaimes (Boston, MA: South End Press, 1992), 175.

44. Turner and Wu, *Environmental Justice and Environmental Racism*, 10.

45. Fairfax et al., *Buying Nature*, 14.

46. For example, Deloria Jr., *God Is Red*; Linda Tuhiwai Smith, *Decolonizing Methodologies* (London: Zed Books, 1999); LaDuke, *All Our Relations*; Winona LaDuke, *Recovering the Sacred: The Power of Naming and Claiming* (Cambridge: South End Press, 2005); Cunningham, "Take Care of the Land."

47. Fairfax et al., *Buying Nature*, 272.

Chapter 4

1. See the InterTribal Sinkyone Wilderness Council Web site, available via the Trees Foundation Web site, http://www.treesfoundation.org/affiliates/specific-22. The following articles also discuss the InterTribal Sinkyone Wilderness Council's development of a precedent-setting intertribal wilderness: Chris Clarke, "Inter-Tribal Sinkyone Park—It Could Happen Soon," *News from Native California* 7, no. 2 (Spring 1993); George Snyder, "Tribes Join for Tribute to Indian Life: 3,800-Acre Wilderness Park Planned," *San Francisco Chronicle*, May 23, 1995; InterTribal Sinkyone Wilderness Council, "The Vision and the Work," *News from Native California* 11, no. 2, Supplement on California Indians and Conservation (1997–1998); William Claiborne, "Native American Tribes Take Back the Land in California," *The Washington Post*, October 7, 1997; "First Wilderness Park Owned by American Indians to Open," *Contra Costa Times*, October 11, 1997; Pacific Forest Trust,

"Sinkyone InterTribal Wilderness," *Pacific Forests*, Winter 1998; William Poole, "Return of the Sinkyone: Long-Contested Forestlands become the First Native American Intertribal Park," *Land and People*, Spring 1998.

2. Claiborne, "Native American Tribes"; *The Run to Save Sinkyone* (film), directed by Jonathan L. Rosales and produced by the InterTribal Sinkyone Wilderness Council, 1994; Gladys A. Nomland, *Sinkyone Notes* (Berkeley: University of California Press, 1935); Chris Clarke, "Maintaining the Wealth: The Inter-Tribal Sinkyone Wilderness," *News from Native California* 7, no. 4 (1994): 45–46; William Poole, "Return of the Sinkyone," *Sierra*, November/ December 1996; Harriet Rhoades, "Relevance of Sinkyone to Local Peoples: Cultural Heritage Explained," *Redwood Times*, April 9, 2008.

3. The exact date of the massacre is unknown.

4. Nomland, *Sinkyone Notes*.

5. Dale Champion, "Conservationists Buy Timberland in Mendocino," *San Francisco Chronicle*, December 31, 1986.

6. *Environmental Information Protection Center, Inc. (EPIC) v. Johnson*, 170 Cal. App. 3d 604, 612 (Cal. App. 1st D. 1985).

7. Ibid.

8. The California Coastal Conservancy is a state agency, but it operates similarly to a land trust in that it purchases parcels for conservation and other public benefits. The conservancy is also charged with mediating between parties to reach mutually acceptable conservation and public benefit outcomes. See the California Coastal Conservancy Web site at http://scc.ca.gov/about.

9. California State Parks, *Sinkyone Wilderness State Park Final General Plan and Environmental Impact Report* (Sacramento: California State Parks, 2006), ES-1.

10. Neal Fishman, personal communication, Oakland, California, February 15, 2008.

11. Ibid.

12. Priscilla Hunter, telephone communication, November 2007.

13. Ricardo Tapia, e-mail message to author, October 1, 2007.

14. Priscilla Hunter, telephone communication, November 2007.

15. Hawk Rosales, telephone communication, July 2007.

16. Neal Fishman, "Sinkyone Lost and Found," *California Coast and Ocean* 12, no. 3 (Autumn 1996).

17. Laurie Wayburn, telephone communication, August 28, 2008.

18. Ibid; Neal Fishman, personal communication, Oakland, California, February 15, 2008.

19. Neal Fishman, "Sinkyone Lost and Found," 18.

20. See http://www.treesfoundation.org/affiliates/specific-22.

21. See Emily Viglielmo, "*The Run to Save Sinkyone*: Local documentary to Be Shown at Sundance Film Festival," *Ukiah Daily Journal*, Friday, December 30–Saturday, December 31, 1994.

22. Priscilla Hunter, telephone communication, November 2007.

23. Tobias Young, "Mendocino Forest Sale OK'd," *The Press Democrat*, March 21, 1995.

24. Michael Corbett, "Native Americans to Acquire Land for a Coast Redwood Park," *Los Angeles Times*, April 12, 1995, Part A (Metro).

25. Laurie Betlach, telephone communication, February 14, 2008.

26. Laurie Wayburn, telephone communication, August 28, 2008.

27. Valued at $1.1 million in 1986, the land price increased to $3.4 million by 1996. By granting the PFT $2 million for an easement, the price dropped to $1.4 million, which the Council paid in 1996 (Neal Fishman, personal communication, Oakland, California, February 15, 2008).

28. Laurie Wayburn, telephone communication, August 28, 2008.

29. See "Sinkyone InterTribal Wilderness," in *Pacific Forests: Private Forest Issues in California, Oregon, and Washington*, Pacific Forest Trust (Winter 1998).

30. Laurie Wayburn, telephone communication, August 28, 2008.

31. Ibid.

32. Neal Fishman, personal communication, Oakland, California, February 15, 2008.

33. Laurie Wayburn, telephone communication, August 28, 2008.

34. "Wood Theft from Sinkyone Property Results in Conviction," *Redwood Times*, April 2, 2008.

35. Laurie Wayburn, telephone communication, August 28, 2008.

36. Sharon Duggan, telephone communication, February 15, 2008. Duggan was one of the lawyers who successfully litigated the *EPIC v. Johnson* case on behalf of the Environmental Protection Information Center and the International Indian Treaty Council.

37. Ibid.

38. Ibid.

39. Ibid.

40. Quote from the conservation easement held by the PFT on land owned by the InterTribal Sinkyone Wilderness Council.

41. Eric Goldsmith, presentation at the Public Interest Environmental Law Conference, University of Oregon, March 7, 2008.

42. Quote from the conservation easement held by Sanctuary Forest on land owned by the InterTribal Sinkyone Wilderness Council.

43. Eric Goldsmith, telephone communication, February 15, 2008.

44. Ibid.

45. Neal Fishman, personal communication, Oakland, California, February 15, 2008.

46. Hawk Rosales, telephone communication, November 2007.

47. Priscilla Hunter, telephone communication, November 2007.

48. Luwana Quitiquit, telephone communication, September 8, 2008.

49. Ibid.

50. Ibid.

51. Hawk Rosales, e-mail message to author, November 2007.

52. Priscilla Hunter, telephone communication, November 2007.

53. Elizabeth Hansen, telephone communication, September 11, 2008.

54. David Edmunds, telephone communication, September 12, 2008.

55. Eric Goldsmith, telephone communication, February 15, 2008.

56. "State Parks Presents ITSWC Director with Award," *Redwood Times*, June 4, 2009.

57. Hawk Rosales, telephone communication, November 2007.

58. Ibid.

59. For example, the Council hosted an intertribal event at Richardson Grove to protect Sinkyone lands and cultural values. It included an afternoon of traditional song and prayer, and Native and non-Native speakers voicing opposition to a CalTrans proposal that would damage the grove. See InterTribal Sinkyone Wilderness Council, "Intertribal cultural event held at Richardson Grove," *Redwood Times*, September 9, 2009.

60. Hawk Rosales, telephone communication, 2009.

61. One source for this information is Ray Raphael and Freeman House, *Humboldt History*, Volume 1: *Two Peoples, One Place* (Eureka, CA: Humboldt County Historical Society, 2007), 17; see also Rhoades, "Relevance of Sinkyone."

62. Atta Stevenson, telephone communication, September 21, 2008.

63. Ibid.

64. Ibid.

65. Ibid.

66. Ibid.

67. Ibid.

68. Hawk Rosales, telephone communication, November 2007.

69. Elizabeth Hansen, telephone communication, September 11, 2008.

70. Eric Goldsmith, telephone communication, February 15, 2008.

71. Laurie Wayburn, telephone communication, August 28, 2008.

72. Eric Goldsmith, telephone communication, February 15, 2008.

73. Hawk Rosales, telephone communication, 2008; Eric Goldsmith, telephone communication, February 15, 2008.

74. Eric Goldsmith, telephone communication, February 15, 2008.

75. Laurie Wayburn, telephone communication, August 28, 2008.

76. Eric Goldsmith, telephone communication, February 15, 2008.

Chapter 5

1. LaDuke, *Recovering the Sacred*.

2. Census 2000, http://factfinder.census.gov/servlet/SAFFFacts?_event=&geo_id=04000US06&_geoContext=01000US%7C04000US06&_street=&_county=&_cityTown=&_state=04000US06&_zip=&_lang=en&_sse=on&ActiveGeoDiv=&_useEV=&pctxt=fph&pgsl=040&_submenuId=factsheet_

1&ds_name=ACS_2008_3YR_SAFF&_ci_nbr=null&qr_name=null&reg= null%3Anull&_keyword=&_industry=. Census data from 2006–2007 reports a much higher number of 689,000, according to "Census figures show slow rise in Native population," May 2, 2008. Available online at http://www .kumeyaay.com/2008/05/census-figures-show-slow-rise-in-native-population/.

3. Kurt Russo, "Introduction to the Native American Lands Conservancy," in *In the Land of Three Peaks: The Old Woman Mountains Preserve* (Valencia, CA: Delta, 2005).

4. Ibid.

5. Russo, "Stewarding a Healing Landscape," in ibid.

6. Kurt Russo, telephone communication, 2008.

7. Dean Mike, presentation to the "Desertlands/Sacred Lands Conference," Palm Desert, California, October 30, 2009.

8. For example, see Steve Lopez, "A Spirit Run for the Desert," *News from Native California* 5, no. 4 (1991): 20–21. Lopez describes a Spirit Run in 1991 to protest the proposed radioactive dump at Ward Valley, in which Native runners ran from Chemehuevi Valley, through the Stepladder Mountains, to Ward Valley, and through Ward Valley to complete the run in the Old Woman Mountains.

9. Philip Klasky, "An Extreme and Solemn Relationship: The Battle against Radioactive Waste Dumping in the Mojave Desert," *News from Native California* 9, no. 2 (1995–1996).

10. For a full geographical and physical description of the Old Woman Mountains, see Kurt Russo, *In the Land of Three Peaks*.

11. See description provided by The Cultural Conservancy: Salt Song Project, http://www.nativeland.org/saltsong.html#songs.

12. Tom Askew, telephone communication, December 31, 2009.

13. Ibid.

14. Kurt Russo, personal communication, Cabazon, California, October 25, 2006.

15. See the NALC Web site, http://www.nalc4all.org.

16. Kurt Russo, e-mail message to author, May 4, 2010.

17. Clifford Trafzer, telephone communication, September 23, 2008.

18. Ibid.

19. Kurt Russo, e-mail message to author, January 4, 2010.

20. Kurt Russo, "Theresa Mike: A Passion for the People." This chapter is slated for inclusion to a book provisionally titled *Activist Minority Western American Women* (Lubbock: Texas Tech University Press, forthcoming).

21. Russo, *In the Land of Three Peaks*.

22. Mike Madrigal, presentation to the "Desertlands/Sacred Lands Conference," Palm Desert, California, October 31, 2009.

23. Tom Askew, telephone communication, December 31, 2009.

24. Ibid.

25. Kurt Russo, telephone communication, 2007.

26. Ibid. In 2009, Russo expanded on this description of the NALC board: "Our board includes Nuwu [Chemehuevi, Paiute, Mojave] people. None are appointed by their councils. It grew out of an intertribal cultural group. It's not political. It's not territorial. It's not bounded. It's spatialized." Presentation to the "Cultural Conservation Easements Workshop," Public Interest Environmental Law Conference, Many Nations Longhouse, University of Oregon, Eugene, Oregon, February 27, 2009. Transcript on file with the author.

27. Kurt Russo, telephone communication, 2007.

28. Ibid.

29. Ibid.

30. Ibid.

31. Ibid. A "Community Note" in *The Press-Enterprise* (Riverside, California, November 24, 2005) announced the NALC's annual golf tournament fundraiser, and it noted that the conservancy "is a group of individuals and tribes who have been actively pursuing conservation for the past five years, and the event is its primary source of funding."

32. Kurt Russo, e-mail message to author, May 4, 2010.

33. Kurt Russo, telephone communication, 2008.

34. Clifford Trafzer, telephone communication, September 23, 2008.

35. Kurt Russo, telephone communication, December 4, 2009.

36. Kurt Russo, telephone communication, 2007.

37. Ibid.

38. Louis Guassac, telephone communication and e-mail messages to author, September-October 2008.

39. Kurt Russo, telephone communication, 2007.

40. Ibid.

41. Ibid.

42. Ibid.

43. The NALC helped the KDLC to complete its 501(c)3 nonprofit application and submit it in March 2010, and the KLDC received its nonprofit status in August 2010. (Kurt Russo, e-mail message to author, May 4 and August 26, 2010.)

44. Kurt Russo, telephone communication, 2007.

45. Barbara E. Hernandez, "Preserving Their History: Tribe's Conservancy Protects New Acreage," *The Press-Enterprise* (Riverside, California), May 4, 2004.

46. Ibid.

47. Benjamin Spillman, "Tribal Coalition Wins Grant for Desert Tract," *The Desert Sun* (Palm Springs, California), January 29, 2004.

48. Kurt Russo, telephone communication, 2007.

49. Askew retired from the NALC Board in 2005 so that he could accept the position of Site Steward in the Old Woman Mountains (Tom Askew, telephone communication, December 31, 2009).

50. Kurt Russo, telephone communication, 2007.

51. Tom Askew, telephone communication, December 31, 2009.

52. Kurt Russo, telephone communication, 2007.

53. Margolin, "California Indians and Conservation."

54. Benjamin Spillman, "Preserving a Piece of History," *The Desert Sun* (Palm Springs, California), March 22, 2005.

55. Ibid.

56. Kurt Russo, telephone communication, 2007.

57. William Madrigal, presentation to the "Desertlands/Sacred Lands Conference," Palm Desert, California, October 31, 2009.

58. Kurt Russo, telephone communication, 2007.

59. "Community Notes, Anza Borrego: Marking Acquisition of Horse Canyon," *The Press-Enterprise* (Riverside, California), April 1, 2005.

60. See Anthony Madrigal, *Sovereignty, Land, and Water: Building Tribal Environmental and Cultural Programs on the Cahuilla and Twenty-Nine Palms Reservations* (Riverside: California Center for Native Nations, History Department, University of California, Riverside, 2008), 40.

61. For more information, see the Salt Song Project Web site, http://www .nativeland.org/saltsong.html.

62. Madrigal, *Sovereignty, Land, and Water*, 14.

63. According to a description of the project provided by the Cultural Conservancy, http://www.nativeland.org/2.html.

64. Kurt Russo, telephone communication, December 4, 2009.

65. Madrigal, *Sovereignty, Land, and Water*, 41.

66. Matthew Leivas, presentation to the "Desertlands/Sacred Lands Conference" Palm Desert, California, October 31, 2009.

67. See, for example, Phil Klasky, "Ward Valley: Sacred Homeland or Nuclear Waste Dump," *Satya* (April 1999).

68. Melissa K. Nelson, "Oral Tradition, Identity, and Intergenerational Healing," in *Cultural Representation in Native America*, ed. Andrew Jolivette (Lanham, MD: AltaMira Press, 2006), 104.

69. Philip M. Klasky, "Awakened Voices," *News from Native California* 14, no. 1 (Fall 2000).

70. Ibid.

71. Ibid.

72. Cultural Conservancy, Storyscape Project, Salt Songs Web site, http:// www.nativeland.org/saltsong.html.

73. Melissa Nelson, telephone communication, December 4, 2009.

74. Ibid.

75. Ibid.

76. Ibid.

77. Ibid.

78. Ibid.

79. Kurt Russo, personal communication, Eugene, Oregon, February 27, 2009.

80. Kurt Russo, telephone communication, December 4, 2009.

81. A. L. Kroeber, "Diegueno and Kamia," in Kroeber, *Handbook*, 709–25; Katharine Luomala, "Tipai-Ipai," in *Handbook of North American Indians*, vol. 8, ed. Robert F. Heizer (Washington, DC: Smithsonian, 1978), 592–618; Bobby Barrett, "The Kumeyaay Have a Well-Established Reputation as Stewards of the Environment," *The Kumeyaay Way* (Winter 2009/2010): 4–5; Florence Connolly Shipek, *Delfina Cuero* (Ballena Press: Menlo Park, 1991); Viejas Band of Kumeyaay Indians. *Viejas Band of Kumeyaay Indians: A Brief History.* Booklet available online at http://www.viejasbandofkumeyaay.org/pdfs/ViejasHistoryBooklet.pdf.

82. See, for example, Beverly Ortiz, "Kumeyaay Netmaking," *News from Native California* 10, no. 3 (Spring 1997).

83. Richard L. Carrico, *Strangers in a Stolen Land: American Indians in San Diego 1850–1880* (Newcastle: Sierra Oaks, 1987), 46–54, 78–85.

84. Kurt Russo, e-mail message to author, January 7, 2010; see also http://www.sandiego.edu/nativeamerican/reservations.html#sycuan.

85. Kurt Russo, e-mail messages to author, January 7 and August 26, 2010.

86. Louis Guassac, telephone communication and e-mail messages to author, September 2008.

87. Florence C. Shipek, "The Impact of Europeans upon Kumeyaay Culture," in *The Impact of European Exploration and Settlement on Location Native Americans*, ed. Raymond Starr (San Diego, CA: Cabrillo Historical Association, 1986), 13–25.

88. Louis Guassac, telephone communication, e-mail messages to author, September 2008.

89. Kurt Russo, e-mail messages to author, January 7 and August 26, 2010.

90. Kuuchamaa is a place where the great Kumeyaay prophet Kuuchamaa lived and taught the people how to live according to the laws set forth by Maayehaa (God). "Help Preserve and Protect the Sacred Mountain and Former Home of Kuuchamaa," brochure produced by the Kumeyaay-Diegueño Land Conservancy, 2009.

91. Larry Kinley, telephone communication, May 4, 2010; Kurt Russo, e-mail message to author, August 26, 2010.

92. Kurt Russo, e-mail message to author, January 7, 2010; Larry Kinley, e-mail message to author, January 7, 2010.

93. Ricci LaBrake (vice chairman, Sycuan Band of Kumeyaay), e-mail message to author, January 7, 2010.

94. Kim Bactad (former vice chairman, Viejas Band of Kumeyaay), e-mail message to author, January 8, 2010.

95. Kurt Russo, e-mail message to author, January 7, 2010.

96. Kurt Russo, telephone communication, 2007.

97. Ibid.

98. Kurt Russo, telephone communication, December 4, 2009.

99. Kurt Russo, telephone communication, 2007.

100. Ibid.

101. Clifford Trafzer, telephone communication, September 23, 2008.

102. Ibid.

103. See, for example, the lists of texts in the recommended Land Trust Alliance library, http://www.landtrustalliance.org/resources/publications/publications.

104. Renee J. Bouplon and Brenda Lind, *Conservation Easement Stewardship* (Washington, DC: The Land Trust Alliance, 2008).

105. Byers and Ponte, *Conservation Easement Handbook*.

106. Wood and O'Brien, "Tribes as Trustees."

Chapter 6

1. See Kurt Russo, ed. *Finding Common Ground* (Yarmouth, Maine: Intercultural Press, 2001).

Chapter 7

1. In 2009, the tribe officially changed its name to the Yocha Dehe Wintun Nation. Yocha Dehe means "home by the spring water" in Patwin. For more on the tribe's story, see http://yochadehe.org/.

2. Ibid. See also Veronica E. Valarde Tiller, ed, *Tiller's Guide to Indian Country* (Albuquerque: BowArrow Publishing, 1996, 2006).

3. Jim Etters, e-mail message to author, January 11, 2010. See also "Home" in the tribe's publication, "Our Story," http://yochadehe.org/heritage/our-story.

4. Tiller, *Tiller's Guide*.

5. For an overview of this process, see the 2009 California Environmental Quality Act Standards and Guidelines, http://www.califaep.org/userdocuments/File/2009%20CEQA%20Statute%20and%20Guidelines2.pdf.

6. Pete Bontadelli, telephone communication, May 2007.

7. The Williamson Act, or the California Land Consolidation Act of 1965, enables agricultural landowners to enter into contract with local jurisdictions (cities or counties) to preserve the rural character of their land. In exchange for a reduced tax rate, landowners commit to not develop their land for a period of time, usually ten years. More information on the Williamson Act is available through the California Department of Conservation.

8. Jim Etters, e-mail message to author, May 6, 2010.

9. Pete Bontadelli, telephone communication, May 2007; Albert Vallecillo, personal communication, Rumsey, California, and telephone communication, 2006–2007.

10 For example, Kiesecker et al. describe the greater effectiveness of conservation easements that establish particular biological targets, or similar clear conservation purposes, which can be specifically monitored. See J. M. Kiesecker et al., "Conservation Easements in Context: A Quantitative Analysis of Their Use by the Nature Conservancy," *Frontiers in Ecology and the Environment* 5, no. 3 (2007): 125–30.

11. Bob Whitney, telephone communication, August 2007.

12. Ibid.

13. Bob Whitney, e-mail message to author, December 10, 2009.

14. Pete Bontadelli, telephone communication, 2008.

15. Bob Whitney, telephone communication, August 2007.

16. Deborah North, telephone communication, September–October 2007.

17. Ibid.

18. Pete Bontadelli, telephone communication, 2007.

19. Bob Whitney, telephone communication, August 2007.

20. Ibid.

21. Pete Bontadelli, telephone communication, 2007.

22. Lynnel Pollock, e-mail message to author, January 4, 2010.

23. Ibid.

Chapter 8

1. For a discussion of the use of executive orders to establish reservations, see Prucha, *American Indian Treaties*, 330.

2. Tiller, *Tiller's Guide*, 274.

3. Ibid.

4. For an overview of SB-18, prepared as part of a training program by the California Office of Planning and Research, see www.opr.ca.gov/programs/training/SB_18_Overview.ppt.

5. Britt Wilson, "Developing Public and Private Land of Tribal Interest/Sacred Sites," paper presented to the "Conserving Indian Country" Environmental Justice Symposium, Boalt Hall School of Law, University of California, Berkeley, March 16, 2007; Britt Wilson, telephone communication and e-mail messages to author, July 2007–August 2008; Madrigal, *Sovereignty, Land, and Water*, 73.

6. Ping Chang et al., "Population," in *The State of the Region* 2007 (Los Angeles: Southern California Association of Governments, 2007), 4; http://www.scag.ca.gov/publications/pdf/2007/SOTR07/SOTR07_Population.pdf.

7. Cuauhtémoc Gonzalez, telephone communication, March 2007.

8. State Health and Safety Code §7050.5.

9. California Public Resources Code §5097.

10. Public Resources Code §5097.9 and 5097.995.

11. Leslie Mouriquand, telephone communication, September 2007.

12. Ibid.

13. Ibid.

14. Britt Wilson, e-mail message to author, August 25, 2008.

15. Leslie Mouriquand, telephone communication, September 2007.

16. Patricia Tuck, e-mail message to author, August 25, 2008.

17. Patricia Tuck, e-mail message to author, May 6, 2010; Leslie Mouriquand, telephone communication, May 6, 2010.

18. Mike Contreras, e-mail message to author, January 8, 2010, telephone communication, January 11, 2010.

19. Britt Wilson, "Developing Public and Private Land of Tribal Interest/ Sacred Sites," paper presented to the "Conserving Indian Country" Environmental Justice Symposium, Boalt Hall School of Law, University of California, Berkeley, March 16, 2007; Britt Wilson, telephone communication and e-mail messages to author, July 2007–August 2008.

20. Leslie Mouriquand, telephone communication, September 2007.

21. Britt Wilson, "Developing Public and Private Land of Tribal Interest/ Sacred Sites," paper presented to the "Conserving Indian Country" Environmental Justice Symposium, Boalt Hall School of Law, University of California, Berkeley, March 16, 2007; Britt Wilson, telephone communication and e-mail messages to author, July 2007–August 2008. For more discussion of the challenges inherent in helping others understand the designation of sites as sacred, see Carol Berry, "National Sacred Sites Day Raises Justice Issues," *Indian Country Today*, July 15, 2009.

22. Ibid.

23. Ibid.

24. Leslie Mouriquand, telephone communication, September 2007.

25. Ibid.

26. Britt Wilson, "Developing Public and Private Land of Tribal Interest/ Sacred Sites," paper presented to the "Conserving Indian Country" Environmental Justice Symposium, Boalt Hall School of Law, University of California, Berkeley, March 16, 2007; Britt Wilson, telephone communication and e-mail messages to author, July 2007–August 2008.

27. Britt Wilson, telephone communication and e-mail messages to author, July 2007–August 2008.

28. Ibid.

29. Leslie Mouriquand, telephone communication, May 6, 2010.

30. Britt Wilson, telephone communication and e-mail messages to author, July 2007–August 2008.

31. Madrigal, *Sovereignty, Land, and Water,* 101.

32. Ibid., 103.

33. Leslie Mouriquand, telephone communication, September 2007.

34. Madrigal, *Sovereignty, Land, and Water,* 85; Mike Contreras, telephone communication, January 11, 2010.

35. Mike Contreras, telephone communication, January 11, 2010.

36. Ibid.

Chapter 9

1. Tiller, *Tiller's Guide;* Little Traverse Bay Bands of Odawa, tribal Web site, http://www.ltbbodawa-nsn.gov/index.html.

2. The 1836 treaty was signed on March 28, 1836, and proclaimed May 27, 1836, by Commissioner Henry R. Schoolcraft. The 1855 treaty was signed on July 31, 1855, and proclaimed on September 10, 1856, by Commissioners

George W. Manypenny and Henry C. Gilbert. Prucha, *American Indian Treaties*, Appendix B ("Ratified Indian Treaties").

3. Little Traverse Bay Bands of Odawa Indians, *Our Land and Culture: A 200 Year History of Our Land Use* (November 2005), http://www.ltbbodawa-nsn.gov/Departments/ArchivesAndRecords/Our%20Land%20and%20Culture%20for%20web.pdf.

4. See Little Traverse Bay Bands of Odawa Web site, "Tribal History," http://www.ltbbodawa-nsn.gov/TribalHistory.html.

5. Tiller, *Tiller's Guide*, 374; James Bransky, e-mail message to author, October 5, 2007.

6. Frank Ettawageshik, telephone communication, September 30, 2008.

7. Ettawageshik is currently executive director of the United Tribes of Michigan (Rachel Smolinski, e-mail message to author, December 4, 2009).

8. See the Little Traverse Conservancy Web site, http://landtrust.org/.

9. *Little Traverse Conservancy Newsletter* 31, no. 4 (Winter 2009–2010): 3, at http://landtrust.org/Newsletters/Winter09-10.pdf.

10. Tom Bailey, e-mail message to author, May 4, 2009.

11. *Little Traverse Conservancy Newsletter* 31, no. 4 (Winter 2009–2010).

12. SB-1004 (2006), (p)(i). For the text of the bill, see http://www.legislature.mi.gov/documents/2005-2006/publicact/pdf/2006-PA-0446.pdf; James Bransky, e-mail message to author, October 2, 2007.

13. See the Michigan Conservation and Historic Preservation Easement Act, Act 187, PA 1980, no. 197, Section 399.253 of Michigan Compiled Laws.

14. James Bransky, e-mail message to author, October 2, 2007.

15. Little Traverse Conservancy, *2008 Annual Report*, http://landtrust.org/Newsletters/AnnualReport2008.pdf.

16. Tom Bailey, telephone communication, July 2007.

17. Ettawageshik was a member of the governing body of the nonprofit beginning in 1985, became chair when the tribe received reaffirmation, and then became chair again in 2001 after a hiatus, and he served until 2009. Ettawageshik has also been a Little Traverse Conservancy board member.

18. Tom Bailey, telephone communication, July 2007; Frank Ettawageshik, telephone communication, September 30, 2008; Rachel Smolinski, telephone communication and e-mail messages to author, March, 2007–December 2008.

19. Tom Bailey, telephone communication, July 2007.

20. Frank Ettawageshik, telephone communication, September 30, 2008.

21. Ibid.

22. Ibid.

23. Tom Bailey, telephone communication, July 2007.

24. Frank Ettawageshik, telephone communication, September 30, 2008.

25. According to the *Department of Justice Title Standards: A Guide for the Preparations of Title Evidence in Land Acquisitions by the U.S.A.*, http://www.justice.gov/enrd/2001_Title_Standards.html.

26. Rachel Smolinski, telephone communication, March 2007.

27. Kieran Fleming, telephone communication, July 2007.

28. Rachel Smolinski, telephone communication, March 2007.

29. Ibid.

30. Ibid.

31. Kieran Fleming, telephone communication, July 2007.

32. As of 2009, the Conservancy held 216 preserves and 208 conservation easements. *Little Traverse Conservancy Newsletter* 31, no. 4 (Winter 2009–2010).

33. Rachel Smolinski, telephone communication, March 2007.

34. Ibid.

Chapter 10

1. Don Ryberg, personal communication, Taylorsville and Nevada City, California, 2007, and telephone communication, May 4, 2010; Farrell Cunningham, personal communication, Greenville, California, 2007. The Ancestral Nexus map spatially renders genealogies to show the different family trees and how they span Nisenan, Concow, and Mountain Maidu territories in the northern Sierra Nevada foothills and mountains. For more information on the map and tribal genealogy, contact the Tsi-Akim tribal office.

2. Don Ryberg, personal communication, Taylorsville, California, and Nevada City, California, 2007.

3. The Tsi-Akim Maidu are collecting resolutions from jurisdictions and organizations, affirming the existence of Tsi-Akim Maidu in support of their bid for recognition. For example, on March 15, 2008, Cunningham presented a resolution to the Maidu Summit for its consideration.

4. Beginning in 1914 (38 Stat. 582–589) and culminating in the 1922 "Purchase of Land for Homeless Indians of California" (42 Stat. 559–567). In 1923, the California State Assembly also passed AB 1333 to set aside lands for the tribes in Plumas, Lassen, and Modoc Counties.

5. "Sus-212 (Old Allick)," Case Files of Land Transactions, 1909–1956, Susanville, Records of the Bureau of Indian Affairs, RG 75, Pacific Region (San Francisco), San Bruno, California, National Archives.

6. Letter filed in the National Archives, Washington, D.C., RG 75, from Greenville Industrial School Superintendant Edgar K. Miller to commissioner of Indian Affairs, dated July 26, 1923.

7. Ibid.

8. The circumstances around this parcel's condemnation and Plumas County's subsequent purchase of it for a county park require more research. The Tsi-Akim Maidu tribe is currently seeking federal recognition based partially upon the illegal condemnation of the land.

9. In a landmark 1983 case, a Pomo woman, Tillie Hardwick, represented seventeen terminated California tribes in a case against the United States for not providing the infrastructure improvements promised when the tribes accepted

termination. *Tillie Hardwick et al. v. United States*, Civil No. C-79–1910-SW (N.D. Cal. 1983). Neither the Tsi-Akim nor the Nevada City Rancheria were eligible to participate in this suit because both tribes were cancelled prior to the termination legislation (HR-108 at the federal level and the California Rancheria Act or Public Law 85–671 at the state level).

10. Aletha Peck, personal communication, Greenville, California, 2006.

11. Ibid. Additionally, Wilhelmina Ives, Vivian Hansen, Marvin Cunningham, Don Ryberg, Lorena Gorbet, Marlene Mullen, Trina Cunningham, Farrell Cunningham, and others voiced their sentiments about the illegal seizure of the site. Personal communications, Greenville, Taylorsville, and Quincy, California, 2003–2008.

12. For a recent article about the Mountain Maidu Bear Dance, see Robert Manlove, "The Mountain Maidu Bear Dance," *News from Native California* 22, no. 3 (Spring 2009).

13. Marty Coleman-Hunt, telephone communication, January 4, 2010. See also the Nevada County Land Trust Web site, http://www.nevadacountylandtrust.org.

14. Wendy Olenick, personal communication, Nevada City, California, January 31, 2007.

15. John Taylor, telephone communication, September 2008.

16. Don Ryberg, personal communication, Nevada City, California, February 2008.

17. John Taylor, telephone communication, September 2008.

18. Dan Macon, telephone communication, 2007.

19. Marty Coleman-Hunt, e-mail message to author, October 2, 2008.

20. A conservation easement can lower property tax rates, but state statutes as well as local assessors determine by how much. Landowners can apply for a tax reduction on property encumbered with a conservation easement, but if the land has been undervalued, this might actually result in a higher tax rate. Byers and Ponte, *Conservation Easement Handbook*, 98–99.

21. Grayson Coney, telephone communication, September 30, 2008.

22. Ibid.

23. Ibid.

24. Ibid.

25. Ibid.

26. Ibid.

27. Ibid.

28. Ibid.

29. Ibid.

30. John Taylor, telephone communication, September 2008.

31. Grayson Coney, telephone communication, September 30, 2008.

32. Wendy Olenick, personal communication, Nevada City, California, January 31, 2007.

33. According to the 2006 Audubon winter bird count.

34. Dan Macon, telephone communication, 2007.

35. Memorandum of Understanding between the Tsi-Akim Maidu and the Nevada County Land Trust, finalized 2008.

36. Don Ryberg, personal communication, Taylorsville and Nevada City, California, 2007

37. Marty Coleman-Hunt, telephone communication, January 4, 2010.

38. Ibid.

39. John Taylor, telephone communication, September 2008.

40. Dan Macon, telephone communication, 2007.

41. Don Ryberg, personal communication, Nevada City, California, February 2008.

42. Dan Macon, telephone communication, 2007.

Chapter 11

1. Alaska Department of Natural Resources. "Fact Sheet: Land Ownership in Alaska." March 2000. Available online at http://dnr.alaska.gov/mlw/factsht/land_own.pdf.

2. Alaska Native Claims Settlement Act (ANCSA), Public Law 92–203.

3. According to Senator Mark Begich (AK), Alaska Native corporations own 90 percent of private land in Alaska. (Introductory remarks for proposed SB-1673, September 15, 2009, on file with author.) For more on the Alaska Native land struggle, and the overlapping state-federal-Native claims, see, for example, Claus-M. Naske and Herman E. Slotnick, *Alaska: A History of the 49th State* (Grand Rapids, MI: William B. Eerdmans Publishing Company, 1979); David S. Case and David Voluck, *Alaska Natives and American Laws* (Fairbanks: University of Alaska Press, 2002); Donald Craig Mitchell, *Take My Land, Take My Life* (Fairbanks: University of Alaska Press, 2001); and William Iggiagruk Hensley, *Fifty Miles from Tomorrow* (New York: Sarah Crichton Books, 2009).

4. 34 Stat. 197, enacted May 17, 1906. Under the ANAA, an Alaska Native could apply for a parcel of nonmineral land of up to 160 acres. Once granted, allotments were not taxable, and they could not be alienated or leased without the permission of the Department of the Interior. Allotment applications trickled in throughout the twentieth century, until 1969 and 1970 when thousands of Alaska Natives applied for allotments, knowing that the ANAA would be repealed under ANCSA in 1971. Many applications were denied, and some people challenged these determinations, calling for reinstatement. In 1980, with the passage of the Alaska National Interest Lands Consolidation Act (ANILCA), Congress approved most of the pending allotment applications (about 8,000). As late as 2001, some allotment applications that had been unfairly cancelled or rejected or had never been reviewed still remained to be adjudicated.

5. In 1980, ANILCA designated 100 million acres of Alaska for national parks, wildlife refuges, and wilderness units. Because of Alaskan Natives' and non-Natives' dependence on subsistence resources, ANILCA directed national park, refuge, and wilderness administrators not to require permits for subsistence

use, and Title 8 of ANILCA established subsistence use of federal lands as a priority unless the resource was in danger.

6. Tom Harris, telephone communication, January 5, 2010.

7. Margie Brown, e-mail message to author, November 27, 2007.

8. Wood and Welcker, "Tribes as Trustees," 414–15.

9. Dune Lankard, Bioneers 2008, available at http://www.youtube.com/watch?v=YemB5BU17u4.

10. See, for example, Rebecca Tsosie, "The Conflict between the 'Public Trust' and the 'Indian Trust' Doctrines: Federal Public Land Policy and Native Nations." *Tulsa Law Review* 39, no. 2 (2003): 301; and Wallace Coffey and Rebecca Tsosie, "Rethinking the Tribal Sovereignty Doctrine: Cultural Sovereignty and the Collective Future of Indian Nations," *Stanford Law and Policy Review* 12, no. 2 (2001).

11. Marie McCarty, e-mail message to author, September 30, 2008. Information about the standards and practices, and steps to formally adopting them, are available on the Land Trust Alliance's Web site, http://www.landtrustalliance.org/learning/sp/land-trust-standards-and-practices.

12. Marie McCarty, e-mail message to author, September 30, 2008.

13. Barbara Seaman, telephone communication, 2007.

14. Ibid.

15. Barbara Seaman, e-mail message to author, October 6, 2008.

16. Margie Brown, e-mail message to author, November 27, 2007.

17. Fred Elvsaas, telephone communication, December 28, 2009.

18. Kachemak Heritage Land Trust Web site, http://www.kachemaklandtrust.org; Barbara Seaman, telephone communication, 2007.

19. By the early 1960s, federal, state, and private land claims in Alaska were putting pressure on Alaska Native lands and resources, and almost no lands had been recognized as Alaska Native lands. Alaska Natives began to organize to push for a settlement of their claims: In 1963, one thousand Native Alaskans from 24 villages sent a petition to Secretary of the Interior Stuart Udall, calling for a freeze on state land selections for all land near their villages. Later, they called for a freeze on the disposition of all disputed lands, including state-selected lands and lands in use by Alaska Natives. In 1966, Udall placed a freeze on all state land claims, oil leases, mining claims, and homesteads, which remained in force until Alaska Native land claims had been settled.

20. PL 84–830 conveyed a one-million-acre land grant to the state of Alaska to benefit Alaska's mentally ill, mandating that the lands be held and managed by the State of Alaska as a public trust. Any proceeds from the sale, lease, mortgage, or exchange of these lands were to be invested to benefit the mentally ill. For information on the program, see the Alaska Mental Health Trust Land Office Web site, http://www.mhtrustland.org.

21. Fred Elvsaas, telephone communication, December 28, 2009. For guidelines for Alaska Native village corporation land selection under ANCSA, see ANCSA 12(b), 43 U.S.C.A. 1611(b).

22. Roger MacCampbell, District Ranger, Kachemak Bay District, Alaska State Parks, telephone communication, May 4, 2010.

23. Barbara Seaman, telephone communication, 2007; Margie Brown, e-mail message to author, November 27, 2007.

24. Roger MacCampbell, District Ranger, Kachemak Bay District, Alaska State Parks, telephone communication, May 4, 2010.

25. Fred Elvsaas, telephone communication, December 28, 2009.

26. Barbara Seaman, telephone communication, 2007.

27. Ibid.

28. Fred Elvsaas, telephone communication, December 28, 2009.

29. Barbara Seaman, telephone communication, 2007.

30. Ibid.

31. Ibid.

32. Ibid.

33. Rita Smagge, statement regarding the Cook Inlet land transfer, provided by Barbara Seaman, telephone communication, 2007.

34. Barbara Seaman, telephone communication, 2007.

35. Ibid.

36. Bruce Oskolkoff, telephone communication, December 2007.

37. Ibid.

38. Ibid.

39. Ibid.

40. Ibid.

41. Ibid.

42. Ibid.

43. Barbara Seaman, telephone communication, October 2008.

44. Marie McCarty, e-mail message to author, October 1, 2008.

45. Barbara Seaman, telephone communication, October 2008.

46. Bruce Oskolkoff, telephone communication, December 2007.

47. Barbara Seaman, telephone communication, October 2008.

48. Bruce Oskolkoff, telephone communication, December 2007.

49. Barbara Seaman, telephone communication, October 2008.

50. Randall Hagenstein, telephone communication, December 2007.

51. Barbara Seaman, telephone communication, October 2008.

52. Elizabeth Manning, "Native Lands at Risk: Coalition Attempts to Save Allotments," *Anchorage Daily News*, December 18, 2000.

53. Nushagak–Mulchatna Wood–Tikchik Land Trust Web site, http://www.nmwtlt.org; Tim Troll, e-mail message to author, November 28, 2007.

54. Tim Troll, e-mail message to author, November 28, 2007.

55. Randall Hagenstein, telephone communication, December 2007.

56. Fred Elvsaas, telephone communication, December 28, 2009.

57. Tim Troll, telephone communication, December 16, 2009.

58. Tim Troll, e-mail message to author, November 28, 2007.

59. Tim Troll, telephone communication, December 16, 2009.

60. The current ANCSA tax provisions were extended by allotments to ANCSA, which was going to begin taxing all Native corporation land (whether or not it was in productive use) 20 years after the start of the Act. The amendments allowed undeveloped Alaska Native corporate lands to remain tax exempt.

61. See the comments of Rep. Don Young (AK) introducing HR 3568, available at http://begich.senate.gov/public/index.cfm?p=SponsoredBills.

62. As Begich noted, "nearly 70 percent of [Native Alaskan communities' food] comes from the land or adjacent waters. For many communities, subsistence is an economic necessity considering both the lack of economic development and the cost and difficulty involved in purchasing food. For example, in Kotzebue, a community in Northwestern Alaska, milk costs nearly $10 per gallon. In Buckland, a village home to approximately 400 people, a pound of hamburger, when it is actually available, costs $14.00." September 15, 2009. Available at http://begich.senate.gov/public/index.cfm?p=SponsoredBills.

63. Ibid.

64. Alaska Statutes Title 34 (Property), chapter 17 of the Uniform Conservation Easement Act (1981).

65. Recall that the value of an easement is calculated by subtracting the value of the land with development restrictions from the value of the land with no development restrictions.

66. See the Land Trust Alliance Public Policy Web site, at http://www
.landtrustalliance.org/policy/taxincentives/federal/policy/advocates/
adv-121809, for the latest information on the conservation tax incentive.

67. Tim Troll, e-mail message to author, November 28, 2007; Tom Harris, telephone communication, January 5, 2010.

68. Tim Troll, e-mail message to author, November 28, 2007.

69. Tom Harris, telephone communication, January 5, 2010.

70. Tim Troll, telephone communication, December 16, 2009.

71. Alex Demarban, "09–39 Urge[s] Creation of Tax Credits or Benefits to Alaska Native Corporations Who Voluntarily Choose to Create Conservation Casements," The Bristol Bay Times, November 10, 2009, and The Arctic Sounder, November 10, 2009.

72. Tim Troll, e-mail message to author, November 28, 2007; Tom Harris, telephone communication, January 5, 2010.

73. For an explanation of the easement and the site, see Tyonek's Web site devoted exclusively to the proposed easement at http://www.chuitnaconservation
.com/about-us.html. For a video with visual and audio information about the proposed easement, see "For the Benefit of All" on the Tyonek Corporation Web site at http://www.tyonek.com/Presentations/TNC_For%20the%20benefit%
200f%20all_WEB-H.264%20300Kbps.mov.

74. Tim Troll, telephone communication, December 16, 2009.

75. Tom Harris, telephone communication, January 5, 2010.

76. See, for example, Don Hunter, "Sullivan, Young Call for Study of Inlet Beluga Whales," *Anchorage Daily News*, December 23, 2009; and Fred Elvsaas, telephone communication, December 28, 2009.

77. Tom Harris, telephone communication, January 5, 2010.

78. See Dwight Kramer, "Just Say 'No' to This Proposed Coal Mine in Alaska Salmon Streams," *Anchorage Daily News*, August 27, 2009; see also Tyonek's film "For the Benefit of All," online at: http://www.tyonek.com/Presentations/ TNC_For%20the%20benefit%200f%20all_WEB-H.264%20300Kbps.mov.

79. The coal-to-gas-to-liquid project would recover energy from coal without an open-pit mine, by initiating a combustion reaction underground, turning the coal into a gas to generate electricity and then into a liquid to provide fuel; see Tyonek's film "For the Benefit of All," online at: http://www.tyonek.com/Presentations/ TNC_For%20the%20benefit%200f%20all_WEB-H.264%20300Kbps.mov. For an alternate view, see Dwight Kramer, "Just Say 'No' to This Proposed Coal Mine in Alaska Salmon Streams," *Anchorage Daily News*, August 27, 2009.

80. Margaret Bauman, "Native Village of Tyonek Opposes Coal Project," in the *Bristol Bay Times*, April 28, 2010.

81. Tom Harris, telephone communication, January 5, 2010.

82. Ibid.

83. Tim Troll, e-mail message to author, November 28, 2007.

84. Under Alaska Statute 16.05.871(a), the Alaska Department of Fish and Game (ADF&G) must "specify the various rivers, lakes and streams or parts of them" where anadromous fish spawn, rear, and migrate. For more information, see the Alaska Department of Fish and Wildlife, *Catalog of Waters Important for the Spawning, Rearing or Migration of Anadromous Fishes"* (Juneau, AK: Habitat Division, Department of Fish and Game, State of Alaska). Also available online at http:// www.sf.adfg.state.ak.us/SARR/AWC/index.cfm/FA/main.overview, or contact J. Johnson at j.johnson@alaska.gov directly for a hard copy; Tim Troll, telephone communication, December 16, 2009.

85. Tim Troll, telephone communication, December 16, 2009.

86. Tim Troll, e-mail message to author, November 28, 2007.

87. Ibid.

88. For an overview of the plan, see the TNC-Alaska Web site: http://www .nature.org/wherewework/northamerica/states/alaska/preserves/art17527.html. The Nushagak Mulchatna Watershed Council was formed in 1998 to bring together stakeholders in the Nushagak watershed. Tribal and city government officials participated, as well as landowners and others. The group aimed to take a regional approach to land conservation. For more information, see Susan Flensburg, "Keeping It Clean: An Alternative Approach to TMDL in Rural Alaska" (paper presented to Getting It Done: The Role of TMDL Implementation in Watershed Restoration, Stevenson, Washington, October 29–30, 2003. Available online at http://www.swwrc.wsu.edu/conference2003/pdf/Proceedings/ Proceedings/Session%204/ABSTRACT_Flensburg.pdf.

89. Press Release: "Koliganek Native LTD Establishes Salmon Reserve on Corporate Lands," November, 2009. Copy on file with author.

90. Fred Elvsaas, telephone communication, December 28, 2009.

91. Randall Hagenstein, telephone communication, December 2007.

92. Ibid.

93. Tim Troll, e-mail message to author, November 28, 2007.

94. Ibid.

Chapter 12

1. See the Jamestown S'Klallam Tribe's History and Culture Web site, http://www.jamestowntribe.org/jstweb_2007/history/hist_jst.htm.; see also Tiller, *Tiller's Guide*, 582.

2. The 1855 Point-No-Point Treaty was signed on January 26, 1855, and proclaimed on April 29, 1859, by Governor Isaac I. Stevens. Prucha, *American Indian Treaties*, Appendix B, "Ratified Indian Treaties."

3. For more information on the Dungeness River Management Team, see http://www.olympus.net/community/dungenesswc/.

4. Tiller, *Tiller's Guide* (1996, 2006).

5. North Olympic Land Trust, "2009 Accomplishments" map, http://www.northolympiclandtrust.org/Graphics/Maps/NOLT_AccompMap_2009.pdf.

6. Greg Good, e-mail message to author, September 18, 2008.

7. For more information on the challenges of restoring the Dungeness floodplain and the benefits of reducing development in it, see the tribe's natural resources websites, beginning at http://www.jamestowntribe.org/jstweb_2007/programs/nrs/nrs_main.htm.

8. Hansi Hals (Jamestown S'Klallam environmental planning manager), telephone communication and e-mail messages to author, May 2007.

9. Greg Good, e-mail message to author, May 7, 2010.

10. Greg Good, e-mail message to author, December 1, 2009.

11. North Olympic Land Trust, "Major Salmon Restoration Funding Announcement," http://www.northolympiclandtrust.org/News/salmon-restoration-funding.html.

12. Lyn Muench, telephone communication, February 1, 2007. Muench had been with the tribe for twenty-one years when she retired in 2007.

13. *Recommended Land Protection Strategies for the Dungeness Riparian Area*, http://www.clallam.net/environment/assets/applets/Protection_Strategy.pdf.

14. Leo Gaten, e-mail messages to author, November 28 and December 1, 2007. See also the Department of Justice Title Standards governing federal land acquisitions, http://www.justice.gov/enrd/2001_Title_Standards.html.

15. Leo Gaten, telephone communication, February 2, 2007.

16. Ibid. As Gaten notes, the tribe also issues waivers when it takes out loans to purchase or develop properties. In this situation, tribal representatives sign a

limited waiver with the lending institution, agreeing to be subject to the local court jurisdiction if they default on the loan terms.

17. "S'Klallam Tribe Reclaiming Hallowed Ground," *North Kitsap Herald* (Poulsbo, Washington), April 16, 2010.

18. Sarah Spaeth, telephone communication, May 5, 2010.

19. Leo Gaten, e-mail message to author, December 1, 2007; for more information on conservation futures, see Greene, "Dynamic Conservation Easements," 893–94.

20. Leo Gaten, e-mail message to author, December 1, 2007.

21. Leo Gaten, e-mail message to author, May 6, 2010.

22. Sarah Spaeth, telephone communication, May 5, 2010.

23. Leo Gaten, e-mail message to author, December 1, 2007. CC&Rs are commonly associated with subdivisions. According to BIA Pacific Region realty specialist Carmen Facio, in some instances, pre-existing encumbrances do not meet the title standards of the U.S. Department of Justice, particularly those encumbrances that restrict land use. Facio suggested that tribes that want to establish certain management restrictions on their lands develop tribal land use ordinances and maintain tribal jurisdiction over those lands, rather than working with land trusts and federal and state agencies to develop conservation easements (Carmen Facio, telephone communication, May 24, 2010). Although tribal land use ordinances are preferred by the BIA, they may not enable access to conservation funds if tribes choose to partner with other entities and develop conservation easements.

24. Leo Gaten, e-mail message to author, December 1, 2007. According to Facio, each BIA trust acquisition is determined on a case-by-case basis (Carmen Facio, telephone communication, May 24, 2010).

25. "S'Klallam Tribe reclaiming hallowed ground," *North Kitsap Herald* (Poulsbo, Washington), April 16, 2010.

26. Sarah Spaeth, telephone communication, May 5, 2010.

27. Ibid; Jamestown S'Klallam Tribe, 2008–2009 *Report to Tribal Citizens* (Sequim, Washington, 2010), 17, available online at http://www.jamestowntribe.org/jstweb_2007/announce/Final%20_008-2009_Report_to_Citizens.pdf.

28. Jeff Chew, "Conservation Panel Wants Jefferson County to Ante for Tamanowas Rock," *Peninsula Daily News* (Port Angeles, Washington), April 20, 2010; Leo Gaten, e-mail message to author, May 6, 2010.

29. See, for example, Jeff Chew, "Conservation Panel wants Jefferson County to Ante for Tamanowas Rock," *Peninsula Daily News* (Port Angeles, Washington), April 20, 2010.

30. Sarah Spaeth, telephone communication, May 5, 2010.

31. Daniel Silliman, "Jimmy Come Lately [sic] Creek Restoration Begins in Blyn," *Peninsula Daily News* (Port Angeles, Washington), January 3, 2003.

32. For a listing of threatened and endangered species in Washington, including the Chum Salmon, Hood Canal sub-species, see http://wdfw.wa.gov/wildlife/management/endangered.html.

33. Hansi Hals, telephone communication, September 2008; and Linda Newberry, "The 'Undevelopment' of Jimmycomelately Creek and Estuary" (report
prepared for the Jamestown S'Klallam Tribe, 2003), http://www.jamestowntribe
.org/jstweb_2007/programs/nrs/nrs_jimmy.htm.

34. Newberry, "'Undevelopment,'" 4.

35. "Sequim: Dungeness Flooding Likely Destroyed Redds," *Peninsula Daily
News* (Port Angeles, Washington), April 7, 2002.

36. This date of contact is from the tribe's history Web site, http://www
.jamestowntribe.org/jstweb_2007/history/hist_jst.htm.

37. Dave Shreffler et al., *Jimmycomelately Ecosystem Restoration: Lessons Learned Report*
(report submitted to Jamestown S'Klallam Tribe, October 31, 2008), 6, http://www
.jamestowntribe.org/jstweb_2007/programs/nrs/jcl-lessionslearned10-31-08.pdf.

38. Ibid.; see also "Jimmycomelately Creek and Estuary Restoration" (brochure), http://www.jamestowntribe.org/jstweb_2007/programs/nrs/070705%
20JCL%20Brochure.pdf.

39. Alan Choate, "Tribe Members Busy Planting Trees, Shrubs, to Reclaim
Area Waterways," *Peninsula Daily News* (Port Angeles, Washington), June 16, 2005.

40. Newberry, "'Undevelopment,'" 4.

41. Ibid., 2.

42. "Jimmycomelately Creek" (brochure), http://www.jamestowntribe.org/
jstweb_2007/programs/nrs/070705%20JCL%20Brochure.pdf.

43. Shreffler et al., *Jimmycomelately Ecosystem Restoration*, 71.

44. Following incursions from settlers that pushed S'Klallam people out of their
homes, a group of S'Klallams were able to raise the funds to buy a 210-acre parcel
near Dungeness, Washington, in 1874. For more information, see the tribe's history website, at http://www.jamestowntribe.org/jstweb_2007/history/hist_jst.htm.

45. Jamestown S'Klallam Tribe, *2008–2009 Report to Tribal Citizens* (Sequim,
Washington, 2010), 20.

Chapter 13

1. Thomas Hatley, telephone communication, November 2007; Tiller, *Tiller's
Guide*, 483.

2. Ibid.

3. This 1819 treaty with the Cherokee was signed on February 27, and
proclaimed on March 10, with Commissioner John C. Calhoun. Prucha, *American
Indian Treaties*, Appendix B, "Ratified Indian Treaties."

4. Finger, *The Eastern Band of Cherokees*, 10.

5. Russell Townsend (Tribal Historic Preservation Officer, Eastern Band of
Cherokee Indians), telephone communication, March 13, 2009.

6. *Cherokee Nation v. Georgia* 30 U.S. (5 Pet.) 1 (1831); *Worcester v. Georgia*, 31
U.S. 515, 8 L. Ed. 483 (1832).

7. The 1835 Treaty of New Echota was signed on December 29, 1835, and
proclaimed on May 23, 1836, with Commissioners William Carroll and John F.

Schermerhorn. Prucha, *American Indian Treaties*, Appendix B, "Ratified Indian Treaties."

8. Finger, *The Eastern Band of Cherokees*, For more on William Thomas, see the Eastern Band of Cherokee Web site, http://www.cherokee-nc.com/index .php?page=65.

9. Tiller, *Tiller's Guide*, 484.

10. Ibid.

11. See the Eastern Band of Cherokee Indians' Web site, http://www .cherokee-nc.com, highlighting tourism opportunities.

12. Sharon Taylor, telephone communication and e-mail messages to author, August 2007.

13. Dennis F. Desmond, *Cowee Mound Baseline Report* (February 23, 2007). On file with the Land Trust for the Little Tennessee.

14. Ibid; Thomas Hatley, telephone communication, November 2007.

15. Thomas Hatley, telephone communication, November 2007.

16. Ibid.

17. Ibid.

18. Ibid.

19. Juanita Wilson, telephone communication, November 8, 2007.

20. Ibid.

21. Thomas Hatley, telephone communication, November 2007.

22. Colin McCandless, "Ancient Mound and Town Site Return to the Cherokee: Land Trust Plays a Key Role in Unique Property Transaction," *The Franklin Press*, October 27, 2006.

23. Jon Ostendorff, "Reclaiming Their Land: Cherokee Indians Buy Undisturbed Indian Mound in Cowee," *Citizen Times*, April 24, 2007.

24. Ibid.

25. Thomas Hatley, telephone communication, November 2007.

26. McCandless, "Ancient Mound."

27. Russell Townsend, telephone communication, March 13, 2007.

28. Ibid.

29. Juanita Wilson, telephone communication, November 8, 2007.

30. Thomas Hatley, telephone communication, November 2007.

31. Desmond, *Cowee Mound Baseline Report*.

32. McCandless, "Ancient Mound."

33. Juanita Wilson, telephone communication, November 8, 2007.

34. Thomas Hatley, telephone communication, November 2007.

35. Sharon Taylor, telephone communication and e-mail messages to author, August 2007.

36. Juanita Wilson, telephone communication, November 8, 2007.

37. Russell Townsend, telephone communication, March 13, 2009.

38. Ibid.

39. Sharon Taylor, telephone communication, May 5, 2010.

40. Thomas Hatley, telephone communication, November 2007.

Chapter 14

1. The treaty was signed between then–Territorial Governor Isaac Stevens and representatives of the Nisqually, Puyallap, Steilacoom, and other Northwest tribes. See Prucha, *American Indian Treaties*, 251–252; Cecilia Svinth Carpenter, *Tears of Internment: The Indian History of Fox Island and the Puget Sound Indian War* (Tacoma, Washington: Tahoma Research Service, 1996).

2. Ezra Meeker, *Pioneer Reminiscences of Puget Sound: The Tragedy of Leschi* (Seattle: Lowman and Hanford, 1905), 248. Meeker notes that the initial treaty promised 1,280 timbered acres, but actually reserved 1,204 acres. Carpenter describes the reserved land as "rocky" and west of the Nisqually River (Carpenter, *Tears of Internment*, 31, 97).

3. For testimonies recalling Leschi's adamant refusal to sign, see Meeker, *Pioneer Reminiscences*, 236, 240–258. Carpenter (*Tears of Internment*, 31) also discusses the refusal, as do Jason Bean-Mortinson, Annalise Duerr-Miller, and Julia Vieau, "Nisqually and Fort Lewis" (April 21, 2009), podcast, http://blogs.evergreen .edu/nativeplace/2009/04/21/nisqually-and-fort-lewis/, and the SHAWL Society, "Honor Chief Leschi," electronic communication (February 7, 2008), http:// mailman2.u.washington.edu/pipermail/nat_issues/2008-February/008032.html.

4. Carpenter, *Tears of Internment*, 39.

5. Ibid., 45–48, 54–55.

6. Ibid., 56–59.

7. Ibid., 100–101; Bean-Mortinson et al., "Nisqually and Fort Lewis"; and Tiller, *Tiller's Guide*.

8. Carpenter, *Tears of Internment*, 101–102; Bean-Mortinson et al., "Nisqually and Fort Lewis," interviews with George Walter and Nisqually elder Zuma McCloud.

9. Lawney L. Reyes, *Bernie Whitebear: An Urban Indian's Quest for Justice* (Tucson: University of Arizona Press, 2006), 73–77.

10. 384 F.Supp. 312, better known as "the Boldt decision," after the name of the U.S. District Court judge who issued the decision.

11. Ibid.

12. Tiller, *Tiller's Guide*.

13. See Tacoma Power Web site, page on the Nisqually River Project, http:// www.mytpu.org/tacomapower/power-system/hydro-power/nisqually-river-project/Default.htm.

14. Jovana Brown, "Salmon, Tribes, and Hydropower Dams in the U.S. Puget Sound" (Olympia, WA: Center for World Indigenous Studies, 1999), online at http://cwis.org/fwj/41/jbsalmo.html.

15. Nisqually Tribal Codes, Title 41 (Settlements), Subchapter I: Implementation of Stipulation and Settlement between the City of Tacoma and the Nisqually Indian Tribe. The March 2003 edition is available at http://www.narf .org/nill/Codes/nisqcode/nisqcode41.htm.

16. Mick Michelutti and John Moudy, "Clear Creek Hatchery" (April 20, 2009), podcast, http://blogs.evergreen.edu/nativeplace/2009/04/20/clear-creek-hatchery/.

17. On December 26, 1854, Governor Isaac Stevens signed the Treaty of Medicine Creek with Nisqually, Puyallup, Steilacoom, and other area tribes. Article 3 of the treaty confirmed the signatories' rights to take "fish, at all usual and accustomed grounds and stations." Prucha, *American Indian Treaties*, 402.

18. *Frontline*, "Salmon Wars: The Battle Over Habitat" (April 23, 2009), http://www.pbs.org/wgbh/pages/frontline/poisonedwaters/clean/.

19. For more information on this process and organization, see http://www.nisquallyriver.org.

20. Jeannette Dorner, telephone communication, November 2007.

21. Frank became chair of the Northwest Indian Fisheries Commission, following the Boldt Decision, and received the 1991 Albert Schweitzer Prize for Humanitarianism, among other honors. See, for example, Reyes, *An Urban Indian's Quest for Justice*, 144.

22. Georgiana Kautz, telephone communication, November 2007.

23. Ibid.

24. The Nisqually Watershed Stewardship Plan can be downloaded from http://www.nisquallyriver.org/.

25. Georgiana Kautz, telephone communication, November 2007.

26. Interview with Georgiana Kautz in "Nisqually Estuary," ed. Emily Gwinn, Jennifer Johnson, and Joe Nance (April 18, 2009), podcast, http://blogs.evergreen.edu/nativeplace/2009/04/18/nisqually-estuary-podcast/.

27. Ibid.

28. Jeannette Dorner, telephone communication, November 2007.

29. Gary Chittim, "Puget Sound Returns to Nisqually Delta," *King 5 News*, November 12, 2009), http://www.king5.com/home/Puget-Sound-Retuns-to-Nisqually-Delta-69907237.html.

30. Ibid.; Gwinn et al., "Nisqually Estuary." A comprehensive Web site about the project is also available athttp://nisquallydeltarestoration.org/about.php.

31. Nisqually Land Trust, *Strategic Direction 2009–2011*, http://www.nisquallylandtrust.org/documents/StrategicPlan.pdf.

32. George Walter, "We Are America's Best Idea," *Nisqually Land Trust Newsletter* (Fall 2009). Available online at http://www.nisquallylandtrust.org/documents/NewsletterFall09Final.pdf.

33. *Nisqually Land Trust Newsletter* (Fall 2009), 10.

34. George Walter, telephone communication, October 2005, and e-mail messages to author, July–October 2007.

35. George Walter, telephone communication, October 2005.

36. Nisqually Tribe Environmental Management Program, http://www.nisqually-nsn.gov/emp.html.

37. Georgiana Kautz, telephone communication, November 2007.

38. George Walter, telephone communication, October 2005.

39. John Babin, Nicholas Croft, and Tyler Luce, "Ohop Creek" (March 23, 2009), podcast, http://blogs.evergreen.edu/nativeplace/2009/03/23/ohop-creek/.

40. Ibid.

41. *Nisqually Land Trust Newsletter* (Winter 2010), 2.

42. Ibid.

43. Jeannette Dorner, telephone communication, November 2007.

44. Ibid.

45. George Walter, telephone communication, October 2005, and e-mail messages to author, July–October 2007.

46. George Walter, telephone communication, October 2005.

47. Ibid.

Chapter 15

1. Jacquelyn Ross, "Bringing the People Back to the Land: The Tending and Gathering Gardening Project," *Regeneration* (Summer 2003).

2. Lynnel Pollock, telephone communication, 2007.

3. According to Cache Creek Conservancy Executive Director Lynnel Pollock, the conservancy can use some of the money set aside by gravel mining companies for restoration, but the county retains much of it for oversight and regulation of mining permits. In a 2008 interview, she reported that the conservancy got $0.05 per ton of gravel sold in Yolo County. In the second quarter of 2008, the amount increased to $0.10 per ton (Lynnel Pollock, telephone communication, October 2008).

4. Jacquelyn Ross et al., "Creating Common Ground: A Collaborative Approach to Environmental Reclamation and Cultural Preservation," in *Partnerships for Empowerment: Participatory Research for Community-Based Natural Resource Management*, ed. Carl Wilmsen, et al. (Sterling, VA: Stylus Publishing, 2008), 5.

5. Lynnel Pollock, telephone communication, November 2006.

6. Thomas C. Blackburn and Kat Anderson, *Before the Wilderness: Environmental Management by Native Californians* (Menlo Park, CA: Ballena Press, 1993).

7. Shannon Brawley, telephone communication, December 6, 2009.

8. Kathy Wallace, personal communication, Davis, California, September 5, 2008.

9. Back in the 1980s, part of the preserve was "reclaimed" for agriculture and then, because of its relatively low elevation, it was converted into about 30 acres of wetlands.

10. Shannon Brawley, telephone communication, December 6, 2009.

11. Kathy Wallace, personal communication, Davis, California, September 5, 2008.

12. Ibid.

13. Ibid.

14. Shannon Brawley, telephone communication, December 6, 2009.

15. Ross et al., "Creating Common Ground," 11.

16. Ibid.

17. Kathy Wallace, personal communication, Davis, California, September 5, 2008.

18. Ibid.

19. Shannon Brawley, e-mail message to author, May 5, 2010.

20. Kathy Wallace, personal communication, Davis, California, September 5, 2008.

21. Ross, "Bringing the People Back," 9.

22. Ross et al., "Creating Common Ground," 3.

23. Ibid., 29.

24. Tribes from California and other states are represented on the committee.

25. Ross et al., "Creating Common Ground," 13. According to the authors, the group includes "biologists, weavers, artists, policy designers, teachers, writers, and account managers."

26. Ibid., 22.

27. Ross "Bringing the People Back," 9.

28. Shannon Brawley, telephone communication, December 6, 2009.

29. Ibid.

30. Ibid.

31. Kathy Wallace, personal communication, Davis, California, September 5, 2008.

32. Shannon Brawley, telephone communication, 2007.

33. Lynnel Pollock, personal communication, Cache Creek Nature Preserve, Yolo County, California, January 6, 2010.

34. Don Hankins, e-mail message to author, December 13, 2009.

35. Kathy Wallace, personal communication, Davis, California, September 5, 2008.

36. Ibid.

37. Ibid. According to Hankins (e-mail message to author, September 12, 2008) and Pollock (telephone communication, 2008), Lowrey was well connected in the fire-fighting community. He was a volunteer with the Capay Valley Fire District and was serving as a commissioner on their board at the time of his death.

38. Ross, "Bringing the People Back," 10.

39. Ibid.

40. Archives partially reviewed by the author at the Cache Creek Conservancy Administrative Office on January 6, 2010. The archives are available to the public by appointment.

41. Shannon Brawley, e-mail message to author, December 19, 2009. See also the *Nisqually Land Trust Newsletter* (Summer 2010), 6.

42. Lynnel Pollock, telephone communication, 2007.

43. Cache Creek Conservancy, Tending and Gathering Garden, "Gathering Protocol," on file with the author and available at Cache Creek Conservancy Nature Preserve.

44. Lynnel Pollock, telephone communication, 2007.

45. Cache Creek Conservancy, Tending and Gathering Garden, "Intellectual Property Rights," on file with the author and available at Cache Creek Conservancy Nature Preserve; and Lynnel Pollock, e-mail message to author, May 6, 2010.

46. Cache Creek Conservancy, Tending and Gathering Garden, "Intellectual Property Rights," on file with the author and available at Cache Creek Conservancy Nature Preserve; and Lynnel Pollock, telephone communication, May 6, 2010.

47. Don Hankins, e-mail message to author, September 12, 2008; Lynnel Pollock, telephone communication, 2008.

48. Lynnel Pollock, telephone communication, 2007.

49. Kathy Wallace, personal communication, Davis, California, September 5, 2008.

50. Ibid.

51. Don Hankins, e-mail message to author, September 12, 2008.

52. Ross, "Bringing the People Back," 10.

53. Kathy Wallace, personal communication, Davis, California, September 5, 2008.

54. Ibid.

55. Ibid.

56. Ibid.

57. According to Hankins, staff restoration ecologist Molly Ferrell did periodic burns of grasses in 2008–2009 (Don Hankins, e-mail message to author, December 13, 2009); Lynnel Pollock, e-mail message to author, May 6, 2010.

58. Don Hankins, e-mail message to author, September 12, 2008.

59. Ibid.

60. "Fall Burn of Grasses in the TGG." *Cache Creek Conservancy News and Events* 34 (December 2008).

61. Lynnel Pollock, telephone communication, 2008.

62. Lynnel Pollock, personal communication, Cache Creek Nature Preserve, Yolo County, California, January 6, 2010.

63. Shannon Brawley, e-mail message to author, December 19, 2009.

64. Lynnel Pollock, personal communication, Cache Creek Nature Preserve, Yolo County, California, January 6, 2010.

Section 3

1. For an example of another collaboration between the NRCS and tribes, this one involving a federal trust easement on tribal trust land, see "A Refuge for Wildlife," *California Heartland*, Program 808 (Sacramento, CA: KVIE Public Television Station). Available from California Heartland, more information online at http://www.californiaheartland.org/. The program describes wetlands owned by the Paskenta Band of Nomlaki Indians in California's northern Central

Valley. The Natural Resources Conservation Service wetland holds a conservation easement on the wetlands. The Clear Creek Sports Club leases the land for a sportfishing and hunting concession, which generates revenue for the tribe.

Chapter 16

1. For more information on this process and the relationship to tribal concerns, see the Indian Nations Conservation Alliance Web site, "Why Tribal Conservation Districts?" http://www.inca-tcd.org/index.php?option=com_content& view=section&layout=blog&id=3&Itemid=63.

2. Reina Rogers's position is statewide, and she is part of an NRCS-CA Outreach Team. The team includes two other American Indian liaisons (one in Southern California and one on the Northwest coast), but Rogers is the only statewide liaison.

3. Reina Rogers, personal communication, Quincy, California, March 2008. Rogers partnered with me to write *Conservation Easements in Indian Country*, which is available from Rogers at the NCRS Quincy field office.

4. Larry Ballew, Coarsegold RCD board member, telephone communication, December 31, 2009.

5. Larry Ballew, e-mail message to author, January 7, 2010.

6. Neil McDougald, telephone communication, September 2008.

7. Tom Wheeler, telephone communication, October 1, 2008.

8. Reina Rogers, personal communication, Quincy, California, March 2009.

9. Christine Elam Ballew, telephone communication, October 3, 2008.

10. Larry Ballew, telephone communications, October 2–3, 2008.

11. Ibid.

12. Ibid.

13. Ibid.

14. Ibid.

15. Ibid.

16. Christine Elam Ballew, telephone communications, October 2–3, 2008.

17. Ibid.

18. Tom Wheeler, telephone communication, October 1, 2008.

19. Neil McDougald, telephone communication, September 2008.

20. Draft easement language for Madera County, provided electronically by Rob Roy, May 2, 2008.

21. Larry Ballew, telephone communication, December 31, 2009.

22. Neil McDougald, telephone communication, September 2008.

23. Tom Wheeler, telephone communication, October 1, 2008.

24. Larry Ballew, telephone communication, December 31, 2009.

25. Regarding California Assembly Bill 1333, Edgar Miller, Superintendent of the Greenville Indian Agency, clipped this April 28, 1923, article from the *Sacramento Bee*. He wrote, "This shows the fine attitude of the Legislature on the Homeless Indians' conditions. This office, with the aid of several prominent

Indians and Assemblyman Matthews, from Susanville, this jurisdiction, is trying to get several pieces of State Land for different groups of Indians." On June 5, 1923, Governor Friend W. Richardson signed the bill. In 1924, the BIA purchased Susanville Rancheria as a home for local Indians.

26. According to the "History of the Susanville Rancheria," there are 1,100 acres in trust status and 240 acres in fee status. See http://sir-nsn.gov/history.html.

27. The NRCS Wetlands Reserve Program guidelines are available online at http://www.nrcs.usda.gov/programs/wrp/.

28. Reina Rogers, telephone communication, May 7, 2010.

29. NRCS' Wetlands Reserve Program guidelines are available online at http://www.nrcs.usda.gov/programs/wrp/.

30. U.S. Environmental Protection Agency, U.S. Department of the Interior, Offices of the Inspector General, *Tribal Successes: Protecting the Environment and Natural Resources*, May 2007, available online at http://www.doioig.gov/upload/2007-G-0020.pdf.

31. Tim Keesey (Susanville Indian Rancheria Environmental Director), telephone communication, 2006.

Chapter 17

1. Blair, *Restoring Native Homelands*.

2. Kurt Russo, presentation to the "Cultural Conservation Easements Workshop," Public Interest Environmental Law Conference, Many Nations Longhouse, University of Oregon, Eugene, Oregon, February 27, 2009. Transcript on file with the author.

3. See Wood and O'Brien, "Tribes as Trustees," 512–13.

4. The preservationist paradigm of creating an untouched wilderness is associated with John Muir and "hands-off" environmentalism. Preservationism does not leave room for subsistence or cultural uses. In chapter 4, Eric Goldsmith, former executive director of Sanctuary Forest, articulated an instance of the differences between stewardship and preservationist approaches: "As a tree-hugger, I might not like to see a tree cut, but I have no need nor place to ask why, unless it was sold, or a case could be made that such action undermines the underlying conservation values articulated in the easement." (telephone communication, February 15, 2008).

5. *Bear Lodge Multiple Use Association v. Babbitt* 175 F.3d (10th Cir. 1999); U.S. Environmental Protection Agency, *Tribal Successes; Access Fund v. U.S. Department of Agriculture* 499 F.3d 1036, 2007 U.S. App., Regarding the judge's decision to uphold the U.S. Forest Service's right to protect historic and cultural resources at Cave Rock, see http://www.washoetribe.us/content/view/24/2/, and the Native American Rights Fund, at http://www.narf.org/nill/bulletins/cta/2007cta.htm.

6. See chapter 7, "Soda Rock/ChuChuYamBa," in Middleton, "'We Were Here.'"

7. Hawk Rosales, telephone communication, July 2007.

8. Madrigal, *Sovereignty, Land, and Water*, 101.

9. Louis Guassac, e-mail messages to author, September 30-October 2, 2008.

10. Beth Rose Middleton, "'Let This All Return to Us': Working to Reclaim Land through the Pacific Forest and Watershed Lands Stewardship Council," *News from Native California*, Winter 2009–2010.

11. Leslie Mouriquand. Telephone communication, May 6, 2010.

12. *Cherokee Nation v. Georgia*, 30 U.S. 1 (1831).

13. For example, in 1953, Public Law 280 gave six states civil and criminal jurisdiction over Indian lands, and it provided other states the option of adopting the law as well. *Oliphant v. Suquamish Indian Tribe*, 435 U.S. 191 (1978) prohibited tribes from exercising criminal jurisdiction over non-Natives who commit crimes within reservation boundaries.

14. Wood and O'Brien, "Tribes as Trustees," 512.

15. Public Law 96–487 (94 Stat. 2371), Alaska National Interest Lands Conservation Act (ANILCA), Title 9, Sec. 905.

16. For more information on the Anadromous Waters Catalog, see http://www.sf.adfg.state.ak.us/SARR/awc/.

17. Mary Christina Wood, e-mail message to author, January 9, 2010.

18. See, for example, the development of Hoopa tribal codes to enable small business development. Beth Rose Middleton and Jonathan Kusel, "Northwest Economic Adjustment Initiative Assessment: Lessons Learned for American Indian Community and Economic Development," *Economic Development Quarterly* 21, no. 2 (2007): 165–78.

19. A copy of the standards and practices is available online at http://www.landtrustalliance.org/learning/sp/lt-standards-practices07.pdf.

20. Kawika Burgess, telephone communication, December 30, 2009.

21. Ibid.

22. For example, see Wood and O'Brien "Tribes as Trustees," 488–92, 530–32; Wood and Welcker, "Tribes as Trustees," 426.

23. The USFWS Tribal Wildlife Grants and Tribal Landowner Incentives Program have been important resources for tribal conservation. For examples of projects funded, including some discussed in this volume, see http://www.fws.gov/grants/NativeAmericanLiaison60807.pdf.

24. List available at http://www.inca-tcd.org/tri_dist.htm.

25. The Indian Nations Conservation Alliance annual meeting is held during the first week in December at the Flamingo Hotel and Casino in Las Vegas, Nevada.

26. Farrell Cunningham, *Land Management Plan*, 28. The full sentence reads: "We may be frightened of outcomes we are unsure of but we should be even more frightened of living in a world where the foundation of injustice is honorable and the perpetuation of that injustice acceptable."

References

Alaska Department of Fish and Wildlife. *Catalog of Waters Important for the Spawning, Rearing or Migration of Anadromous Fishes.* Juneau, AK: Habitat Division, Department of Fish and Game, State of Alaska. Also available at http://www.sf.adfg .state.ak.us/SARR/AWC/index.cfm/FA/main.overview.

Alaska Department of Natural Resources, Division of Mining, Land, and Water. "Fact Sheet: Land Ownership in Alaska" (March 2000). http://dnr.alaska.gov/ mlw/factsht/land_own.pdf.

Aldrich, Rob, and James Wyerman, with Chris Soto and Anne W. Garnett. "Land Trust Alliance: 2005 National Land Trust Census Report." http://www .landtrustalliance.org/about-us/land-trust-census/census.

Alvarez, Michelle. "Mount Shasta: A Question of Power," *News from Native California* 8, no. 3 (Winter 1994–1995): 4–7.

Anderson, M. Kat. *Tending the Wild: Native American Knowledge and the Management of California's Natural Resources.* Berkeley and Los Angeles: University of California Press, 2005.

Babin, John, Nicholas Croft, and Tyler Luce. "Ohop Creek" (March 23, 2009). Podcast. http://blogs.evergreen.edu/nativeplace/2009/03/23/ohop-creek/.

Barker, Joanne. "For Whom Sovereignty Matters." In *Sovereignty Matters*, edited by Barker. Lincoln: University of Nebraska Press, 2005.

Barrett, Bobby. "The Kumeyaay Have a Well-Established Reputation as Stewards of the Environment." *The Kumeyaay Way* (Winter 2009/2010): 4–5.

Bean Mortinson, Jason, Annalise Duerr-Miller, and Julia Vieau. "Nisqually and Fort Lewis" (April 21, 2009). Podcast. http://blogs.evergreen.edu/ nativeplace/2009/04/21/nisqually-and-fort-lewis/.

Berry, Carol. "National Sacred Sites Day Raises Justice Issues." *Indian Country Today*, July 15, 2009.

Blackburn, Thomas C., and Kat Anderson. *Before the Wilderness: Environmental Management by Native Californians*. Menlo Park, CA: Ballena Press, 1993.

Blackie, Jeffrey A. "Conservation Easements and the Doctrine of Changed Conditions." *Hastings Law Journal* 40, no. 6 (1989): 1187–1222.

Blair, Bowen. "Introduction." *Restoring Native Homelands: An Anniversary Project Gallery*. San Francisco, CA: The Trust for Public Land, 2009.

Bouplon, Renee J., and Brenda Lind. *Conservation Easement Stewardship*. Washington, DC: The Land Trust Alliance, 2008.

Brown, Jovana. "Salmon, Tribes, and Hydropower Dams in the U.S. Puget Sound." Olympia, WA: Center for World Indigenous Studies, 1999. http://cwis.org/fwj/41/jbsalmo.html.

Byers, Elizabeth, and Karin Marchetti Ponte. *The Conservation Easement Handbook*. Washington, DC: Land Trust Alliance and Trust for Public Land, 2005.

California Heartland. "A Refuge for Wildlife." Program 808, KVIE Public Television Station, Sacramento, California. http://www.californiaheartland.org.

California State Parks. *Sinkyone Wilderness State Park Final General Plan and Environmental Impact Report*. Sacramento: California State Parks, 2006.

Carpenter, Cecilia Svinth. *Tears of Internment: The Indian History of Fox Island and the Puget Sound Indian War*. Tacoma, Washington: Tahoma Research Service, 1996.

Carrico, Richard L. *Strangers in a Stolen Land: American Indians in San Diego 1850–1880*. Newcastle: Sierra Oaks, 1987.

Case, David S., and David Voluck. *Alaska Natives and American Laws*. Fairbanks: University of Alaska Press, 2002.

"Census Figures Show Slow Rise in Native Population." May 2, 2008. Available at http://www.kumeyaay.com/2008/05/census-figures-show-slow-rise-in-native-population/.

Champion, Dale. "Conservationists Buy Timberland in Mendocino." *San Francisco Chronicle*, December 31, 1986.

Chang, Ping. *The State of the Region 2007*. Los Angeles: Southern California Association of Governments, 2007. http://www.scag.ca.gov/sotr/index.htm.

Cheever, Frederico. "Public Good and Private Magic in the Law of Land Trusts and Conservation Easements: A Happy Present and a Troubled Future." *Denver University Law Review* 73, no. 4 (1996): 1077–1102.

Chew, Jeff. "Conservation Panel Wants Jefferson County to Ante for Tamanowas Rock." *Peninsula Daily News* (Port Angeles, Washington), April 20, 2010.

Chittim, Gary. "Puget Sound Returns to Nisqually Delta." *King 5 News*, November 12, 2009. http://www.king5.com/home/Puget-Sound-Retuns-to-Nisqually-Delta-69907237.html.

Choate, Alan. "Tribe Members Busy Planting Trees, Shrubs, to Reclaim Area Waterways." *Peninsula Daily News* (Port Angeles, Washington), June 16, 2005.

Christian-Smith, Juliet, and Adina M. Merenlender. "The Disconnect between Restoration Goals and Practices: A Case Study of Watershed Restoration in the Russian River Basin, California." *Restoration Ecology* 17, no. 7 (2009): 95–102.

Churchill, Ward. "The Earth Is Our Mother." In *The State of Native America*, edited by Annette Jaimes. Boston, MA: South End Press, 1992.

Claiborne, William. "Native American Tribes Take Back the Land in California." *The Washington Post*, October 7, 1997.

Clarke, Chris. "Inter-Tribal Sinkyone Park—It Could Happen Soon." *News from Native California* 7, no. 2 (1993): 47.

———. "Maintaining the Wealth: the InterTribal Sinkyone Wilderness." *News from Native California* 7, no. 4 (1994): 45–46.

Clifford, James. *On the Edges of Anthropology (Interviews)*. Chicago: Prickly Paradigm Press, 2003.

Coffey, Wallace, and Rebecca Tsosie. "Rethinking the Tribal Sovereignty Doctrine: Cultural Sovereignty and the Collective Future of Indian Nations." *Stanford Law and Policy Review* 12, no. 2 (2001): 191–221.

"Community Note." *The Press-Enterprise* (Riverside, California), November 24, 2005.

"Community Notes, Anza Borrego: Marking Acquisition of Horse Canyon." *The Press-Enterprise* (Riverside, California), April 1, 2005.

Corbett, Michael. "Native Americans to Acquire Land for a Coast Redwood Park." *Los Angeles Times*, April 12, 1995, Part A (Metro).

Cornell, Stephen, and Joseph P. Kalt. "Sovereignty and Nation-Building: The Development Challenge in Indian Country Today." *American Indian Culture and Research Journal* 22, no. 3 (1998): 187–214.

———, eds. *What Can Tribes Do? Strategies and Institutions in American Indian Economic Development*. Los Angeles: American Indian Studies Center, University of California, Los Angeles, 1992.

Crum, Steven J. "Pretending They Didn't Exist: The Timbisha Shoshone Tribe of Death Valley, California, and the Death Valley National Monument Up to 1933," *Southern California Quarterly* 84, no. 3/4 (2002): 223–40.

Cunningham, Farrell. *Maidu Summit Land Management Plan*. Submitted to the Pacific Forest and Watershed Lands Stewardship Council, San Mateo, California, July 2007.

———. "Take Care of the Land and the Land Will Take Care of You: Traditional Ecology in Native California." *News from Native California* 18, no. 4 (2005): 24–34.

Cutter, S. L. "Race, Class, and Environmental Justice." *Progress in Human Geography* 19, no. 1(1995): 111–22.

Deloria Jr., Vine. *Custer Died for Your Sins*. London: Collier-Macmillan Limited, 1969.

———. *God Is Red: A Native View of Religion*. Golden, CO: Fulcrum Publishing, 1994.

Demarban, Alex. "09–39 Urge Creation of Tax Credits or Benefits to Alaska Native Corporations Who Voluntarily Choose to Create Conservation Easements." *The Bristol Bay Times*, November 10, 2009, and *The Arctic Sounder*, November 10, 2009.

Desmond, Dennis F. *Cowee Mound Baseline Report*. Submitted to the Land Trust for the Little Tennessee, February 23, 2007. On file with the Land Trust for the Little Tennessee (Franklin, North Carolina).

Drummer, Marina. "Endangered Cultures, Endangered Species, and the Law." *News from Native California* 15, no. 2 (2001/2002): 33.

Edwards, Victoria. *Dealing in Diversity: America's Market for Nature Conservation*. Cambridge, United Kingdom: Cambridge University Press, 1995.

Fairfax, Sally K., Lauren Gwin, Mary Ann King, Leigh Raymond, and Laura A. Watt. *Buying Nature: The Limits of Land Acquisition as a Conservation Strategy, 1780–2004*. Cambridge, MA: MIT Press, 2005.

"Fall Burn of Grasses in the TGG." *Cache Creek Conservancy News and Events* 34 (2008).

Fenner, Randee G. "Land Trusts: An Alternative Method of Preserving Open Space." *Vanderbilt Law Review* 33, no. 5 (1980): 1039–99.

Finger, John R. *The Eastern Band of Cherokees, 1819–1900*. Knoxville: University of Tennessee Press, 1984.

"First Wilderness Park Owned by American Indians to Open." *Contra Costa Times*, October 11, 1997.

Fishman, Neal. "Sinkyone Lost and Found." *California Coast and Ocean* 12, no. 3 (1996). http://www.coastalconservancy.ca.gov/coast&ocean/archive/SINKYONE .HTM.

Fixico, Donald. *Termination and Relocation: Federal Indian Policy 1945–1960*. Albuquerque: University of New Mexico Press, 1986.

Flensburg, Susan. "Keeping It Clean: An Alternative Approach to TMDL in Rural Alaska." Paper presented at the conference Getting It Done: The Role of TMDL Implementation in Watershed Restoration, Stevenson, Washington, October 29–30, 2003.

Freedman, Eric. "When Indigenous Rights and Wilderness Collide." *American Indian Quarterly* 26, no. 3 (2002): 378–92.

Frontline. "Salmon Wars: The Battle Over Habitat." Aired April 23, 2009. http:// www.pbs.org/wgbh/pages/frontline/poisonedwaters/clean/.

Geisler, Charles. "Property Pluralism." In *Property and Values: Alternatives to Public and Private Ownership*, edited by Charles Geisler and Gail Daneker. Covelo, CA: Island Press, 2000.

Getches, David H., Charles F. Wilkinson, and Robert A. Williams, Jr. *Cases and Materials on Federal Indian Law*. 4th ed. St. Paul, MN: West Group, 1998.

Giles-Rankin, Juliann Elizabeth. "An Ethnohistorical Reconstruction of the Greenville Indian Industrial School." Master's Thesis, California State University, Chico, 1983.

Goldberg, Carole, and Duane Champagne, "Status and Needs of Unrecognized and Terminated California Indian Tribes." In *A Second Century of Dishonor: Federal Inequities and California Tribes*, edited by Goldberg and Champagne. UCLA: Native American Studies Center, prepared for the Advisory Council on California Indian Policy, Community Service, Governance, Census Task Force Report, March 27, 1996.

Greene, Duncan M. "Dynamic Conservation Easements: Facing the Problem of Perpetuity in Land Conservation." *Seattle University Law Review* 28, no. 3 (2005): 883–924.

Greensfelder, Sara. "The Nature Conservancy." *News from Native California* 6, no. 1 (1991/1992): 28.

Gulliford, Andrew. *Sacred Objects and Sacred Places: Preserving Tribal Traditions*. Boulder: University Press of Colorado, 2000.

Gwinn, Emily, Jennifer Johnson, and Joe Nance. "Nisqually Estuary" (April 18, 2009). Podcast. http://blogs.evergreen.edu/nativeplace/2009/04/18/nisqually-estuary-podcast/.

Hall, Stuart. "Race, Articulation, and Societies Structured in Dominance." In *Critical Race Theories: Text and Context*, edited by Philomena Essed and David Theo Goldberg. Malden, MA: Wiley-Blackwell Publishers, 2001.

Heiman, M. K. "Race, Waste, and Class: New Perspectives on Environmental Justice." *Antipode* 28, no. 2 (1996): 111–21.

Heizer, Robert. *Languages, Territories, and Names of California Indian Tribes*. Berkeley and Los Angeles: University of California Press, 1966.

Hensley, William Iggiagruk. *Fifty Miles from Tomorrow: A Memoir of Alaska and the Real People*. New York: Sarah Crichton Books, 2009.

Hernandez, Barbara E. "Preserving Their History: Tribe's Conservancy Protects New Acreage." *The Press-Enterprise* (Riverside, California), May 4, 2004.

Hoopes, Chad L. *Domesticate or Exterminate: California Indian Treaties Unratified and Made Secret in 1852* (Loleta, CA: Redwood Coast Publications, 1975).

Hunter, Don. "Sullivan, Young Call for Study of Inlet Beluga Whales." *Anchorage Daily News*, December 23, 2009.

InterTribal Sinkyone Wilderness Council. "Intertribal Cultural Event Held at Richardson Grove." *Redwood Times*, September 9, 2009.

———. "The Vision and the Work." *News from Native California* 11(2) (1997–1998): 13–14 (supplement on California Indians and Conservation).

Jacoby, Karl. *Crimes Against Nature: Squatters, Poachers, Thieves, and the Hidden History of American Conservation*. Berkeley and Los Angeles: University of California Press, 2001.

Jamestown S'Klallam Tribe, 2008–2009 *Report to Tribal Citizens* (Sequim, Washington, 2010). http://www.jamestowntribe.org/jstweb_2007/announce/Final%20_008-2009_Report_to_Citizens.pdf.

Johnston-Dodds, Kimberly. *Early Laws and Policies Related to California Indians*. California Research Bureau: California State Library. September 2002. Available at http://www.library.ca.gov/crb/02/14/02-014.pdf.

Kiesecker, J. M., et al. "Conservation Easements in Context: A Quantitative Analysis of Their Use by the Nature Conservancy." *Frontiers in Ecology and the Environment* 5, no. 3 (2007): 125–30.

King, Mary Ann. "Co-Management or Contracting? Agreements between Native American Tribes and the U.S. National Park Service Pursuant to the 1994 Tribal Self-Governance Act." *Harvard Environmental Law Review* 31, no. 2 (2007): 475–530.

King, Mary Ann, and Sally Fairfax. "Public Accountability and Conservation Easements: Learning from the Uniform Conservation Easement Act Debates." *Natural Resources Journal* 46, no. 1 (2006): 65–129.

Klasky, Philip. "Awakened Voices." *News from Native California* 14, no. 1 (2000): 32–33.

———. "An Extreme and Solemn Relationship: The Battle against Radioactive Waste Dumping in the Mojave Desert." *News from Native California* 9, no. 2 (1995–1996): 9–11.

———. "Ward Valley: Sacred Homeland or Nuclear Waste Dump." *Satya*, April 1999. Satya ceased publication in 2007, but information on how to order back issues is available at http://www.satyamag.com/.

"Koliganek Native LTD Establishes Salmon Reserve on Corporate Lands." Press Release, November, 2009.

Korngold, Gerald. "Privately Held Conservation Servitudes: A Policy Analysis in the Context of In-Gross Real Covenants and Easements." *Texas Law Review* 63, no. 3 (1984): 433–95.

Kramer, Dwight. "Just Say 'No' to This Proposed Coal Mine in Alaska Salmon Streams." *Anchorage Daily News*, August 27, 2009.

Kroeber, Alfred L. *Handbook of the Indians of California*. Berkeley: California Book Company, 1925.

Kueter, Lawrence R., and Christopher S. Jensen. "Conservation Easements: An Underdeveloped Tool to Protect Cultural Resources." *Denver University Law Review* 83, no. 4 (2006): 1057–67.

Kumeyaay-Diegueño Land Conservancy. "Help Preserve and Protect the Sacred Mountain and Former Home of Kuuchamaa." Brochure. San Diego: Kumeyaay-Diegueño Land Conservancy, 2009.

LaDuke, Winona. *All Our Relations: Native Struggles for Land and Life.* Boston, MA: South End Press, 1999.

———. *Recovering the Sacred: The Power of Naming and Claiming.* Cambridge, MA: South End Press, 2005.

Land Trust Alliance. "Land Trusts: Finding the Answers that Save the Land." Washington, DC: Land Trust Alliance, 1990.

Lesko, Lawrence M., and Renee G. Thakali. "Traditional Knowledge and Tribal Partnership on the Kaibab National Forest with an Emphasis on the Hopi Interagency Management." In *Trusteeship in Change: Toward Tribal Autonomy in Resource Management*, edited by Richmond Clow and Imre Sutton. Norman: University of Oklahoma Press, 2001.

Liegel, Konrad, and Gene Duvernoy. "Land Trusts: Shaping the Landscape of Our Nation." *Natural Resources and Environment* 17 (2002): 95–97, 125–129.

Little Traverse Bay Bands of Odawa Indians. *Our Land and Culture: A 200 Year History of Our Land Use* (Harbor Springs, MI: Little Traverse Bay Bands of Odawa Indians, 2005). http://www.ltbbodawa-nsn.gov/Departments/ArchivesAndRecords/Our%20Land%20and%20Culture%20for%20web.pdf.

Lopez, Steve. "A Spirit Run for the Desert." *News from Native California* 5, no. 4 (1991): 20–21.

Luomala, Katharine. "Tipai-Ipai." In *Handbook of North American Indians*. Vol. 8: *California*, edited by Robert F. Heizer. Washington, DC: Smithsonian Institution, 1978.

Madrigal, Anthony. *Sovereignty, Land, and Water: Building Tribal Environmental and Cultural Programs on the Cahuilla and Twenty-Nine Palms Reservations.* Riverside: California Center for Native Nations, University of California, Riverside, 2008.

Mahoney, Julia D. "Perpetual Restrictions on Land and the Problem of the Future." *Virginia Law Review* 88, no. 4 (2002): 739–88.

Manlove, Robert. "The Mountain Maidu Bear Dance." *News from Native California* 22, no. 3 (2009): 14–19.

Manning, Elizabeth. "Native Lands at Risk: Coalition Attempts to Save Allotments." *Anchorage Daily News*, December 18, 2000.

Margolin, Malcolm. "California Indians and Conservation." *News from Native California* 11, no. 2 (1997–1998): 2–50 (supplement on California Indians and Conservation).

McCandless, Colin. "Ancient Mound and Town Site Return to the Cherokee: Land Trust Plays a Key Role in Unique Property Transaction." *The Franklin Press* (Franklin, North Carolina), October 27, 2006.

McLaughlin, Nancy A. "Rethinking the Perpetual Nature of Conservation Easements." *Harvard Environmental Law Review* 29, no. 2 (2005): 421–521.

Meeker, Ezra. *Pioneer Reminiscences of Puget Sound: The Tragedy of Leschi.* Seattle: Lowman and Hanford, 1905.

Michelutti, Mick, and John Moudy. "Clear Creek Hatchery" (April 20, 2009). Podcast. http://blogs.evergreen.edu/nativeplace/2009/04/20/clear-creek -hatchery/.

Middleton, Beth Rose. "'Let This All Return to Us': Working to Reclaim Land through the Pacific Forest and Watershed Lands Stewardship Council," *News from Native California,* Winter 2009–2010.

———. "Seeking Spatial Representation: Mapping Mountain Maidu Allotment Lands." *Ethnohistory* 57, no. 3 (2010): 363–88.

———. "'We Were Here, We Are Here, We Will Always Be Here': A Political Ecology of Healing in Mountain Maidu Country." PhD diss., University of California, Berkeley, 2008.

Middleton, Beth Rose, and Jonathan Kusel. "Northwest Economic Adjustment Initiative Assessment: Lessons Learned for American Indian Community and Economic Development." *Economic Development Quarterly* 21, no. 2 (2007): 165–78.

Mitchell, Donald Craig. *Take My Land, Take My Life.* Fairbanks: University of Alaska Press, 2001.

Morgan, Ryan. "Valmont Butte Offer on Horizon: Preservation Groups to Make Offer for at Least Part of Land Parcel." *The Daily Camera* (Boulder, Colorado), July 21, 2006.

Naske, Claus-M., and Herman E. Slotnick. *Alaska: A History of the 49th State.* Grand Rapids, MI: William B. Eerdmans Publishing Company, 1979.

National Archives Branch Depository for the Pacific Region, San Bruno, California. Case Files of Land Transactions, 1909–1956 from Susanville, Records of the Bureau of Indian Affairs. Sus-212 (Old Allick); RG 75.

Nelson, Melissa K. "Oral Tradition, Identity, and Intergenerational Healing." In *Cultural Representation in Native America,* edited by Andrew Jolivette. Lanham, MD: AltaMira Press, 2006.

Neumann, Roderick P. "Ways of Seeing Africa: Colonial Recasting of African Society and Landscape in Serengeti National Park." *Ecumene* 2 (1995): 149–69.

Newberry, Linda. "The 'Undevelopment' of Jimmycomelately Creek and Estuary." Report prepared for the Jamestown S'Klallam Tribe. 2003.

Nomland, Gladys A. *Sinkyone Notes*. Berkeley and Los Angeles: University of California Press, 1935.

Ortiz, Bev. "Kumeyaay Netmaking." *News from Native California* 10, no. 3 (1997): 9–10.

Ostendorff, Jon. "Reclaiming Their Land: Cherokee Indians Buy Undisturbed Indian Mound in Cowee." *Citizen Times*, April 24, 2007.

Ottaway, David B., and Joe Stephens. "Big Green: Inside The Nature Conservancy." *The Washington Post*, May 4, 2003.

Pacific Forest Trust. "Sinkyone InterTribal Wilderness." *Pacific Forests* Winter 1998.

Parker, Dominic P. "Land Trusts and the Choice to Conserve Land with Full Ownership or Conservation Easements." *Natural Resources Journal* 44, no. 2 (2004): 483–518.

Parker, Patricia, and Thomas King. "National Register Bulletin 38: Guidelines for Evaluating and Documenting Traditional Cultural Properties." 1990, revised 1992, 1998. http://www.nps.gov/nr/publications/bulletins/nrb38/.

Paton, Robert J. "Back into the Park: California Desert Protection Act Offers Hope to Timbisha Shoshone." *News from Native California* 8, no. 4 (1995): 50–51.

Phillips, George Harwood. *Indians and Indian Agents: The Origins of the Reservation System in California, 1849–1852*. Norman: University of Oklahoma Press, 1997.

Poole, William. "Return of the Sinkyone." *Sierra*, November/December 1996.

———. "Return of the Sinkyone: Long-Contested Forestlands Become the First Native American Intertribal Park." *Land and People* (a publication of Trust for Public Land), Spring 1998.

Powers, Stephen. *Tribes of California*. Berkeley and Los Angeles: University of California Press, 1976. Reprint of 1877 *Contributions to North American Ethnology*. Vol. 3. Washington, DC: Department of the Interior, U.S. Geographical and Geological Survey of the Rocky Mountain Region.

Prucha, Francis Paul. *American Indian Treaties*. Berkeley and Los Angeles: University of California Press, 1994.

Raphael, Ray, and Freeman House. *Humboldt History*. Vol. 1: *Two Peoples, One Place*. Eureka, CA: Humboldt County Historical Society, 2007.

Reyes, Lawney L. *Bernie Whitebear: An Urban Indian's Quest for Justice*. Tucson: University of Arizona Press, 2006.

Rhoades, Harriet. "Relevance of Sinkyone to Local Peoples: Cultural Heritage Explained." *Redwood Times*, April 9, 2008.

Ring, Ray. "Write-Off on the Range." *High Country News*, May 30, 2005.

Rissman, Adena, and Adina M. Merelender. "The Conservation Contributions of Conservation Easements: Analysis of the San Francisco Bay Area Protected Lands Spatial Database." *Ecology and Society* 13, no. 1 (2008): 40. http://www .ecologyandsociety.org/vol13/iss1/art40/.

Rollins, William H. "Imperial Shades of Green: Conservation and Environmental Chauvinism in the German Colonial Project." *German Studies Review* 22, no. 2 (1999): 187–213.

Romm, Jeff. "The Coincidental Order of Environmental Justice." In *Justice and Natural Resources: Concepts, Strategies, and Applications*, edited by Kathryn Mutz, Gary Bryner, and Douglas Benner. Washington, DC: Island Press, 2002.

Ross, Jacquelyn. "Bringing the People Back to the Land: The Tending and Gathering Gardening Project." *Regeneration* 3, no. 2 (2003): 8–10.

Ross, Jacquelyn, Shannon Brawley, Jan Lowrey, and Don Hankins. "Creating Common Ground: A Collaborative Approach to Environmental Reclamation and Cultural Preservation." In *Partnerships for Empowerment: Participatory Research for Community-Based Natural Resource Management*, edited by Carl Wilmsen, Larry Fisher, Gail Wells, Jacquelyn Ross, and William Elmendorf. Sterling, VA: Stylus Publishing, 2008.

Ross, Timberly. "Indian Tribes Buy Back Thousands of Acres of Lands." Associated Press, December 27, 2009.

Royster, Judith V., and Michael C. Blumm. *Native American Natural Resources Law*. Durham, NC: Carolina Academic Press, 2002.

Russo, Kurt, ed. *Finding Common Ground*. Yarmouth, ME: Intercultural Press, 2001.

———. *In the Land of Three Peaks: The Old Woman Mountains Preserve*. Valencia, CA: Delta, 2005. Available via http://www.nalc4all.org.

———. "Theresa Mike: A Passion for the People." In *Activist Minority Western American Women*. Lubbock: Texas Tech University Press, forthcoming.

"Sequim: Dungeness Flooding Likely Destroyed Redds." *Peninsula Daily News* (Port Angeles, Washington), April 7, 2002.

Shipek, Florence C. "The Impact of Europeans upon Kumeyaay Culture." In *The Impact of European Exploration and Settlement on Local Native Americans*, edited by Raymond Starr. San Diego, CA: Cabrillo Historical Association, 1986.

———. *Delfina Cuero*. Menlo Park: Ballena Press, 1991.

Shreffler, Dave, et al. *Jimmycomelately Ecosystem Restoration: Lessons Learned Report*. Sequim, WA: Jamestown S'Klallam Tribe, 2008. http://www.jamestowntribe .org/jstweb_2007/programs/nrs/jcl-lessionslearned10-31-08.pdf.

Silliman, Daniel. "Jimmy Come Lately Creek Restoration Begins in Blyn." *Peninsula Daily News* (Port Angeles, Washington), January 3, 2003.

"Sinkyone InterTribal Wilderness." *Pacific Forests: Private Forest Issues in California, Oregon, and Washington* (former newsletter of the Pacific Forest Trust), Winter, 1998.

"S'Klallam Tribe Reclaiming Hallowed Ground," *North Kitsap Herald* (Poulsbo, Washington), April 16, 2010.

Slagle, Allogan. "Unfinished Justice: Completing the Restoration and Acknowledgement of California Indian Tribes." *American Indian Quarterly*, Special Issue, "The California Indians" 13, no. 4 (1989): 325–45.

Smith, Linda Tuhiwai. *Decolonizing Methodologies: Research and Indigenous Peoples.* London: Zed Books, 1999.

Snyder, George. "Tribes Join for Tribute to Indian Life: 3,800-Acre Wilderness Park Planned." *San Francisco Chronicle*, May 23, 1995.

Spence, Mark. *Dispossessing the Wilderness: Indian Removal and the Making of the National Parks.* New York: Oxford University Press, 1999.

Spillman, Benjamin. "Preserving a Piece of History." *The Desert Sun* (Palm Springs, California), March 22, 2005.

———. "Tribal Coalition Wins Grant for Desert Tract." *The Desert Sun* (Palm Springs, California), January 29, 2004.

"State Parks Presents ITSWC Director with Award." *Redwood Times*, June 4, 2009.

Suagee, Dean. "The Cultural Heritage of Indian Tribes and the Preservation of Biological Diversity." *Arizona State Law Journal* 31, no. 2 (1999): 483–538.

Tarlock, Dan, and Holly A. Doremus. *Water War in the Klamath Basin: Macho Law, Combat Biology, and Dirty Politics.* Covelo, CA: Island Press, 2008.

Taylor, Dorceta. "American Environmentalism: The Role of Race, Class, and Gender in Shaping Activism 1820–1995." *Race, Gender, and Class* 5, no. 1 (1997): 16–62.

Tiller, Veronica E. Valarde, ed. *Tiller's Guide to Indian Country: Economic Profiles of American Indian Reservations.* Albuquerque, NM: BowArrow Publishing, 1996, 2006.

Tsosie, Rebecca. "The Conflict between the 'Public Trust' and the 'Indian Trust' Doctrines: Federal Public Land Policy and Native Nations." *Tulsa Law Review* 39, no. 2 (2003): 271–312.

Turner, Robin, and Diana Pei Wu. *Environmental Justice and Environmental Racism: An Annotated Bibliography and General Overview Focusing on U.S. Literature, 1996–2002.* Berkeley Workshop on Environmental Politics Bibliography No. B 02–7. Institute of International Studies, University of California, Berkeley. 2002.

U.S. Environmental Protection Agency, U.S. Department of the Interior, Offices of the Inspector General. *Tribal Successes: Protecting the Environment and Natural Resources.* May 2007. http://www.doioig.gov/upload/2007-G-0020.pdf.

"Valmont Butte Heritage Alliance." *The Daily Camera* (Boulder, Colorado), November 10, 2007.

VanDevelder, Paul. *Coyote Warrior: One Man, Three Tribes, and a Trial that Forged a Nation.* New York: Little, Brown, and Company, 2004.

Viejas Band of Kumeyaay Indians. "Viejas Band of Kumeyaay Indians: A Brief History." Booklet available online at http://www.viejasbandofkumeyaay .org/pdfs/ViejasHistoryBooklet.pdf.

Viglielmo, Emily. "'The Run to Save Sinkyone': Local Documentary to Be Shown at Sundance Film Festival." *Ukiah Daily Journal* (Ukiah, California), December 30–31, 1994.

Walter, George. "We Are America's Best Idea." *Nisqually Land Trust Newsletter*, Fall 2009: 4.

Whyte, William. *The Last Landscape.* Garden City, NY: Doubleday, 1968.

———. "Securing Open Space for Urban America: Conservation Easements." *Urban Land Institute Technical Bulletin*, no. 36 (1959).

Wilkinson, Charles F. *American Indians, Time, and the Law.* New Haven, CT: Yale University Press, 1987.

Wood, Mary Christina, and Matthew O'Brien. "Tribes as Trustees Again (Part II): Evaluating Four Models of Tribal Participation in the Conservation Trust Movement." *Stanford Environmental Law Journal* 27, no. 2 (2008): 477–544.

Wood, Mary Christina, and Zachary Welcker. "Tribes as Trustees Again (Part I): The Emerging Tribal Role in the Conservation Trust Movement." *Harvard Environmental Law Review* 32, no. 2 (2008): 373–432.

"Wood Theft from Sinkyone Property Results in Conviction." *Redwood Times* (Garberville, CA), April 2, 2008.

Young, Tobias. "Mendocino Forest Sale OK'd." *The Press Democrat* (Santa Rosa, CA), March 21, 1995.

Index

Internal Revenue Service (IRS), 67;
501(c)(3) status, 88–89
Intertribal Cultural Resources Working
Group, 117–18
InterTribal Sinkyone Wilderness, 45,
49, 241, 273n27; conservation easements, 51–56, 238; plans for, 58–60;
support for, 50–51
InterTribal Sinkyone Wilderness
Council, xxi(map), 20, 43, 62, 232,
235–37, 238, 248, 274n59; alliances,
49–50; easement structure, 51–56;
goals, 56–57; land trust, 54–55;
members, 45–46, 57–58; and NALC,
224–28; plans, 58–60; support,
48–49

Jamestown S'Klallam Tribe, xxi(map),
23, 24, 30, 40, 230, 232, 233, 234;
collaboration, 164–73; Dungeness
River Audubon Center, 167–68, 229;
fishing rights, 163, 174
Jefferson Land Trust: and Tamanowas
Rock, 169–72
Jimmycomelately Estuary, 172–74, 233

Kachemak Heritage Land Trust
(KHLT), xxi(map), 139, 140,
243, 245; and Alaska Natives,
149–50, 231; Cook Inlet Region,
Inc., 143–45; and Seldovia Native
Association, 141–43
Kenai Peninsula, 145–46
Kenaitze Indian Tribe, 143, 145, 231
Klamath Trinity Resource Conserva-
tion District, 214
Klasky, Phil, 78–79
Koliganek Natives, LTD, 160, 234
Koncor Forest Products, Inc., 142
Kumeyaay-Diegueño Land Conser-
vancy (KDLC), xxi(map), 43, 72,
73, 276n43; NALC and, 81–84, 225
Kumeyaay-Diegueño Unity Bands, 82,
225, 226, 237
Kumeyaay Nation, 69, 225, 226

Kuuchamaa, Mt., 83, 278n90

landowners: conservation easements,
12–14, 15, 16, 20, 41–42, 122, 123;
relationships with, 28–29
landscapes: healing, 65, 68–69,
133–34; preserving, 130–31; sacred,
x, xii, 72, 73–84, 95, 110, 113–15
Land Trust Alliance (LTA), 4, 7, 26,
40, 80, 86, 139, 155, 243, 248–49,
261n5; tax incentives, 9, 14
Land Trust for the Little Tennessee
(LTLT), xxi(map), 30, 176–77;
Cowee Mound, 180, 182–83; and
EBCI, 177–78, 183–84, 230, 231,
232, 233, 248
land trusts, xv, xvi, xvii, 1, 2, 4, 6,
7, 8–9, 13, 63, 153, 223, 224–26,
238–39, 248, 258n16, 263–64n43,
266n93; collaboration, 127–28,
228–35; cultural values, xix–xx;
definitions of, 25–27; InterTribal
Sinkyone Wilderness, 54–55;
Jamestown S'Klallam, 164–74;
NMWTLT, 158–59; and tribes, xxii,
29–31, 80, 99
land use, 12–13, 15–16, 19–20, 21
Lankard, Dune, 19, 139
Lannan Foundation, 51, 52
Leivas, Matthew, x, 70, 77, 78
Little Traverse Bay Bands of Odawa
Indians (LTBBOI), xxi(map), 21,
119, 120, 229, 231, 232, 238;
conservation easements, 24, 121–27,
229; Hoag Natural Area, 20, 124;
partnership, 246–47
Little Traverse Conservancy (LTC),
xxi(map), 21, 120, 231, 232;
conservation easements, 121–27,
229; partnership, 246–47
living cultural center: Maidu, 30–31,
131, 132–35
Lorenzo, Paula, 107, 198
Lowrey, Jan, 107, 197, 198, 199, 200,
202, 206, 233, 297n37

Maidu, xiii, xiv, 219, 283n1; cultural resources, 131–37; land issues, xviii–xix, 21

Maidu Active Cultural Center (MACC), 131; development of, 132–35

Maidu Summit Consortium, xix, xxi(map), 19, 20, 73

Memoranda of Understanding (MOU): Burton Homestead, 132, 135–36, 230; Cahuilla "Fish Traps" Site, 75–76, 227; conservation districts, 214, 215

Michigan, 4, 119, 120–21, 250

Michigan Department of Environmental Quality, 124, 126, 128

Mike, Dean, 66, 67, 79

Mike, Theresa, 66, 67, 68, 79, 97

mining, 133–34, 196

mitigation, 30, 102–4, 114–15, 246–47

monitoring, 14, 51, 55, 232–33, 246–47

Mono Rancheria, 215–16

Morongo Band of Mission Indians/ Reservation, xxi(map), 30, 118, 234; and SB-18, 109–17, 241–42

Mountain Maidu, xiii, xiv, xvii, 129

National Park Service, 36, 37–38, 72, 83, 269n14

Native American Land Conservancy (NALC), x, xxi(map), 26, 31, 43–44, 238, 239, 276nn26, 31, 49; as 501(c)(3), 89–95; formation of, 66, 67–68; functions of, 65–66, 73–76, 84–86, 224–28, 276n43; governance of, 69–71; operations of, 68–69, 72–73, 235, 236, 237; partnerships, 76–84, 95–96

Native Conservancy Land Trust, 19, 139

Native Village of Tyonek, 155, 156–57

Natural Resources Conservation Service (NRCS), 2, 14, 30, 173, 211, 213, 214–15, 249–50, 299n2; and

Susanville Indian Rancheria, 219–22; tools, 235, 245–46; wetlands preservation, 220–21

Nature Conservancy, The (TNC), xiv–xv, 7, 13, 27, 67, 267n100; Alaska Natives, 147, 149, 150, 152, 155, 158; cultural knowledge, 159–60

Needmore Tract, 178, 182

Nevada County Land Trust (NCLT), xxi(map), 130–31, 230, 240–41; cultural center, 30–31, 131–37

New Mexico, 21, 22

Nicholson Short Plat, 169–70

Ninilchik Natives Association, Inc. (NNAI), 147, 148

Nisqually Indian Tribe, xxi(map), 23, 40, 185, 232, 234, 235, 268n117; fish hatcheries, 186–87; land restoration, 186–88; and Nisqually Land Trust, 191–94, 229–30; reservation, 185–86; and USFWS, 189–90; watershed protection, 30, 187–89

Nisqually Land Trust (NLT), xxi(map), 187, 188, 189, 190, 233; and Nisqually Tribe, 191–94, 229–30

Nisqually River, 185, 187–88

Nisqually River Citizens Advisory Committee, 188

Nisqually River Council, 187–88, 189, 191, 194

Nisqually River Task Force, 187, 230

North Carolina, 4, 34, 182–83, 250

North Carolina Clean Water Management Trust Fund (CWMTF), 180, 182

Northern Michigan Ottawa Association, 119, 120

North Olympic Land Trust (NOLT), xxi(map), 164–65, 230, 232, 233

Nushagak–Mulchatna Wood–Tikchik Land Trust (NMWTLT), xxi(map), 139, 141, 162, 225, 226, 234, 242–43; Alaska Native, 150–53, 158–61; governance, 157–58, 245

INDEX   319

U.S. Fish and Wildlife Service
(USFWS), 36, 73–74, 107, 160,
189–90, 221, 227, 250
U.S. Forest Service, 36, 221, 266n92

Wallace, Kathy, 197, 198–200, 203,
204–5, 206–7
Washington, 4, 34, 163, 185, 187, 250,
260n3
Washington Department of Fish and
Wildlife (WDFW), 165, 166–67,
168
Washington Department of Natural
Resources, 167, 172–73
Washington Salmon Recovery
Funding Board, 190

watersheds: protection of, 30, 158,
165, 182, 187–89; restoration of,
172–74, 189–90, 192–93
Wetlands Reserve Program (WRP), 14,
25, 30, 212, 220–21, 235, 247
Whitebear, Bernie, 186
wilderness areas, 45, 50–51, 300n4
Wilson, Britt, 110, 112, 113–14, 116

Yocha Dehe Wintun Nation, xxi(map),
30, 101, 246, 279n1; Cache Creek
Conservancy, 106–7, 198, 199,
202, 203, 208, 240; conservation
easement, 231–32; GSLC, 104–6,
108; partnerships, 102–4
Yolo Land Trust, 105
Yurok, 37–38

About the Author

Beth Rose Middleton is of Afro-Caribbean and Eastern European descent, and she was born and raised in rural northern California, specifically the Mokulumne watershed of the central Sierra Nevada foothills, Miwuk country. After completing her undergraduate degree at the University of California, Davis, in Nature and Culture in 2001, she worked as an intern for the Sierra Institute for Community and Environment on rural environmental justice and rural resource-based economic development research and policy. She also began working with the Maidu Culture and Development Group (MCDG). In 2002, Beth Rose entered graduate school at UC Berkeley in Environmental Science, Policy, and Management—Society and Environment. She continued to work with the MCDG as an intern, focusing on land claims research, the Maidu Stewardship Project, and fundraising; and with the Maidu Summit Consortium on Maidu land history, land claims, and stewardship. She also worked as a grant writer and kids' camp director for the Roundhouse Council Indian Education Center, and she served on the board of The Jefferson Center, a social justice/popular education organization.

Beth Rose's dissertation, "'We Were Here, We Are Here, We Will Always Be Here': A Political Ecology of Healing in Mountain Maidu Country," completed in 2008, utilizes participatory research and GIS mapping, among other methods. It focuses on both intergenerational trauma and the need for healing in Maidu natural resource activism. An ongoing project related to the dissertation is an interactive GIS map of Indian allotments in Plumas and Lassen counties that Maidu tribal governments, individuals, and organizations can use in land claims and genealogical research.

Beth Rose has published on Native economic development in the *Economic Development Quarterly*, on political ecology and healing in the *Journal of Political Ecology*, on Native California resource issues in *News from Native*

California, and on qualitative GIS mapping in *Ethnohistory*. From 2008 to 2010, she was a UC President's Postdoctoral Fellow in the UC Davis departments of Environmental Science and Policy and Native American Studies. In fall 2010, Beth Rose became an assistant professor in the UC Davis Department of Native American Studies, where she has developed courses on Native public health, Native environmental policy, and federal Indian law.

Her research interests include Native green entrepreneurship, using environmental statutes for cultural preservation, qualitative GIS mapping of Indian allotment lands, Afro-indigenous populations, and Native activism to bring cultural concerns into natural resource policies.

About the Contributors

Kurt Russo received his doctorate in history from the University of California, Riverside, his MS in forestry at the University of Washington, and his BS in forestry from the University of Montana. He works with Indigenous communities throughout the American West as well as with Indigenous communities in the Caribbean region, Mexico, Guatemala, Chile, and Brazil. He works on poverty reduction programs for the Lummi Indian tribe of Washington State, is Executive Director of the Native American Land Conservancy based in southern California, and is a Research Fellow at the California Center for Native Nations (University of California, Riverside). His publications include *In the Land of Three Peaks: The Old Woman Mountains Preserve* (Delta, 2005); "Lummi Indians of the Pacific Northwest," in *Endangered Peoples of North America* (University of Nebraska Press, 2003); and *Finding Common Ground: Insights and Applications of the Value Orientation Method* (Intercultural Press, 2001). He is a contributor to *The Making of the American West* (Routledge, forthcoming).

Clifford E. Trafzer is Professor of History at the University of California, Riverside, where he holds the Rupert Costo Chair in American Indian Affairs. He is on the board of the Native American Land Conservancy.

www.ingramcontent.com/pod-product-compliance
Lightning Source LLC
Chambersburg PA
CBHW021848020426
42334CB00013B/240